Religious Education and (Realism

Religious Education and Critical Realism: Knowledge, Reality and Religious Literacy seeks to bring the enterprise of religious education in schools, colleges and universities into conversation with the philosophy of critical realism. This book addresses the problem, not of the substance of our primal beliefs about the ultimate nature of reality and our place in the ultimate order-of-things, but of the process through which we might attend to questions of substance in more attentive, reasonable, responsible and intelligent ways. This book unpacks the impact of modern and post-modern thought on key topics whilst also generating a new critically realistic vision. Offering an account of the relationship between religious education and critical realism, this book is essential reading for students, scholars and practitioners interested in philosophy, theology and education.

Professor Andrew Wright researches and teaches at UCL Institute of Education, UK and London School of Theology, UK.

New Studies in Critical Realism and Spirituality

Religious Education and Critical Realism

Knowledge, reality and religious literacy

Andrew Wright

Routledge
Taylor & Francis Group

LONDON AND NEW YORK

First published 2016 by Routledge

2 Park Square, Milton Park, Abingdon, Oxfordshire OX14 4RN

52 Vanderbilt Avenue, New York, NY 10017

Routledge is an imprint of the Taylor & Francis Group, an informa business

First issued in paperback 2020

British Library Cataloguing in Publication Data
A catalogue record for this book is available from the British Library

Library of Congress Cataloging in Publication Data
Wright, Andrew, 1958–
Religious education and critical realism : knowledge, reality and religious / Andrew Wright.
New studies in critical realism and spirituality
Religious education–Philosophy. | Critical realism.
LCC BV1464 .W75 2016 | DDC 268.01–dc23
2015021307

ISBN: 978-0-415-55987-4 (hbk)
ISBN: 978-0-367-59770-2 (pbk)

Typeset in Times New Roman
by Wearset Ltd, Boldon, Tyne and Wear

In Memoriam
Roy Bhaskar
1944–2014
friend, scholar, sage

He took out the package and unwrapped the battered book. 'This one has been scraped and gnawed at,' he said. 'I wonder what agonies have settled here.... Here we are – this oldest story. If it troubles us it must be that we find the trouble in ourselves.' 'I haven't heard it since I was a child,' said Adam.

John Steinbeck, *East of Eden*

Contents

Introduction

Religious Education and Critical Realism: Knowledge, Reality and Religious Literacy seeks to bring the enterprise of religious education in schools, colleges and universities into conversation with the philosophy of critical realism. In doing so it has a dual audience in mind. First teachers, academics, religious ministers and politicians who carry the burden of responsibility for overseeing the cultivation of the religious literacy of children and young adults, and hence of the future religious literacy of society as a whole. Second, the philosophical community of critical realists who are at the forefront of a renaissance in our understanding of ourselves and the world we indwell that has the potential to overcome the tired dichotomy between modernity and post-modernity, reformulate our understanding the heritage of both the pre- and post-Enlightenment past, and under-labour for more truthful ways of being and flourishing as persons-in-community.

The intentionality underlying the identification of two different sets of implied readers is twofold. First, to overcome a tendency of *some* religious educators towards an inward-looking parochialism that fails to locate the subject in its broader historical, cultural and intellectual contexts. Failure to properly understand these various contexts opens the door to the accommodation of the subject to prevailing norms in a manner that occludes the possibility of the subject challenging and transforming such norms for the better. In short, if the argument of this book is viable, then the possibility of a religious education capable of proactively changing the world for the better, and in the process undercutting the objections of its cultured despisers, is equally viable. Second, to overcome a tendency amongst *some* philosophers of critical realism not to take the full implications of their emergent philosophy seriously. Critical realism has generated a set of powerful and compelling arguments that demonstrate beyond reasonable doubt that the epistemic assumptions of much modern and post-modern thought are fundamentally flawed. Now if the epistemic assumptions that generated the various worldviews of modernity and post-modernity have been found wanting, there is every reason to question the veracity of the worldviews constructed by such deeply flawed epistemic tools. However, the equation flawed epistemology, therefore (possibly) flawed ontology, has not always been afforded the seriousness it deserves: the level of resistance to the so-called 'spiritual turn' in critical realism, which effectively recognised that the world-views constructed by flawed epistemic foundations can no longer simply be taken for granted, was significantly high.

The book is primarily about process rather than substance. It addresses the question, not of the *substance* of our primal beliefs about the ultimate nature of reality and our place in the ultimate order-of-things, but of the *process* through which we might attend to questions of substance in more attentive, reasonable, responsible and intelligent ways. Hence it under-labours for the pedagogic emergence of a religiously, philosophically and spiritually literate society. The book deals in turn with questions of philosophy, theology, education in general and religious education in particular. Each set of questions is addressed in parallel chapters, the first of which seeks to unpack the impact of modern and post-modern thought on its given topic, and the second of which seeks to generate a new critically realistic vision.

Religious Education and Critical Realism: Knowledge, Reality and Religious Literacy has had a long gestation. During the process of writing, debates within the community of critical realists regarding critical realism's so-called 'spiritual turn' revealed the urgent need for an account of the relationship between Christian theology and critical realism. hence I found myself abandoning this book and writing *Christianity and Critical Realism: Ambiguity, Truth and Theological Literacy* instead (Wright 2013). Having lived with the current book far longer than intended or anticipated, it is with equal delight and relief that I find myself typing the final words and anticipating opening a rather expensive bottle of single malt by way of reward. Before doing so, I must pause to acknowledge many debts of gratitude. To my previous friends and colleagues at King's College London, and to my new friends and colleagues at UCL Institute of Education and London School of Theology. To my current doctoral students: Mustapha Cabir Altintas, Katie Clemmey, Lisa Cornwell, Ayse Demirel, Ciro Genovese, Johnny Go, Angela Goodman, Thomas Pemberton, Johanna Wood-cock Ross, John Seymour and Adrian Smith. To my wife, Dr Elina Wright, Regent's Park College University of Oxford for making me think. To Alexis for correcting my mistakes. And to Flora for sharing her songs of Zion. On taking up my present post at UCL Institute of Education, I was delighted to discover that I had been allocated a room adjacent to Roy Bhaskar's. Sadly, within weeks delight had turned to deep sadness and the choice of this book's dedicatee had been made for me. And, finally: mere expressions of gratitude cannot possibly recompense the unconditional love, care, support and encouragement graciously gifted by Elina, and by Juliana, Mariana, Becky and Liz.

1   The epistemic fallacy

Our planet is spherical and does not change its shape in response to our shifting beliefs. The fact that in the past many believed it to be flat does not mean it once was flat. Ontological realism recognises, correctly, that reality trumps our epistemic beliefs about reality: the world does not change in order to conform to our beliefs; rather, it is our beliefs that must change in order to conform to the world. The epistemic fallacy forces reality into the straightjacket of our preferred ways of knowing, despite the fact that the primacy of ontology over epistemology requires us to allow reality to shape our epistemic endeavours. The inversion of the proper relationship between the knower and the object of knowledge leads directly to forms of alienation and pathological behaviour, since imagined worlds inevitably clash with the actual world. This is why there is an intellectual, moral and spiritual imperative to pursue truth and truthful living in harmony with the ways things actually are in reality. This chapter narrates a story of the progressive impact of the epistemic fallacy on post-Enlightenment Western thought, speech and action: from the assertion of the sovereignty of consciousness, via epistemic foundationalism and the ensuing displacement of fact from value, to the emergence of a pervasive and hegemonic secular liberal ontology.

The sovereignty of consciousness

Rational autonomy is a critical marker of modern identity. René Descartes insisted that we are fundamentally rational creatures: *cogito ergo sum*, I think, therefore I am. Immanuel Kant maintained that the proper exercise of reason requires our independence from any external constraint: *sapere aude*, have the courage to think for yourself. On this reading, reason and autonomy constitute the fundamental principles of modern selfhood, tempered only by the responsibility to act tolerantly towards others whenever the exercise of rational autonomy leads to a clash of interests. Viewed from the vantage point of post-modernity, the modern notion of human beings as rational, dispassionate, self-reliant and self-possessed seekers after truth and truthfulness appears little more than an ephemeral dream. Michel Foucault's genealogical account of the construction of the modern self seeks to demonstrate that the notion was largely arbitrary, the product of the chance configuration of a variety of socio-cultural power structures. This claim, coupled with the failure of the modern self to fulfil the emancipatory hopes of the Enlightenment, lead Foucault to conclude that 'we have had to abandon all those discourses that once led us to the sovereignty of consciousness' (Foucault 1972: 202). Though 'you may have killed God beneath the weight of all that you have said', he cautions the advocates of modernity, 'don't imagine that, with all that you are saying, you will make a man that will live longer than he' (ibid.: 211). For post-modern philosophers the constructed self of modernity is merely 'a momentary "fold" in the fabric of knowledge, an episode brought about by the enlightenment need to think of man as the rational, autonomous dispenser of his own moral laws' (Norris 1987: 221). As such, it is destined to be 'erased, like a face drawn in sand at the edge of the sea' (Foucault 1989: 387).

In *Madness and Civilization* Foucault charts the emergent polarisation of madness and sanity generated by the triumph of modern reason (Foucault 1971). The medieval Christian understanding that all human beings are loved unconditionally by a gracious God, despite the fact that all fall short of perfection when measured against divine standards, meant that the dividing line between madness and reason was not firmly drawn. Because the outcasts, sinners and demon-possessed took pride of place in the Kingdom of God, Christendom celebrated the court jester and proverbial village idiot as 'holy fools', set apart from society by virtue of their paradoxical closeness to the divine. A litany of Renaissance texts, from Brant's *The Ship of Fools* through Erasmus' *In Praise of Folly* and Shake-speare's *King Lear* to Cervantes' *Don Quixote*, together with the woodcuts and paintings of Bosch and Dürer, testified to the fact that 'folly held pride of place in the catalogue of human weakness' (Boyne 1990: 22). The displacement of Christian faith by secular reason led to a loss of this sense of the sanctity of unreason: insanity was no longer deemed a 'space of pure vision', and madness no longer constituted 'a primitive force of revelation' (Foucault 1971: 38ff.). Instead reason now sought to illuminate and control 'the fantastic and terrible territory of the Other' (Boyne 1990: 16). Where previously a discourse *between* reason and madness had flourished, this was now replaced with a 'monologue of reason *on* madness' (Sarup 1988: 69). This resulted first in policies of incarceration designed to protect society from the mentally ill, and then in the humanitarian *treatment* of the insane through various emergent medical and therapeutic practices.

The transition from medievalism to modernity was the product of a diverse range of interlinked causes: the Renaissance oversaw the recovery of pre-Christian classical culture; the Reformation, with its commitment to the priesthood of all believers, challenged the authority of the Roman Catholic hierarchy and nurtured dreams of individual freedom and responsibility; the notion of the divine right of monarchs to rule gave way to notions of representative government by and for the people; exploration and colonisation served to relativise the supposedly normative status of European culture; the scientific revolution undermined the Christianised Aristotelian worldview of scholastic natural philosophy; economic developments paved the way for a transition from feudalism to capitalism; advances in literature and the fine arts, financed by the emergent mercantile classes, undermined the hegemony of the Church's previous monopoly on culture.

Such changes were prefigured and precipitated by the nominalist turn in late medieval philosophy and theology. William of Ockham dismissed the received scholastic synthesis of faith and reason on the grounds that any attempt, however limited, to make God accountable to human reason risked compromising divine sovereignty (Ockham 1983, 1990; cf. Freddoso 1999; Spade 1999). His nominalist distinction between the reality of particulars and non-reality of universals effectively drove a wedge between the historical Jesus and the Christ of faith. Though this enabled him to assert the absolute transcendence, otherness and freedom of God, it also denied theological discourse any secure purchase on reality. For Ockham, 'the idea of divine omnipotence thus means that human beings can never be certain that any of the impressions they have correspond to an actual object' (Gillespie 1996: 18). This undermined confidence in the Christian account of an all-loving and all-gracious God intimately involved with his creatures in the person of the incarnate, crucified and resurrected Christ. Some Protestant Reformers inferred from Ockham's dual insistence on the absolute sovereignty of God and utter inability of human beings to engineer their own salvation the doctrine of double-predestination, according to which God – in a manner that from the human perspective appears utterly arbitrary – elects some to eternal life and others to eternal damnation. This opened up the visage of a nihilistic world, devoid of any ultimate stability and security, and administered by an all-powerful, arbitrary and unpredictable divine despot. Once the 'holy fool' is dislocated from the orthodox Christian belief in the unbounded grace of an all-loving God and associated instead with an omnipotent tyrant, she ceases to be an object of reverence and becomes instead a potential demonic threat.

It is here that we encounter a key source of modernity. If the failure of reason leads not to a loving God but to an arbitrary despot, then reason must not be allowed to fail. Hence the philosophers of the Enlightenment,

> facing the possibility that all their given reality and perception were illusory, arbitrary and liable to negation at any moment by the Creator, decided to assert themselves and make stable their values, thereby securing a world that a perverted theology had so explicitly abandoned.
>
> (Blond 1999: 234; cf. Wright 2004: 12)

Descartes' *Meditations* take the form of spiritual confession, in which the Cartesian soul contemplates human finitude and struggles with the very real possibility of a descent into chaos:

> The terrifying quality of the journey is reflected in the allusions to madness, darkness, the dread of waking from a self-deceptive dream world, the fear of having 'all of a sudden fallen into deep water' where 'I can neither make certain of setting my feet on the bottom, nor can I swim and so support myself on the surface', and the anxiety of imagining that I may be nothing more than the plaything of an all-powerful evil demon.
>
> (Bernstein 1983: 17; cf. Descartes 1967a: 149)

Descartes' spiritual pilgrimage drives him into an intellectual wilderness in which he must confront the arbitrary God of late-medieval nominalism and wrestle with the demons of madness and chaos.

> Reading the *Meditations* as a journey of the soul helps us to appreciate that Descartes' search for a foundation or Archimedean point is more than a device to solve metaphysical and epistemological problems. It is the quest for some fixed point, some stable rock upon which we can secure our lives against the vicissitudes that constantly threaten us.
>
> (Descartes 1967a: 18)

The potential menace underlying this Cartesian anxiety is such that Descartes is in no position to compromise: '*Either* there is some support for our being, a fixed foundation for our knowledge, *or* we cannot escape the forces of darkness that envelop us with madness, with intellectual and moral chaos' (ibid.: 18).

In the *First Meditation* Descartes sets out, in the light of 'the multitude of errors that I had accepted as true in my earliest years', to make 'a clean sweep for once in my life, and beginning again from the very foundations ... establish some secure and lasting result' (Descartes 1970: 61). He employs a method of systematic doubt, a hermeneutic of suspicion, an epistemology of deconstruction in his attempt to identify a secure foundation both for himself and for his knowledge of the world. Suppose, he argues, in response to Pierre Gassendi's objection, a man

> had a basket of apples, and fearing that some of them were rotten, wanted to take those out lest they make the rest go bad, how could he do it? Would he not turn the whole of the apples out of the basket, and look over them one by one, and then having selected those which he saw were not rotten, place them again in the basket and leave out the others?
>
> (Descartes 1967b: 282)

Descartes' *Discourse on Method* begins by proclaiming the Cartesian soul's emancipation from history, tradition and any received intellectual authority. In 'noticing many things that seem to us extravagant and ridiculous, but are none the less commonly accepted and approved', he learned 'not to believe too firmly anything that I had been convinced about only by example and custom' (Descartes 1970: 13). He offers a negative evaluation of his scholastic education tempered by Renaissance humanism, as delivered by his Jesuit teachers, and questions the value of his study of languages, classics, oratory, poetry, mathematics, ethics and theology. 'And yet I was in one of the most celebrated schools in Europe; and I thought there must be learned men there, if there were such in any part of the globe' (ibid.: 9). He concludes:

> But as soon as I had finished the whole course of studies at the end of which one is normally admitted among the ranks of the learned ... I found myself

embarrassed by so many doubts and errors, that it seemed to me that the only profit I had had from my efforts to acquire knowledge was the progressive discovery of my own ignorance.

(ibid.)

According to Ernst Cassirer, 'it is customary to consider it a major shortcoming of [the Enlightenment] epoch that it lacked understanding of the historically distant and foreign', so that 'in naive overconfidence it set up its own standards as the absolute, and only valid and possible, norm for the evaluation of historical events' (Cassirer 1951: x). In rejecting the authority of received tradition it affirmed the sovereignty of the consciousness of the isolated self, abstracted from the world, dislocated from tradition, and reliant on its own standards of rationality. Thus according to Kant, 'Enlightenment is man's emergence from his self-incurred immaturity', an immaturity marked by 'the inability to use one's own understanding without the guidance of another' (Kant 1997: 54). However, there were tensions inherent in this negative reading of the past. As a child of the Renaissance's rediscovery of classical antiquity, the Enlightenment combined a fascination for the past with a concern to establish a critical distance from it. It was not any lack of interest in, or insensitivity towards, the past that was a hallmark of the Enlightenment, but rather the way in which the past was *used* (Cobban 1960). Peter Gay argues that it is entirely wrong to ignore the Enlightenment's recognition of the past as both 'useful' and 'beloved': it juxtaposed a reverence for classical antiquity with an antipathy towards the Judaeo-Christian tradition (Gay 1973a: 31ff.). Though classical antiquity could not be trusted as a valid source of knowledge, it nevertheless provided the philosophers of the Enlightenment with a certain sense of congeniality: just as a dominant stream of the Enlightenment sought to replace Judaeo-Christian faith with secular philosophy, so pagan antiquity offered – especially in the writings of Lucretius and Cicero, forerunners of the modern 'spirit of criticism' – a historical example of the triumph of reason over myth. Though the earlier triumph of classical reason had subsequently been undermined by the scholastic synthesis of medieval Christianity, the time was now right to forge a new victory of science over myth, reason over faith, and philosophy over religion. Far from being insensitive to the past, the Enlightenment's use of history to undermine the epistemic authority of the received testimony of religious myth was eminently sophisticated.

No longer reliant on the testimonial authority of received tradition, Descartes was free to appeal to first person testimony and confession:

Certain paths that *I* have happened to followed ever since *my* youth have led *me* to considerations and maxims out of which *I* have formed a method; and this, *I* think, is a means to a gradual increase in *my* knowledge that will raise it little by little to the highest point allowed by the mediocrity of *my* mind and the brief duration of *my* life.

(Descartes 1970: 8, my emphasis)

The hermeneutic of suspicion, in dislocating the self from its cultural heritage, forces the Cartesian soul back onto its own resources: the more he doubts the authority of tradition the more he is separated from it, and the more he is separated from it the more he must rely on his own cognitive resources. This process is replicated in Descartes' empirical experience of the physical world, including that of his own body. Though he is aware of sense data in his mind, he cannot be certain that it derives from physical objects in the external world: the Kantian distinction between the noumenal realm of things-in-themselves and the phenomenal realm of things-as-they-appear-to-us is already present here in embryonic form. Since there are times when his empirical sense experiences clearly deceive him, he cannot be certain that they do not deceive him all of the time. Though he holds out the possibility that ideas generated by his sense experiences might be true – if not the composite ideas of sirens and satyrs, then at least those of cats and dogs – he has no way of knowing for certain whether or not they are merely the illusionary products of a dream. Hence his turn from external experience to internal reflexivity and from complex to simple ideas:

> At this rate we might be justified in concluding that whereas physics, astronomy, medicine, and all the other sciences depending on the consideration of composite objects, are doubtful; yet arithmetic, geometry, and so on, which treat only of the simplest and most general subject-matter, and are indifferent whether it exists in nature or not, have an element of indubitable certainty.
>
> (ibid.: 63)

The fact that two plus three equals five is surely true, whether he is awake or dreaming. But what if he is being deceived on this point by a malignant demon? What if two plus three actually equals seven? What if the apparently ordered world of mathematics is ultimately lawless? What if reality is not grounded in an all-powerful and all-knowing God, the benevolent dispenser of natural and moral law? What if our language is purely nominal and utterly disconnected from an ordered, structured and meaningful reality? What if there is no line of demarcation between madness and reason? What if all is anarchy and chaos? And here we arrive at the heart of the matter: even if this were the case, Descartes himself would have to exist in order to be deceived in this way. Whatever the extent of disorder in the world, so long as Descartes is able to question the limits of his knowledge and the extent of his sanity, he must exist to do so: 'I am', 'I exist', 'I am something' (ibid.: 67). Here, in the assertion of the inalienable sovereignty of immediate self-consciousness, lies the foundation and possibility of both intellectual certainty and spiritual security; here, in its self-assertive and self-protective response to Cartesian anxiety, the modern rationally autonomous self engineers its own creation; here, in the drive to impose internal reason on the external world, lies the source of the modern version of the epistemic fallacy.

Epistemic foundations

In affirming the sovereignty of consciousness Descartes claimed to have identified *the* basic self-evident truth that would provide a secure foundation for the positive reconstruction of indubitably certain knowledge in the wake of the termination of the negative deconstructive programme of systematic doubt. However, his use of the phrase *cogito ergo sum* makes a number of assumptions – about language, meaning, communication, thought, identity and being – that appear to have been artificially protected from the hermeneutic of suspicion. As Anthony Kenny points out:

> It is notable how much of Cartesian metaphysics is latent in the arguments for Cartesian doubt ... the sceptical arguments gain their full force only if the reader is prepared to entertain the Cartesian system as possible from the outset.
>
> (Kenny 1968: 38f.)

Despite this, the image of the dislocated mind seeking to reconnect with the world in a manner that avoids any subjective distortion of objective reality came to pervade Western philosophy from the Enlightenment onward: 'there can be little doubt that the problems, metaphors and questions that he bequeathed to us have been at the very center of philosophy since Descartes' (Bernstein 1983: 17). Richard Rorty picks up this theme:

> It is pictures rather than propositions, metaphors rather than statements, which determine most of our philosophical convictions. The picture that holds traditional philosophy captive is that of the mind as a great mirror, containing various representations – some accurate, some not – and capable of being studied by pure, non-empirical methods.
>
> (Rorty 1980: 12)

The dislocated mind seeking to reconnect with the world is envisaged as a mirror capable of reflecting reality; the task facing philosophy is to ensure that the images of reality contained in the mind are properly understood and comprehended, and the burden of responsibility for achieving this rests with the mind itself.

> Without the notion of the mind as mirror, the notion of knowledge as accuracy of representation would not have suggested itself. Without this later notion, the strategy common to Descartes and Kant – getting more accurate representations by inspecting, repairing, and polishing the mirror, so to speak – would not have made sense.
>
> (ibid.)

The very real danger of the mind projecting its own subjective assumptions onto reality meant that the process of reconstructing knowledge must proceed with extreme caution. Because the affirmation of the sovereignty of consciousness could not rule out subjective distortion, it was deemed necessary to set in place a second tier of foundational epistemic principles. The failure to reach agreement on these secondary principles set in chain an ongoing dispute between empiricism, idealism and romanticism.

(1) *Empiricism* sought to establish epistemic certitude by subjecting sense experience of the external world to sustained critical scrutiny. A complex statement was deemed true only if it correctly referenced simple ideas contained in the mind, and if these ideas could be shown to converge with objects in the external world. The danger of misidentification led to the epistemic privileging of simple ideas over complex ones. Complex ideas were viewed as mental constructions derived from simple ideas. Thus the complex idea of 'cat' is basically an assemblage from a set of simple atomistic ideas – colour, shape, feel, sound, smell, movement, etc. The act of construction ran the risk of combining simple ideas in ways unwarranted by the empirical evidence, thereby producing imaginary creatures – unicorns, centaurs, etc. To counter this danger it was necessary to curtail the imagination and seek to maintain a direct ostensive relationship between ideas, words and objects in the world. This required the rejection of all forms of rhetorical and metaphorical expression, since such embellishments could only serve to fuel the imagination and obscure the relationship between words and ideas. The correct linguistic identification of simple ideas still left open the question of their convergence with the external world. How could it be known for certain that mental ideas, however clear, simple and basic, are the product of sense impressions generated by the external world?

Because a thoroughgoing hermeneutic of suspicion could always leave open the idealist possibility that ideas are innate or self-generating, it was necessary to distinguish between 'pure' sense experience and 'impure' ideas generated by the mind's misreading or distortion of such experience. This was achieved by the rigorous cross-referencing of ideas and experiences: regular patterns and conjunctions of verifiable sense data could be attributed to the impact of the external world on the mind; irregular patterns and conjunctions of ideas, especially ideas closed to empirical verification, indicated a potential misapprehension or abuse of sense data. The notion of explaining constellations of sense experience with reference to underlying causal mechanisms was dismissed on the grounds that such mechanisms were not directly observable. The ongoing verification of ideas against sense experience thus constituted the primary means of obtaining true knowledge of the external world. The constant danger was that the mind would irrationally or imaginatively distort atomistic sense data, either by claiming to discern occult causal mechanisms behind empirical objects and events, by combining the data in fanciful ways, or by appealing to aesthetic, moral, metaphysical, or theological concepts closed to empirical verification. The need to guard against such misuse and abuse required surface readings of empirical data that generated reductive accounts of a reality devoid of causal properties, moral value, aesthetic worth, metaphysical depth and theological meaning.

(2) *Idealism*, grounded in the notion of the mind's possession of innate ideas, appeared to offer a path beyond the simplistic and reductionist claims of empiricism. Once emancipated from the problem of the relationship between ideas and the external world, the criterion for truth shifted from the external *convergence* of truth claims with empirical reality to the internal *coherence* of ideas and rational constructs. The mirror of the mind must be inspected, repaired and polished, not to enable it to reflect the empirical world more effectively, but to generate a deeper understanding of ideas and concepts already present within it. If the constructive activity of the mind need no longer be restricted by regular conjunctions of sense data, then it could be embraced as a positive virtue rather than approached cautiously as a potential vice. According to Kant, we obtain knowledge by actively constructing meaning under the guidance of rational categories inherent in the mind's basic make-up (quantity, quality, relation and modality with respect to space and time). The idealist philosopher could avoid simplistic descriptions of surface appearances because there was no longer any danger of exceeding the evidence and trespassing into the illegitimate sphere of metaphysics; on the contrary, metaphysics was the very lifeblood of idealist philosophy. Similarly, idealism could avoid reductionism, since the realms of morality, aesthetics and theology employed rational categories that were inherently meaningful and not reliant on empirical verification.

Idealism claimed a further advantage over empiricism: whereas the latter dealt largely with contingent objects and events, idealism dealt directly with the necessary truths of reason. The heritage of Platonism, with its distinction between eternal necessary forms and temporal contingent objects, was played out in terms of the dispute between empiricism and idealism. Whereas empiricism was faced with the challenge of inferring necessary laws from its observation of contingent events without recourse to causal inference or metaphysical speculation, idealism was faced with the challenge of relating its necessary laws to contingent events. Hegelian dialectic offered a means of making sense of historical contingency by battening historical events down onto an idealised logical structure and thereby accounting for historical contingency in terms of the necessary being-as-becoming of Absolute Spirit via a dialectic of thesis, antithesis and synthesis.

From the empiricist perspective, the crucial question for Hegel, as for all idealist philosophers, was the relationship between internal ideas and external reality, since it was by no means self-evident that the coherence of any given set of ideas necessarily guaranteed a fit with the way things actually are. Kant's moral system might require God to exist in order to ensure that ultimately good will be rewarded and evil punished, but if God does not exist, and if there is no ultimate justice in the world, then no set of logically coherent ideas can alter that state of affairs. Further, if logical coherence is the basic criterion for truth, one is faced with the illogical possibility of affirming the equal truth of two equally coherent, yet ontologically incommensurate, idealist systems.

(3) *Romanticism*, in appealing to the self-evident truth of moral, aesthetic and spiritual feeling, intuition and sensibility, provided an alternative set of epistemic

foundations to rival those of empiricism and idealism. Given that any attempt to live the good life necessarily requires an engagement with the realm of value that transcends the merely 'factual' and 'rational', the emergence of romanticism was perhaps inevitable. Even Hume, the archetypal embodiment of the Enlightenment's commitment to rationally ordered empirical facts, recognised that to live the good life *required* the adoption of a set of values, even if such values are merely the pragmatic products of social convention. To live the good life, for Hume, was essentially a matter of cultivating the sentiment of good taste, regardless of its lack of any objective grounding: in the sphere of human conduct judgements of sentiment and taste are always right, 'because sentiment has a reference to nothing beyond itself, and is always real, wherever a man is conscious of it' (Hume, quoted in Cassirer 1951: 307). Romanticism was essentially the child of idealism: sense was eclipsed by sensibility as appeals to the self-evident truth of rational ideas gave way to appeals to the self-evident truth of emotive feelings. In the romantic realm artists, poets, musicians and spiritual seers replaced empirical scientists and rational philosophers as the high priests and mediators of reality. The latter provided either an atomistic, reductive and truncated vision of the empirical world, or a reified and rationalistic vision of an ideal world, both of which were devoid of contact with the emotions and feelings central to the human condition. The former, on the other hand, allowed access to a holistic vision of the breadth and depth of spiritual experience, one that encapsulated a sense of the intrinsic beauty and goodness of the world and of the sacred, sublime and Transcendent.

Hans-Georg Gadamer views romanticism as a mirror-image of the Enlightenment: the 'reversal of the enlightenment's [rational] presupposition results in the paradoxical tendency to restoration ... culminating in the recognition of the superior wisdom of the primaeval age of myth' (Gadamer 1979: 242f.). Just as reflexive sense gave way to intuitive sensibility, so 'belief in the perfectibility of reason' gave way to 'the perfection of the "mythical" consciousness' (ibid.: 243). Thus Rousseau, having established as an 'incontrovertible rule' that 'the first impulses of nature are always right [since] there is no original sin in the human heart', viewed rationally ordered society as a primary source of human ills, and advocated – via a negative education designed to protect children from the corrosive forces endemic in society and empower them to develop according to their natural dispositions – a return to a primal state of natural goodness (Rousseau 1986: 56).

Despite their fundamental differences, empiricism, idealism and romanticism were all committed to a distinctively modern metaphysic of presence that affirmed the sovereignty of the self-conscious Cartesian ego: the immediate presence in the mind of self-evident foundational truths, whether in the form of empirically sourced sense data, rationally ordered concepts or intuitively grounded sensibility, promised both epistemic certainty and intellectual, aesthetic, moral and spiritual security. All commit the epistemic fallacy of forcing reality into the straightjacket of immediate empirical, rational or intuitive awareness. According to post-modern critics, the modern pursuit of the unachievable goal of epistemic certitude resulted in a premature epistemic closure that led directly to a descent into various forms of totalitarianism: the over-reaching of epistemic boundaries could only be achieved by resorting to hegemonic economies of power: (1) *Empiricism* degenerated into forms of scientism that asserted the applicability of the epistemic tools of natural science to all strata of reality and sought salvation in their technological fruits. The epistemic fallacy of reductively forcing the realms of moral, aesthetic and spiritual value into the procrustean bed of nature had a devastating effect: 'When reason turned totally instrumental, a function solely of power, it legitimated the construction of a totalitarian state and engineered a Holocaust' (Levin 1988: 4). (2) *Idealism*, building on the Enlightenment's self-designation as the moment of transition from an age of superstition to an age of reason, generated totalitarian accounts of the teleological progress of history: for Hegel the realisation of Absolute Spirit and consummation of history were coterminous with the appearance of his own dialectical system. Thus Karl Popper views idealism as a chief cause of totalitarianism and a major enemy of open societies (Popper 1996a, 1996b). (3) *Romanticism*, the sentimental face of idealism, invited the emplotment of historical events within a mythical narrative of the past loss and future recovery of a golden age of primal innocence: through heroic and sacrificial struggle the Nazi Aryan race, the Marxist proletariat, or the stardust-and-golden hippies of the 1960s counter-culture, would eventually return to the mythic Garden of Eden. Each vision, insofar as it proclaims the inevitability of victory, is marked by a totalitarian teleology. The failure of romanticism is all too apparent in the Nazi gas chambers, the Soviet gulags, and the terroristic activities of the likes of the Manson Family and Symbionese Liberation Army. Prior to the advent of postmodern critiques, Bertrand Russell and Isaiah Berlin had already identified a link between romanticism, epistemic closure and totalitarianism (Russell 1946: 701ff.; Berlin 1997: 553ff.).

Just as empiricism subsumes the realm of value within the realm of fact, and idealism subsumes the realm of fact within the realm of value, so 'the romantic reversal of [the empiricist and rationalistic] criterion of the Enlightenment actually perpetuates the abstract contrast between myth and reason' (Gadamer 1979: 243). The dualistic division between objective fact and subjective value remained firmly in place, the only difference being that, in the romantic economy, the realm of subjective value, which had previously been viewed with suspicion as empirically vacuous and rationally dubious, was now celebrated and valorised. If 'Kant severed the connection between science and faith, depriving faith of any objective or ontological reference and emptying it of any real cognitive content', then the neo-Kantian romantic appeal to the self-evident truth of moral, aesthetic and spiritual sensibility generated 'a romantic idealism where the human spirit could range at will, uncontrolled by scientific evidence or knowledge' (Torrance 1980: 27). Appeals to the self-authenticating nature of romantic intuition tended to ignore the fact that our emotive responses to the world are frequently misplaced, often inappropriate and at times profoundly wrong: if intensity of feeling and depth of conviction are criteria for truth, then the emotive responses to the world of the racist, sexist, homophobe and paedophile must be deemed legitimate. Romanticism, in falling prey to the epistemic fallacy of 'trying to make the world fit the agents' feelings, rather than the other way round', is guilty of the 'sentimental falsification of human possibilities' (Kekes 1999: 198, 203).

Dislocated from all meaningful relationships, the Cartesian ego was thrust back on its own resources, and forced to trust its own experiences, reasons and intuitions. As David Levin points out, this triumph of epistemology over ontology, of subjective reason (whether in empiricist, idealistic or romantic mode) over objective reality, had dire consequences: as 'people slowly began to lose sight of the difference between reason and power', so 'reason, increasingly asserting itself in self-destructive ways, began to think of itself as the will to truth' (Levin 1988: 4).

> When subjectivity triumphed [the epistemic fallacy], it imposed its will on things and brought into being a world ruled by objectivity [the ontic fallacy]. But in a world of objectivity, there is no place, no home, for the subject, whose subjectivity – that is to say, experience – is denied value, meaning, and ultimately any truth or reality. This triumph of subjectivity has been self-destructive; we can now see how the subject falls under the spell of its objects; how it becomes subject to the objectivity it set in power. The subject is in danger of losing touch with itself.... The triumph of subjectivity is self-destructive, because it has inflated the human ego without developing self-respect, the true basis of agency, and the social character of human vision.
>
> (ibid.: 4)

Post-modern philosophers identify the Cartesian ego's self-aggrandisement in pursuit of its own security as a root cause of the totalitarian thrust of modernity. The post-modern call to abandon logo-centrism and ontotheology, reject the metaphysic of presence, deconstruct any stable connection between language and reality, attend to the voices of alterity and otherness, and forgo all meta-narratives is a direct response to the totalitarian thrust of modernity. If the human quest for truth and epistemic certitude inevitably degenerates into a network of hegemonic power games, then the only viable alternative is to abandon the pursuit of truth and embrace a thoroughgoing epistemic relativism. Significantly, the abandonment of certitude and security did not plunge the new post-modern self back into Cartesian anxiety: where Descartes feared drowning in a torrent of epistemic uncertainty, post-modern philosophers celebrated the white-water ride of intellectual relativism and made it the centrepiece of the post-modern cultural theme park. Once the Cartesian self-ego is deconstructed, and personal identity perceived as necessarily ephemeral and changeable, there is no capital to be gained in attempting to secure it from the ravages of fate; instead we are free to playfully construct, deconstruct and reconstruct our preferred identities in a cycle of eternal recurrence devoid of any ultimate meaning or teleological goal.

The rhetoric of post-modernity frequently disguises its reliance on the legacy of modernity: once disconnected from any essential ideal or mythic vision of a lost-yet-recoverable golden age, the romantic commitment to intuitive sensibility, reformulated in terms of unconstrained desire, remains firmly in place. Post-modernity does not mark the passing of modernity, but rather the *radical extension* of its romantic wing. The abandonment of the pursuit of truth and deconstruction of the Cartesian ego is rooted in precisely the same primal spiritual concern that drove Descartes and the prophets of modernity: namely, to secure the freedom of the self from all hegemonic powers, both externally imposed social, political and cultural power structures, and internally self-imposed psychological forces. Paradoxically, the deconstruction of the essential modern ego functions to secure the freedom of the nominal post-modern self from self-delusion: once we escape the fantasy that we possess some fixed empirical identity, ideal essence or innate romantic potential that we have a duty to identify and actualise, we are free to become whatever we desire to be.

This reflects the paradox at the heart of post-modernity: namely, its affirmation of the truth that we have no access to truth, and the claim to know with indubitable certainty that indubitably certain knowledge is unobtainable. In rejecting the pursuit of truth and dismissing the essential ego in favour of a vision of a directionless ephemeral self, post-modernity falls prey to the hegemonic forces of unconstrained psychological desire and material consumption: forces encapsulated in the economy of consumer capitalism. And in doing so, it embraces the very same totalitarian thrust it rejected in modernity. Ironically, 'the underlying [post-modern] ideal is some variant of that most invisible, because it is the most pervasive, of all *modern* goods, unconstrained freedom' (Taylor 1992: 489, my emphasis). Ironically, both Descartes and Derrida celebrate 'the prodigious power of subjectivity to undo all the potential allegiances which might bind it: pure untrammelled freedom' (ibid.: 489). Post-modernity inherits from Descartes a concern to emancipate the individual from all external and internal tutelage: such untrammelled freedom constitutes 'the fundamental principle for understanding what it means to be human in the modern (and post-modern) era', and as such 'serves as the ultimate warrant for human actions, desires and interests and as the fundamental reference-point for the justification of our actions, desires and interests' (Schwöbel 1995: 57).

Post-modernity may have swept away the empirical experiences, idealist concepts and romantic intuitions that promised to provide the essential Cartesian ego with secure epistemic foundations, and asserted instead the freedom of the deconstructed Cartesian self to generate its own ephemeral identity on the basis of its own interests, preferences and desires, but in doing so it simply reconfirms the dislocated self at the very centre of reality: the empirical ego ('I experience, therefore I am') and rational ego ('I think, therefore I am') morph, first into the romantic ego ('I feel, therefore I am') and then into the post-modern ego ('I desire/consume, therefore I am'). Whether the dislocated Cartesian self elects to secure itself from the ravages of fate by experiencing, thinking, feeling or desiring, the result is the same: entrapment in the epistemic fallacy of forcing reality to conform to the mind's experiences, reasons, emotions and preferences.

The displacement of value

Colin Gunton suggests that 'the divorce of the natural and moral universes is perhaps the worst legacy of the Enlightenment, and the most urgent challenge facing modern humankind' (Gunton 1985: 25). This divorce and its consequences are a direct result of the epistemic fallacy: the failure to provide morality, aesthetics and spirituality with the same supposedly secure epistemic status as that enjoyed by the natural sciences lead directly to their dislocation from the intransitive ontological realm of objective reality and relocation in the transitive epistemic realm of subjective human responses to reality.

(1) *Cosmology.* Thomas Aquinas' synthesis of Christian theology and Aristotelian philosophy generated a vision of an intrinsically purposeful and value-laden cosmos, one temporally bounded by the events of creation and eschatological consummation, and spatially ordered in a hierarchical chain of being that flowed from the Creator down through his creation. Under the grace of God the cosmos was being transformed and everything in it relocated to its proper place: the ultimate purpose of creation was the establishment of divinely ordained harmonious and beatific relationships, both within creation and between creation and its Creator. However, with the advent of Copernicus' heliocentric account of the universe and Kepler's discovery of the laws of planetary motion, the cosmos could 'no longer be comprehended within that clearly defined scheme which classical cosmology possessed' (Cassirer 1951: 37). Building on the work of Copernicus and Kepler, Newton distinguished between 'absolute mathematical time and space and relative apparent time and space' (Torrance 1980: 24).

> Through clamping down the former, regarded as an unchangeable, inertial framework, upon the world of observations and appearances, characterised by relative apparent time and space, he was able to bring mathematical order into phenomena, and so to expound the immutable laws of nature in terms of the causal and mechanical connections that constitute the system of the world.
>
> (ibid.: 24)

He went on to identify absolute space-time with the divine sensorium, the mind of the eternal and immutable God, within which the universe is contained and from which it receives its inherent order and rationality. The task of God was to establish and sustain the rational order of the universe, an order open to scientific measurement and testing. This constituted a theological shift from theism to deism: God was transformed from the personal creator, sustainer and redeemer of the universe into the impersonal first principle that ensured its rational order. No longer a personal agent, he becomes instead the impersonal structure on which the cosmos is grounded and from which it receives its being. The God of ancient Greek natural theology, which functioned as the ultimate underlying principle (ἀρχή, *archē*) and source of rational order (λόγος, *logos*) in the cosmos, effectively replaced the personal, gracious and merciful God of the revealed Abrahamic faiths (Gerson 1994: 5ff.). Despite his significantly different cosmology, Albert Einstein remains firmly within this tradition: 'I do not believe in the God of theology who rewards good and punishes evil. My God created laws that take care of that. His universe is not ruled by wishful thinking, but by immutable laws' (Jammer 1999: 123).

The emergence of modern natural science from pre-modern natural philosophy, with its commitment to empirical observation, mathematical measuring, experimental testing and inductive modelling, appeared to require 'the discarding by scientific thought of all considerations based upon value concepts, such as perfection, harmony, meaning and aim' (Koyré 1957: 276). Viewed from the perspective of critical realism, both the natural order-of-things and the methods used to investigate it are far from value-neutral: scientific progress via retroductive modelling requires abductive leaps of imagination – reasoning *secundum imaginationem* – in response to the inherent order, beauty and simplicity of nature. However, the remarkable success of natural science generated the fallacious assumption that the epistemic tools developed by natural science in response to the ontological demands of the natural order-of-things were not only neutral, but also universal and generic, and as such transferable and applicable to *all* strata of reality. The strategy of universalising the methods of natural science and giving them hegemony over all other emergent strata of reality served to further exacerbate the devalualisation of being: not only were the realms of human consciousness and culture deemed to be devoid of value, but also those Transcendent realities investigated by metaphysics and theology. Little consideration was given to the fact that non-natural strata of reality make ontological demands that required the development of significantly different epistemic tools, sensitive to moral, aesthetic and spiritual realities: one cannot use an oscilloscope to discern the sublime beauty of a Mozart piano concerto, or an algometer to measure Adolf Hitler's moral character.

Aristotle recognised that both 'science and art come to men *through* experience', and that though the senses 'give the most authoritative knowledge of particulars', they 'do not tell us the "why" of anything – e.g. why fire is hot; they only say that it is hot' (Aristotle 1984: 1552f.). He maintained that discerning the 'why' of things 'involves theoretical and causal explanations and thus goes beyond empirical evidence' (Grant 2007: 215). Having emerged from natural philosophy, natural science, once freed from empiricist and positivist constraints, provided a powerful tool for elucidating the 'why' of nature by explaining how causal mechanisms not directly accessible to the senses generate and configure different objects and events in the physical, chemical and biological realms. However, it cannot, without employing reductive strategies rooted in the epistemic fallacy of making reality conform to our ways of knowing, explain a rich vein of intellectual *aporia*: the aesthetic 'why' of the ontological nature of beauty; the moral 'why' of the ontological nature of good and evil; the metaphysical 'why' of the ultimate origin, nature and purpose of being-qua-being; the spiritual 'why' of the ultimate meaning and purpose of reality; the theological 'why' of the ontological reality of God and his self-revelation to humankind.

The epistemic fallacy of granting the methods and tools of natural science's absolute hegemony over all strata of reality generated reductive accounts of aesthetics, morality and spirituality and denied metaphysics and theology intellectual legitimacy. A particular set of epistemic procedures thus shaped a specific, value-free and teleologically vacuous ontology:

> The infinite Universe of the new Cosmology, infinite in Duration as well as in Extension, in which matter in accordance with eternal and necessary laws moves endlessly and aimlessly in eternal space, inherited all the ontological attributes of Divinity. Yet only those ... all the others the departed God took away with Him.
>
> (Koyré 1957: 276)

(2) *Aesthetics.* In the medieval world it was taken for granted that all manifestations of beauty have their ontological source in God. According to Augustine, God is 'Truth, Goodness and Beauty, all intertwined in ineffable unity' (O'Connell 1978: 49). At the onset of the Enlightenment beauty was deemed to be inherent in nature and reflected in humankind's artistic endeavours. Art was conceived as an imitation of nature, and as such was, like nature, 'to be measured and tested by the rules of reason' (Cassirer 1951: 279). Aesthetics constituted 'an eminently logical system, which scorns the waywardness of unschooled genius, values reason above imagination and knowledge above persons' (Chambers 1932: 80). In principle, 'the proportion of a human figure and the proportions of the architectural order are both reducible to a regulated mathematical system' (ibid.: 80). In practice, the correlation of reason and art proved difficult to sustain, since the affinity between them was 'too dimly felt for expression in precise and definite concepts' (Cassirer 1951: 276). Romanticism sought to break free from the constraints of such classicism: as the mirror image of the rational Enlightenment it valorised imagination, inspiration and artistic genius. Whereas the classical artist was constrained by the rules of her art form and the order of nature, the romantic artist was free to transgress both (Coleman 1971: 52). Romanticism claimed to 'discover heights and depths of the human spirit that the older philosophy had hardly dared dream of' (Chambers 1932: 163). In romantic art, the 'value and charm of aesthetic appreciation do not lie in precision and distinctness but in the wealth of associations which such appreciation comprises' (Cassirer 1951: 300). If the brilliance of Mozart's classicism lay in his ability to hide himself and allow beauty to reveal itself through the established structures and rules of classical composition, as evidenced in his late symphonies and piano concertos, the genius of Beethoven's romanticism lay in his ability, especially in his late string quartets and piano sonatas, to reveal his inner life of joy and despair, loss and fulfilment, by deconstructing classical forms and

employing fugue, theme and variation to allow melodic simplicity and moments of harmonic dissonance to repeatedly turn back on themselves in a process of ever-deepening introspection and self-expression (Wright 1998: 62, n. 24). It was the subjective focus on aesthetic self-expression that gave birth to the romantic notion of troubled artistic genius, of whom Beethoven was the musical archetype (Sonneck 1954: 230; Dahlhaus 1993: 31).

This progressive shift in the primary focus of aesthetics, from God via nature to the human spirit, had profound consequences for the developing understanding of the ontological basis of art and beauty:

> The concept 'nature' has now undergone a characteristic change of meaning. For the 'nature of things' (*natura rerum*), to which aesthetic objectivism had been orientated, is no longer the guiding star; it has now been superseded by the nature of man.
>
> (Cassirer 1951: 298)

If beauty was no longer perceived to be grounded in the objectivity of God or nature, but rather in subjective human genius and sensibility, could it claim any lasting or stable ontological status? The romantic image might be grasped as an epiphany of transcendent beauty, 'a radiant truth out of space and time'; but it could just as easily be dismissed as the prosaic expression of ephemeral subjective sentiment (Kermode 1971: 30). Characteristically, Hume was in no doubt as to the answer: 'beauty is no quality of things in themselves: it exists merely in the mind which contemplates them, and each person perceives a different beauty' (Hume 1963: 268). On this reading art ceases to possess the profundity of primal revelation: it is reduced to mere entertainment, and its appreciation to the expression of personal taste. 'Intelligence considers what things are in themselves, according to their essence, without relation to ourselves. Taste, on the contrary, occupies itself solely with objects as they are related to ourselves' (Charles Batteux, quoted in Coleman 1971: 23). Kant placed the appreciation of beauty on the same level as the appreciation of good food: 'I try the dish with my own tongue and palate, and I pass judgement according to their verdict, not according to universal principles' (Kant, quoted in Nahm 1975: 326). In effect, aesthetics is disconnected from objective ontology and reduced to subjective epistemology, and judgemental rationality is reduced to the expression of personal preference. If, as Cassirer points out, 'all value judgements as such are concerned not with the thing in itself and its absolute nature', but with our relationships with the object 'as perceiving, feeling, and judging subjects', then values are devoid of all ontological significance and reduced to expressions of subjective preference (Cassirer 1951: 306f.).

(3) *Morality.* The Abrahamic faiths find the source of all goodness in the being of God. If this led them to affirm absolute standards against which to measure human character and behaviour, it also resulted in the recognition of human fallibility and moral failure. Belief in God's all-loving and all-merciful nature enabled these faiths to develop practices of prayer, worship and spiritual

discipline designed to draw believers into relationship with God and aid their stumbling attempts to allow God to transform their lives for the better. The transition from theism to deism meant that, in the absence of a personal God, goodness was seen as a natural phenomenon. As a result, prayer, worship and spiritual discipline became redundant, and human beings were forced to pursue goodness through their own efforts. According to Locke, we can infer from the animal kingdom that the good life is constituted by the pursuit of happiness and avoidance of suffering: 'Things then are Good or Evil, only in reference to Pleasure or Pain' (Locke 1975: 229). He sought to move beyond the simple ideas of pleasure and pain, via the complex ideas of good and evil, to the universal principles, or natural laws, on which human conduct should be based. Though Locke suggested that the relationship between moral law and its divine source was in principle open to rational demonstration, he does not develop any extended account of the divine source of our moral obligations. Instead he is content to offer only a brief sketch of how such an account might be developed: the existence of God can be established through rational argument; since we are dependent on God for our existence, he possesses rightful authority over us; since God is benevolent and desires our happiness, we are under an obligation to obey his will; since the ultimate ground of our happiness lies in such obedience, it is irrational not to seek to obey God's commands (ibid.: 351ff.). The fact that this skeletal argument is not developed in any depth reflects the progressive dislocation of the moral order from any theological source or legitimation. The later claim that nature, 'red in tooth and claw', did not actually reflect any moral order, whether its own or God's, opened the door to the utilitarian and pragmatic rejection of any theological or naturalistic grounding for morality and the insistence that morality is essentially a human construct.

This distinctively modern subjective turn in moral thinking is most clearly visible in the thought of Kant. Though the substance of his moral vision has deep Christian roots, its form is profoundly anthropocentric: the evil in human nature is overcome by human effort and self-transformation rather than divine grace.

> The proximate source of this transformation of the will is not God, but the demands of rational agency itself which lie within me. The fact that ultimately, in Kant's view, it is God who designed things this way doesn't mitigate the central status given to human dignity.
>
> (Taylor 1992: 366)

> Kant explicitly insists that morality can't be found in nature or in anything outside the human rational will.... We cannot accept that the cosmic order, or even the order of ends in human 'nature', should determine our normative purposes. All such views are heteronomous; they involve abdicating our responsibility to generate the law out of ourselves.
>
> (ibid.: 364)

Kant claimed to have identified a self-evident deontological categorical imperative: 'act only in accordance with that maxim through which you can at the same time will that it become a universal law' (Kant 1998: 31). Charles Taylor notes the fragility of Kant's concept of 'a noumenal rational agent', and suggests that our 'growing inability to hold on to it creates something of a spiritual crisis in our civilization' (Taylor 1992: 367). The stringent challenge of upholding deon-tological moral norms invited a turn to more pragmatic and consequentialist ethical systems. It is significant that both Descartes and Locke were content to affirm provisional moral values designed to enable humankind to function on pragmatic lines until such time as universal moral principles could be estab-lished. In the *Discourse on Method*, Descartes undertakes to obey the customs of his country, act resolutely even on the basis of doubtful opinions, and allow the world to shape his desires until he has completed his journey of self-instruction (Descartes 1970: 24ff.). In similar vein, Locke appeals to the twin principles of freedom and tolerance as an interim ethic, designed to avoid a descent into social anarchy and establish an environment conducive to the ongoing pursuit of moral truth (Locke 1993a, 1993b). The fact that comprehensive liberals reified these principles and turned them into ends in themselves, thereby *equating* the good life with the exercise of personal autonomy tempered by the practice of toler-ance, serves to highlight tensions between modern deontological and consequen-tialist ethics (Wright 2007: 29ff.). What both ultimately have in common, however, is a shared conviction that moral values are essential human constructs radically disconnected from both God and nature.

(4) *Spirituality.* In previous books I have sought to defend a critically realistic understanding of spirituality as 'the developing relationship of the individual, within community and tradition, to that which is – or is perceived to be – of ulti-mate concern, ultimate value and ultimate truth' (Wright 1998: 88; cf. Wright 1999, 2000). In medieval Christendom spiritual identity was understood *sub specie aeternitatis* – under the aspect of eternity. Christian doctrine and praxis provided a sacred canopy under which it was possible 'to "locate" human phe-nomena within a cosmic frame of reference' (Berger 1990: 35). The modern embargo on metaphysics and theology sought to expose the illusionary nature of all such sacred canopies. Douglas Porpora suggests that this resulted in 'a cultur-ally pervasive lack of orientation in metaphysical space, an inability to place ourselves meaningfully in the cosmos' (Porpora 2001: 152). Attempts to fill this void generated a subjective turn in spirituality, in which ultimate spiritual concern was understood in terms of the subjective experiences of the dislocated Cartesian self, rather than in terms of any substantial relation to the ultimate order-of-things.

This transition from objective to subjective spirituality is reflected in the early stages of Ludwig Wittgenstein's spiritual quest. In the *Tractatus Logico-Philosophicus* he argues that reality consists of the totality of facts and states of affairs in the world, and that ideas are logical pictures of facts and states of affairs which can be expressed as meaningful propositions (Wittgenstein 1974). However, knowledge of facts and states of affairs fails to resolve the riddle of life: 'We feel that even when all *possible* scientific questions have been answered, the problems of life remain completely untouched' (ibid.: 73). To approach the world *sub specie aeternitatis* and view the totality of facts and states of affairs as a limited whole raises spiritual *aporia*: 'It is not *how* things are in the world that is mystical, but *that* it exists' (ibid.). Since the world consists of nothing more than the totality of facts and states of affairs, we cannot ask spiritual questions of our relation to that which lies beyond it, and if the question of the meaning of life cannot be asked then the riddle of existence does not exist. In which case, the 'solution of the problem of life is seen in the vanishing of the problem' (ibid.).

> My propositions serve as elucidations in the following way: anyone who understands me eventually recognizes them as nonsensical, when he has used them – as steps – to climb up beyond them. (He must, so to speak, throw away the ladder after he has climbed up it).... He must transcend these propositions, and then he will see the world aright.
>
> (ibid.: 74)

To see the world aright is to experience reality as a totality *sub specie aeternitatis*. The mystical manifests itself to us, even though it can never be put into words: 'What we cannot speak about we must pass over in silence' (ibid.).

Unlike the logical positivists, Wittgenstein is clearly unwilling to allow their mutual rejection of metaphysics to occlude spiritual *aporia*, and he seeks to counter this possibility by appealing, albeit implicitly, to the romantic tradition of intuitive, pre-linguistic experience. At the heart of such romanticised spirituality is the consciousness of being part of a greater limited whole – a state of consciousness words can never express adequately, if at all. This effectively shifts the locus of spirituality from the ontological actuality of ultimate reality to the individual's subjective epistemic intuitions and experiences. Since romantic intuition is essentially pre-linguistic it is necessarily closed to judgemental rationality: if it is impossible to evaluate the epistemic authority and veracity of intuitive experience without recourse to language, then any assessment of spiritual intuition must be wholly reliant on further spiritual intuition. This subjective turn in spirituality is a direct consequence of the denial that spiritual language possesses any meaningful ontological referent, a denial that forced spiritual intuition to claim self-legitimation and consequently focus attention on the 'inner space' of subjective spiritual experience rather than on any objective relationship with the ultimate order-of-things. This subjective turn is reflected in the definition of spirituality proposed by Her Majesty's Inspectorate as the basis for spiritual education in English and Welsh schools:

> The spiritual area is concerned with the awareness a person has of those elements in existence and experience which may be defined in terms of *inner feelings and beliefs* ... concerned with matters at the heart and root of existence.
>
> (DES/HMI 1977, my emphasis; cf. Wright 1999: 9)

Michael Grimmitt's functional account of such a subjective spirituality offers a vision of spirituality as the dislocated Cartesian self's capacity for creative self-transcendence, in a manner devoid of any objective relationship to any greater reality.

> In speaking of human spirituality, therefore, I am referring to a human capacity for a certain type of awareness ... the activation of the human capacity for self-transcendence and movement towards a state of consciousness in which the limitations of human finite identity are challenged by the exercise of the creative imagination.
>
> (Grimmitt 1987: 125)

This is yet another manifestation of the epistemic fallacy: in the absence of theological or metaphysical knowledge of the ultimate order-of-things, the spiritual quest is no longer an objective search for ultimate truth and truthful living *sub specie aeternitatis*, but instead a subjective process of self-identification and realisation.

The ontological matrix

To recap: Cartesian anxiety created a desire for epistemic certitude; the desire for epistemic certitude led to empiricist, idealist and romantic forms of epistemic foundationalism; and epistemic foundationalism generated a dualistic distinction between objective fact and subjective value. Post-modernism, as a reactionary mirror-image of modernity, abandoned the quest for certitude and rejected epistemic foundationalism. However, this simply reinforced the fact–value divide: cut adrift from any ontological mooring, values became free-floating objects of subjective preference.

It is tempting to hold post-Enlightenment culture culpable for the occlusion of ontology. This, however, would be a gross distortion of the truth: in reality it generated a relatively clear ontology, though one that was rendered invisible to many by virtue of its pervasive scope and hegemonic authority. If a closed society is one that 'lives in a charmed circle of unchanging taboos, of laws and customs which are felt to be as inevitable as the rising of the sun, or the cycle of the seasons', then, contrary to its rhetoric of emancipation, the liberal society generated by the Enlightenment is, in many respects, remarkably closed (Popper 1966a: 57). Locke's vision of an 'open' political liberalism, in which adherents of contested accounts of reality could participate together in an ongoing pursuit of truth and truthful living, gradually gave way to a 'closed' comprehensive liberalism, in which the 'facts of disagreement themselves frequently go unacknowledged, disguised by a rhetoric of consensus' (MacIntyre 1988: 2).

The ontology matrix of naturalism, secular humanism and neo-liberalism sketched in this section can be read as a direct product of the epistemic fallacy: the foundational epistemic criteria required to overcome Cartesian anxiety produced a particular understanding of reality, effectively forcing ontology into an epistemic straightjacket. Critical realism offers an alternative account of the relationship between ontology and epistemology: since the intransitive ontological realm exists apart from our transitive epistemic discernment of it, ontology is necessarily prior to epistemology. Since knowledge is constituted by the relationship between the knower and the object of knowledge, the attainment of knowledge requires the mind of the knower to adapt itself to, or allow itself to be adapted by, the ontological demands made by the object itself. When a new knowledge relationship is established the transitive mind of the knower is transformed, while the intransitive reality of the object of knowledge remains constant – apart, that is, from the (generally relatively inconsequential) fact that the object has now become an object known by the knower.

The epistemic fallacy reverses this polarity by giving epistemology priority over ontology, on the false assumption 'that statements about being can be reduced to or analysed in terms of statements about knowledge … ontological questions can always be transposed into epistemological terms … being can always be analysed in terms of our knowledge of being' (Bhaskar 2008: 36). In the Preface to the second edition of his *Critique of Pure Reason* Kant rejects the realistic claim 'that our cognition must conform to the objects', and proposes instead that 'the objects must conform to our cognition' (Kant 1934: 12).

> Reason must approach nature with the view, indeed, of receiving information from it, not, however, in the character of a pupil, who listens to all that his master chooses to tell him, but in that of a judge, who compels the witness to reply to those questions which he himself thinks fit to propose.
>
> (ibid.: 10f.)

Since 'reason only perceives that which it produces after its own design', it must resist following 'the leading-strings of nature' and instead 'proceed in advance with principles of judgement according to unvarying laws' (ibid.: 10). Because observation of the accidents of nature cannot generate universal laws, reason must proceed from a set of a priori categories to which 'all the objects of experience must necessarily conform' (ibid.: 12). The fact–value divide is a direct product of the epistemic fallacy: because the spheres of aesthetics, morality and spirituality are not amenable to the close measuring and testing employed by the natural sciences, they are effectively dislocated from the realm of objective reality and reassigned to the realm of subjective opinion. For the logical positivists the unverifiable nature of value statements meant that they must be dismissed as quite literally meaningless, since they could not possibly enjoy any cognitive purchase on the actual order-of-things: the process of forcing ontology into the procrustean bed of positivist epistemology required the dismemberment of reality.

The epistemic fallacy lays the foundation for the ontic fallacy, which 'views knowledge as an unproblematic, direct mapping between subject and being' (Shipway 2011: 64). Where the epistemic fallacy ignores the ontological givenness of reality in the intransitive domain, the ontic fallacy ignores the epistemic relativity of knowledge claims in the transitive domain. Though they may appear to be direct opposites, the two fallacies are actually mutually dependent, since it is only by committing the epistemic fallacy of forcing a complex and never-fully-comprehended reality into a simplistic and fully-comprehended set of epistemic assumptions that it is possible to claim to possess an unmediated and comprehensive knowledge of reality.

> The epistemic fallacy projects the external world onto a subjective phenomenal map, then the ontic fallacy projects the phenomenal entities of that subjective map back out on the world as objective sense data, of which we have direct perceptual knowledge. So reality independent of thought is first subjectified, then the subjectified elements are objectified to explain and justify our knowledge.
>
> (Irwin 1997)

The rest of this section will outline the basic contours of the post-Enlightenment liberal ontology generated by the epistemic and ontic fallacies. Karl Popper identifies the ontological reality of three interlinked worlds: *World 1* consists of the material world of organic and inorganic nature; *World 2* consists of the domain of the consciousness in sentient beings; *World 3* consists of the cultural artefacts, linguistic ideas and social structures generated by sentient human beings as they engage with nature (Popper 1972; cf. Niiniluoto 1999: 23ff.). To these we can add, whilst recognising that its existence is contested, *World 4*: a more primal and basic Transcendent ontological domain or reality (e.g. God, YHWH, Trinity, Allah, Nirvana, Brahman, Plato's Forms, Bhaskar's meta-Reality) that constitutes the original source, teleological destination, transcendent canopy and/or ontological ground of the interlinked network of Popper's Worlds 1–3.

World 1: the natural order-of-things. If, as Descartes claimed, the basic criterion for truth is immediate self-conscious awareness, then awareness of empirically generated data provided secure access, once tested and verified, to World 1. The post-Enlightenment world was dominated by the success of natural science in explaining the natural order-of-things and enabling a vast range of technological advances. Optimistic assessments of our ability to understand and control nature helped dissipate Cartesian anxiety and secure a sense of our proper place within the natural world. Such optimism is clearly evident in Francis Bacon's 'Great Instauration', his project designed to help humankind return to a paradisiacal state through the exercise of reason and promotion of natural science (Bacon 1974, 2012; cf. Gaukroger 2001: 132ff.). This generated a tendency to identify natural science as the provider of *the* overarching meta-narrative, against which all other accounts of reality must be measured. Thus the realms of aesthetics and morality could either be incorporated within the natural scientific narrative, so that talk of good and evil was reduced to reifications of the animal instinct to seek pleasure and avoid pain, or disbarred from the narrative and dismissed as emotive expressions devoid of any ontological purchase on reality. At the same time, the emergent recognition that natural science employed a posteriori empirical observation led to the rejection of metaphysics and theology as a priori non-empirical disciplines whose claims were closed to empirical verification and/or refutation. This served to reinforce the growing assumption that nature could be understood without an appeal to any Transcendent agency or mechanism, and gave birth to naturalistic and materialistic assumptions that the natural order-of-things constitutes the ultimate bedrock of reality, the primal stratum beyond which there is no need to look for any further explanation.

The metaphysical question of being-qua-being was effectively disqualified: it was deemed sufficient merely to *describe* the primal natural forces present at the origins of the universe, rather than *explain* the 'why' of their existence. Recognition that the technological fruits of natural science could be used for great evil as well as for great good led to a reassessment of natural science in the post-modern era. Though Paul Feyerabend's attempt to deconstruct and relativise natural science proved attractive to some post-modernists at a theoretical level, it had little impact on scientific practice or the conduct of ordinary life: the ability of scientific narratives to explain and manipulate the natural world was simply too powerful to ignore (Feyerabend 1987). Instead a new eco-politics emerged that, rather than advocating its deconstruction, sought to limit the hegemony of natural science by asserting the pragmatic utility of non-scientific discourses, advocating a greater moral input into the process of scientific investigation, and campaigning for a greater respect for the natural world and deeper recognition of our dependence on it – a process that, in some New Age and neo-pagan circles, extended to the deification or semi-deification of nature. Though eco-politics produced a revised understanding of our relationship with nature, it did little to displace the increasingly naturalistic and materialistic assumption that the natural order-of-things constitutes the basic ontological bedrock of reality, and that any more extensive aesthetic, moral or spiritual understanding of the world must necessarily operate within the boundaries imposed by the strata of reality described by natural science. Thus naturalism provided the bedrock of the dominant post-Enlightenment ontological matrix.

World 2: human consciousness. If the basic criterion for truth is immediate self-conscious awareness, then such awareness enables direct unmediated access to World 2. If we can be relatively certain of the external natural world described by natural scientists, then we can be equally certain about the internal world of our immediate thoughts, feelings and desires. The extent to which other sentient minds may be aware of our inner consciousness is a disputed issue. Ancient Greek philosophy distinguished between a person's outward appearance (πρόσωπον, prosopon) and underlying ontological ground (ὑπόστᾰσις, hypostases). In Platonism the identification of the ultimate ontological ground of human beings with the impersonal Platonic Forms led to a devaluation of those personal traits and characteristics that marked the outward appearance of embodied individuals. Thus in neo-Platonism, when the body dies the immortal soul loses its distinctive personal identity and is absorbed back into the eternal 'One'. In Greek tragedy the hero typically struggles to secure his personal identity in the face of the impersonal ravages of fate: the mask (προωπεῖον, prosopeion) he wears on stage tragically *both* affirms his transient ephemeral identity *and* disguises his lack of any secure ontological ground (Zizioulas 1985: 27ff.). Christian theology challenged this dualistic distinction between appearance and reality. Working from their conviction that Jesus of Nazareth was *essentially* God rather than a mere fleeting manifestation of the divine, the first Christian theologians insisted on the identity of Jesus' external appearance (πρόσωπον) and underlying ontological ground (ὑπόστᾰσις). In the person of Jesus, the incarnate Christ, fully human and fully divine, there is no distinction between outward appearance and underlying ontological reality. The Trinitarian God consists of three persons (Father, Son and Holy Spirit) existing in the indivisible unity of the one Godhead: though the distinctive identity of each person is irreducible, all three are indissolubly united in a bond of reciprocal love, so that the distinctive and irreducible identity of each person is grounded in the reciprocal relations within the Triune Godhead. Two things follow from the belief that 'God created humankind in his own image' (Genesis 1:27). First, personal identity is ontologically secure: we are created as persons in the image of God, held in being eternally by our Creator, and devoid of any debilitating dualistic divide between appearance and reality. Second, personal identity is essentially relational: just as the distinctive identities of the persons of the Trinity are grounded in their reciprocal loving relationships with one another, so we are the people we are insofar as we relate, not merely to ourselves, but also to other-persons-in-community, to the natural order-of-things, and to God. Descartes' epistemology of systematic doubt sought to secure the first of these features (ontological identity), but did so only at the expense of abandoning the latter (relational identity): if the hermeneutic of suspicion sought to establish and secure the ontological reality of the Cartesian ego, it did so at the expense of dislocating it from any substantial relationships with any external reality.

With the eclipse of the *imago dei*, human identity was no longer understood as ontologically grounded in, and reflective of, the reciprocal loving relationships that constitute the identities of the persons of the Trinity. Instead, personhood was understood with reference to the natural order: human identity was deemed to be constituted (1) by our dependence on a natural order incapable of sustaining us for more than a brief period of time, and (2) by the fact that we are set apart from other animals by virtue of our capacity to reason. The Christian 'I am loved by God, therefore I am' was replaced by the Cartesian 'I think, therefore I am.' Thus the autonomous exercise of reason, emancipated from all relational constraints other than those necessarily imposed by the natural order, became the distinguishing mark of human identity in the modern era. The transition to post-modernism via romanticism led to the replacement of rationality first with intuitive sensibility ('I feel, therefore I am') and then with the capacity for self-creation ('I desire, therefore I am.') Throughout this process the vision of the dislocated Cartesian self remained constant: whether through sense and reason, sensibility and feeling, or desire and creativity it remained the measure of its own identity. This brings us full circle back to the anthropology of ancient Greek philosophy: in terms of our outward appearance, we secure our personal identities by thinking, feeling and acting autonomously; in terms of our under-lying ontological ground we are, as embodied persons, utterly dependent on the ontological primacy of the natural order that brings us into being and sustains our lives, if only for a brief period of time. Just as the neo-Platonic self was des-tined to be absorbed back into the eternal 'One', so the post-Enlightenment self is destined to be absorbed back into the natural order as its body decays after death. The image of the autonomous individual, fighting tragically and heroically (ancient Greece), stoically and courageously (modernity), or playfully and joy-fully (post-modernity) to affirm and secure his existence in the face of his inevit-able death and extinction, constitutes, alongside the bedrock of the natural order-of-things, the second basic component of the post-Enlightenment onto-logical matrix.

World 3: culture. If the basic criterion for truth is immediate self-conscious awareness, then the reality of World 3 cannot be avoided, though its meaning is inevitably more ambiguous than the certainties afforded by awareness of Worlds 1 and 2. The Enlightenment generated a divide between scientific and non-scientific culture (Snow 1959). Where empiricists tended to be sceptical of the value of non-scientific culture, idealists and romantics adopted an altogether more appreciative stance, especially towards the creative arts, which were deemed to reveal sublime dimensions of reality untouched and unrecognised by natural science. This opened up the possibility of distinguishing between 'high' and 'low' culture, and establishing a canon of artistic works of inspired genius. F.R. Leavis, for example, identified a 'Great Tradition' in the English novel, marked by moral commitment and a recognition of the complexity of life, that centres on the works of Jane Austen, George Eliot, Henry James and Joseph Conrad (Leavis 1972). The post-modern response was to dismiss all such canons as hegemonic: since there are no secure standards for distinguishing between works of art, readers must be free to consume whatever they like, and make judgements on the basis of personal preference and taste. This led both to a flattening-out of culture, so that no single work could be deemed better or worse than any other, and to the abandoning of notions of the revelatory power of art, which could be consumed for entertainment or edification without any expecta-tion that it might illuminate profound truths about the human condition.

Underlying this democratisation of art lay the eclipse of 'political' liberalism by 'comprehensive' liberalism. John Locke had wrestled with the reality that tensions between conflicting beliefs and values frequently descend into violence. His response was to advocate a form of 'political' liberalism designed to enable members of diverse traditions to embrace their distinctive visions whilst partici-pating in a common pursuit of truth. To that end he advocated an interim ethic predicated on the exercise of reason, freedom of belief, and tolerance of the beliefs of others. Over time Locke's political liberalism was reified into a com-prehensive liberal worldview, in which the principles of freedom and tolerance functioned as *ends in themselves* rather than as a means of securing the con-ditions necessary for the ongoing pursuit of truth and truthful living. In such an economy the right to believe, desire and do whatever one wishes, provided one accepts the duty not to harm others in the process, constitutes the greatest human good. In the comprehensive liberal economy of rights and duties Locke's epistemic virtues are effectively transformed into ontological norms: the ontological autonomy of the Cartesian self has absolute priority, and all other beliefs and values are reduced to cultural objects that may be consumed or refused according to personal taste. Emerging from, and dependent upon, the value-free and teleologically vacuous process of natural evolution, the Cartesian self, as the highest ontological entity known to exist in the cosmos, stands at the apex of reality and enjoys the freedom to pursue its own cultural desires and construct its own cultural identities within the limits imposed by the natural order-of-things. The realm of human culture presents a host of possibilities that the autonomous self is free to utilise and consume at will, provided that it does so in a tolerant manner that avoids doing harm to others (Rorty 1989).

World 4: Transcendence. If the basic criterion for truth is immediate self-conscious awareness, then access to World 4 becomes problematic, since we have no direct empirical access to it (as we do for Worlds 1 and 3, nature and culture), and no unmediated awareness of it (as we do for World 2, sentient mind). The term 'Transcendence' is used here to refer to a primal ontological reality underlying Worlds 1–3, rather than to the human capacity for self-transcendence. Popper's failure to identify World 4 implies that religious and spiritual experience in World 2 (sentient mind), and religious and spiritual ideas, artefacts and institutions in World 3 (human culture), do not provide epistemic purchase on, or ontological grounding in, any ultimate Transcendent reality, and that by default World 1 (nature) constitutes the primal ontological reality. Though the comprehensive liberal principle of freedom allows for Transcendent beliefs and practices, it views them as essentially private affairs lacking in ontological significance, and consequently tends to seek to exclude them from rational debate and public life. The reasons behind the occlusion of World 4 (Transcendence) and positioning of World 1 (nature) and World 2 (human consciousness) as default substitutes will be explored in the next chapter. Here it is sufficient to make three preliminary observations. First, the assumption that religious beliefs and practices have no rational basis, threaten to undermine human freedom if taken too seriously, and challenge humankind's place at the apex of reality is a direct product of the ontic and epistemic fallacies that generate and sustain the post-Enlightenment ontological matrix. Second, despite its antipathy toward all forms of hegemony, comprehensive liberalism assumes the self-appointed task of policing religious traditions: if the principle of freedom allows religious adherents to subscribe to whatever beliefs they choose, then the principle of tolerance requires that religious expression and practice is largely confined to the private sphere, where it can do less harm to non-adherents. Third, critical realism, in challenging the epistemic and ontological assumptions on which the post-Enlightenment ontological matrix of naturalism, secular humanism and neo-liberalism rests, opens the door to the possibility that religious beliefs may be intellectually warranted, that the practice of autonomy is not necessarily the greatest human good, that humankind is not necessarily positioned at the apex of reality, and that religion, spirituality and theology have the potential to transform the public sphere for the greater good of all.

This chapter offered an account of the impact of the epistemic fallacy on post-Enlightenment Western culture: Cartesian anxiety generated a desire for certitude; the desire for certitude spawned epistemic foundationalism; epistemic foundationalism engineered a fact–value divide; and the fact–value divide gave birth to a post-Enlightenment ontological matrix which holds: (1) that the natural order-of-things constitutes the primal bedrock of reality (naturalism); (2) that sentient human beings are the highest entities to have evolved from the bedrock of nature (secular humanism); and (3) that consequently they have the inalienable right to think, speak and act with complete autonomy in the transitive realm of culture, provided they recognise their duty to avoid causing harm to others when doing so.

2   Critical realism

Critical realism, acting as an under-labourer across a wide range of intellectual disciplines, offers philosophical tools capable of challenging the epistemic fallacy and re-establishing the primacy of ontology over epistemology. The triumvirate of ontological realism, epistemic relativity and judgemental rationality provide an antidote to the various pathologies associated with the premature epistemic closures of modern essentialism and post-modern nominalism. By allowing reality itself to guide and structure our ways of knowing, it becomes possible to make informed, though necessarily contingent, judgements about the nature of reality in a manner that makes possible the advancement of learning and human flourishing. This chapter offers a presentation of the basic contours of critical realism, in the context of a critique of the Cartesian account of the dislocated self driven by a hermeneutic of suspicion, and its replacement by a vision of the embodied self driven by a hermeneutic of trust.

Indwelling the world

Bhaskar identifies a lack of seriousness prevalent in philosophical discourse that generates inconsistencies between theory and praxis, and leads to alienation and pathological behaviour (Bhaskar 1994: 62ff.). Though logical positivists might claim that moral discourse is literally meaningless, they cannot avoid engaging in meaningful moral relations with other human beings. Their failure to attend to the inconsistency between their theory and praxis betrays a lack of philosophical seriousness. It is certainly true that the positing of hypothetical counterfactual scenarios has potential heuristic value: 'What if our moral discourse *is* empirically unverifiable and therefore meaningless?' And equally true that the meticulous, consistent and serious working-through of the implications of such hypothetical scenarios can yield positive results: 'We must abandon *either* our moral relationships – if such an option is possible – *or* the claim that moral discourse is meaningless.' Failure to do so leads directly to the dislocation of thought from action: 'We will continue to engage in meaningful moral relationships despite our belief that to do so is meaningless.' Similarly, the anti-realist philosopher who denies that scientific theory enjoys any epistemic purchase on reality is under an intellectual obligation to account for the accomplishments of natural science: if 'the theoretical claims of the natural sciences were not correct, their massive empirical success would appear to be totally accidental, or at best a stunning concatenation of coincidences' (McGrath 2001: 73). The disparity between the absence of any adequate explanation of the success of science and the anti-realist philosopher's practical inability to avoid utilising the technological fruits of science betrays a fundamental lack of philosophical seriousness.

> Even the most dedicated anti-realist philosopher, crossing the Atlantic Ocean to deliver an eagerly-awaited intellectual demolition of realism, will be forced to concede that the airplane boarded to reach that destination flies – and it flies, at least in part, on account of the relation between pressure and kinetic energy first set out by Daniel Bernoulli in 1738.
>
> (ibid.: 72)

In the *Grammar of Assent* John Henry Newman detects a similar lack of seriousness in John Locke's account of how we establish knowledge of the world. Locke, he suggests, 'takes a view of the human mind, in relation to inference and assent, which to me seems theoretical and unreal' (Newman 1979: 139).

> Reasonings and convictions which I deem natural and legitimate, he apparently would call irrational, enthusiastic, perverse, and immoral; and that, as I think, because he consults his own ideal of how the mind ought to act, instead of interrogating human nature, as an existing thing, as it is found in the world.
>
> (ibid.)

Locke provides an account of how he thinks the mind *ought* to set about the task of establishing knowledge, but fails to assess his claims in the light of how the mind *actually* establishes knowledge. All serious accounts of epistemology, including accounts designed to revise received practices, must attend to the 'human mind as we find it, and not as we may judge it ought to be' (ibid.: 177). If there is to be continuity between theory and practice, epistemology must at some point engage in a 'phenomenological analysis of the process of belief-formation [that] describes how the mind works within real-world environments' (Aquino 2004: 58).

In the previous chapter we saw how Cartesian anxiety generated a hermeneutic of suspicion that resulted in the dislocation of the self from the world. The ensuing affirmation of the sovereignty of consciousness led to the establishment of a set of foundational epistemologies concerned with distinguishing between the certitude of knowledge and ambivalence of belief, which in turn spawned a dualistic differentiation between objective fact and subjective value. The philosophers of the Enlightenment dreamt of a timeless and transcendent universal reason, set on indubitable objective foundations, uncontaminated by the contingent spatio-temporal accidents of history and culture, and capable of providing a god's-eye 'view from nowhere' (Nagel 1986). Isolated in his stove-heated room and 'at full liberty to discourse with myself about my own thoughts', Descartes took time to lament the deficiencies of humankind's knowledge of the world through an extended architectural analogy. Our knowledge, he conjectures, is akin to

> those ancient cities which were originally mere boroughs, and have become large towns in process of time ... [and which] are as a rule badly laid out ... in view of their arrangements – here a large one, there a small – and the way they make the streets twisted and irregular, one would say that chance has placed them so, not the will of men who had the use of reason.
>
> (Descartes 1970: 15)

But what, he speculates, if the ancient cities were torn down and replaced by new towns 'laid out by a designer on an open plan to suit his fancy' (ibid.)? Those 'buildings undertaken and carried out by a single architect are generally more seemly and better arranged than those that several hands have sought to adapt' (ibid.). Thus the philosophers of the dawning age of reason have the opportunity to discard the untrustworthy knowledge accumulated by the accidents of history and start the epistemic endeavour afresh.

A major problem with this vision of new knowledge constructed on firm foundations is that it bears little resemblance to our actual ways of knowing in real-world environments. In practice we know the world by virtue of our immersion in received communal traditions, not by isolating ourselves and attempting to reconstruct knowledge anew from first principles. Further, the vision is disconnected from the actual status of knowledge: as rational-yet-fallible human beings we possess substantial knowledge of the world, despite the fact that such knowledge is always partial, provisional and contingent. The binary opposites of objectively certain knowledge and subjectively uncertain belief do not accurately reflect the actual standing of our knowledge of the world: we may not know all there is to know about nature, morality and aesthetics, but we certainly know enough to walk on the moon, recognise genocide as a great evil and appreciate the sublimity of Mozart's music. There is a basic inconsistency between the theoretical ideals and aspirations of the Enlightenment project and the actuality of its epistemic practices and their results. Thus, for example, the actual procedures employed by natural scientists differ significantly from the accounts provided by empiricist philosophers. In practice natural science does not generally proceed along the Humean path of deducing natural laws from the observation of regular occurrences of objects and events under experimental conditions. Instead, as Roy Bhaskar and other critical realists point out, abductive encounters with the natural world enable scientists to retroductively generate and iteratively refine theoretical models designed to explain the natural world through the identification of casual mechanisms underlying empirical objects and events (Bhaskar 2008).

The failure of many modern philosophers to identify and problematise the disparity between theory and practice reflects a lack of philosophical seriousness that has grave consequences: in particular, it engenders a version of the epistemic fallacy that reduces reality to that which is open to empirical observation, measurement and verification, and thereby allows for the alienation of objective fact from subjective value. Wittgenstein came to recognise this state of affairs during the course of his philosophical journey. We have already seen how, in the *Tractatus Logico-Philosophicus*, he set out to describe an ideal monophonic language capable of providing a comprehensive account of the totality of reality (Wittgenstein 1974). In the *Philosophical Investigations* he recognised the inconsistency between this ideal and the polyphonic ways in which language is actually utilised in practice, noting (in an apparent allusion to Descartes' conjecture noted above) that:

> Our language can be seen as an ancient city: a maze of little streets and squares, of old and new houses with additions from various periods; and this surrounded by a multitude of new boroughs with straight regular streets and uniform houses.
>
> (Wittgenstein 1968: 8)

If one of the functions of language is to act as a tool through which we engage with and seek to understand the world, then our actual use of language in real-world environments suggests that epistemology cannot ignore the received wisdom of the past, the interpersonal nature of communal knowing, or the relativity of knowledge. Thomas Nagel, in insisting that epistemology cannot rightfully claim to occupy an idealised 'view from nowhere', suggests that if 'one of the strongest philosophical motives is the desire for a comprehensive picture of objective reality' then 'the natural place to begin is with our position in the world' (Nagel 1986: 13). As Thomas Kuhn points out, we learn science not by isolating ourselves from the scientific community and attempting to replicate the history of scientific achievement from scratch, but by consulting scientific textbooks that enable us to access the rich heritage of scientific knowledge (Kuhn 1970). If 'there is no "vantage point" from which we can view and evaluate our beliefs' other than 'our already existing beliefs', then we have no option other than to embrace a contextual epistemology that proceeds from the knowledge that communities-of-knowing already give assent to (McGrath 2002: 35).

Michael Polanyi draws an important distinction between 'tacit' and 'explicit' knowledge. We employ tacit knowledge in the course of our everyday lives, responding immediately and intuitively to particular situations without necessarily stepping back to reflect explicitly on what we are thinking, doing and saying. This tacit knowledge extends to the physical and linguistic tools we utilise, so that they form virtual extensions of our minds and bodies in psychosomatic unity. Just as the blind person's white stick and sculptor's chisel function as tacit extensions of themselves, so our language, beliefs and values function as tacit extensions of ourselves. We indwell the world, both physically and mentally: 'we pour ourselves out into [physical and linguistic tools] and assimilate them as parts of our own existence ... [accepting] them existentially by dwelling in them' (Polanyi 1958: 59). Knowledge flows from 'our community with and indwelling within, not our disembodied contemplation of, the real universe of which we are a part' (Gunton 1985: 44). We indwell the world not as isolated individuals, but as communal beings who mutually share beliefs, values and languages (Polanyi 1958: 212). Such tacit and interpersonal engagement 'commits us, passionately and far beyond our comprehension, to a vision of reality' (ibid.: 64). The 'roots of personal knowledge' are to be found in primal encounters with the world 'which lie beyond the operations of a scientific formalism' (ibid.).

Polanyi recognises that our tacit knowledge can be mistaken, and that the secondary process of making primary tacit knowledge explicit and critically assessing it constitutes a key means of avoiding epistemic error. Crucially, such critical reflection functions as an under-labourer to tacit knowledge rather than as a foundational alternative to it. If critical reflection is allowed to override rather than serve tacit knowledge there is a constant danger that it will debilitate effective thought, speech and action. The pianist whose focal awareness falls on the interaction of her fingers with the keyboard rather than the music she is producing is unlikely to perform as well as a pianist only tacitly aware of the technical issues surrounding her playing: whereas the playing of the former is likely to be mannered, stilted and overly self-conscious, the playing of the latter is likely to be better precisely because of her ability to spontaneously lose herself in the music she is producing. The philosophers of the Enlightenment, insofar as they sought to artificially break loose from the tacit spontaneity of everyday existence and build knowledge afresh on the foundation of explicit self-conscious reflection, effectively dislocated the Cartesian ego from the practice of ordinary life. Though critical reflection has a vital under-labouring role to play in everyday life, any attempt to replace the latter with the former will inevitably lead to inconsistent thought and pathological action.

Critical thinking and rational reflection must proceed from the lifeworlds and real-world environments we indwell and inhabit, rather than seek to replace them with an abstract and artificial ideal. Tom Wright suggests that our worldviews embrace tacit assumptions about the nature of reality that generally function at a pre-reflective and pre-cognitive level: (1) they provide the stories through which we make sense of reality; (2) they answer a set of primal questions (Who am I? Where am I? What is wrong? What is the solution?); (3) they employ distinctive cultural symbols that express communal identity; and (4) they embrace a distinctive praxis or way-of-being in the world (Wright 1992: 123f.). Thus the worldview of the United States of America: (1) tells the *story* of the birth of a democratic nation in which all citizens have the right to life, liberty and the pursuit of happiness, and of the need to protect such rights from internal and external attacks; (2) answers *primal questions* by identifying an American citizen as an autonomous individual ('Who am I?'), living in a democratic polity ('Where am I?'), under real or potential threat, internally and externally, from undemocratic totalitarian forces ('What is wrong?'), that must be actively resisted in order to secure the basic rights of American citizens ('What is the solution?'); (3) embraces *distinctive symbols*, such as the saluting of the American flag and celebration of Independence Day; and (4) encourages a praxis organised around the freedom of individuals to determine for themselves what constitutes the good life (the accumulation of money, the nurturing and protection of family life, obedience to the will of God, etc.), provided that in doing so they remain within the law. Though lifeworlds can be inhabited tacitly, there are significant advantages in encouraging adherents to make their stories, questions, symbols and praxis explicit, even though such a process carries with it the possibility of iteratively refining, radically reforming or even completely rejecting them.

Truth and Method, Hans-Georg Gadamer's *magnum opus*, presents an account of the hermeneutics of knowledge and understanding that seeks to explicate actual hermeneutical practices rather than advocate an ideal: 'I am *not proposing a method*, but I am describing *what is the case*' (Gadamer 1979: 465). It is, he suggests, a phenomenological reality that 'long before we understand ourselves through the process of self-examination, we understand ourselves in a self-evident way in the family, society and state within which we live' (ibid.: 245). Knowledge is rooted in the given, pre-reflective horizons of meaning of the lifeworlds we inhabit, and within which we live out our everyday lives. Ordinary pre-reflective knowledge takes epistemic precedence over abstract reflective knowledge: we are political beings before we engage in political philosophy, moral beings before we engage in moral reflection, and religious beings before we engage in theological science. The process of reflection, whether it takes place during the course of everyday life or in the reified atmosphere of the academy, does not provide the epistemic foundations of ordinary life; rather, it serves as an under-labourer, enabling us to evaluate, refine, revise and even abandon the knowledge and beliefs that inform our everyday living, and thereby empowering us to live more authentic and truthful lives.

The priority of the pre-reflective life over the reflective life means that it is 'the prejudices of the individual, far more than his judgements, [that] constitute the historical reality of his being' (ibid.). It follows that knowledge inevitably proceeds from *Die Vorurteile* – prejudice, presupposition, pre-understanding. This being the case, the epistemic category of pre-understanding, which had been unequivocally rejected by most Enlightenment philosophers, must be rehabilitated. The hermeneutic of suspicion set out to rid the knower of all prejudices inherited from the authority of tradition and hegemony of received institutional opinion: within the Enlightenment project the pursuit of knowledge requires knowers to think for themselves, have the courage to trust their own reason, and set aside their biases and presuppositions. The 'fundamental prejudice of the enlightenment is the prejudice against prejudice itself, which deprives tradition of its power' (ibid.: 239f.). Gadamer argues that if knowledge is rooted in the pre-reflective lifeworld and dependent on the authority of received testimony, then it follows that 'there is no … unconditional antithesis between tradition and reason' (ibid.: 250). Just as reason engages with the raw material of received tradition, so understanding proceeds from faith, and knowledge emerges from assent.

The 'recognition that all understanding inevitably involves some prejudice gives the hermeneutical problem its real thrust' (ibid.: 239). A 'person who is trying to understand a text is always performing an act of projecting': whenever we encounter an object or event that we do not immediately understand we respond by projecting a potential meaning onto it, which we then either revise or abandon in favour of an alternative possibility in the light of our ongoing engagement with, and contemplation of, the object or event in question (ibid.: 236). If we are too quick to impose our projected meaning onto an object or event we risk committing the epistemic fallacy by forcing it to conform to our established knowledge and ways of knowing. If, on the other hand, we are open to the possibility of the object or event resisting our initial projection, asserting its truth against our prejudices, and thereby transforming our understanding, we open up the possibility of a realistic engagement with reality. If 'reason is concerned to adjust our beliefs to conform to the world' then acknowledgement of our beliefs, recognition of their fallibility, and openness to their potential revision is a necessary factor in the pursuit of knowledge (Bhaskar 1994: 66).

Gadamer suggests that philosophical seriousness is dependent on the epistemic priority of the unreflective lifeworld. If we participate in a sporting contest, it is the 'seriousness in playing [that] makes the play wholly play': the person 'who does not take the play seriously' undermines the integrity of the game (Gadamer 1979: 92). If a sporting contest is to be authentic we 'must accept the primacy of play over the consciousness of the player' (ibid.: 94). Bill Shankly, one time manager of the Liverpool football team, once famously observed: 'Some people believe football is a matter of life and death ... I can assure you it is much, much more important than that' (LiverpoolFC.TV 2012). As in sport, so in life! It is precisely because philosophical reflection both flows from and impacts upon the challenge of inhabiting our lifeworlds authentically and living the good life truthfully, that philosophy is, or ought to be, a serious business. To view the dislocation of the philosopher from the game of life as a necessary prerequisite for philosophical reflection is to invite unserious, inconsistent and pathological philosophy.

The 'grammar of assent'

The Cartesian search for epistemic certitude grounded in secure foundational principles generated a split between objective knowledge and subjective belief. This in turn engendered a critique of enthusiasm, the enthusiast being a person of deep aesthetic, moral or spiritual commitment who insists on treating their subjective beliefs as if they possessed the status of objective knowledge, and refuses to confine their commitments to the private sphere (Locke 1993a, 1993b). In a liberal economy grounded in notions of freedom and autonomy, the expressions and actions of the enthusiast constitute potential threats to the moral order (Kekes 1999; Thiessen 2011). To insist on the objective truth of a subjective belief in the public sphere is to threaten the principle of tolerance, which functions to mitigate the impact of the inevitable clash of human interests generated by the exercise of personal autonomy. Given that, by definition, a subjective belief is closed to rational demonstration, the proclamation and propagation of such beliefs in the public sphere requires the use of persuasion and force. This liberal suspicion of enthusiasm runs up against the fact that tolerance is a morally neutral concept: a blanket undifferentiated tolerance requires tolerance of racism, sexism, homophobia and paedophilia. Hence, as Karl Popper points out, the tolerant liberal paradoxically claims 'in the name of tolerance, the right not to tolerate the intolerant' (Popper 1966a: 265). The paradox lies in the fact that the question of the criteria by which decisions regarding what is and what is not worthy of tolerance can only be answered by appealing to subjective value judgements. In Locke's day, as in our own, such criteria tend to focus pragmatically on the issue of potential threats to the moral and political fabric of society. For Locke the practice of tolerance required the proactive intolerance of Roman Catholics, just as today it requires the proactive intolerance of so-called 'radical' Islam. One of the major problems with this pragmatic resolution of the paradox is that it valorises a status quo that may be both unjust and misinformed, and severely restricts progressive and revolutionary beliefs and actions. The enthusiast thus becomes the person who, for good or ill, seeks to change the status quo and hence threatens the established order. The liberal embargo on public enthusiasm thus acts as an impediment to social change and intellectual transformation. On this reading, enthusiasm, like tolerance, is a morally neutral concept: it is not tolerance per se that is the solution to society's ills, since some societies may be in urgent need of intolerant citizens (e.g. Nazi Germany, apartheid South Africa); by the same token it is not enthusiasm per se that is the problem, since enthusiasm can be a source of both good and ill, but rather morally and intellectually degenerate instances of enthusiasm. This raises the question of the criteria through which we might judge the moral and intellectual integrity of a set of enthusiastically held beliefs, and brings us back to the heart of the matter: the Enlightenment's assumption that our aesthetic, moral and spiritual commitments constitute subjective beliefs that are *closed* to moral and intellectual scrutiny.

Despite being theologically motivated, John Henry Newman's *An Essay in Aid of a Grammar of Assent* is essentially an exercise in secular philosophy (Newman 1979). Newman asks how ordinary people in real-world environments can legitimately assent with assurance to beliefs in the absence of demonstrable proof. Though his central concern is for the epistemic warrant of Christian beliefs, the tenor and substance of his argument clearly extends to all beliefs, religious and secular alike, across all spheres of human knowing. Newman argues that belief formation is primarily the product of ordinary everyday life, and that it is driven and informed by the *organum investigandi*: an 'illative sense' that guides and directs 'a non-rule-governed process of reasoning, which accumulates probabilities and renders informed assessment about concrete matters' (Aquino 2004: 48).

> As a complex belief-producing process, the illative sense enables people to
> be certain about concrete matters without epistemic access to how the mind

justifies knowledge. Explicit awareness of the grounds of belief is not a pre-condition for forming rationally acceptable beliefs.

(ibid.: 5)

On the basis of our illative sense we may legitimately believe with certitude that time and space are relative, the natural world is dynamically structured, the music of Mozart sublime, Auschwitz an abominable evil, and God is the creator and redeemer of the world, despite both the absence of a full and comprehensive understanding of nature, beauty, goodness and Transcendence, and the inability of natural science, aesthetics, moral philosophy and theological science to provide demonstrable proofs of their various truth claims. Paradoxically, such certitude cannot rule out the possibility of doubt, nor can it guarantee the truth of our convictions. Though I may be absolutely certain that critical realism consti-tutes a more powerful philosophical tool than positivism, idealism, pragmatism or anti-realism, this does not preclude me from questioning my convictions and does not guarantee that I am correct; nevertheless, my illative sense provides sufficient warrant for my continuing to hold fast with certitude to my critically realistic beliefs.

Newman's argument proceeds from observation of the actual real-world con-ditions in which we assent to beliefs, rather than from any idealised or formal-ised conditions that philosophy might seek to impose or demand. He suggests that in real-world environments it is virtually impossible to avoid subscribing with certitude to beliefs that cannot be fully understood or adequately defended. Though such beliefs may be mistaken, we normatively assent to them and act on them on the assumption that they are true. In the case of many of our more con-sequential beliefs, such as those in the spheres of aesthetics, morality and spiritu-ality, the lack of demonstrable proof appears insurmountable. Despite this, many – though by no means all – human beings appear capable of making informed aesthetic, moral and spiritual judgements, and of acting appropriately in accord-ance with them.

The refusal to make such judgements on the grounds that they will inevitably fall short of demonstrable proof, appears to entail a lack of aesthetic, moral and spiritual seriousness that undermines the possibility of consistent belief and action. This suggests that there is considerable virtue in the medieval scholastic formula of faith-seeking-understanding, and places a question mark over the Enlightenment principle of understanding-seeking-faith. Negatively, Newman opposes philo-sophers such as Descartes, Locke and Hume, who deny any legitimate epistemic warrant for holding beliefs that cannot be fully comprehended and properly demonstrated; his chief target is the thoroughgoing scepticism engendered by the Enlightenment, which he views as an artificial construct that undermines the pursuit of truth and cultivation of truthful living. Positively, Newman argues that epistemic certitude in real-world environments is derived from informed assent to propositions regarding realities external to our minds; such propositions are derived from non-rule-governed inferences-to-the-best-possible-explanation of our immediate experiences of reality. Newman's argument is twofold: (1) In Part One of the *Grammar*, 'Assent and Apprehension', he argues that we can legitimately assent to propositions that we cannot fully understand; (2) in Part Two, 'Assent and Inference', he argues that we can legitimately subscribe to beliefs we cannot demonstrably prove.

(1) *Assent and apprehension.* Newman begins, then, by arguing that we can legitimately assent to propositions that we cannot fully understand. Contra Descartes' insistence that knowledge must be based on clear and distinct ideas, Newman claims an epistemic warrant for assenting to propositions that are not fully and comprehensively understood. Such assent is dependent on the proper use of the illative sense. For example, we can employ our illative sense to judge a person's character despite not having a comprehensively clear and distinct understanding of them. In everyday life it is often possible to observe the maturity of a person's illative sense, for example when we recognise them to be a 'good judge of character', 'socially insightful', 'trustworthy', 'philosophically sharp' or 'politically astute'. Though the illative sense is a natural component of our humanity, like Aristotle's 'phronesis' or practical wisdom it requires cultivation and refinement through experience, education and practice. Because the illative sense cannot be taken for granted, we have a moral and intellectual duty to seek to cultivate it, both in ourselves and others.

How then might the illative sense pan out epistemologically? In real-world environments a person in possession of a mature illative sense will recognise that propositions proffering cognitive truth claims about reality are open to three possible responses: assent, inference and doubt. Though doubt is a natural and necessary means of testing our beliefs, it is immature to equate it with a thoroughgoing scepticism that will inevitably lack philosophical seriousness and prove epistemically counterproductive. Since we can only question that which we or others already believe to be the case, both assent and inference enjoy epistemic priority over doubt. Inference, despite eschewing any narrowly conceived formalism or logic when operating in real-world environments, is necessarily conditional, since the act of inference requires us to draw our experiences together into meaningful wholes. Assent, on the other hand, is unconditional, since it requires us to affirm the truth of a proposition directly, without any need to infer conclusions from prior experiences. Assent thus takes epistemic precedence over both doubt and inference.

But *can* we legitimately assent to propositions we do not fully understand? In order to assent to the truth of a proposition it is clearly necessary to apprehend its meaning. Apprehension 'is simply an intelligent acceptance of the idea, or of the fact which a proposition enunciates' (Newman 1979: 36). Crucially, apprehension is not the same as understanding, which requires a deeper level of discernment and comprehension. Newman insists that it 'is possible to apprehend without understanding' (ibid.). We can apprehend the order of nature, the beauty of music, the evils of genocide, and the reality of God despite the fact that such apprehension falls short of a full and comprehensive understanding. In real-world environments we can and do assent to propositions we do not fully understand, and we possess a legitimate epistemic warrant for doing so. If this were not the case, we would need to possess the omniscient mind of God in order to assent to any proposition or state of affairs; since we are self-evidently fallible creatures, the requirement of full and comprehensive understanding means that we could never assent to any proposition; however, since we *do* assent to propositions, and in many cases are self-evidently correct to do so, full and comprehensive understanding cannot be a condition for informed assent.

Newman distinguishes between *real apprehension* of objects and events external to our minds, and *notional apprehension* of thoughts and ideas contained within our minds: real apprehension determines the intrinsic meaning of things and enables us to explore actual events and objects in depth, whilst notional apprehension considers the relationship between things and provides our understanding with a breadth of vision. It is important to recognise that for Newman real apprehension cannot be reduced to the perception of empirical sense data, but rather involves the discernment and cognition of deep ontological realities underlying surface appearances. Together, real and notional apprehensions constitute distinct-yet-related dimensions of our way-of-knowing in real-world environments. However, real apprehension enjoys epistemic priority over notional apprehension, because it is concerned with actual objects rather than conceptual abstractions, and because notional apprehension (like inference) entails degrees of assent (on a continuum from profession through opinion to speculation) excluded from the real apprehension of immediate objects and events. Nevertheless, the real apprehension of actual objects runs the constant risk of deluded and wayward assent. Consequently notional apprehension, despite possessing second-order epistemic status, remains a vital and necessary component of the epistemic process: reflective critical thinking, through which we doubt, question, test and assess the veracity of our propositional truth claims, constitutes a major means of avoiding the dangers of delusion and waywardness in our real, immediate and direct apprehensions of reality.

An authentic Christian life possesses both a spiritual and a theological dimension. In the spiritual dimension Christians participate in the religious beliefs and practices of Christian communities and give real assent to them; in the theological dimension Christians critically test and iteratively refine the doctrinal propositions that sustain Christian belief and give notional assent to them. A similar pattern repeats itself in the secular world: ordinary everyday life in real-world environments is guided and supported by the under-labouring activities of intellectuals within the academy. In a world of increasing intellectual specialisation, it is impossible for ordinary citizens to engage in the specialist activities of the academy, and within the academy it is impossible for specialists in one field to be specialists in other fields. This means that, in the vast majority of cases, we have no option other than to take the fruits of epistemic under-labouring in the academy on trust. An epistemology of assent to testimony does not, however, imply the hegemony of testimonial authority: a mature mind will be attuned, receptive and attentive to the relative status of epistemic testimony, whilst an immature mind will either be artificially resistant to all testimonial authority ('have the courage to think for yourself') or else naively and simplistically accepting of a single authority – both options being alternate sides of the same coin.

(2) *Assent and inference.* Having demonstrated an epistemic warrant for assenting to propositions that cannot be fully understood, Newman now turns to his central question: Can we legitimately subscribe to beliefs we cannot demonstrably prove?

Whereas the act of 'assent is in its nature absolute and unconditional', the act of inference is necessarily conditional (ibid.: 135). Newman accepts that it *appears* inconsistent to hold 'that an unconditional acceptance of a proposition can be the result of its conditional verification' (ibid.). He distinguishes between simple and complex assent: the former generates *material* certitude, whilst the latter generates *interpretative* certitude (ibid.: 174). We give simple assent to beliefs that we take to be self-evidently true without reflection and complex assent to beliefs that are placed on 'an argumentative footing' and require inferential support (ibid.: 175). Though there is value in questioning beliefs grounded in simple assent, 'introspection of our intellectual operations' is not the primary source of our beliefs (ibid.: 177). The habit of questioning, of substituting assent with inference, can all too easily slip into artificial forms of scepticism that are inconsistent with our ways of knowing in real-world environments.

Recognising that our convictions can be either true or false, Newman defines certitude as 'a right conviction' (ibid.: 181). He sets out three conditions for certitude: that it is grounded in informed discernment that transcends mere fancy and prejudice; 'that it is accompanied by a specific sense of intellectual satisfaction and repose' that transcends mere inference; and that it is subject to a level of irreversibility that transcends mere conviction (ibid.: 207). Formal inference, 'considered in the sense of verbal argumentation, determines neither our principles, nor our ultimate judgements', and as such 'is neither the test of truth, nor the adequate basis of assent' (ibid.: 229). Our belief that Britain is an island is not the product of formal inference, though formal inference can help test its veracity; rather it is derived from informal discernment within the real-world environments we indwell. Thus, contra appearances, it *is* consistent to assent unconditionally to propositions despite the conditional nature of the inferential arguments supporting them. We *can* legitimately subscribe with certitude to various beliefs – e.g. that Britain is an island, that genocide is evil, that Mozart's music is sublime, or that God exists – even if we are not in a position to offer demonstrable proof. The sceptical retort, 'But where is your *proof* that Britain is an island, genocide is evil, Mozart's music is sublime or God exists?' lacks intellectual seriousness. This immediately becomes clear when we invoke a counter-question: 'But where is your *proof* that Britain is *not* an island, that genocide is *not* evil, that Mozart's music is *not* sublime or that God does *not* exist?'

Informal discernment is generally implicit and tacit, and requires the personal engagement of the knower with the object of knowledge in a manner that is too delicate and intricate to be reduced to formal inference. Informal inference flows from the cumulation of probabilities, independent of each other, arising out of the nature and circumstances of the particular case which is under review; probabilities too fine to avail separately, too subtle and circuitous to be convertible into syllogisms, too numerous and vast for such conversion, even were they convertible.

(ibid.: 230)

In short, we know more than we can explain. Our assent to the sublime nature of Mozart's music flows directly from our personal and attentive engagement with it; our irreversible certitude that our assent is right and proper is the product of informal inferences that cannot be reduced to formal arguments, and which manifest themselves in the aesthetic satisfaction provided by the music itself. No amount of argument can convince the person tone-deaf to the beauty of the music; because 'our most natural mode of reasoning is, not from propositions to propositions, but from things to things, from concrete to concrete, from wholes to wholes', all we can do is encourage them to listen attentively (ibid.: 260). It is this 'illative sense' that enables us to properly assent with certitude to scientific, moral, aesthetic, religious and spiritual beliefs in the absence of demonstrable proof and formal inference.

What warrant have we for trusting our illative sense? Newman argues that knowledge proceeds from that which we already know by virtue of our embeddedness in the world. In real-world environments we 'are conscious of the objects of external nature, and we reflect and act upon them' (ibid.: 272).

We are in a world of facts, and we use them; for there is nothing else to use. We do not quarrel with them, but we take them as they are, and avail ourselves of what they can do for us.

(ibid.)

Consequently we employ a basic hermeneutic of trust, not just in the external world but also in ourselves in-relation-to the external world: 'a basic self-acceptance, a communion with the concrete individual that I am, [is] a necessary condition of [the] possibility of self-realization' (Norris 1977: 97). Knowledge does not proceed from an artificial hermeneutic of suspicion, in which we deconstruct our antecedent knowledge and seek to reconstruct it on secure foundational principles. It is because our natural way-of-knowing takes precedence over artificial ways-of-knowing that we have a primal warrant to trust our illative sense and assent to our beliefs despite the absence of full understanding and demonstrable proof, and to continue to do so until such time as a more powerful account of our experiences and of the world we indwell becomes available to us. The phenomenological givenness of our actual knowledge relationships should ground our epistemic reflections. To reverse this sequence and 'propose a normative account of rationality independent of an empirical analysis of belief-formation' is to commit the epistemic fallacy of making the 'world of facts' subservient to our chosen ways of knowing (Aquino 2004: 59). Philosophical reflection has the under-labouring role of iteratively refining our actual epistemic procedures, not the over-labouring role of establishing them. There is no consistent alternative: Cartesian scepticism is not neutral, since it embraces scepticism as a *positive dogmatic principle* and fails to be sceptical about the epistemic value of scepticism itself (Newman 1979: 294). Rather than turn all the apples out of the basket in the suspicion that one might be rotten and contaminate the others, we ought to inspect each individual apple and only discard those that are becoming putrid. In 'the true way of learning' we 'begin with believing everything that is offered to our acceptance' and then proceed to test the veracity of our beliefs by seeking out and discarding errors (ibid.). 'The illative sense is the elastic logic of thought, the living rule by which people judge issues in various fields of knowledge' (Aquino 2004: 68). Judgemental rationality is not the same as thoroughgoing scepticism: just as one false belief does not justify abandoning all beliefs, so one instance of faulty reasoning does not justify abandoning reason.

> Within real-world environments, reliable belief-forming processes, instantiated in communally established practices, furnish the proper context for examining the nature and function of our constitutive faculties.
>
> (ibid.: 61)

Newman holds that, though the illative sense is a natural property of all human beings, it is possible, through formal and informal education, for individuals to refine and seek to perfect it, and that they have a moral duty to do so to the best of their ability. Though the illative sense is generic, it pans out in specific epistemic contexts: just as some people are better at 'reading' an individual's character and motivations than others, so some can 'read' music, art, religion, politics, the natural world, etc. better than others. We refine our illative sense by immersing ourselves in communities of practice and learning from those whose illative sense is more advanced than ours. In specialist fields in which we have no expertise we have no option other than to trust the testimony of experts, and do so by applying our illative sense to the question of the veracity of the secondary testimony rather than the primary object of such testimony. Provided we have acted reasonably to refine our illative sense to the best of our ability, we have an epistemic warrant to hold fast to our beliefs, despite the absence of demonstrable proof. Thus the 'ordinary' atheist or religious believer is entirely justified in holding their epistemic beliefs with certitude, despite the ontological possibility that they may be mistaken, provided they have employed, to the best of their natural ability, judgemental rationality to iteratively test them in the light of their own experiences and the testimony of experts. This does not of course mean that atheists and theists are necessarily correct to hold the beliefs they do, since atheism and theism are ontologically incommensurate; it does however mean that they have a legitimate epistemic warrant to do so. The pursuit of knowledge thus proceeds not by way of an artificial hermeneutic of suspicion grounded in an illusory rational objectivity, but by way of a cultivated hermeneutic of trust that proceeds from and through faith to deeper, faith-based

understanding. Faith is not a subjective leap beyond objective reason to be tolerated provided it remains firmly within the private sphere; rather it is the necessary
public basis of all knowledge, both religious and secular.

We possess a tacit ability, however embryonic or well honed, to make
informal-yet-informed judgements. Newman links such judgements to Aristotle's notion of *phronesis* or practical wisdom (Newman 1979: 277). Intellectual
virtues such as humility, prudence, responsibility, attentiveness and reasonableness are central to our epistemic endeavours, and cannot be reduced to the technical skill of obeying a rule or following a set procedure. Informed inference
combines both implicit and explicit features: it proceeds from explicit concrete
situations, but requires implicit instinctual and abductive reasoning in response
to a mass of problems and possibilities. Our minds reason 'in spontaneous,
subtle and dynamic ways' that 'cannot be captured fully by logical rules or
formal analysis' (Aquino 2004: 72).

Any given object or event will generate a vast range of data. Whilst individual
items of data might possibly be open to rational demonstration, the illative sense
enables us to recognise patterns and connections within the data as a whole that
would not otherwise be available to us. Just as the strength of a rope lies in the
combination of separate strands that are not strong enough individually to bear
the load carried by the rope as a whole, so the strength of a cumulative explanation flows from the combination of a range of data and inferential arguments that
are rarely strong enough individually to support the explanation as a whole. It is
our illative sense of the cumulation of probabilities, each independent of one
another, which enables us to generate rich explanations of the phenomena under
investigation. Such explanations are the result of an ongoing attentive, intelligent, reasonable and responsible contemplation and discernment of the object of
study (Lonergan 1973: 231). Such contemplation and discernment necessarily
proceeds from within the framework of antecedent assumptions the interpreter,
operating within an interpretative community, brings to bear on the phenomenon. Since knowledge is predicated on the knower entering into a truthful relationship with the object of knowledge, the investigator must be humble enough
to allow the object to transform her antecedent framework, committed enough to
hold fast to her antecedent framework, and wise enough to discern which of
these two options is demanded by the reality of the object itself.

A refined illative sense will be able to grasp aspects of reality unavailable to
an unrefined sense. If one person's certitude is another person's unknowing, then
the possibility of epistemic progress lies in the maturity of their respective illative senses rather than their propensity for scepticism. A person who has not
engaged with Mozart's music attentively would be wise to accept the positive
judgement of the musician who has, rather than simply dismiss it out of hand.
Similarly in the sphere of spirituality and religion, the sceptic would be wise to
attend carefully to the beliefs, experiences and practices of spiritual and religious
persons and communities, as well as the accounts of philosophical and theological experts in the field, when seeking to confirm, refine and revise their own
antecedent judgements. The notion that religious belief can be debunked without

careful scrutiny of the lives of religious believers and the formulations of theologians lacks intellectual seriousness: the absenting of due attentiveness, intelligence, reasonableness and responsibility in making spiritual, religious and theological judgements is justifiable only to the extent that the epistemic fallacy that generates a dualistic distinction between public object knowledge and private subjective belief is justifiable.

Reality, relativity and reason

The philosophy of critical realism proceeds from our embodied indwelling of reality in real-world environments, and asks what the world must be like for us to experience it in the ways we do. It claims that the most comprehensive and powerful answer to this question involves the postulation of three core principles: ontological realism, epistemic relativity and judgemental rationality. Ontological realism affirms that the world exists largely independently of our knowledge of it; epistemic relativity affirms that our knowledge of the world, however substantial, is always limited and often mistaken; judgemental rationality affirms that through the exercise of reason and cultivation of wisdom it is possible to pursue truth and live more truthful lives. There is nothing particularly remarkable about these principles. They are views that we might reasonably assume people of common sense across diverse cultural, geographic and historical divides subscribe to. Whatever their philosophical convictions and regardless of their cultural locations, most teachers assume students live independent lives beyond the classroom (ontological realism), recognise that their knowledge of the world is limited (epistemic relativity), and accept the challenge of helping them to extend and deepen it (judgemental rationality).

Of course, not everyone accepts that such views are reasonable: 'common sense' is itself an epistemically relative concept. There are those who reject (1) ontological realism, (2) epistemic relativity or (3) judgemental rationality. (a) anti-realists deny the *existence* of an external world, whilst epistemic sceptics deny access to *knowledge* of an external world. However, the fact that it appears impossible for anti-realists and epistemic sceptics to live out their lives without engaging with the external world – if they are hungry and thirsty they will intentionally seek food and drink – suggests a deep inconsistency between their beliefs and their actions; (b) similarly, religious and secular fundamentalists who deny epistemic relativity and claim access to secure knowledge of the whole of reality cannot easily account for their ignorance on particular matters – if they are lost they will ask for directions – or explain why they have privileged access to knowledge unavailable to other, apparently highly intelligent, human beings; (c) by the same token, those who reject judgemental rationality and deny the power of reason to resolve disputes nevertheless do not respond in completely arbitrary ways to situations that require specific choices – not least in their rational decision to abandon reason. Thus, though the affirmation of the triumvirate of ontological realism, epistemic relativity and judgemental relativity is itself epistemically relative and subject to iterative revision, critical realists identify it as the most powerful account of the relationship between ontology and epistemology currently available, and consequently elect to work with it until such time as they have good reason to abandon it in favour of an alternative. It is the balance between these three principles that gives critical realism its cutting edge: remove any one from the equation and we arrive at a less comprehensive and powerful answer.

Having established these three basic principles, critical realists go on to ask how we come to understand the world. We do so, they suggest, in precisely the same way in which we arrive at these three core principles: by constructing explanatory narratives that provide comprehensive and powerful explanations of our antecedent experiences of the world. This is the case both for our everyday experiences in real-world environments, and for our reflective attempts to theorise our everyday experiences in academic settings. We obtain knowledge of the world via a process of retroductive reasoning that proceeds from our experience of any given object or event and seeks to infer the best possible *explanation* – as opposed to description or probabilistic prediction – of such experience. Retroduction functions as a 'mode of inference in which events are explained by postulating (and identifying) mechanisms which are capable of producing them' (Sayer 1992: 107). The deliberations of a jury in a court of law typically take the form of retroductive reasoning: given the evidence available to them, they are required to identify the best possible explanation of the actions of the defendant, and thereby to judge them guilty or innocent within the bounds of reasonable doubt.

Contra Descartes, this process of retroductive explanatory narration does not begin anew with each succeeding generation and each individual learner; on the contrary, individuals-in-community receive retroductive stories from tradition, so that learning about the world begins with the reception of testimony from the past. We learn natural, social and theological science not by devising experiments from scratch and attempting to replicate for ourselves the history of humankind's scientific endeavours, but by consulting scientific textbooks which make available to us a scientific heritage from which our knowledge of science proceeds. This does not mean that our retroductive knowledge is inextricably bound to the past, since retroductive explanations remain open to iterative refinement and abductive modification. Iteration involves 'the successive and incremental revision of how we see or understand something in the light of insights disclosed through the process of engagement itself' (McGrath 2009: 32). Abduction enables us to take account of new experiences, and as such is 'fundamentally innovatory and creative, generating new ideas and insights in response to "surprising facts"' (ibid.: 44). Abductive reasoning may require us to reformulate our established retroductive frameworks in order to do justice to new experiences. The very nature of epistemic discovery means that abductive reasoning takes the form of 'a proleptic conception, an anticipatory glimpse, a tenuous and subtle outreach of the understanding with a forward thrust in cognition of something quite new' (Torrance 1984: 114). Whilst iterative fine-tuning allows prosecution and defence counsels to refine the retroductive narratives they plan to set before a jury, abductive revision in the light of surprising new evidence may lead to them the generation of entirely new retroductive explanations.

We make sense of the world we indwell, and which exists in the main independently of us, by constructing retroductive explanations of our encounters with reality. Such explanations infer aspects of reality beyond our immediate and past experiences. Roy Bhaskar here draws an important distinction between the domains of the 'empirical', 'actual' and 'real': (1) the *empirical domain* consists of the sum total of our individual and collective experiences of the world, both past and present; (2) the *actual domain* consists of all that actually exists in the world, regardless of whether human beings have experience of it or not; (3) the *real domain* consists of the causal mechanisms that generate different configurations of objects and events in the actual world and make possible experience of them in the empirical world. A powerful retroductive account is one that penetrates beyond the domains of the empirical and actual and offers explanations in the domain of the real.

1   In the empirical domain, our experience of the world is dependent on our five senses. Without the capacity to see, touch, hear, taste and smell we could not relate to or know anything. We are not born with innate knowledge already present in our minds, though we do appear to possess the genetically inbuilt potential to develop certain kinds of knowledge (e.g. the capacity to use language). Further, our experience of the world is holistic rather than atomistic: we do not see a black shape, hear a purring sound and surmise the existence of a cat; rather, we experience cats directly as cats. Some of our experience is direct: if we get caught in a thunderstorm we have first-hand experience of the weather. Most of our knowledge, however, is indirect: if we have never met the President of the United States we must rely on information mediated by the testimony of others, via newspaper reports, video-clips, etc. (Lackey and Sosa 2006).

2   The actual domain consists of all objects and events that exist in reality, whether we (directly or indirectly) experience them or not. Our empirical experience of this domain is severely limited: we have indirect mediated experience of only a tiny proportion of the world's population, direct unmediated experience of an even smaller proportion, and enjoy deep personal relationships with only a tiny minority. Though I may have direct experience of a thunderstorm in London, and by checking weather reports may gain indirect experience of sunshine in Crete, this will not give me complete knowledge of all past and present weather systems across the globe. It is a mistake to draw the conclusion that because I do not possess direct or mediated knowledge of the weather in Cape Town there is no actual weather in Cape Town. This would be to commit the epistemic fallacy of equating reality with my direct and mediated experience of reality. It is far more reasonable to infer that the residents of Cape Town are currently experiencing some form of weather than that they are not. The suggestion that the residents of Cape Town cannot experience the weather unless I

am directly or indirectly aware of their experience is extraordinarily egocentric and profoundly lacking in either explanatory power or intellectual seriousness. Further, even if we *did* possess total knowledge of all past and present weather systems our understanding of the weather would not be complete: we would still not understand *how* and *why* different weather systems occur.

3   The real domain consists of the diverse forces, structures and causal mechanisms that generate and constitute various configurations of objects and events in the actual domain and make possible experience of them in the empirical domain. At a deeper level than my experience of the weather (direct or mediated), and the totality of different weather systems (experienced or not), are a complex set of causal mechanisms – chemical reactions in the sun, temperature changes, pressure in the Earth's atmosphere, the gravitational pull of the moon, etc. – that are continually generating actual weather systems and have the potential to generate new weather systems in the future. It follows that we do not learn about reality merely by establishing a greater *quantity* or *breadth* of knowledge through the expansion of our empirical experiences: a rich and powerful understanding of reality also requires a greater *quality* or *depth* of knowledge. Such knowledge must penetrate beyond surface appearances and engage with issues not merely of 'What?', but more fundamentally of 'How?' and 'Why?' If 'primitive' natural science proceeds by classifying different types of objects in the world, then 'sophisticated' natural science seeks to understand why objects behave in the way they do; similarly, if 'primitive' social science describes the configuration of society, then 'sophisticated' social science seeks to explain the causal mechanisms – including both social structures and personal agents – that configure societies in particular ways. A person with encyclopaedic knowledge of every song Elvis ever recorded may be a useful member of a pub quiz team; however, this does not necessarily mean that they possess the same deep understanding of Elvis' music of a person able to contrast the raw emotion of his innovative early recordings for Sun Records with the somewhat sentimental and derivative nature of much of his later output.

Retroductive explanations seek to provide true accounts of reality in the domains of the empirical, actual and real, and to enable truthful living in relation to the way things actually are in the world. There is no denying that the pursuit of truth is wrapped up in a range of power structures that frequently militate against its success. However this does not justify the suggestion that the so-called 'pursuit of truth' is nothing more than an exercise in the adjudication of human interests. Given the basic human desire to seek truth and avoid being duped by lies and falsehoods, it is reasonable, if at times exceedingly difficult, to seek to identify ways in which human interests serve to distort and obscure truth, and thereby to rescue the latter from the former. Bhaskar distinguishes between the alethic and propositional truth: at the risk of oversimplification, the former refers to ontological reality itself while the latter refers to epistemic accounts of that reality (Bhaskar 1993: 214ff., 1994: 26, passim; cf. Groff 2004: 71ff.). Thus it is alethically true that the Earth is a sphere, and that this was the case long before human beings gave expression to that truth in the proposition 'the Earth is a sphere'. This raises the question of the relationship between alethic truth and propositional truth. Here Bhaskar holds that (epistemic) propositional truth claims seek to *refer* to (ontological) alethic realities. However, he rejects a 'correspondence' theory of the relation between the two in favour of an 'expressive' one. This does not mean that Bhaskar has abandoned questions of the reference of propositions to the realities they refer to, and opted instead for a 'coherence' or 'consensus' theory, according to which propositions may be deemed 'true' if they are internally coherent or embraced by a consensus of interested individuals. On the contrary, Bhaskar maintains consistently that a 'proposition is true if and only if the state of affairs that it expresses (describes) is real' (Bhaskar 2008: 249). Language is not the same as the objects language refers to: because words and the objects they seek to describe are distinct ontological entities it is wrong to expect a one-to-one correspondence between them. The fact that many of the entities identified by natural scientists are inferred rather than directly observed makes a one-to-one correspondence between word and object impossible to sustain, so that descriptions of them are forced to employ metaphorical language. Such metaphor is an essential component of scientific explanation, and as such cannot be reduced to the status of expendable rhetorical decoration. We refer to 'chaperone proteins' and 'factory cells' because the biological realities we encounter demand this, or something similar, of us: the metaphor might change ('supervisory proteins', 'manufacturing cells') but the *meaning* expressed by the metaphor and demanded by the alethic reality of the object to which the metaphor refers remains the same. Thus our retroductive models seek to refer to the real world using a heuristic language that expresses alethic truth in a manner that cannot be reduced to a crass one-to-one correspondence between word and object, but instead gives us access to deep knowledge and understanding that would not otherwise be available to us.

How can we distinguish between true and false retroductive propositions and explanations? The question suggests the necessity of an either/or choice between binary opposites. However, few of our beliefs are absolutely mistaken, even though many may be profoundly misplaced. The ancient who believed the Earth to be flat and the modern who believes it to be a sphere are both responding to the same reality: though the latter may possess greater truth, the former is not *utterly* devoid of meaning. Few of our beliefs are either absolutely true or absolutely false; most are located on a continuum between greater and lesser degrees of truthfulness. The fact that in many cases it is exceedingly difficult to adjudicate with absolute certainty between true and false propositions does not warrant a thoroughgoing relativism that abandons judgemental rationality. Critical realism is highly suspicious of attempts to evaluate truth claims against pre-established foundational criteria: a statement cannot properly be deemed to be true simply because we can verify it through our senses, identify its internal coherence or are emotionally committed to it. The danger of such criteria is that they commit us to the epistemic fallacy of reducing reality to our preferred means of knowing reality, thereby negating the priority of ontology over epistemology. If an object exists ontologically, if it possesses alethic truth, then it does so regardless of our epistemic capacities and tools. As Bhaskar points out, 'reason is concerned to adjust our beliefs to conform to the world', and it is fallacious to attempt to adjust the world to conform to our beliefs (Bhaskar 1994: 66). This means that we must be continually open to the possibility of the ontological reality of an object or event forcing us to abandon our pre-established epistemic criteria and ontological assumptions. Though Einstein's field equations suggested that the universe was expanding contrary to Newton's notion of absolute space and time, he initially resisted this conclusion by adding a 'cosmological constant' to his equations; it was his eventual recognition of the cumulative weight of the retroductively configured evidence, as demanded by the universe itself, that led him to abandon his prior beliefs about the nature of space and time. In a non-foundational epistemology, such as that espoused by critical realism, any criteria for truth must be internal to the object under investigation: there can be no legitimate appeal to criteria beyond the demands imposed by reality itself. Further, any criteria for truth must flow from the *nature* of the object under investigation: we cannot measure social, moral, aesthetic or theological truth in the same way we measure the weight of a physical object.

> It is part of our situation that we are inevitably and inseparably *inside* the knowledge relation, from the start to the end, and so cannot step outside of ourselves to an indifferent standpoint from which to view and adjust the relations of thought and being.
>
> (Brown 1953: 170; cf. Torrance 1969: 1)

Knowledge is grounded in our capacity to engage attentively, intelligently, reasonably and responsibly with the object under investigation, and to construct the best possible inferential explanation that the object itself allows and demands. When faced with conflicting retroductive explanations of the same object or event we cannot legitimately appeal to any external criteria to adjudicate the dispute; instead, we have no option other than to return to the object itself and contemplate it in the light of the conflicting interpretations, make a provisional judgement call regarding the relative virtues of divergent explanations, and then continue the dialogue in the hope that iterative refinement and/or abductive reformulation will enable us to move toward a deeper understanding of the nature of the object itself. This may be unwelcome to those moderns driven by a need for Cartesian certitude, and might lead those post-moderns mesmerised by Cartesian certitude to embrace a reactive and thoroughgoing relativism; however, it is the only way open to us for the resolution of such disputes, and the only one consistently practised in the mainstream academy. If sub-atomic neutrinos exceeding the speed of light *have* been detected, then Einstein's established theory of special relativity requires major iterative revision;

if, on the other hand, evidence of the existence of the Higgs boson particle *does* prove forthcoming, then the Standard Model of particle physics will be significantly enhanced: the fact that, at the time of writing, the evidence on both counts remains uncertain and the scientific community remains undecided, is not an epistemic problem, but rather the very lifeblood of the ongoing pursuit of truth.

Critical realism does not offer a 'total philosophy': one does not need to become a critical realist or convert to critical realism in order to garner its fruits. Critical realism is self-consciously an 'under-labouring' enterprise, offering informed advice on how best to engage effectively with a range of intellectual problems and possibilities. As such it offers cognitive tools and insights to adherents of a range of different worldviews, both religious and secular, and to practitioners of a variety of academic disciplines. The core advice it offers is minimal: distinguish between ontology and epistemology, seek informed judgements rather than demonstrable proofs, generate deep retroductive explanations of the object under investigation, and adjudicate conflicting truth claims by attending a posteriori to the intrinsic ontological reality of the object under investigation rather than imposing a priori any extrinsic epistemic criteria. At the same time, however, such minimal procedural advice *has* generated a range of substantial insights into the nature of reality – albeit not to the extent of generating a specific 'critically realistic' worldview – to which we now turn.

(1) *Reality is stratified and pluriform.* It is possible to provide multiple explanatory accounts of the same reality: the physicist, chemist, psychologist, sociologist, historian, geographer, artist, poet, philosopher and theologian are all able to provide diverse retroductive explanations of the same person, object or event. Given a commitment to ontological realism and epistemic relativity, this raises the question as to which, if any, of these diverse explanations may legitimately be identified as 'true'. This question can be answered in one of three distinctive ways.

First, multiple explanations can be explained away on the grounds that none actually engages cognitively with the object under investigation, so that each explanation merely skims the surface of reality. On this reading the hierarchy of disciplines established in the academy is the product of economies of power generated and driven by diverse human interests, rather than a reflection of the fact that reality itself is stratified and pluriform. This being the case, the various academic disciplines can tell us little of value about reality, though much about the psychological, sociological, political and economic forces operating in institutes of higher education and across society as a whole.

Second, multiple explanations of reality can be explained reductively, so that one particular explanation or cluster of explanations is privileged over all others. On this reading what appears to be a moral explanation of the actions of an individual agent can be reduced to a psychological explanation, and what appears to be a psychological explanation can be reduced to a biological explanation. If our moral choices are determined by our psychological make-up, and our psychological make-up is determined by our biological make-up, then moral discourse disguises the brute reality that we are ultimately conditioned to behave in the ways we do by our genes. Here biology trumps both psychology and morality. On the larger scale, the arts are reduced to the humanities, the humanities to the social sciences, and the social sciences to the natural sciences. The closer we get to the natural sciences, the closer we get to objective truths and secure facts; conversely, the closer we get to the arts, the closer we get to subjective opinions and ephemeral values. Consequently it is to physics – and to physics alone (or, perhaps, if we allow metaphysics into the equation, to the mathematics under-girding physics) – that we should look for a total explanation of everything. If physics is *the* privileged discourse, then the Higgs boson particle *is* potentially a 'God particle', the discovery of which will enable us to move closer to a total explanation, not merely of the stratum of reality investigated by physicists, but of all strata of reality.

Richard Rorty effectively combines these first two explanations: on the one hand, he affirms a reductive account of the academic disciplines that privilege natural science, arguing that it is self-deceptive to think 'that we possess a deep, hidden, metaphysically significant nature which makes us "irreducibly" different from inkwells or atoms'; on the other hand, he affirms an anti-realistic and non-cognitive understanding of the arts and humanities, arguing that they provide the raw material for the pragmatic task of living the good life by pursuing our desires in a manner that avoids cruelty to others (Rorty 1989).

Third, critical realism suggests an alternative option, one that *both* affirms the cognitive purchase on reality of all intellectual disciplines *and* resists any form of reductive explanation. On this reading reality is itself *intrinsically stratified and pluriform*, so that we are *simultaneously* moral, psychological and biological beings, and our moral, psychological and biological discourses are *complementary* to one another. In real-world environments we do indeed relate to one another on a moral level and cannot avoid making moral decisions. In the reflective domain of the academy, the experts properly qualified to explore our moral lives are not biologists qua biologists or psychologists qua psychologists, but rather moral philosophers. The suggestion that somehow morality is less 'real' than psychology, and psychology less 'real' than biology is a direct product of the epistemic fallacy of identifying reality with our capacity to accurately measure and quantify it. The fact that the biologist, the psychologist and the moral philosopher offer powerful retroductive explanations of specific strata of reality does not mean that we must choose between them; on the contrary, if reality is ontologically stratified and pluriform, then explanations of different strata of reality are complementary rather than mutually exclusive.

(2) *Reality is ordered and structured.* The fact that we inhabit a reality that is ordered and structured is a basic presupposition of both our real-world environments and the natural and human sciences. If this were not the case events would be entirely arbitrary, our lives devoid of any pattern or meaning, and scientific investigation impossible. Though we cannot predict the weather with any degree of certainty, we can nevertheless anticipate that the weather will normally behave according to certain recognisable patterns. Our experiences in the *empirical domain* reflect patterns of meaning in the *actual domain* that are generated

by the complex interaction of different causal mechanisms in the *real domain*. Empirical descriptions of regular configurations of objects and events fall short of deep explanations that identify the causal mechanisms that generate and sustain them. The empirical fact that plants tend to wilt when deprived of light is best explained by the causal mechanism of photosynthesis, through which light energy is converted into chemical energy by living organisms. Similarly, the fact that we cannot normally use newspaper as a form of currency, avoid paying our taxes without becoming vulnerable to certain legal consequences, or ordain women in the Roman Catholic Church is the result of social mechanisms established by the collective intentionality of particular societies and sub-groups within society.

Knowledge of such natural and social structures opens up the possibility of transformative praxis. Knowledge of the causal mechanisms that produce certain diseases opens up the possibility of adopting healthy lifestyles in order to maintain physical wellbeing. Similarly, the causal link between economic deprivation and poor health opens up the possibility of engineering social change, whether through increased welfare provision within the structures of capitalism, or the structural replacement of a capitalist economy with a socialist one. Though we cannot change the causal mechanisms operating in the natural world, we can in certain circumstances intervene to replace one set of causal mechanisms with another, for example by prescribing drugs or removing cancerous cells. In the social world it is possible through individual and collective agency to change both the structures of society and the causal mechanisms underlying them, for example by replacing dictatorships with democracies. The fact that different causal mechanisms operate on different strata of reality means that solutions to the problems faced by humanity normally require a diverse range of interrelated responses. Contra behaviourism, it is not the case that a person's lifestyle choices are determined purely by their genetic make-up: many other factors, such as their upbringing, economic circumstances, moral commitments and religious beliefs also need to be taken into account. The maintenance of a healthy lifestyle might require not only a change in economic circumstances but also better education and a renewed sense of self-worth.

(3) *Reality is emergent and dynamic.* The order and structure inherent in reality is not fixed, and the causal mechanisms operating within nature and society do not take the form of deterministic causal laws. Though there is a causal link between smoking and lung cancer, some people contract lung cancer without exposure to cigarette smoke, while some smokers never contract the disease. Though knowledge of causal mechanisms enables us to explain the world and intervene within it, it does not enable us to predict events with any degree of certainty. If we drop a wine glass on a hard surface we reasonably expect it to break; however, it is not the case that glass *necessarily* shatters under such circumstances, and when it does shatter, it is *impossible* to predict the precise patterns formed by the broken shards. The nature and interaction of the various causal mechanisms that generate particular weather systems is such that the systems themselves are ordered-yet-open. The same can be said of events in

the social sphere: though the game of football is played under fixed rules, every moment in every game is unique. Despite this, the actual outcome of some games is relatively predictable – though we can never be absolutely certain that Manchester United will *always* defeat Accrington Stanley.

Reality is dynamic in its order and open in its structure. This is reflected in the phenomena of 'emergence'. Nature is capable of generating objects 'greater' than the mechanisms that produce them. Human beings are an emergent species: as sentient creatures, capable of reflecting on ourselves and our environment, we evolved from non-sentient life-forms and are irreducible to them. Though entity β may depend on entity α for its existence, and though fundamental changes in α can bring about fundamental changes in β, the emergence of β as a separate entity is such that β is irreducible to α. The emergence of β 'implies some form of disjuncture between α and β such that β cannot be translated, explained or predicted from α alone' (Morgan 2007: 166). Though I am dependent on my biological make-up, and biological changes will impact on my person, my identity cannot – contra behaviourism – be explained purely by my biology.

The dynamic and emergent nature of reality is such that there is nothing fundamentally deterministic about the emergence of human life on Earth: it is entirely possible for sentient life *not* to have evolved, or for it to have evolved in a form significantly different from that possessed by human beings. This notion of a dynamic and emergent universe is central to contemporary physics, chemistry and biology, not least with respect to the emergence of life on Earth. The social sciences recognise that the various causal mechanisms that generate the regularities, patterns and tendencies evident in society do not follow fixed deterministic laws. The fact that Europe experienced a shift from absolute monarchy to democracy does not make a democratic outcome of the 'Arab Spring' inevitable. Similarly, the fact that there is nothing inevitable about the global dominance of capitalism opens up the possibility of turning to alternative economic systems. Bhaskar refers in this context to the 'TINA' syndrome: an ironic reference to Margaret Thatcher's defence of her monetarist economic policies on the grounds that 'there is no alternative'. The social and economic structures we inhabit are neither determined nor inevitable – there are real alternatives.

(4) *Reality is value-laden.* We have already seen how the epistemic fallacy impacted negatively on the realms of moral, aesthetic and spiritual value. The notion of scientific investigation as objective and dispassionate generated an understanding of the material world as intrinsically value-free, driven by impersonal casual mechanisms and possessing no original purpose or teleological meaning beyond the accidental dialectic of structure and emergence visible in the natural order-of-things. With regard to aesthetic values, the beauty discerned in the natural world, as well as in human beings and their cultural artefacts, was either dismissed as meaningless by virtue of its immunity to close measurement and empirical verification, or attributed to emotive constructs imposed on objects deemed beautiful by subjective human sensibility ('beauty is in the eye of the beholder'). Similarly, in the field of morality, our moral dispositions, discourses and actions were either dismissed as cognitively meaningless, or reduced to

human constructs generated by human desires driven by utopian visions or pragmatic concerns. By the same token spirituality was reduced from a discernment of our place within ultimate (divine or natural) order-of-things, and either dismissed as unverifiable and unmeasurable twaddle, or limited to expressions of human aspiration and desire. The common feature here is a strategy of limiting value to the empirical domain of human experience: any notion that moral, aesthetic and spiritual values might enjoy an ontological status in the actual domain, apart from human perception and experience, or function as casual mechanisms apart from human agency, was generally dismissed out of hand.

The recognition that we know the world through retroductive modelling grounded in our illative sense invites a fundamental reconsideration of the ontological nature and status of values. Beauty, goodness and spirituality now appear as substantial ontological realities embedded within a value-laden world. The love of a mother for her new born child, the beauty of Mozart's music, the splendour of the natural order, and presence of injustice and suffering in the world constitute substantial ontological realities that exist regardless of our ability to know or comprehend them. Abused children remain abused, even if the individual, group or society perpetuating the abuse has no comprehension that such actions are morally reprehensible. The natural world is intrinsically and ontologically beautiful, regardless of our ability to discern its magnificence. The willingness of an animal to protect its offspring at the expense of its own life and the devotion of a dog to his owner would appear to reflect an embryonic moral order. True, such behaviour might be dismissed in reductionist fashion as mere biologically determined behaviourism; however, when we attribute such behaviour to the 'survival of the fittest', we cannot avoid introducing some form of value system into our discourse. The repost that the notion of the 'survival of the fittest' is intended not as a value judgement regarding the notion of 'fitness', but merely as a description as the inevitable outcome of value-free evolutionary causal mechanisms, merely raises the question of the *absence* of value in the natural world. According to Bhaskar, 'absence' is itself a causal mechanism, one that allows us to identify the ontological significance of the absence of beauty, goodness and spirituality in certain contexts. If our genes are indeed ontologically 'selfish', as Richard Dawkins would have us believe, then they are ontologically marked by the absence of 'unselfishness'. Just as the contentment of a lion basking in the sun is ontologically marked by the absence of discontentment, so the pain experienced by the cornered fox ravaged by hounds is marked by the absence of pleasure. Andrew Collier argues cogently, in the context of a discussion of Spinoza, that both the natural and human worlds are imbibed with 'worth', regardless of whether we recognise this fact or not (Collier 1999). Far from being meaningless, or constructs imposed by our sensibility, goodness, beauty and ultimate spiritual meaning are best seen as states of affairs and networks of relations in the world that we encounter and discover rather than construct and create.

(5) *Reality is dialectically open to transformation and change.* Bhaskar's turn to dialectical critical realism was driven by the conviction that philosophy must

be a serious enterprise. It is not sufficient to merely describe or explain the world: we have an aesthetic, moral and spiritual duty to seek to seek to change the world for the better. By identifying the structural and agential mechanisms that configure society in different ways, Bhaskar established the ground for a shift beyond surface description and pragmatic response to retroductive explanation and emancipatory praxis. The fact that reality is not merely ordered and structured, but also dynamic and emergent, suggests that the world is in process of becoming. Unlike the deterministic dialectical philosophies of Hegel, and to a lesser extent Marx, dialectical critical realism recognises the essential openness of the emergent world to the future.

In *Dialectic: The Pulse of Freedom* Bhaskar argues that the future-oriented process of transformation and change passes through four stages (Bhaskar 1993).

1   Bhaskar begins with the recognition of the non-identity of objects in the world. The ontological structures of reality are such that there is an irreducible difference between things: I am not you, and you are not me, and our identities cannot be subsumed under the generic category 'human being'.

2   Bhaskar then affirms a dispositional ontology in which the being-in-becoming of the world is driven and marked by absence. Each object and event in the world is simultaneously marked not merely by what is present but also by that which is absent. Thus the *absence* of a recently deceased relative at a family gathering constitutes an ontological reality that will impact directly on the family members. Bhaskar suggests that absence is a causally significant aspect of reality. There can be no change without negation, whether this entails the negating of the absence of something by making it present, or of the negating of the presence of something by making it absent. Just as justice is absent from an unjust society, so justice can only emerge if injustice is removed. Ontological monovalence seeks to restrict meaning to that which is actually present, and in doing so generates the TINA syndrome in which the status quo is taken as normative, inevitable and unavoidable. Ontological polyvalence opens meaning to both the absence and presence of states of affairs, and opens the door to the transformation of society. Emancipatory change and transformative praxis is dependent on the negation of the givenness of a particular situation via the introduction of a new state-of-affairs.

3   Bhaskar goes on to suggest that, altogether, objects in the world are irreducibly different; they are also unavoidably related. Reality consists of the totality of interrelated objects and events in the actual domain, together with the various causal mechanisms in the real domain which generate, configure and change them. Given the absence of proper moral, aesthetic and spiritual relations in the world, reality falls short of what it could and should be. The process of being-as-becoming is neither entirely random nor absolutely determined. Though natural and social structures establish both the limits and possibilities of human action and wellbeing, human agents are able to

alter their relationships with the natural world and work together to change social structures – whether for better or worse – in a dialectic process of absenting and making present.

4   Bhaskar focuses finally on the role of human agency in transformative praxis. Because changing causal relationships in different strata of reality have the capacity to change the totality of reality, human agents have the capacity to act to help transform the world they indwell. If social structures simultaneously restrict some human actions and make possible others, human agents can work together to transform social structures in order to maximise human flourishing and restrict human suffering. In order to transform social structures it is necessary to transform human agents, so that they are better equipped, more capable and more willing, to engineer positive change. The recognition of the need to transform human nature led to the so-called 'spiritual turn' in critical realism, which, not without controversy, introduced fundamental metaphysical and theological questions and issues into the debate. Since this book is concerned with spiritual, religious and theological education, the spiritual turn warrants its own chapter. However, before proceeding to do so, we must pause to consider the impact of the epistemic fallacy on spirituality, religion and theology in the modern and post-modern eras.

3 The subjugation of Transcendence

The first chapter recounted a story of misplaced attempts to secure humankind's place in the world by forcing reality to conform to a set of preferred ways of knowing. The resulting distinction between objective knowledge and subjective opinion gave rise to a closed comprehensive liberal worldview, in which the natural world and the Cartesian self are seen as ontologically basic, and individuals are free to pursue their own subjective visions of ultimate reality and the good life. The second chapter suggested that this worldview constitutes only one amongst many potentially viable ways of understanding our place in the ultimate order-of-things; and one that, given its various flaws, is not self-evidently the most powerful currently available. This being the case, the pervasive presence of comprehensive liberalism within contemporary culture means there is a genuine danger of it becoming an unquestioned ideology. Replacing the image of the dislocated self driven by a hermeneutic of suspicion with a vision of the embodied self driven by a hermeneutic of trust opens up a new set of possibilities: in particular, the possibility of rejecting an epistemology that forces reality to conform to pre-established ways of knowing in favour of an epistemology driven by an attentive, intelligent, reasonable and responsible engagement with the actual order-of-things. This opens up the further possibility of cultivating a genuinely plural society in which adherents of a range of incommensurable worldviews (epistemic relativity) engage in the pursuit of truth and the cultivation of truthful living (judgemental rationality) in relation to the ultimate nature of reality (ontological realism) on the basis of an open political liberalism guided by the underlabouring resources of critical realism.

We turn now from philosophy to theology. The current chapter tells a story of the subjugation and accommodation of religion under the auspices of an epistemic fallacy that required both theological and philosophical accounts of Transcendence to be evaluated in the light of a priori epistemic criteria rather than a posteriori ontological encounters. As we have seen, these criteria required the dislocated Cartesian self to provide empirically, rationally or experientially *certain proof* of the veracity of Transcendent truth claims through the exercise of *rational autonomy* against a background of *thoroughgoing scepticism*. The struggle of both natural and revealed theology to hold their ground in the face of sustained critique led, on the one hand to the self-protective retreat of religious believers into private fideistic and fundamentalist ghettos, and on the other hand to a reductive accommodation of religion to the norms of comprehensive liberalism grounded in an appropriation of the romantic category of the self-evident certainty of spiritual experience and intuition.

Natural and revealed theology

The generic category 'theism' embraces a range of conflicting accounts of the being and nature of God: deistic, theistic, pantheistic, panentheistic, etc. The traditions of Western theism inherited by the Enlightenment flowed from two overlapping sources: the natural theology of ancient Greek philosophy and the revealed theology of the three major Abrahamic religious traditions (Judaism, Christianity and Islam). Blaise Pascal famously distinguished between the God of the philosophers and scholars, and the God of Abraham, Isaac and Jacob (Pascal 1966: 309). Similarly Joseph Butler differentiated between natural and revealed religion in his *Analogy of Religion* (Butler 1884). The God of the philosophers and natural theology is the impersonal first principle (ἀρχή, archē) of reality, and source of the rational order (λόγος, logos) in the cosmos (Gerson 1994: 5ff.); the God of Abraham and revealed religion is a personal deity who intentionally creates the world and actively seeks the eternal salvation of humankind. Knowledge of the God of the philosophers is implicit in the natural world and human souls, and can be made explicit through the exercise of reason and critical reflection; knowledge of the God of Abraham, though similarly implicit throughout creation, is made explicit through particular historical acts of divine self-revelation. Because of his direct personal concern for the wellbeing of humanity, the God of revealed theology has an existential significance for religious adherents largely absent in the relationship between the God of natural theology and philosophers. The God of Abraham invites human beings to enter into relationship with him through prayer and worship, provides a set of moral norms for them to obey, and offers mercy, forgiveness and reconciliation to those who repent of their failure to adhere to them; the God of the philosophers provides the foundation of the rational and moral order inherent in the universe, and leaves human beings to engineer their own happiness and wellbeing.

Though the instinct of the ancient Greeks to look for rational order in the universe might lead us to anticipate a thoroughgoing monotheism, Greek mythology offered instead 'a most luxuriant polytheism' (Kitto 1957: 194). If a basic function of myth in antiquity was to position humankind meaningfully within the universe, then Greek mythology identified, reified, personified and divinised a diverse range of primal forces – natural, social and personal – operative within the cosmos. The result was a pantheon made up of a largely dysfunctional and unscrupulous divine family, whose power struggles and love affairs simultaneously impacted upon and mirrored the world of human experience. Though a range of associated cultic practices sought to placate the gods and control these primal forces, the recognition that even the gods were subject to the higher power of fate served to revealed the simultaneous poverty and richness of Greek mythology: if its theological poverty lay in the failure to understand this higher power in monotheistic terms, its enduring moral and aesthetic richness is reflected in classical Greek literature's unparalleled dramatic and poetic exploration of the human struggle for fulfilment in the face of the ravages of fate.

A key achievement of Greek philosophy was to discern rational order behind the primal forces fêted in Greek mythology, and thereby oversee a transition from polytheism to monotheism. According to Heraclitus, 'fire', the underlying *logos* of the universe, is marked by change, motion, war and strife, so that the whole exists in a constant state of flux; in sharp contrast Parmenides identified the underlying rational order as timeless, permanent, uniform and stable (Parmenides 1984; Heraclitus 2001). Ontologically, Heraclitus attributed priority to the immanent 'many', whilst Parmenides gave precedence to the Transcendent 'One'. Epistemically, where Heraclitus affirmed the inevitable contingency of human knowledge, Parmenides distinguished between the way of truth, which leads to the Transcendent realm of unchanging Being, and the way of opinion, which leads only to the demi-reality of the immanent realm of contingency and change (Parmenides 1984: 53). Greek natural theology followed the Parmenidean way of truth: God, as we have already noted, is ultimate reality and absolute Being, the first principle and source of all rational, moral and aesthetic order in the cosmos. This led inevitably to the emancipation of philosophy from mythology: if 'God is not the cause of all things, but only of the good', then Homer's poetry, which identifies Zeus as 'dispenser alike of good and of evil to mortals', can have no place in the education system of Plato's ideal Republic (Plato 1963a: 626f.).

According to Plato the underlying principle of all reality is the intelligible, immaterial, unchanging and Transcendent 'Form of the Good'. Human beings are trapped in the demi-reality of the sensible, material, contingent and immanent universe, and when unschooled in reason have access only to shadowy intimations of the ultimate ground of reality. Plato's natural theology is not, however, either fully monotheistic or entirely emancipated from mythology: if God, the Form of the Good, is the eternal and unchanging bedrock of reality, then he/it cannot possibly *act* to bring the cosmos into being; consequently, the creation of the universe is attributed to the Demiurge, a pre-existent lesser god whose intellect ($voῦς$, nous) enables him to contemplate the Form of the Good and use it as a celestial blueprint when imposing form on pre-existent formless matter. If a pure monotheism in which God is timeless and unchanging is unable to account for the act of creation, the mythical positing of the pre-existence of both the Demiurge and formless matter alongside the Form of the Good appears to contradict the latter's status as the ultimate, eternal and divine source of all reality.

Aristotle's attempted solution to this theological conundrum was to reject the Platonic Forms in favour of Aristotelian categories. The categories of actuality ($ἐντελέχεια$, entelecheia) and potentiality ($δύναμις$, dynamis) constitute the basic rational ground of being. Though all created objects possess actuality (they are what they are) and potentiality (they will become what they will become), their actuality is antecedent to their potentiality (they must first *be* in order to *become*).

This leads Aristotle to conceive reality as a great chain of being-as-becoming. In order to explain this (and, according to many later philosophers, to avoid any notion of infinite regress) he posits a 'First Cause', or 'Unmoved Mover', existing as pure actuality and devoid of all potentiality (Aristotle 1984: 1688ff.). As pure actuality, Aristotle's God is the Supreme Being: not dependent on any antecedent cause, its essence is simply to exist in eternal passive self-contemplation of its own perfection. As such, it is necessarily impersonal and devoid of will, since the possibility of an intentional act of will carries with it the potential for change. The Unmoved Mover moves, the impersonal God creates, purely passively: as perfect being it is the ultimate object of desire, provoking responses from the (apparently pre-existent) heavenly bodies without any effort on its part. Just as we might be emotionally 'moved' by the intrinsic beauty of an impersonal and passive sunset, so the heavenly bodies are 'moved' by virtue of the intrinsic beauty and attractiveness of God: 'The object of desire and the object of thought ... move without being moved' (ibid.: 1694). As with Plato, Aristotle employs mythical categories to account for the emergence of the universe from a God who is the ultimate source of the order in the material universe, but not the ultimate source of matter per se.

The turn from natural to revealed theology takes us on a significant journey: from the academy to the synagogue, church and mosque; from small intellectual elites to vast popular movements; from reason to faith; from philosophical language to the idioms of myth, legend, parable and historical reportage; from locutionary to illocutionary and perlocutionary speech-acts; and (at the risk of improperly disparaging the existential import of academic philosophy) from abstract theory to embodied practice. The Abrahamic faiths have their roots in historical events rather than philosophical reflection. The origins and development of Israelite religion, and of its Christian and Islamic offshoots, though not always completely transparent, are nevertheless relatively well documented. Though the God of Abraham is common to Jews, Christians and Muslims, his precise nature, character and actions are disputed. The ontological incommensurability of Jewish, Christian and Islamic accounts of God cannot be ignored without doing violence to the self-understanding of the adherents of each tradition. Thus, for example, the Christian doctrines of Trinity and incarnation are irreconcilable with Jewish and Islamic theology: it is utterly anathema to both Jewish and Islamic monotheism to claim that God is a Trinity of persons united in a single Godhead, and that God chose to live on Earth as a human being. Despite their differences, Jews, Muslims and Christians agree that the God of Abraham is essentially a *personal* God rather than an abstract Platonic Form or impersonal Aristotelian Unmoved Mover.

The source of the Abrahamic conviction that God is a personal being lies, not in philosophical speculation, but in God's self-revelation mediated through historical events and scriptural texts. The Abrahamic traditions make little reference to direct unmediated experience of God: Transcendence is normally discerned within the immanent realm of human history and culture. In the terminology of critical realism, revealed theology has its roots in a range of abductive historically specific events and experiences that served to transform previously held understandings of the being and acts of God. Attempts to make retroductive sense of such abductive experiences were situated in the developing faith and praxis of particular religious communities. Unlike their Canaanite neighbours, who discerned deities operating within the repetitive cycle of the seasons, the early Israelites discerned the hand of God in unique historical events: not least in the escape of a group of Israelites from slavery in Egypt and their long walk to freedom through the Sinai wilderness. The belief that God was Lord of Israel gradually extended into a belief that he was also Lord of all human history and of the natural world. If the creation myths of the ancient Near East tend to view time in terms of the repetitive cycle of the seasons and recount stories of the struggles of a pantheon of gods to gain control over the primal forces of nature, the Israelite creation myth embraces a linear understanding of time and tells the story of God calling all that exists into being, and imbibing it with God-given meaning, direction and purpose. The Abrahamic cosmos is structured rather than chaotic, open rather than deterministic, and eschatological – oriented towards the consummate reconciliation of fallen humanity with its divine Creator. Such abductive encounters generated retroductive understandings of God as essentially just, faithful, loving, and – especially in the Judaeo-Christian traditions – consumed with passion for the flourishing of humankind. This passionate God, intimately engaged with the contingencies of history and concerned for the lives and destinies of groups and individuals, was also the creator and sovereign ruler of the entire cosmos.

Israel's historical narratives, prophetic proclamations, legal texts, wisdom books and psalms of praise sought to retroductively express and iteratively refine the nation's abductive ontological encounters with God (Brueggemann 1997). This emergent body of literature appeared to the Israelites to provide a more powerful explanation of their collective experiences than any other accounts available to them. As a result, a canon of authoritative scripture gradually emerged that functioned to reveal the nature of God and his dealings with creation in general and the people of Israel in particular. The belief that Hebraic scripture proffered alethically truthful accounts of Israel's ongoing relationship with God, rather than mere projections of the nation's fears and aspirations, led to the conclusion that scripture constitutes a divinely ordained witness to God's self-revelation in history. Though they recognise that God reveals himself in the majesty and order of the created natural world, the Abrahamic faiths insist that it is primarily in historical acts and sacred texts that God's nature and purpose is most fully revealed: whether through the Covenant with Israel recorded in the Torah, the incarnation of Jesus Christ witnessed to in the New Testaments, or the Holy Qur'an revealed to the prophet Mohammed by the angel Gabriel. The personal God of the Abrahamic tradition is known because he proactivly elects to make himself known to human beings in particular events and specific circumstances; and he does so because, as a supra-personal (rather than merely supra-natural) deity, he is committed to the flourishing and eternal salvation of humankind.

Of course, affirmations of divine self-revelation are necessarily epistemically relative: the possibility of misreading and misappropriating divine revelation, or of discerning revelation when no revelation is present, is intrinsic to the self-understanding of all three Abrahamic faiths. To worship God inappropriately, or to worship idols instead of God, constitutes a constant danger; indeed, given human fallibility and sin, *all* attempts to discern God must recognise that human knowledge necessarily falls short of final and comprehensive understanding. The central thrust of the prophetic tradition in Israel was to warn against false understanding and thereby open the door to more authentic discernment. Epistemic relativity extends beyind the borders of particular religious communities, and in doing so inevitably raises the question of the truth of their claims to revelation. Modern scholarship recognises that it is possible to recount the history of the Abrahamic religious traditions in immanent secular terms, and explain their emergence and development in terms of political, economic, social, cultural and psychological causal networks. Theologians, whilst recognising the value of describing and explaining the religious histories of Judaism, Christian and Islam in this way, seek to supplement them with theological descriptions and explanations that take seriously the possibility that the abductive encounters and iteratively refined retroductive explanations contained within scripture may actually embody alethic theological truth. From a theological perspective to limit description and explanation to a non-theological network of immanent causes and effects is inherently reductionist, since it rules out a priori the possibility that the Transcendent theological claims inherent within the scriptural text may actually be true.

During the late-Hellenistic and medieval eras, scholastic philosophers and theologians combined the contrasting theologies of Greek philosophy and the Abrahamic faiths into an uneasy synthesis that produced the God of 'classical theism'. The initial impetus was provided by Augustine's Platonic reading of Christianity, though the synthesis reached its zenith in the assimilation of Aristotelian philosophy by first Islamic and later Jewish and Christian scholars, such as Abu Ibn-Sīnā (Avicenna), Maimonides and Aquinas. This resulted in a hybrid version of the Gods of natural and revealed theology: an omnipotent and omniscient divinity, *both* the timeless and utterly Transcendent source of the natural and moral order inherent in the world, *and* a personal agent proactivly seeking the perfection of creation and salvation of humankind: 'a person without a body (i.e. a spirit) who is eternal, free, able to do anything, knows everything, is perfectly good, is the proper object of human worship and obedience, the creator and sustainer of the universe' (Swinburne 1993: 1). The fundamental innovation here is the reintroduction into the Greek concept of God of those personal categories that the demythologising strategy of Greek philosophy had sought to expunge. True, the personal God of classical theism is a marked advance on Zeus: omnipotence and omniscience; absolutely free from the constraints imposed by pre-existent matter, rational necessity, eternal Forms and the ravages of fate; and, above all, perfectly just, good, benevolent and loving – attributes which make him both worthy of worship and closed to all forms of cultic appeasement and magical manipulation. Nevertheless, to speak of God in personal terms required, however minimally, the reintroduction of mythological language into theological discourse, since to speak of realities beyond direct empirical observation, whether in the realms of theology or natural science, requires the use of analogical, metaphorical and tropic language. As we shall see below, it was precisely this reintroduction of myth into the Greek concept of God that the philosophers of the Enlightenment took such exception to.

For all its considerable achievements the medieval synthesis generated a host of theological problems: How can a timeless God act in time? How can an utterly transcendent God engage immanently with the world? How can an impersonal rational principle care for humanity? Why does an omnipotent, omniscient and all-loving God allow human beings to suffer? The roots of the fragmentation of classical theism lay in the Renaissance's rediscovery of classical art and literature untouched by the influence of the Abrahamic faiths. Further impetus was provided by the Reformation, as Protestant theologians sought to recover a pristine theology grounded in God's self-revelation alone and uncontaminated by Platonic and Aristotelian influences. The Enlightenment, in rejecting the God of revealed theology and attempting a deistic restatement of natural theology, added further to the breakup of the medieval synthesis. The differentiation between these very different philosophical and theological accounts of God has had a significant impact on recent debate.

On the theological side, Colin Gunton has sought to recover an understanding of the Trinitarian God of Christianity emancipated from the tradition of classical theism, arguing that the failure to properly distinguish the two is a major source of the theological crisis facing Western Christianity in the modern age (Gunton 1978: 11ff.; cf. 1991, 2003). He suggests that the flaws of classical theism become transparent once it is differentiated from Trinitarian theology. Thus, for example, classical theism is unable to account for either the ontological or epistemic relationship between God and creation: if God is timeless, he must ontologically transcend our time-bound universe in a dualistic manner; and if he is impersonal, he can have no motive to epistemically reveal himself in the world. However if God is, as Christianity proclaims, an eternal and personal Triune agent, three persons united together in a reciprocal bond of love, then there is no difficulty in affirming a salvific relationship between the Father and his creation mediated by the Son and the Holy Spirit, and no problem in explaining why he should choose to reveal himself in the incarnate Christ in an act of gracious and unconditional love.

On the philosophical side, the notion of a Transcendent principle underlying the rational order discernible in the universe remained attractive to many unwilling to accept any form of personal God. The philosophers of the Enlightenment sought to demythologise the God of classical theism and recover a vision of God as the impersonal source of the rational order inherent in the universe. Peter Gay interprets the Enlightenment as the rise and near-triumph of a reconstituted 'pagan' natural theology, grounded in the differentiation of the God of Abraham from the God of the philosophers and the rejection of the former in favour of the latter:

The philosophes' experience ... was a dialectical struggle for autonomy, an attempt to assimilate the two pasts they had inherited – Christian and pagan – to pit them against one another and thus to secure their independence ... the philosophes' rebellion succeeded in both its aims: theirs was a paganism directed against their Christian inheritance and dependent upon the paganism of classical antiquity, but it was also a *modern* paganism, emancipated from classical thought as much as from Christian dogma.

(Gay 1973a: xi)

Similarly, Michael Buckley's account of the origins of modern atheism argues cogently that the philosophers of the Enlightenment were quick to bypass the God of Abraham and focus their theological deliberations almost entirely on the God of the philosophers (Buckley 1987). Positively, the mainstream Enlightenment affirmed a deistic God, a divine watchmaker who constructs the mechanical clock of the universe, winds it up, and then leaves it to its own devices; negatively, the radical Enlightenment's affirmation of atheism was grounded almost exclusively in the rejection of this deistic God, since the God of Abraham had long since ceased to warrant their attention.

'Paganism' in this context refers to the reverence afforded to forces and mechanisms operative within the universe that are beyond the immediate control of humanity: powers that human beings must seek either to manipulate (insofar as they are able) or resign themselves to. In antiquity such forces tended to be personified and mythologised as divine or semi-divine beings that must either be placated through sacrificial rites or submitted to as agents of fate and destiny. With the advent of modernity these were recast as the impersonal forces of nature (and, albeit to a lesser extent, the forces of 'lower' human nature and reified social structures). The Enlightenment's commitment to human freedom generated a trenchant critique of revealed theology, one that sought to emancipate humankind from the (potentially demonic) power and authority of the Abrahamic God. This created space for a deistic version of natural theology, in the form of an impersonal or semi-personal God responsible for generating the forces of nature, and left the forces of nature as the only remaining substantial threat to human freedom. Francis Bacon's vision of the 'Great Insurrection' envisaged humankind finally learning to control and manipulate the natural world for its own ends, both through the exercise of autonomous reason and by drawing on the technological fruits of the emergent natural sciences (Bacon 1974, 2012; Gaukroger 2001: 132ff.). Deism sparked briefly, only to be subjected to a similarly trenchant critique: since positing a deity as the source of the physical world did nothing to illuminate understanding of the natural order-of-things, it appeared superfluous and lacking in explanatory power. The apparent redundancy of appeals to a divine source of the natural order-of-things thus paved the way for a thoroughgoing secular naturalism. Insofar as both deism and naturalism made humankind ultimately responsible for their own destiny, they affirmed the Enlightenment dream of individual freedom and autonomy in a manner that the Abrahamic call for obedience and submission to the will of a benevolent personal God could never hope, or desire, to achieve. The identification of the God of natural theology as a redundant hypothesis in turn generated a conviction that metaphysical questions about the ultimate structures of reality underlying the natural order-of-things were illegitimate. Metaphysics was dismissed as a purely speculative exercise, and primal metaphysical questions about the nature and existence of 'Being' itself, and of the best explanation of the actuality of the existence and contingent order of the physical universe, were dismissed as unverifiable and therefore nonsensical. It was enough that natural science could explain *how* the natural order works: questions about *why* it exists and *why* it works as it does must be excluded. Any hope of answering them lay not in metaphysics, natural theology or revealed theology, but in the emergent insights of natural science itself. Once again we come face-to-face with the epistemic fallacy: to bracket-out metaphysical questions on the grounds of unverifiability, and exclude metaphysical answers until such time as natural science generates them is to make the a priori assumption that the physical world is self-explaining, self-generating, self-rationalising and self-sustaining.

Critiques of revealed theology

Our review of the Enlightenment's critique of revealed theology must necessarily be selective and indicative. We will focus on five key objections: (1) that it improperly sought to generate eternal truths from historically contingent events; (2) that its appeal to scriptural authority undermined the principle of rational autonomy; (3) that its reliance on metaphor undercut the epistemic necessity of grounding knowledge on simple ideas and atomistic sense data; (4) that its appeals to miracle contradicted natural law and depended on the second-hand authority of received testimony; and (5) that its requirement of obedience to God's will undermined moral autonomy.

(1) *Historical contingency.* In the orthodox Christian tradition knowledge of the Trinitarian, God is the product of God's self-revelation, grounded in his Spirit-driven covenantal relationship with Israel and culminating in the incarnation of Jesus Christ. The hypostatic union of God and humanity in the person of Jesus Christ constitutes the still point around which the entire economy of creation revolves: the ultimate mystery, meaning and purpose of the totality of reality rests on the contingent historical events surrounding the life, death and resurrection of Jesus of Nazareth. Christianity does not proclaim a timeless truth exemplified or partially reflected in the person of Jesus of Nazareth; on the contrary, Christianity is committed to the particularity of God's active engagement in history, and insists that contingent historical events are real-in-themselves and as such possess an ontological significance that cannot be reduced to the level of mere shadows, reflections or ciphers of some greater Transcendent reality. If even the most insignificant event impacts, however slightly, on the whole, then *the* most significant event can and must impact on the whole decisively and fundamentally. This understanding of God as a personal agent acting within history rather than an impersonal structure transcending history contradicted a

fundamental assumption of the philosophers of the Enlightenment. Both the idealist and empiricist currents of the Enlightenment resisted any substantial connection between contingent events and eternal truths: a position given classical expression in Gotthold Lessing's dictum that 'accidental truths of history can never become the proof of necessary truths of reason' (Lessing 1957: 53).

Enlightenment idealism had its roots in the Platonic appropriation of Parmenides' identification of a timeless uniformity underlying the contingencies of history. From this perspective, the demi-reality of the universe of flux and change is but a pale reflection of the ultimate reality of the fixed and eternal Platonic Forms. A God capable of entering into reciprocal personal relationships with human beings is a God capable of change, and a God capable of change cannot possibly be the eternal First Principle of reality. The Christian response, that it is the reciprocal self-giving-and-receiving-in-love that binds the three persons of the Trinity together in eternal unity which constitutes the First Principle of creation, and that such love can be constant even in relation to the contingencies of history and vagaries of human behaviour, was largely ignored by Enlightenment philosophers. If God is identified with the necessary truths of reason, then a 'God' actively engaged in the contingencies of history cannot possibly be *that* God. Even Hegelian dialectic, open as it was to the notion of historical progress towards the realisation of Absolute Spirit, rejected any notion that contingent historical events are capable of generating, constituting or perfectly embodying eternal truths: at best, history might exemplify eternal truth or reflect progress towards eternal truth. On this reading the life of Jesus Christ might, at best, faintly shadow some eternal moral or spiritual value on the wall of the cave of the cosmos to which human beings have been consigned.

Enlightenment empiricism departed from idealism in identifying the empirical realm as fundamentally real-in-itself, rather than as a demi-reality falling short of the ultimate reality of absolute Transcendent truth. If truth is to be found, it must be located *within* Heraclitus' ephemeral cosmos, marked as it was by constant flux, motion and change. It is here that the success of modern science came into its own: where Heraclitus saw mere chaos, Isaac Newton discerned the inherent order of a mechanistic universe governed by the laws of nature. Even the sceptical tradition of Humean empiricism found evidence of natural law in its observation of regular conjunctions of empirical objects. Crucially however, unique historical events, though real-in-themselves, possessed no intrinsic significance beyond that of their necessary obedience to natural law. Consequently there could be nothing especially significant about the life of Jesus Christ: despite Christian claims to the contrary, it must necessarily be bound by the laws of nature and part of the repetitive pattern of regular events that order human affairs. Empirical philosophers knew in advance that contingent historical events must be explained in terms of the impersonal structures of natural law rather than the personal actions of a divine agent.

Any suggestion that Jesus Christ possessed eternal significance by ontologically embodying and epistemically revealing God's essential nature inevitably transgressed the established boundaries of both idealism and empiricism: the accidental truths of the life of Jesus of Nazareth could never become proofs of the eternal and necessary truths of reason. If the Gospels retained any value, it lay in the ability of Jesus' moral teachings to exemplify eternal moral truths that could be established independently on rational grounds; Jesus' theological teachings, together with the theological narrative with which the Gospels frame their account of his life, must be demythologised, deconstructed and dismissed as rank superstition. Such readings of the life of Jesus commit the epistemic fallacy by forcing historical interpretation to conform to an established set of assumptions regarding the potential significance of historical events: the philosophers of the Enlightenment embraced the a priori assumption that contingent historical events could not possibly embody or constitute eternal Transcendent truths and as a result dismissed out of hand the a posteriori retroductive response of the first Christians to their abductive encounters with Jesus. Thus the ground rules of the Enlightenment denied any possibility of a theological reading of history: a timeless and unchanging God could not possibly be incarnate in a time-bound and contingent world.

(2) *The authority of scripture.* The three main Abrahamic faiths all possess sacred scriptures that, albeit in different ways and to different degrees, enjoy authoritative status as divine revelation within their respective communities. The Enlightenment's negative hermeneutic of suspicion directed towards all forms of external authority, together with its positive insistence that readers of texts must have the courage to trust their own reason when interpreting them, inevitably resulted in the wholesale questioning of the authority of scripture. As Thomas Paine insisted in *The Age of Reason*, the hermeneutical key for interpreting scripture is simple: 'My own mind is my own church' (Paine 2004: 22). Colin Gunton points out that this rules out in advance any possibility of divine revelation: 'If reason is autonomous and self-sufficient, we do not need revelation'; and if truth is 'something lying within the control of the human rational agent', any appeal to revelation necessarily 'takes away our autonomy and leaves us in thrall to the authority of others' (Gunton 1995: 21). As Johann Gottlieb Fichte argued in his *Attempt at a Critique of All Revelation*, if appeals to reason take precedence over appeals to revelation then any revealed knowledge of God must necessarily also be accessible through the independent exercise of autonomous reason (Fichte 2010). However, particular historical events cannot possibly be known independently of either direct experience or mediated testimony. It follows that to claim that knowledge of God must be independently accessible by autonomous reason is necessarily to rule out a priori the possibility of historical revelation. This is a clear instance of the epistemic fallacy of forcing knowledge of reality to conform to established epistemic assumptions. The critically realistic alternative is to insist that our epistemic procedures must be progressively honed and polished a posteriori, in response to the realities we actually encounter. It was the first disciples' encounter with Jesus of Nazareth that led Christianity to lay claim to knowledge of God revealed through contingent historical events and mediated through sacred scripture. The Enlightenment's rejection of both historical revelation and scriptural authority was predicated on a priori epistemic and ontological assumptions.

Paine's account of revelation assumes a direct transaction between God and human beings: 'Revelation when applied to religion, means something communicated immediately from God to man' (Paine 2004: 23). He has in mind a direct empirical hearing of the oracular voice of God, and appears unaware of the Judaeo-Christian understanding of revelation as *indirectly mediated* through historical events and communal experiences (Gunton 1995: 18f.). On the latter reading, Christian scripture may be seen as a divinely sanctioned witness to the ontological actuality of God's self-revelation in history: generated by abductive revelatory events that have been subjected to retroductive explanation and iterative refinement by human authors under the guidance of the Holy Spirit. As such, scripture can legitimately be interpreted as *both* the product of fallible human authors *and* the revealed Word of God. For many Christians the authority of scripture rests on the ontological fact that it is God's Word revealed to humankind; this Word is mediated by the Bible's human authors who, under the inspiration of the Holy Spirit, produced the most powerful and authoritative retroductive explanations of the events surrounding the life, death and resurrection of Jesus of Nazareth available to humankind. Epistemic access to this ontological reality is possible because of the intrinsic explanatory power of the text itself: for Christians the authority of the Bible is intrinsic to the Biblical text itself, and not imposed by any extra-Biblical authority.

Paine hints that if he were to receive an immediate revelation in the form of a face-to-face encounter with an angel he might, on the grounds of the sovereignty of his own conscious experience, have a legitimate epistemic warrant to affirm its truth. However, 'I did not see the angel myself, and therefore I have a right not to believe it' (Paine 2004: 24). Appeals to revelation are appeals to 'revelation to the first person only, and *hearsay* to every other, and, consequently, they are not obliged to believe it' (ibid.: 23). Given the sovereignty of the experience of the Cartesian self, appeals to revelation can have currency only if revelation is direct and unmediated; revelation mediated through scriptural texts is necessarily dependent on illicit second-hand testimonial authority.

Paine distinguishes between external authority attributed to scripture and internal authority intrinsic within scripture itself. The external authority of scripture is dependent on fallible human testimonial authority: the New Testament canon emerged when theologians 'decided by *vote* which of the books out of the collection they had made, should be the WORD OF GOD, and which should not' (ibid.: 32). Such authority is the product of 'hearsay upon hearsay, and I do not chuse to rest my belief upon such evidence' (ibid.: 24). Appeals to the internal authority of scripture fare no better: working with a positivistic understanding of history as the recounting of historical facts in chronological order, and drawing on the fruits of modern historical scholarship, he views the Bible as a collection of historically inaccurate narratives overlaid with layers of mythical speculation. The Christian account of reality expressed in the Bible constitutes a mythical fable 'which for absurdity and extravagance is not exceeded by anything that is to be found in the mythology of the ancients' (ibid.: 28).

If a 'thing which everybody is required to believe, requires that the proof and evidence of it should be equal to all, and universal', then appeals to divine revelation and the authority of scripture fall woefully short (ibid.: 27). If there are no rational grounds for accepting the authority of revelation and scripture, then those who seek to uphold them must be driven by more sinister motives: 'All national institutions of churches, whether Jewish, Christian, or Turkish [i.e. Muslim], appear to me no other than human inventions set up to terrify and enslave mankind, and monopolize power and profit' (ibid.: 22). To embrace the authority of revelation and scripture is to submit to the hegemony of religious institutions and refuse the God-given right to think for ourselves.

(3) *Myth and metaphor.* Theological science, like natural science, seeks to describe and explain aspects of reality closed to direct empirical observation: the God of Abraham, like the hydrogen and oxygen in water, cannot be directly seen, smelt, heard, touched or tasted. Consequently, both disciplines employ analogical, metaphorical and tropic modes of expression that seek to refer to substantial ontological realities in indirect non-literal ways. Ancient and medieval natural philosophy employed a mixture of philosophical reflection and empirical observation to identify hidden, invisible or 'occult' objects and forces in the natural world. With the emergence of modern natural science, systematic methods of empirical observation, experimental testing, mathematical measurement and explanatory modelling took priority over philosophical speculation. The success of modern natural science enabled astronomy and chemistry to replace the occult sciences of astrology and alchemy, and generated a tendency to reduce the natural world to that which is perceptible by the five senses. As a result the 'occult' gradually became associated with hidden, speculative, esoteric knowledge of mystical realms and supra-natural realities beyond empirical observation: knowledge that all reasonable people ought to dismiss as the product of rank superstition. This is reflected in Auguste Comte's account of humankind's intellectual progress from religious through metaphysical to positivistic explanations of reality (Comte 1988). Whereas pre-modern attempts to explain the causes and mechanisms underlying empirical reality appealed initially to invisible gods and spirits and later to unseen metaphysical forces, modern positivistic science was content to offer surface explanations of empirical phenomena without recourse to any underlying occult forces, whether religious, metaphysical or natural. Logical positivism dismissed both theological and metaphysical discourse as essentially meaningless, and rejected attempts to identify natural causal mechanisms operating beneath the surface appearances of phenomena, on the grounds that all three were closed to empirical verification.

This attempted reduction of reality to the objects of sense experience had a direct impact on the Enlightenment's understanding of the nature and function of language. If knowledge is constituted by clear and distinct ideas immediately present in the mind, and if these clear and distinct ideas enjoy a direct ostensive relationship with observable empirical objects, then metaphorical language must be dismissed as unnecessary rhetorical embellishment that threatens to obscure clear and distinct expressions of meaning. According to John Locke, the use of eloquent figurative language serves only 'to insinuate wrong *Ideas*, move the Passions, and thereby mislead the Judgement' (Locke 1975: 508). To employ figurative language when constructing complex ideas from simple ideas is to run the risk of generating fabulous configurations unwarranted by the empirical data: unicorns and centaurs rather than cats and dogs. Objectivity demands a direct ostensive connection between objects and the words we employ to identify them; metaphor occludes such ostensive reference and gives free range to the subjective imagination.

Such a literalistic understanding of the proper use and function of language lies behind Paine's assertion of the 'absurdity and extravagance' of Christian mythology (Paine 2004: 28). All talk about God must necessarily employ figurative speech, since the absence of direct empirical experience precludes literal ostensive language; yet – and once again the epistemic fallacy comes into play – Paine knows *in advance* that figurative speech necessarily lacks cognitive purchase on ontological objects. True, he is happy to commend the genius of Homeric myth *qua* myth, since 'the merit of the poet will remain, though the story be fabulous' (ibid.: 92). However, when faced with the poetry of the Bible and its claim to describe ontological realities, he insists on a literalistic reading and consequently finds only the work of charlatans and imposters in accounts 'such as that of talking with God face to face, or that of the sun and moon standing still at the command of a man' (ibid.). The difference is that whereas Homer seeks merely to entertain through the stimulus of the fantastical imagination, the Bible claims access to ontological truths, and as such must be read literalistically and positivistically, since literalism and positivism are our only means of accessing truth. Consequently the mythical language employed in the Bible, such as the account of Christ's 'ascension … several miles high into the air' can be discarded, not because of the inadequacy of the theological claims expressed in mythic terms, but because of the absence of verifiable empirical evidence and incompatibility with natural law (ibid.: 77). Paine's argument is representative of a literalistic strain of thought within the Enlightenment that found in the metaphorical and mythological language present within sacred texts a priori evidence of the absence of any viable truth claims. It is precisely this literalism that gave birth to the distinctively modern phenomenon of scriptural fundamentalism, which ironically seeks to resist modernity by embracing the modernist criterion of literal ostensive definition as a necessary requirement of all truth claims.

Some liberal theologians responded to the Enlightenment's critique of theological metaphor by attempting to demythologise theological language: if theological metaphor and myth could be stripped away then a pristine theological truth might be revealed, one capable of speaking to modern humankind in a language uncontaminated by pre-modern mythic superstition. The problem with such a strategy lay in the fact that if God can only be described analogically, then to abandon analogy was necessarily to abandon talk of God and recast accounts of the Transcendent realm as disguised accounts of the immanent realm of nature, culture and human minds. Joseph Campbell identified four basic functions of myth: cosmological, explaining the ultimate nature of the universe; mystical, expressing experiences of awe and wonder; sociological, validating a particular social order; and pedagogic, guiding the living out of the good life (Campbell 2011). To demythologise theological discourse was to abandon the cosmological function of myth on the understanding that natural science, rather than theology or metaphysics, offers the best explanation of the ultimate nature of the universe. This effectively reduced theological discourse to its mystical, sociological and pedagogic functions: expressing spiritual experience, sustaining religious communities and providing guidance for practical living. As a consequence, religious discourse was increasingly driven in an anti-realistic direction: the spiritual experiences and lifestyles nurtured by religious communities were increasingly seen as devoid of any cognitive purchase on Transcendent ontological realities, and religious traditions increasingly evaluated in terms of their pragmatic utility rather than their cognitive truth claims.

With the benefit of hindsight, it is clear that the reduction of reality to that which is open to direct empirical experience, together with the reduction of language to the role of literal ostensive definition, constitute classic examples of the epistemic fallacy of forcing reality to conform to pre-established understandings of our ways of knowing and speaking. The a priori epistemic ground rules regarding the methods and modes of expression of natural science, as theorised by empiricist and positivist philosophers (though rarely practised by natural scientists themselves), denied theology and metaphysics any cognitive purchase on reality. Roy Bhaskar has been at the forefront of attempts to expose the poverty of such theory. There is more to reality than we can see, taste, hear, smell and touch: we know that interactions in the natural and social worlds are, at least in part, products of invisible ('occult') causal mechanisms (gravity, economic forces, personal desires, etc.) that cannot be directly discerned and whose existence we surmise from their affects in a process of 'inference to the best possible explanation' (Lipton 2004). Retroductive explanations of aspects of reality that appeal to underlying causal mechanisms have proved far more powerful than surface descriptions that refuse to trespass beyond empirically verifiable facts. Crucially, retroductive explanations of entities that are not open to direct empirical verification *necessarily* utilise metaphorical language: natural science is as replete with metaphor as any other human discourse ('particles', 'waves', 'chaperone proteins', 'factory cells', 'big bangs', etc.), and yet rightfully claims cognitive access to ontological entities not directly accessible to the five senses.

(4) *The improbability of miracles.* The critique of miracles quickly became a central plank of the Enlightenment's attack on revealed religion. Two factors help explain this emphasis. First, the remarkable success of modern natural science, allied to the deistic assumption that having created the natural order-of-things God elected not to engage further with it, effectively established the laws of nature as 'the fundamental determinants of what happens' in the world (Swinburne 2010: 86). Hume's definition of miracle as a 'violation of the laws of nature' followed directly from the assumption that any action of God in the world must necessarily take the form of an occult or supra-natural intervention

within the observable natural order (Hume 1902: 114). Second, the Enlightenment's insistence that knowledge must be based on indubitably secure foundations generated the assumption that the primary function of miracle was to *demonstrate* the truth of revealed religion – this despite the virtual absence of appeals to the epistemic function of miracle in Christian scripture and the early Church (Wright 2013: 274ff.). Thus according to Hermann Reimarus, it 'is always a sign that a doctrine or history possesses no depth of authenticity when one is obliged to resort to miracles *in order to prove its truth*' (Voysey 1879: 74f., my emphasis). Similarly, John Mackie's critique of miracles draws the conclusion 'that it is pretty well impossible that reported miracles should provide *a worthwhile argument* for theism' (Mackie 1982: 27, my emphasis). Consequently the inherent implausibility of reports of supra-natural violations of the laws of nature were deemed to provide clear evidence of the poverty of the truth claims of revealed religions.

David Hume offered the most thorough and influential Enlightenment critique of miracles (Hume 1902: 109ff.; cf. Mackie 1982: 13ff.). Recognising that some truth claims possess greater epistemic warrant than others, he insisted that we can only legitimately subscribe to beliefs in proportion to the strength of the available evidence, and offers two reasons why belief in miracles should be rejected. First, miracles are *intrinsically improbable* because we have good reason to assume the inviolability of natural law. Given that our understanding of interactions between objects 'are founded merely on our experience of their constant and regular conjunction', it is highly unlikely that miracles ever occur (Hume 1902: 111). Indeed, since 'a uniform experience amounts to a proof, there is here a direct and full *proof*, from the nature of the fact, against the existence of any miracle' (ibid.: 115). Second, historical accounts of miracles are *inherently untrustworthy*. Our beliefs about the past are reliant on the primary testimony of eyewitnesses and the secondary transmission of their evidence. In assessing testimonial evidence we must strike a balance between trust and suspicion: before accepting evidence at face value, we must be alert to the possibility of intentional or unintentional deception. 'We have particular reason to exercise suspicion whenever witnesses contradict each other, are of a doubtful character, have a vested interest in persuading us to believe their stories, or deliver their testimony with undue hesitation or excessive assertiveness' (Wright 2013: 259). Because miracles are intrinsically improbable, the burden of proof rests on those who testify to miraculous events.

> When anyone tells me, that he saw a dead man restored to life, I immediately consider with myself, whether it be more probable, that this person should either deceive or be deceived, or that the fact, which he relates, should really have happened.
>
> (Hume 1902: 116)

Given the gullibility of the uneducated masses, it is no surprise that 'the generality of mankind ... believe and report, with the greatest vehemence and assurance, all religious miracles' (ibid.: 119). Belief in miracles is common 'among ignorant and barbarous nations', and those who continue to believe in them are reliant on the uneducated testimony of their superstitious ancestors (ibid.). Hume holds that 'no testimony is sufficient to establish a miracle, unless the testimony be of such a kind, that its falsehood would be more miraculous, than the fact, which it endeavours to establish' (ibid.: 115f.). To shift the balance of probability in favour of miracles would require testimony of extraordinary authority and power; however, 'there is not to be found, in all history, any miracle attested by a sufficient number of men, of such unquestioned good-sense, education, and learning' to tilt the burden of proof in favour of the miraculous (ibid.: 116).

Two brief concluding observations must suffice here. First, the Christian appeal to miracle is not epistemically driven by a desire to prove the truth of Christianity but rather by an ontological desire to better understand the nature of God. Thus in John's Gospel, Jesus' miracles are understood not as proofs of his divinity but as 'signs' of his theological significance (John 2:11). Second, contra standard empiricist assumptions, we understand the natural world not by offering surface descriptions of regularly occurring events, but by producing retroductive explanations of the underlying causal mechanisms that combine to generate such events. Christian appeals to miracle do no more than acknowledge the actions of God as constituting a more primal causal mechanism than the processes of nature. Richard Swinburne acknowledges that it 'is immensely improbable that [miracles] would ever have happened if laws of nature were the fundamental determinants of what happens' (Swinburne 2010: 86). However, if God is more fundamental than the laws of nature, it follows that 'all events occur only because God allows them to occur ... all laws of nature operate only as long as God determines that they shall' (ibid.: 85). This being the case, it is perfectly reasonable to suppose that what Hume terms 'violations' of the laws of nature can be brought about by God. It follows that provided we have good reason to believe in God and to trust the reliability of witnesses, and are able to explain why God might have brought about a miraculous event, we have a legitimate reason to believe in miracles. Here miracles that Hume interprets as violations of the laws of nature are revealed as divine actions through which God heals and restores his fallen creation.

(5) *Debased morality.* The modern critique of revealed religions sought the moral high ground. Paine records how, having listened to a sermon entitled 'Redemption by the death of the Son of God',

> I revolted at the recollection of what I had heard, and thought to myself that it was making God Almighty act like a passionate man, that killed his son, when he could not revenge himself any other way.
>
> (Paine 2004: 65)

Similarly, according to Christopher Hitchens,

> Once you assume a creator and a plan, it makes us objects, in a cruel experiment, whereby we are created sick, and commanded to be well.... And over

us, to supervise this, is installed a celestial dictatorship, a kind of divine North Korea.

(Hitchens 2010)

Both examples have the advantage of avoiding, at least in part, the crass apologetics of scriptural proof-texting beloved of religious and secular fundamentalists alike, and attempting instead to respond to the Christian narrative holistically. That said, both betray a remarkable lack of understanding of Christian doctrine. Paine's suggestion that God killed his son in an act of revenge is anathema to orthodox Christian soteriology, which insists that *God* himself was incarnate in Christ and suffered and died in an act of unconditional and reconciliatory love (Moltmann 1974; Fiddes 1992). Hitchens' suggestion that 'we are created sick and commanded to do well' is the polar opposite of orthodox Christian teaching which affirms humankind's utter reliance on the grace of God, and his notion of a 'celestial dictatorship' is incompatible with the orthodox Christian doctrine of incarnation – prior to his death, there was little evidence of any intention on the part of Kim Il-sung to sacrifice his life for the good of his American enemies!

Paine does, however, identify the heart of the problem in his recognition that in the Christian narrative God acts 'like a passionate man'. Many philosophers of the Enlightenment were willing to embrace a deistic God devoid of passion and personality only to the extent of imbuing his creation with an intrinsic rational and moral order. The notion of a God capable of laughing and crying is anathema to Greek natural theology: Plato's Form of the Good can no more laugh than Aristotle's Unmoved Mover can cry. Yet it is this notion of a passionate God that lies at the very heart of the Judaeo-Christian theological tradition. We might, for heuristic purposes, suggest that if Feuerbach is right, and theology is essentially an act of projection, then Greek natural theology projects a God who mirrors the rational order of nature, whilst revealed theology projects a God who mirrors human passions; and if God is identified as the highest supranatural being and humankind the highest natural being, then any project ought, at the very least, to project God as supra-human and not merely supra-natural. However, such abstract speculation fails to do justice to the epistemic ground of the Judaeo-Christian tradition, which posits a personal God, not on the basis of metaphysical speculation, but rather in response to God's self-revelation in historical events.

Crucially, a personal God who, as the omnipotent and omniscient Creator of the universe, invites his creatures to enter into a personal relationship with him constitutes an immediate threat to their moral autonomy, since his essential being embodies deontological moral standards that human beings cannot alter. Even if such a personal God approaches his creatures as a servant, under-labouring for their wellbeing and acting only out of gracious, self-giving and unconditional love, the notion that we do not stand at the apex of the created order, and that a higher authority invites, calls and empowers us to transcend our limitations, is experienced as morally, aesthetically and spiritually repugnant – a direct threat to the modern liberal ideal of personal autonomy. The heart of the Enlightenment's moral objection to Abrahamic faith lies in the latter's claim that God rather than the Cartesian ego stands at the summit of reality, and that consequently humankind is ontologically subservient to a moral order it did not create and over which it has no control.

Critiques of natural theology

The critique of revealed theology continues to simmer and occasionally, as in the contemporary debate surrounding the so-called 'New Atheism', boil over (Harris 2006; Dawkins 2007; Dennett 2007; Hitchens 2007; cf. Poole 2009; McGrath 2011). The mainstream Enlightenment however, secure in its belief that revealed theology had been successfully deposed, quickly turned its attention to what appeared to be the more intellectually promising task of articulating a redux natural theology. To demythologise the hybrid God of classical theism, strip away the vestiges of revealed religion, and reject the uneasy synthesis of Greek philosophy and Abrahamic theology was to open the door, not to atheism, but to a recovery of the pristine God of the philosophers, the First Cause of all that has being and First Principle of the natural and moral order of the universe.

The first comprehensive statement of deism is found in Herbert of Cherbury's *De Veritate* (first published in 1624), and notable subsequent expositions are found in the writings of Thomas Paine, Hermann Reimarus, Matthew Tindal and Voltaire (Bedford 1979; Byrne 2013). Negatively, deism was marked by an anti-clerical suspicion of organised religion and latitudinarian rejection of religious dogma: the God of the deists does not reveal himself in authoritative scriptures, nor does he intervene miraculously, prophetically or supra-naturally in the world. Positively, deism affirmed a demi-personal God who acts to create the universe and imbue it with rational and moral order, only to depart from it and leave it to its own devices. The God of deism remains utterly transcendent of the subsequent course of nature and wholly aloof from human affairs, leaving humankind the freedom and responsibility to utilise its God-given reason to manage its own affairs and engineer its own salvation. Though deism fell short of invoking the impersonal God of Plato's Form of the Good and Aristotle's Unmoved Mover, the concern to limit the personal characteristics of the deity was unmistakable: if God is the demi-personal watchmaker who constructs the great mechanism of nature, winds it up and then takes his leave, then that God's personal disinterest in humanity allowed humanity to reciprocate with a personal disinterest in the character of God. If God leaves us to our own devices and makes no demands on us, then we are free to organise our own lives and engineer our own salvation: a conclusion that resonated positively with the Enlightenment ideal of personal autonomy.

(1) *The Copernican turn in natural theology.* In a previous chapter we left Descartes meditating on his certainty of his own existence, despite the best efforts of a hypothetical malignant demon to convince him otherwise. But how could he translate such self-certainty into certainty about the external world?

How could he avoid leaving the recently secured Cartesian ego adrift on a sea of chaos? Cartesian epistemology would remain a fragile affair unless the demon of doubt could be successfully exorcised, and only a God incapable of deception could possibly achieve this feat. Descartes' strategy was 'to proceed from certainty of himself to certainty of God to certainty of the external world' (Byrne 1996: 63). The 'proof of God's existence is, for Descartes, an essential step in the secure reconstruction of human knowledge' (Mackie 1982: 31).

In his *Third Meditation* Descartes argued that the existence of a perfect God is necessary to explain the presence of the idea of a perfect God in his mind. Descartes embraces without argument the God of the philosophers: 'By the word "God" I mean a substance that is infinite, independent, supremely intelligent, supremely powerful, and the Creator of myself and anything else that may exist' (Descartes 1970: 85). But where did his clear and distinct idea of such a God come from? Ideas have causes: they do not come from nothing. Some ideas are generated by empirical experience (e.g. sound and weight), some are products of the imagination (e.g. mythical creatures), and others are innate to the mind. The idea of God cannot possibly be the product of empirical experience, since Descartes has neither seen, heard, smelt, touched nor tasted God. Neither can the idea of God be the product of his imagination: since an effect cannot be greater than its cause, Descartes' imperfect mind cannot possibly create the idea of a perfect being:

> I did not derive it from the senses ... and it is not my own invention, for I can neither add anything to it nor subtract anything from it. So it can only be innate in me, just as the idea of myself is.
>
> (ibid.: 90)

Since only a perfect God can cause the idea of a perfect God, 'it is not surprising that God, when he created me, should have implanted this idea in me, to be as it were an artist's mark impressed on his work' (ibid.). Our concern here is not with the veracity of Descartes' argument, which has been subject to a range of trenchant criticisms: that it is circular (the idea of a perfect God exorcises the malignant demon/the malignant demon deceptively implants the idea of a perfect God); that the notion of physical causality is not transferrable to the mental realm; that it is not possible to comprehend perfection; that experience of imperfection can generate the idea of perfection, etc. Rather our interest lies elsewhere, in the *epistemic ramifications* of his arguments (he also offers a version of Anselm's ontological argument in the *Fifth Meditation*) for God's existence: 'I am confident that the human mind can know nothing more certainly or more evidently' than the existence of God; consequently, 'I can see [with equal confidence] the impossibility of God's ever deceiving me' (ibid.: 92). This being the case, the malignant demon of doubt is effectively exorcised, Cartesian anxiety assuaged, and the hermeneutic of suspicion transformed into a hermeneutic of trust in the power of humankind's cognitive faculties. This does not mean that Descartes cannot be mistaken, since he is capable of misusing his God-given capacity to reason; it does however mean that if he strives to use that faculty aright, and learns the habit of trusting only clear and distinct ideas, then the knowledge that flows from such actions will be inherently trustworthy. 'Thus today I have learnt, not only what to avoid, so as not to be deceived, but also what to do, so as to attain the truth' (ibid.: 100).

As Hans Küng points out, Descartes' argument marked a Copernican revolution in theology, an '*epochal turning point*' in the history of Western thought, not because of its substance but because of its function (Küng 1980: 15). If the traditional function of revealed theology was to locate humanity within God's universe, Cartesian natural theology now sought to locate God within the world of humankind. The move from theocentrism to anthropocentrism meant that:

> Certainty is no longer centered on God, but on man ... the medieval way of reasoning from certainty of God to certainty of the self is replaced by the modern approach: from certainty of the self to certainty of God.
>
> (ibid.: 15)

The function of theology was no longer to give an account of God's gracious justification of fallen humanity, but to utilise God as a tool for the justification of the supremacy of human reason. Contra some critics, Descartes' argument for the existence of God is *not* circular: the triumph of the *cogito*, the assertion of his existence as a thinking being, *precedes* the proof of God's existence. God functions to confirm, secure and buttress the power of human reason, and thereby to impress a mark of approval on the Enlightenment project itself. Descartes' decision to submit the *Meditations* for approval to the Sorbonne, the theological faculty of the University of Paris, was not driven by any concern to establish its Christian orthodoxy; rather it was a political move designed to enlist support for his philosophy (ibid.: 17). Descartes' theology was an academic exercise far removed from the real-world environment of Christian faith as practised by ordinary believers. His exorcism of the arbitrary God of late-medieval nominalism signified the death of the God of Abraham and the resurrection of the God of the philosophers.

(2) *Natural theology and metaphysics.* Both Descartes and the philosophers of the Enlightenment had no doubt that human reason could and should address ontological questions regarding the ultimate source and order of the universe. Deistic reasoning had two original sources: metaphysics and natural philosophy. According to Aristotle, the task of metaphysics was to answer ultimate *aporiai* concerning the Transcendent and unchanging structures of reality that enable the immanent and contingent natural and moral orders-of-things to be and function as they do. In modern parlance, metaphysical *aporiai* are concerned not with the natural and social sciences per se, but with the more basic or primal question as to what reality must ultimately be like for us to experience nature and human relationships in the ways that we do. Natural philosophy (*philosophia naturalis*), the precursor of modern natural science, was concerned with the immanent world of physics rather than the Transcendent realm of metaphysics. It sought to

explain the workings of nature through a combination of (largely unsystematic) empirical observation and philosophical speculation. The rise of deism in the seventeenth century paralleled the emergence of modern natural science from pre-modern natural philosophy. Natural science *assumed* the givenness of material reality and sought to *explain* how it functioned: the former entailed an implicit rejection of forms of Platonic idealism that reduced the material world to a mere demi-reality; the latter attempt at explanation effectively negated a priori metaphysical arguments, that had previously dominated natural philosophy's attempts to understand the natural world, in favour of Francis Bacon's method of a posteriori inductive reasoning. Nevertheless, the expanding knowledge of the nature of the universe provided by Isaac Newton, Galileo Galilei and many other pioneering natural scientists served to enhance rather than diminish the importance of metaphysical *aporiai*. Two basic metaphysical questions predominated: Why is there something rather than nothing? Why is that 'something' ordered and structured in a manner open to rational explanation?

These questions, first asked by the ancient Greeks (though they focused predominantly on the latter rather than the former), were not initially displaced by the emergent natural sciences. On the contrary, both metaphysics and natural science were seen as necessary and interrelated means of making sense of the universe. If the proper object of study of metaphysics was the realm of the Transcendent, then the proper object of study of natural science was the immanent realm of nature. Despite a gradual recognition of the autonomy of both disciplines and increasing differentiation of their tasks and responsibilities, the positivistic rejection of metaphysics, denial of Transcendence, and consequent reduction of reality to the realm of nature still lay in the future. During the seventeenth century, if the emergent inductive natural sciences were called on to explain *how* the universe functions, then metaphysics was still deemed necessary to explain *why* it is inherently open to rational explanation and, more fundamentally, *why* it exists at all. For most Enlightenment philosophers, answers to the 'why' questions of the existence and inherent rationality of the universe were beyond the scope of natural science and as such could only be answered by natural theology.

First: 'why is the universe ordered and structured in a manner open to rational explanation?' In the *Timaeus* Plato sought to answer this question by positing a supremely wise Demiurge that used the Platonic Forms as a blueprint when imposing form on pre-existent matter. Aristotle invoked a perfect Unmoved Mover, whose intrinsic beauty and rationality passively shaped the pre-existent heavenly bodies and ordered the contingent universe. In insisting that the material world is not intrinsically rational but rather receives its rationality from a greater divine or quasi-divine being, Plato and Aristotle laid the foundations for Thomas Aquinas' teleological argument for God's existence, which proceeds from his recognition of 'the governance of the world' (Aquinas 1920: 26). Natural bodies are rationally ordered or governed: they do not behave completely randomly, but rather tend to act in particular ways and towards particular ends. Yet they lack intelligence, and 'whatever lacks intelligence cannot move towards an end, unless it be directed by some being endowed with knowledge and intelligence' (ibid.: 27). Just as an arrow hits its target only by virtue of the purposeful intelligence of an archer, so natural objects behave in rationally discernible ways because 'some intelligent being exists by whom all natural things are directed to their end; and this being we call God' (ibid.).

The advent of modern natural science, with its increasingly rich understanding of the natural order-of-things, generated a more complex version of Aquinas' position, in the form of the 'argument from design'. Newton's mechanical account of the universe invited mechanical accounts of its design: thus, according to William Paley, just as we properly infer the existence of a watchmaker if we find a watch lying on the ground, so we legitimately infer the existence of a creator God when we discern order and structure in the universe. As David Hume has Cleanthes argue in the *Dialogues Concerning Natural Religion*, since the

> curious adapting of means to ends, throughout all nature, resembles exactly, though it much exceeds, the productions of human contrivance ... we are led to infer, by all the rules of analogy ... the existence of a Deity, and his similarity to human mind and intelligence.
>
> (Hume 1947: 143)

Hume's critique of Cleanthes, placed in the mouth of the sceptic Philo, proceeds through five stages: the analogy between God and nature, and human beings and human artefacts is remote; even if the universe is designed, a creator God is only one among many alternative hypothetical causes; even if God did create the universe, the existence of a complex divine mind requires explanation; further, the existence of a benevolent deity does not explain the reality of evil; and, finally, the positing of a deity tells us nothing substantial about the universe itself and has no existential significance for our moral and spiritual wellbeing. The advent of Darwinian evolutionary theory appeared to undermine the teleological argument:

> One of the most impressive categories of apparent marks of design, the detailed structures of plant and animal bodies and their adaptation to conditions and a way of life, could be explained better by the theory of evolution through natural selection.
>
> (Mackie 1982: 133)

It is unclear, however, whether an explanation of how higher entities emerged from lower entities sufficiently answers the more primal metaphysical question as to why the universe *is* actually ordered in such a way as to be able to produce and sustain natural selection, and in a manner open to rational discernment.

Second: 'why is there something rather than nothing?' This question, addressed by the cosmological argument for God's existence, is more basic than the question of the inherent rationality of the universe: in order to ask why the universe is rationally ordered, it is first necessary to assume the existence of something rather than nothing. Even if we accept – as we surely must – some form of evolutionary theory as the best (currently available) retroductive biological explanation of the way in which plant and animal bodies adapt to their environments, the brute fact remains that 'something' must have previously existed for plants and animals to evolve from. The being-in-becoming of the emergent material cosmos is dependent on underlying physical, chemical and biological causal mechanisms that appear to be necessary preconditions of the evolutionary process. Even if we posit such causal mechanisms as transitive rather than intransitive, so that the forces and processes underlying evolution are themselves subject to emergence, development and change, at the very least they must have been 'something', however primal or chaotic, from which these causal mechanisms emerged. If reality, including both primal organic and sub-organic matter and the causal mechanisms that enabled them to evolve, were to be shown to have originated out of chaos, the *actuality* of such chaos would still need to be explained. Regardless of the extent and scope, depth and breadth, origins and end of the totality of being – of the 'something' that actually exists – it remains possible to counterfactually imagine a state of absolute nothingness. Even if time and space are infinite, so that that-which-exists has no spatial or temporal boundaries and there is no longer any need to invoke a 'First Cause', it remains a brute fact that these spatio-temporal coordinates exist and host various objects and events. The actuality of any existent reality, including the most primal particle, force, spatial point or temporal moment, constitutes a metaphysical *aporia* that demands explanation.

To ask the most basic ontological question of being-qua-being – why is there something rather than nothing? – is to assume, on the principle of sufficient reason, the possibility of a rational answer. To refuse an answer on the grounds that the available evidence is insufficient is to slip into the epistemic fallacy: retroductive explanation proceeds, not by deferring attempts at explanations, but by inferring explanations from the evidence currently available and evaluating the respective merits of competing explanations. This being the case, the alternative to the theological claim that God created the universe out of nothing is not explanatory deferral, but rather the construction of an explanation as to why the universe is best seen as self-generating, self-sustaining and self-rationalising.

The ancient Greeks struggled to account for the existence of something rather than nothing. Plato's explanation of creation in the *Timaeus* posits three primal realities: the Forms, pre-existent matter and the Demiurge responsible for imposing order onto chaotic matter using the Forms as a blueprint. Aristotle's account posits two primal entities: the Unmoved Mover and pre-existent celestial bodies. Plato and Aristotle were primarily concerned to explain *how* and *why* a perfect, immaterial and unchanging being (whether the Platonic Forms or the Aristotelian Unmoved Mover) *could* or *would* create lesser imperfect, material and contingent beings. If perfect being is changeless it cannot act (since – given that an already perfect being cannot become *more* perfect – to act would be to change and thereby move away from perfection), and if perfect being is impersonal it can have no motivation to act. The solution, of positing the pre-existence of primal matter or celestial bodies alongside perfect immaterial being, and explaining their order and movement with reference to the Demiurge or the intrinsic attractiveness of perfect being, begs the question: 'what caused these apparently unnecessary entities to exist?' The notion of a perfect and unchanging object, whose very essence *is* to exist, might possible explain the existence of the Forms or the Unmoved Mover; but neither primal matter, celestial bodies or the Demiurge possess the characteristics of such a necessary being. The Abrahamic faiths offered a solution to this dilemma, though – given their rejection of revealed theology – one that was no longer available to Enlightenment philosophers. The Christian doctrine of creation *ex nihilo* posited the Trinitarian God, united in a bond of reciprocal love, as the only uncreated and necessary being, responsible for bringing the entire spatio-temporal-bound created order into being out of nothing in a perfect and intentional act of love. Such an act does not undermine God's perfection, since if perfection is constituted by unconditional love, then to act out of love constitutes rather than diminishes perfection.

At its most basic, the cosmological argument runs as follows: the universe exists; every finite object in the universe has a cause; a causal chain cannot be infinite; therefore there must be a first cause or necessary being whose very essence *is* to exist – namely, God. In terms of modern cosmology, this raises the question of the origin and cause of the Big Bang. We might posit three possible answers. First, the Big Bang was self-generating, so that time, space, primal objects and primal causal mechanisms emerged spontaneously out of nothing. Second, the Big Bang was caused by the implosion of a previous universe, in which case *that* universe was either self-generating or generated by a still earlier universe, thus raising the possibility of infinite regress and an infinite number of universes. Third, the Big Bang was caused by God, a necessary being whose very essence *is* to exist.

According to Gottfried Leibnitz's principle of sufficient reason, every existing object must have a *reason* for being, so that the fact that there is something rather than nothing ultimately requires a necessary object whose *reason* for existing is intrinsic to itself (Leibniz 1973: 211ff., 220ff.). This leaves us with three possibilities: the Big Bang is self-generating, an infinite chain of exploding and imploding universes is infinitely self-generating, or God is self-generating. This raises (quite literally) metaphysical questions that natural science, restricted as it is to investigation of the natural strata of reality, appears unqualified to answer. Theoretical physics hypothesises that the Higgs boson particle causes movement in the Higgs field, raising it above its ground state and enabling fundamental particles such as quarks and electrons to take on mass. Higgs boson has been dubbed the 'God particle' in the popular media because it explains how objects come to possess mass and hence how material objects emerge out of non-material forces. This, however, falls far short of explaining the self-generation of the universe *ex nihilo*: the theory presupposes mathematical values, quantum fields, presence in space, movement in time, and either primal order or a primal potential for order to emerge from chaos. However close scientists come to explaining the origins of the Big Bang, they must necessarily begin by positing *something* primal – some particle, force or spatio-temporal point – rather than pure nothingness. On this reading, if natural science explains *how* the universe works, it cannot explain *why* the universe exists to be investigated, *why* there is something rather than nothing, without moving beyond physics into the realm of metaphysics. Even if the cosmological arguments fail to provide the epistemic certitude demanded of it by Enlightenment philosophers, it still raises fundamental questions that demand rational answers.

(3) *The demise of deism.* Deism is far from dead: there are many who hold fast to a belief that the universe was created and ordered by a higher power. Nevertheless, the demise of deism and natural theology from its highpoint in the Enlightenment is an unmistakeable reality. This is not to deny the existence of robust defences of natural theology (e.g. Swinburne 1971, 1993, 1998, 2004, 2005). However, the discipline of natural theology is no longer at the centre of the intellectual pursuits of philosophers, and for many the persistence of theism in the face of trenchant criticism is nothing short of 'miraculous' (Mackie 1982). But, given the fact that highly intelligent scholars continue to defend natural theology robustly, and that their arguments are countered by similarly robust counter-arguments, we cannot explain its demise merely by appealing to the poverty of intellectual argument: though the claims of natural theology may be contested, they have not yet been shown to be completely devoid of explanatory force.

Ironically, one of the major causes of the demise of natural theology has been the criticism directed against it by some adherents of the Abrahamic faiths. They argue that the God of the philosophers is an idol who falls significantly short of the God of Abraham: unworthy of worship, making no existential demands of humankind, and offering nothing of value to them. Karl Barth's reasoned 'no' to natural theology, in the first volume of the *Church Dogmatics*, insists that God can only be known insofar as he elects to make himself known to humanity, namely though the incarnate Christ (Barth 1975: 130ff.). It follows that natural theology, when approached in the light of the actuality of the incarnation, is epistemically impossible: if God reveals himself as *this* particular being (the Trinitarian God) in this particular set of circumstances, then he cannot also reveal himself as a significantly different kind of being (the God of deism) in a significantly different set of epistemic circumstances. Barth's critically realistic theology precedes on the premise that knowledge of any given object is possible only a posteriori by virtue of our epistemic encounters with it: in all spheres of knowledge, including the theological sphere, it is the nature of the object of knowledge itself that establishes the ways and means through which it can be known (La Montagne 2012; McCormack 1997). Just as we cannot establish knowledge of the natural world on the basis of epistemic decisions taken independently of our actual encounters with nature, so we cannot establish theological knowledge on the basis of epistemic criteria established independently of our actual encounters with God (Moore 2003). Since God elects to actively disclose himself to humankind, any attempt to secure knowledge of God independently of God's self-revelation constitutes an act of hubris that can only lead to idolatry. 'Trying to know God apart from God's revelation is to attempt the impossible, because it ignores the fact that God's self-revelation is the only condition for the possibility of knowing God' (Schwöbel 2000: 32). To seek God independently of the nature and acts of God is to commit the epistemic fallacy of forcing God into the straitjacket of a set of a priori epistemic assumptions. For Barth, natural theology falls into the trap Feuerbach cautions against, namely of creating a God after our own image. This is precisely the same trap Descartes falls into when he invokes a God designed to secure and maintain the power of his own cognitive faculties.

Secular critiques of natural theology follow a similar line of thinking insofar as they look beyond the specifics of the arguments proffered by natural theologians and question the very possibility of natural theology. As we have already noted, the crucial step in the emergence of natural science from natural philosophy was the turn to systematic empirical observation and abandonment of philosophical speculation. At the time of the Enlightenment this did not rule out metaphysical investigation as a separate intellectual endeavour with its own specific object of knowledge transcendent of the natural world. However, positivism took a further step beyond the entirely legitimate rejection of metaphysics as a tool for use within the natural sciences, to the entirely illegitimate rejection of the very possibility of metaphysics per se. Positivism held that if knowledge of the natural world is dependent on systematic empirical observation, testing and verification, then knowledge of God and Transcendence must also be dependent on the exact same process; and since God and Transcendence are closed to empirical observation, testing and verification, it follows that theological and metaphysical statements must be dismissed as quite literally meaningless. This is yet another example of the epistemic fallacy: one particular set of epistemic procedures successfully applied to one particular stratum of reality because the nature of that particular stratum demanded it is artificially universalised and imposed indiscriminately on *all* strata of reality. Theological, aesthetic and moral knowledge is thus forced into the straitjacket of the epistemic procedures of natural science.

The inevitable result is a form of reductionism that limits reality to objects and forces in the natural world and reduces all theological, metaphysical, moral and aesthetic claims to the level of arbitrary and subjective opinion. Metaphysical *aporiai* are deemed pseudo-questions because there is nothing beyond the physical world open to direct empirical verification; and because there is nothing *epistemically* beyond the physical world open to empirical verification, there is, quite literally, *nothing ontologically* beyond the physical world. In effect reality is reduced to our means of knowing, and our means of knowing is limited to our means of knowing one particular stratum of reality. The assumption that natural science possesses the potential to provide a comprehensive explanation of the totality of reality is both reductive and lacking in sufficient reason: reductive, because natural science can only explain the emergent strata of moral, aesthetic and spiritual values by reducing them to the level of physical, chemical and biological events; lacking in sufficient reason, because the *aporiai* of the existence of being-qua-being and its inherent rationality are not the objects of natural scientific investigation but rather the preconditions of *all* scientific investigation, including investigation in the natural, social and theological spheres.

The extension of the methods of natural science beyond the boundaries of their proper object of investigation constitutes an act of hubris just as illegitimate as the intrusion of theological, metaphysical, moral and aesthetic investigation into the sphere of natural science. This is not to suggest that natural science should be devoid of a moral framework, merely that such a moral framework cannot legitimately override that close empirical observation, mathematical measuring, experimental testing and retroductive modelling that constitutes our primary means of expanding knowledge of the natural order-of-things. Despite the collapse of positivism, the fact that its judgements regarding the possibility of metaphysics retain significant currency is reflected in the suspicion articulated by many critical realists regarding Roy Bhaskar's so-called 'spiritual turn' to metaphysical and theological questions, and this despite their frequent willingness to accept moral and aesthetic realism (Wright 2013: 21ff.).

Natural theology continues to flourish, albeit in a marginalised academic sphere. However, the rejection of the very possibility of legitimately pursuing natural theology, as asserted by many theologians and secular philosophers, remains a dominant position. The reasons for this rejection may, however, prove highly significant: whereas the theological critique appeals to the critically realistic principle that knowledge must be ground in a posteriori epistemic encounters with the object of knowledge, the secular critique appeals to a set of a priori epistemic assumptions dislocated from the object of knowledge.

The liberal accommodation of religion

The Enlightenment critique of revealed theology and post-Enlightenment rejection of natural theology appeared to many people to sound the death knell of religion. Revealed theology had been shown to be both irrational and immoral, and the speculative metaphysics of natural theology had failed to provide any viable alternative. Consequently, the path appeared open to a thoroughgoing atheism capable of nurturing naturalistic accounts of the ultimate order-of-things and generating a new secular humanistic moral order. However, the combative zeal with which defenders of the so-called 'New Atheism' are currently obliged to pursue their project suggests that this is not the end of the story. When viewed globally, the Abrahamic faiths, alongside a range of other religious and spiritual traditions, are not, contra the predictions of secularisation theory, in terminal decline (Taylor 2007). One reason amongst many for this complex state of affairs is the emergence of forms of theological apologetic that refuse to operate with the empiricist, positivist, romantic and pragmatic assumptions engendered by the Enlightenment, but instead offer robust defences of theological truth claims informed by a critically realistic understanding of the relationship between ontology, epistemology and rationality. We will consider these in greater detail in the following chapter. A more immediate reason for the persistence of religion within Western-style post-Enlightenment culture, however, was the willingness and ability of secular liberalism to accommodate religion within its own liberal polity: the twin principles of freedom of belief and tolerance of the beliefs of others enabled liberalism to house religion despite its perceived lack of rational warrant. The offer of residence was not, of course, unconditional: religious communities must first demonstrate that their value systems did not pose a threat to liberal polity, since the offer of liberal tolerance was not extended to the intolerant and illiberal. Hence religious traditions faced a moral, political and intellectual imperative to adapt themselves to liberal norms and values.

It was romanticism that provided theologians with the primary means of accommodating traditional revealed religions to modern liberal polity. In the nineteenth century, liberal Protestant theologians, accepting the force of the Enlightenment's critique of revealed and natural theology, sought to recast Christianity within a romantic framework. If the sovereignty of the Cartesian ego disallowed any appeal to the external authority of revealed scripture, the romantic grounding of aesthetics, morality and spirituality in the epistemic categories of experience, intuition and sensibility appealed directly to the immediate self-legitimating consciousness of the Cartesian ego, and as such offered a means of rehabilitating theological discourse in a post-Enlightenment liberal milieu. Historically, Christianity had been committed to a cognitive-propositional model of theological discourse. Christian doctrines, that is to say, offered cognitive accounts of the ultimate order-of-things in the form of propositions that claimed epistemic purchase on Transcendent ontological realities. As we have seen, the material substance of such descriptions increasingly were seen to conflict with emergent scientific accounts of the natural world, especially as natural science shook off the vestiges of the metaphysical substructure previously provided by natural philosophy and emerged as a fully independent discipline. At the same time, the metaphorical and figurative linguistic forms through which such descriptions were necessarily articulated, identified by Enlightenment philosophers under the general rubric of 'myth', were increasingly seen as rhetorical threats to accurate descriptions of reality grounded in clear and distinct ideas. The historical progression from mythical through metaphysical to positivistic explanations of reality entailed the abandonment of realistic theological discourse.

The failure of theologians to provide a rational warrant for cognitive-propositional doctrines in line with the epistemic norms championed by the Enlightenment led to the emergence of a revised understanding of religious language. The cognitive-propositional model was replaced with an experiential-expressive model that viewed religious doctrines as linguistic expressions of pre-linguistic spiritual experience rather than propositional descriptions of cognitively accessible ontological realities. According to the cognitive-propositional model, religious doctrines are 'informative propositions or truth claims about objective realities'; according to the experiential-expressive model, they are 'noninformative and nondiscursive symbols of inner feelings, attitudes, or existential orientations' (Lindbeck 1984: 16). The suggestion that religious language referred primarily to a person's internal spiritual experiential awareness, rather than any external ontological object that may or may not have generated such awareness, effectively immunised theological discourse from the Enlightenment's critique of both revealed and natural theology. Because spiritual experience is in the immediate possession of the Cartesian ego it is essentially self-authenticating and as such no longer reliant on any rational defence or appeal to scriptural authority.

According to Friedrich Schleiermacher, the founder of modern liberal Protestant theology, religions are not doctrinal or moral systems 'craving for a mess of metaphysical and ethical crumbs' (Schleiermacher 1958: 31). In true romantic fashion he insists that the Cartesian ego possesses an intuitive pre-linguistic awareness of the Infinite and Transcendent: a primal pre-rational sense of being absolutely dependent on God. This universal human capacity for spiritual awareness, which grounds and generates particular religious traditions, is 'neither a Knowing nor a Doing, but a modification of Feeling, or of immediate self-consciousness' (Schleiermacher 1976: 5). Religion is grounded in profound spiritual sensibility that cannot be reduced to any dogmatic or moral system. 'Christian doctrines' are not descriptions of the ultimate ontological structures of reality, but rather 'accounts of the Christian religious affections set forth in speech' (ibid.: 76). This opens the door to a theological accommodation with modernity: first, because immediate awareness of the Transcendent meets the criterion that knowledge must be grounded in the immediate self-consciousness of the Cartesian ego; and second, because the romantic affirmation of the primal significance of pre-linguistic and pre-rational sensibility effectively bypasses rationalistic critiques of revealed and natural theology. If the myths of the theologians serve to give poetic expression to primal spiritual experience they cannot properly be dismissed as pseudo-scientific descriptions of reality. The spiritual intuition of the religious seer possesses the same status as the aesthetic perception of the poet, artist and musician, all of whom enjoy deeper and more profound insights into the human condition than the stilted rationalism of the philosophers and scientists.

Rudolph Bultmann's attempt to demythologise Christian doctrine is a classic example of the application of the experiential-expressive model (Bultmann 1969, 1985; cf. Miegge 1960; Roberts 1976). Bultmann's central contention was that the mythological language of the New Testament – in which the Earth, populated with angelic and demonic powers and marked by miraculous events, forms the middle layer of a three-decker universe located between heaven above and hell below – is no longer viable or meaningful. However, the strategy of dismissing the New Testament as outmoded superstition occludes the perennial wisdom of the New Testament authors. Their mythological statements give expression to an experientially grounded existential self-understanding that only becomes apparent once the Biblical text is demythologised and literalistic readings abandoned. Bultmann's Christ calls individuals to an existential decision between authentic and inauthentic modes of existence, and invites them to choose between a life oriented toward the petty affairs of the world and a life lived *sub specie aeternitatis*. The language of myth, when appropriated within a realistic frame of reference, invites us to reify God as a supranatural object-above-the-world rather than envisage the divine as the Ground of our Being and source of our Ultimate Concern.

This romantic turn in theology was to have far-reaching consequences. Rudolf Otto's *The Idea of the Holy* sought to provide a phenomenological account of the universal human capacity for the pre-rational and pre-sensory apprehension of the 'holy' or 'numinous', understood as a majestic (*majestas*), mysterious (*mysterium*), fascinating (*fascinans*) and awe inspiring (*tremendum*) reality transcending both the self and the world (Otto 1931). Mircea Eliade's distinction between the 'sacred' and 'profane' drew directly on Otto's work. He argued that human beings in pre-modern societies were *homo religiosus*, striving to make sense of their lives *sub specie aeternitatis*, under the aspect of the Transcendent or sacred. 'Man becomes aware of the sacred because it manifests itself, shows itself, as something wholly different from the profane' (Eliade 1987: 11). Hierophany, the moment of the manifestation of the sacred, occurs in ordinary profane contexts:

> From the most elementary animism, in which the sacred manifests itself in ordinary objects such as stones or trees, through to the most developed religious systems, such as the Christian belief in the incarnation of God in Jesus Christ, the sacred manifests itself in and through profane realities.
>
> (Wright 2004: 210)

Eliade's account became the paradigmatic framework for the phenomenological study of religion: the eidetic essence of religious phenomenon was identified as a *sui generis* intentionality towards the sacred or Transcendent.

The suggestion that human beings are essentially *homo religiosus*, hardwired to experience the numinous, was given some credence by empirical research that revealed spiritual experience to be a remarkably widespread phenomenon not restricted to religious adherents. Drawing on this raft of evidence, David Hay suggested that we possess a natural disposition for spiritual experience that has been occluded by a modern hermeneutic of suspicion which has enabled rationalism to colonise our intuitive 'inner space': 'We have difficulty hanging on to the spiritual, because "really" the fundamentals of the world are particles and space' (Hay 1985: 140). This resonates strongly with Roy Bhaskar's philosophy of meta-Reality, which advocates a spiritual re-enchantment and re-awakening through entry into a ground state in which we experience the world of non-duality and are in harmony with the totality of all things (Bhaskar 2002). Similarly, forms of New Age spirituality hold that we can escape from debilitating social conventions by cultivating an inner spiritual sensibility that constitutes 'the source of authentic vitality, creativity, love, tranquillity, wisdom, power, authority and all those other qualities which are held to comprise the perfect life' (Heelas 1996: 19).

For many orthodox Christians, the experiential-expressive model tends towards the reductive and anti-realistic. The intransitive and Transcendent Triune God is denied ontological status as the creator and redeemer of the world and reduced to the epistemic status of immanent human subjectivity. The experiential-expressive model is especially vulnerable to Feuerbach's critique that religion is merely an expression of human ideals and aspirations (Feuerbach 1957). In the terminology of critical realism, if theological language is limited to the expression of human feeling and emotion it is necessarily restricted to the transitive empirical domain of human experience and as such cannot retain epistemic purchase on the intransitive domains of the actual and real. The cognitive-propositional model, on the other hand, retains the possibility of generating realistic retroductive explanations, truthful or otherwise, of Transcendent reality. If the experiential-expressive model of religious discourse claims immunity from rationalistic critiques of natural and revealed theology, it does so only at the cost of embracing a model of language whose only secure ontological purchase is on human feelings and emotions. On this reading, the question as to whether such feelings and emotions are authentic responses to the ultimate order-of-things, or merely products of the human capacity for self-deception, can be answered only through appeals to the personal conviction of the Cartesian self. However, intensity of feeling is not a sufficient criterion of truth, unless we are willing to attribute truth to the inner convictions of the racist, homophobe and paedophile.

There can be little doubt that the experiential-expressive model of religion loosens the purchase of theological language on reality. Though the capacity for spiritual experience is universal, it is inevitable that different individuals and groups will express such experience in the language and thought forms provided by their particular cultural contexts. The suggestion that Buddhists, Christians, Hindus, Jews, Muslims, Sikhs and others express a common universal experience of the Transcendent in various culturally bound ways invites the conclusion that the specific doctrinal claims of particular religious traditions are culturally relativistic rather than culturally relative. If cultural relativism views attempts to employ judgemental relativity to differentiate between more and less truthful accounts of the ultimate order-of-things as redundant, cultural relativity recognises the task as both intellectually possible and spiritually significant. Cultural relativism is clearly visible in John Hick's universal theology, which claims that different religious traditions offer a range of equally valid means of accessing Transcendence, and suggests that, as a consequence, their doctrinal formulations lack any cognitive purchase on Transcendence per se, but instead refer only to religious adherents' *experiences* of Transcendence (Hick 1977a, 1989). Thus the Christian doctrine of incarnation does not identify and describe an actual ontological event, but rather functions instrumentally to express an experience of Transcendence generated by the first disciples' encounter with Jesus of Nazareth, and to further stimulate similar experiences amongst later generations of

Christians (Hick 1977b, 1993). The question as to whether Jesus Christ was actually God incarnate is ultimately irrelevant: what matters spiritually is that the myth of God incarnate has the potential to stimulate experiences of Transcendence.

The anti-realistic thrust of the experiential-expressive model of religious discourse becomes explicit in post-modern theology. For some post-modern theologians the post-structural rejection of occidental reason appeared 'to herald the end of theology's long intellectual marginalisation' (Berry 1992: 4). If discourse was assessed on its pragmatic utility and ability to enhance the human condition, rather than on its truth and truthfulness, then theology could reclaim legitimacy on the grounds of its pragmatic spiritual value rather than its ability to describe Transcendent realities. This was the path followed by Don Cupitt. In *Taking Leave of God* he argues that cognitive-propositional theology, insofar as it claims epistemic purchase on ontological realities, is intrinsically immature and potentially dangerous by virtue of its implicit authoritarian and totalitarian thrust (Cupitt 1980). Humanity must learn to recognise that 'God' is not an objective being to whom human beings must make obeisence, but rather 'the religious concern reified; the demands and promises of spirituality in coded form' (Cowdell 1988: 18). 'The highest and central principle of spirituality (the religious requirement, as it is often called) is the one that commands us to become spirit, that is, precisely to attain the highest degree of autonomous self-knowledge and self-transcendence' (Cupitt 1980: 9). This possibility is dependent on the abandonment of the objective God of onto-theology and its replacement by a God constructed according to human aspirations and needs.

> Once we have become fully conscious of our languages and other forms of symbolic communication as sign-systems through which every thinkable and knowable is mediated, then we see that there can be no sense in the idea of transcending language.
>
> (Cupitt 1985: xi)

This anti-realist turn entails the recognition that 'there is no longer any absolute Beginning, Ground, Presence or End in the traditional metaphysical sense' (Cupitt 1987: 7).

The outcome of the liberal accommodation of religion is transparent. On the basis of the liberal commitment to autonomy and the sovereignty of the Cartesian ego, individuals are free to embrace their spiritual experiences on their own terms and make their own decisions regarding their truth, value and utility. And on the basis of the liberal commitment to tolerance, they must be allowed to do so without coercion, provided that their subjective commitments are confined to the private sphere and not allowed to impact on the world of public affairs. Religious belief and spiritual experience is thus effectively accommodated within the polity of secular liberalism, on the strict condition that subscribers to subjective beliefs do not attempt to lay claim to possession of publically accessible truth.

The subjugation of religion described here appeared to confront religious adherents with a stark choice: between the Scylla of holding fast to their orthodox beliefs at the expense of a retreat into a fideistic (and potentially anti-intellectual or fundamentalist) ghetto, and the Charybdis of seeking an accommodation with the culture of modernity at the expense of accepting revisionary and reductive accounts of their traditional beliefs. A third option, of employing critical realism in an under-labouring role to challenge the epistemic and ontological assumptions of post-Enlightenment culture and rehabilitate their orthodox beliefs, is the subject of the following chapter.

4 Theological realism

The strategy of employing the under-labouring services of critical realism to defend an approach to religious education critically oriented toward the pursuit of ultimate truth and cultivation of truthful living *sub specie aeternitatis* inevitably looks to the triumvirate of ontological realism, epistemic relativity and judgemental rationality. Of the three, epistemic relativity is certainly the least controversial. The affirmation, revision or rejection of a range of different spiritual, religious and theological beliefs is highly contentious, and hence necessarily epistemically relative, both within and across different religious and secular traditions. Ontological realism is slightly more problematic. 'There is no getting around the fact that people who express their religious convictions are in so doing referring to a specific – usually divine or divinely instituted – reality and intend to assert something as true of it' (Pannenberg 1976: 327; cf. Byrne 2003). However, we cannot ignore the emergence, largely under the influence of post-modernism, of a plethora of non-realistic readings of religion that seek to employ religious language and practices as pragmatic tools for the enhancement of spiritual wellbeing, whilst denying they enjoy any epistemic purchase on Transcendent ontological reality. This does not, however, rule out ontological considerations. Those who reject the ontological reality of God or Transcendence, regardless of whether they go on to either affirm or deny the pragmatic utility of religious beliefs and spiritual practices, will necessarily embrace, whether explicitly, implicitly or by default, some form of immanent or naturalistic understanding of the ultimate order-of-things. Thus the absenting of God or Transcendence constitutes a critical move that necessarily involves some form of ontological commitment. Judgemental rationality is by far the most contentious. The positivistic assumption that Transcendent truth claims are closed to rational investigation remains influential today, both in popular culture and amongst a minority of academics. This despite the fact that academic theologians and philosophers continue to subject Transcendent truth claims to rigorous rational investigation.

This chapter assumes that most religious adherents are ontological realists, and that those who deny religious truth claims any purchase on ontological reality cannot legitimately avoid ontological commitments. The terms of the debate may have shifted from a pre-modern conversation between incommensurable Transcendent truth claims to a modern conversation between incommensurable Transcendent truth claims *and* a range of immanent altern- atives, but the critical ontological question of our place in the ultimate order-of- things and the challenge of living truthful lives *sub specie aeternitatis* (whether this entails the affirmation or absenting of Transcendence) remains. It also assumes that all ultimate truth claims are necessarily epistemically relative. This is not to affirm a thoroughgoing relativism in which all Transcendent truth claims are deemed equally true/false, but rather a provisional relativity in which conflicting truth claims are seen as ontologically incommensurate rather than ontologically redundant. Given the possibility of false consciousness, the task of adjudicating between conflicting truth claims and striving to differentiate between more and less powerful explanations of the ultimate order-of-things becomes an intellectual, moral and spiritual imperative. Hence the central importance of cultivating forms of judgemental rationality and establishing and maintaining appropriate levels of religious, spiritual and theological literacy, *both* amongst those who affirm *and* amongst those who deny the ontological reality of Transcendence. Given critical realism's rejection of epistemic founda- tionalism, there is no need here to demonstrate that the application of judge- mental rationality to Transcendent truth claims rests on secure epistemological foundations. Since we always reason from within particular traditions and seek to better understand that which we already believe we know, there is no need to provide any antecedent justification of our attempts to understand and assess our established beliefs and practices. The fact that adherents of both Transcendent and immanent worldviews subject their beliefs and practices, and the beliefs and practices of others, to critical scrutiny, in an ongoing and as yet unresolved process of enquiry, is sufficient condition for the debate to proceed. Understand- ing seeking faith may require the establishment of secure antecedent epistemic foundations, but faith seeking understanding simply embarks from our given sit- uatedness in particular faith traditions, whether religious or secular.

The issue is not whether it is possible to employ judgemental rationality in evaluating our religious and secular beliefs, and the religious and secular beliefs of others, since it is a phenomenological fact that many religious and secular believers do precisely that. Rather, the issue is that of the quality, richness and depth of the judgemental rationality we employ. Even the most cursory review of the attempts of academic theologians and philosophers to apply judgemental rationality to Transcendent claims reveals the presence of genuine quality, rich- ness and depth, marked by attentiveness, intelligence, reasonableness and responsibility. Indeed, the absence of these factors in the academy is most clearly visible in the remarkable failure of a number of contemporary critics of religion to engage with the corpus of theological and philosophical literature when pre- senting their arguments, despite the established academic protocol of attending closely to the best available version of a position one seeks to debunk. Despite the rhetorical flourishes that are perhaps justifiable in a semi-popular polemical text, the following words of Alister McGrath, in the context of a close reading of the work of Richard Dawkins, are worth quoting here:

Richard Dawkins ... knowing nothing about Christian theology, rushes headlong into the field, and tells theologians what they really mean.... There is a total failure on Dawkins' part to even begin to understand what Christian theology means by its language. It really does make it difficult to take his judgements concerning its alleged failures with any degree of ser- iousness.... Now perhaps Dawkins is too busy writing books against reli- gion to allow him time to read works of religion. On the rare occasions when he cites classic theologians, he tends to do so at second hand, often with alarming results.

(McGrath 2005: 99)

Given that McGrath holds doctorates in both molecular biophysics and theology, he cannot easily be accused of a lack of attentiveness to the field of natural science within which Dawkins couches his arguments; unfortunately, the same cannot be said of Dawkins' attentiveness to the intricacies of Christian theology. McGrath goes on to point out that 'the classic Christian tradition has always valued rationality, and does not hold that faith involves the complete abandon- ment of reason or believing in the teeth of the evidence', and identifies a range of contemporary Christian philosophers, apparently unknown to Dawkins, whose work reveals a 'passionate commitment to the question of how one can make "warranted" or "coherent" statements concerning God' (ibid.: 99).

In the absence of epistemic foundationalism, the only way to adjudicate between conflicting truth claims is to bring them into critical conversation and assess the relative strengths of their explanatory power. If McGrath is right in his critique of Dawkins, then the problem lies not in the failure of Christian theolo- gians to employ judgemental rationality, but in the absence of any sustained attempt on Dawkins' part to engage with their endeavours. The legitimacy of Christian truth claims cannot properly be assessed without a close and attentive engagement with those claims, both with regard to their ontological substance and epistemic warrant. The fact that Christian theologians *do* attempt to employ judgemental rationality is an undeniable fact; the extent to which they do so suc- cessfully remains an open question. In order to assess the extent of their success or failure it is necessary to attend to what they actually say rather than conduct an abstract debate on whether it is legitimate for them to speak in the first place. This being the case, the task before us in this chapter must be simply to *show* concrete examples of Christian theologians employing judgemental rationality and let their endeavours speak for themselves, rather than attempt to construct and defend a foundational Christian epistemology.

The poverty of secular paganism

The assumption that religious truths claims lack intellectual warrant is closely linked to secularisation and secularisation theory. The impulse toward seculari- sation, viewed as a historical process and social phenomenon, is an undeniably global reality. However, we need to exercise caution in assessing its extent and potency, and especially in attributing to it any measure of historical inevitability. Charles Taylor's *A Secular Age*, whilst accepting the reality of secularisation, questions whether there was anything necessary about its emergence, challenges inflationary perceptions of its extent and suggests that its future development is far from secure (Taylor 2007). Taylor identifies three interlinked accounts of the phenomenon of secularisation. The first equates secularism with the privatisation of religious institutions, theological beliefs and spiritual attitudes and their withdrawal, whether enforced or voluntary, from the public sphere, so that civic spaces are 'allegedly emptied of God, or of any reference to ultimate reality' (ibid.: 2). Though such privatisation is clearly a significant tendency in the post-Enlightenment era, it is neither universal, comprehensive, nor necessarily progressive: a significant number of nation states possess religious constitutions, and many more retain formal connections with religious traditions; politicians cannot avoid addressing religious issues and appealing to religious constituents; religious education forms part of the state-sponsored curriculum of many liberal democracies; and the 'God question' is regularly raised and debated in the public media. Taylor's second account equates secularism with a 'falling off of religious belief and practice, in people turning away from God, and no longer going to Church' (ibid.: 2). Again, though this has undoubtedly been a significant tendency in the modern era, it is largely, though by no means exclusively, restricted to Western culture in general and northern Europe in particular. Viewed from a global perspective, contemporary society is marked by a widespread resurgence of religion and spirituality, both within and beyond the institutional structures of organised religious communities, and by a significant theological renaissance in the academy. Taylor's third account, which he sets out to defend, identifies secularisation as 'a move from a society where belief in God is unchallenged and indeed, unproblematic, to one in which it is understood to be one option among others, and frequently not the easiest to embrace' (ibid.: 3). This has the virtue of recognising the reality of secularisation whilst avoiding extravagant claims about its extent, potency and historical necessity: though religious institutions, beliefs and practices are undoubtedly contested, and certainly no longer normative in many societies, the global evidence does not warrant the conclusion that they are in terminal decline. This more nuanced stance helps explain the phenomenon of so-called 'New Atheism', a movement whose proponents, incredulous of the persistence of religion, strive proactivly and evangelically to bring about the *thoroughgoing* secularisation anticipated by the radical atheistic wing of the Enlightenment.

Secularisation theory seeks to *explain* the historical process and social phenomenon of secularisation in terms of modernisation and rationalisation. Modernisation, the cluster of social, political, cultural, technological and economic mechanisms of 'progress' that emerged in the wake of the Enlightenment, had a direct impact on religious institutions, theological truth claims and spiritual attitudes. The success of modern science led to unforeseen technological advances that promised to secure the eudemonic flourishing of humankind. This in turn generated a sharp division between the realms of objective scientific fact and subjective moral, aesthetic and spiritual value, and reduced consideration of the latter to mundane pragmatic and utilitarian levels. As a result the world became disenchanted, and collective consciousness, insofar as it attended to ultimate questions of truth and truthful living, became fragmented. No longer living under a common sacred canopy, individuals were faced with the challenge of securing their own personal sense of meaning and purpose. Politically this led to forms of liberalism that advocated autonomy of belief and freedom of action, limited only by the pragmatic duty to avoiding causing harm to others. This ran hand-in-hand with the emergence of a capitalist economy in which individual freedom was predicated on private consumption, driven by the twin hegemonies of personal desire and market forces, and tempered only by the duty to care for the economically disempowered via either altruistic acts of charity or collective forms of social welfare. This panned out ontologically in the form of a comprehensive liberalism that affirmed the absolute primacy of the self-determining and self-constructing individual. Cast adrift in his own personal space, forced back onto his own resources, devoid of any answers to the ultimate questions of truth, meaning and purpose, and entrapped in the hegemony of a capitalist cycle of desire and material satisfaction, it was no wonder that the Cartesian ego either took his leave of religion and immersed itself in the cultural goods and opportunities provided by modernity, sought refuge in the security offered by various forms of religious and secular fundamentalism, or else struggled with a profound sense of spiritual absence and alienation.

Concomitant with modernisation, rationalisation sought to explain the rise of secularisation in terms of the intellectual poverty of religious beliefs. The secular wing of the Enlightenment told a story of progress in which humankind gradually and inevitably progressed from explanations of reality grounded in religious myth, via explanations grounded in philosophical metaphysics, to explanations grounded in positivistic science. In antiquity religious myth, as propounded by Greek poets and Hebrew prophets, had been exposed and summarily dismissed as crass superstition by Greek philosophers. However, despite the best efforts of enlightened philosophy, the authority of religious myth was perpetuated in the medieval period by a scholastic synthesis of philosophy and theology. The Enlightenment's recovery of the Greek philosophical spirit of criticism was foreshadowed in the seventeenth century: despite paying lip-service to their Christian heritage, Francis Bacon, Isaac Newton and René Descartes elected not to place any significant weight on the epistemic authority of the religious myths of revealed theology. Their God was the God of the philosophers, a version of the God of Aristotle and prototype of the God of the Enlightenment deists. Newton held fast to a metaphysical concept of God as the creator of nature and its rational laws, and identified absolute time and space with the *divine sensorium* – the mind and presence of God within which the created order lived, moved and had its being. Despite this metaphysical commitment, he questioned Descartes' and Leibnitz's assumption that it is possible to determine the nature of matter through a priori philosophical argument, and in so doing paved the way for the emergence of natural science as an a posteriori discipline, grounded in empirical observation, mathematical measuring, experimental testing and inductive theo-rising, and emancipated from the metaphysical claims of natural philosophy (Janiak 2010: 117f.). The success of natural science encouraged a reductive account of the cosmos, one that effectively limited reality to its physical, chem-ical and biological components, and in doing so pronounced the disciplines of metaphysics and theology redundant. The ancient Greek spirit of criticism was recovered not by metaphysicians opposed to theology, but by natural scientists opposed to both metaphysics and theology. On this reading both the natural theology of the metaphysicians and the revealed theology of the theologians were dismissed as outmoded epistemic tools, philosophically naive and reli-giously superstitious in equal measure. If there were no viable grounds for theo-logical discourse in either its philosophical or religious guises, then this fact would inevitably filter through to the lifeworlds of ordinary uneducated citizens, who in turn would come to embrace a secular world devoid of religious institu-tions, theological dogmas and spiritual dispositions.

In *Theology and Social Theory: Beyond Secular Reason* the Anglican theolo-gian John Milbank offers a full-frontal attack on both modernity and the ration-alisation supporting it. Drawing on the work of Michel Foucault, he suggests that the story of secularisation, like all such stories, is a construction that cannot be completely isolated from human interests, but which nevertheless stands or falls by virtue of its truth or falsehood. The narrative of secularisation has its roots in the trenchant desire of those on the radical secular wing of the Enlight-enment to debunk Christianity, and as such served the self-interest of those com-mitted to an anti-Christian secularist ideology. 'The secular *episteme* is a post-Christian paganism, something in the last analysis only to be defined, nega-tively, as a refusal of Christianity and the invention of an "Anti-Christianity"' (Milbank 1990: 280).

> It accepts the basic forces of the world as brute givens of fate, fortune and chance. The self-interest of nation states, the individual's drive for survival, the impersonal working of market forces – all of these are like the will of the gods in pre-Christian Greek myth. We can't live without them, but they are not directed towards any harmonious vision of the good, or any recon-ciliation of the different parts of our life. However much they are dressed up as something else, at bottom they are simply expressions of a blind will-to-power.
>
> (Shakespeare 2007: 10)

Milbank contends that secularisation is grounded in an 'ontology of violence', in which the brute forces of nature, society and individual agency perpetuate ever-increasing cycles of violence and counter-violence, only thinly disguised behind an increasingly vacuous rhetoric of progress, emancipation and reason. Despite claims to ideological neutrality and empirically grounded universal reason, secular social science is a highly value-laden enterprise, one that, having bracketed-out the reality of God, finds its organising principle in the violent interface of various natural, social, political, economic and ideological casual mechanisms, which it seeks to explain and contain through strategies of counter-violence. Though it presents itself as a neutral, rationally grounded account of the world, secularism is at root a pagan religion, worshipping at the altar of the brute forces of nature and human society in a vain attempt to placate and contain them. The tragedy of contemporary Christianity lies in its misplaced veneration of the gods of modern paganism, as manifest in revisionary liberal attempts to accommodate Christianity *within* modernity, and reactionary fundamentalist attempts to rescribe Christianity *in opposition to* modernity. Milbank's positive contention is that a radically orthodox Christian theology, ontologically grounded in the bond of reciprocal love that unites the persons of the Holy Trinity, the divine creator, sustainer, redeemer and sanctifier of an ordered, emergent and purposeful cosmos, provides an alternative retroductive model to that proffered by secular paganism, one possessing superior explanatory power by virtue of its greater intellectual discernment, moral profundity and aesthetic beauty.

Transcendence reclaimed

Douglas Porpora's critically realistic response to secularisation proceeds from the assumption that any authentic sense of personal identity must be relationally located in social, moral, metaphysical and critical space. It is not a sufficient condition of a rich and fulfilled life merely to seek to 'get by' or 'muddle through' gregariously in social space. Our interpersonal relationships make moral demands on us and ask ultimate questions of us, and we can only respond authentically to them by learning to locate ourselves emotionally, reflectively and responsibly within both moral and metaphysical space. These two spaces are mutually independent, since we can only understand ourselves as moral beings by understanding our place in the cosmos as a whole. Despite this, both 'sociologists and the lay public tend to situate identity entirely in social space', and in so doing tend to adopt instrumental attitudes that occlude any deep sense of moral purpose or spiritual identity (Porpora 2001: 57). Such instrumentalism is directly related to an inability to locate ourselves within moral and metaphysical space: 'moral purpose must be emotionally and conceptually grounded in some larger worldview', yet we 'so lack any articulated worldview that arguments about the cosmos strike us as ponderously irrelevant' (ibid.: 57f.). Porpora's empirical research reveals 'a culturally pervasive lack of orientation in metaphysical space, an inability to place ourselves meaningfully in the cosmos' (ibid.: 152). This situation is exacerbated by the failure to locate ourselves in critical space: if we 'refrain from the search for truth' and 'choose to die with the beliefs we were born with', then 'our identity in critical space will only be a void' (ibid.: 23). This secular refusal of moral, metaphysical and critical space rebounds on the individual: the all-pervasive void generated by such refusal engenders 'an equally pervasive void in our own sense of self', since 'we cannot lose our place in the cosmos without losing ourselves as well' (ibid.: 152).

In *Transcendence: Critical Realism and God* Margaret Archer, Andrew Collier and Douglas Porpora set out a critically realistic case for the rehabilitation of theological discourse in the public sphere. They insist that to ask the question of the existence of God is to ask a realistic ontological question: 'talk about God should be interpreted realistically so that statements about God, like most statements in science and everyday life, must be treated as either true or false' (Archer *et al.*: 6). This is consistent with the standpoint of the vast majority of theistic believers and of those atheists who reject theistic beliefs. Contra positivism, theological statements cannot be summarily dismissed as intrinsically meaningless on the assumption that they are closed to empirical verification. Positivism is a redundant philosophical position: we do not have to delve deeply into the realm of theoretical physics to identify objects and mechanisms not directly open to empirical observation, since on a far more mundane level we know that water is made up of hydrogen and oxygen despite being unable to taste, smell or see either. Contra forms of post-modernity, the referent of theological discourse cannot be restricted to expressions of personal desire or communal self-understanding. The post-modern reduction of discourse to non-realistic communal language games is an increasingly indefensible philosophical position: natural scientists intend to describe reality, not weave pragmatically useful or socially cohesive fictions; and provided we address the issue with the seriousness it deserves, we have every reason to judge that their efforts, though at times mistaken and certainly far from complete, have been remarkably successful.

As Archer *et al.* point out: 'Ontological realism about God in the intransitive dimension is consistent with epistemic or experiential relativism in the transitive dimension' (ibid.: 5). Our understanding of the cosmos is necessarily historically and socially situated, and our individual and collective experiences of God or the Transcendent – whether direct or mediated, putative or real – inevitably vary. The existence of God is contested, both in ordinary real-world environments and in the reified milieu of the academy. In intellectual debate, when we:

> often reach a point where the arguments for certain claims are so strong that we are ready to consider the case as being virtually settled ... we consider ourselves to have arrived at what critical realists call alethia or alethic truth, the truth of reality as such.
>
> (ibid.: 2)

Though different religious and secular traditions claim to access such alethic truth with regard to the ultimate order-of-things, there is little agreement between them. In most academic disciplines the tension between secure and contested truth claims provides the drive for cutting-edge research. The case of theology is a peculiar one: on the one hand the question of God continues to be contested both in real-world environments and at the highest intellectual level, whilst on the other there are those who consider the truth of naturalistic atheism to be so self-apparent that they regard theistic claims, like the claims of alchemists and astrologers, to be utterly devoid of intellectual warrant. It is no surprise that members of the latter group tend to be non-theologians largely ignorant of academic theology, since if they were conversant with theological literature they would have little option other than to recognise that it is largely the product of intelligent people proffering intelligent arguments, and thereby acknowledge the reality of a phenomenon they currently seek to deny on a priori grounds (McGrath 2005: 99f.; Wright 2011). Most academics rightly display great caution in entering into intellectual debate in areas beyond their field of expertise, and most recognise the intellectual imperative to be particularly attentive, intelligent, reasonable and responsible when doing so.

This somewhat curious phenomenon, of intellectuals being dismissed by fellow intellectuals as anti-intellectuals on a priori grounds, demands explanation. Archer *et al.* draw attention to the 'implicit structures of discursive privilege' (Archer *et al.* 2004: 5). 'It is an unexamined legacy of the enlightenment that we privilege atheism as the intellectual baseline and make religious belief alone something which is to be explained or defended' (ibid.: 5). Equally unexamined is the Cartesian-inspired assumption that any such defence must provide secure epistemic foundations, offer demonstrable proofs, and generate epistemic certainty. Yet the principle of presumptive trust, as explicated in Newman's illative sense, suggests that we are justified in embracing and affirming our own individual and communal experiences until such time as we are given good reason to abandon them. This being the case, we could equally privilege theism as the intellectual baseline, make atheism something to be to be explained and defended, and require of atheists secure epistemic foundations and clear demonstrable proof, to the point of epistemic certitude, of the non-existence of God.

They go on to argue that it 'is not intellectually appropriate to privilege any belief – not even a religious belief – in such a way that it becomes immune to judgemental rationality' (ibid.: 16). In the debate between theism and atheism 'public argument remains inconclusive and the ultimate truth indeterminate' (ibid.: 3). Consequently both theists *and* atheists are under an intellectual obligation to defend their respective positions. Critical realism's affirmation of the possibility of judgemental rationality vis-à-vis theology proceeds by rejecting epistemic foundationalism. Since ontology logically precedes epistemology, to identify epistemic criteria in advance of any engagement with the object of investigation is to commit the epistemic fallacy of forcing reality into the procrustean bed of a set of prior epistemic assumptions. The Enlightenment asserted specific foundational epistemic criteria: knowledge must be indubitable, certain and secure; not derived from any external authority; and grounded in either sense experience (empiricism), a set of internally coherent ideas (idealism), or intuitive insight and apprehension (romanticism). Critical realism proposes an alternative approach to epistemology: knowledge can never be absolutely secure; is communally generated and frequently derived from third-party testimony; and is produced through retroductive modelling, which seeks to establish inferentially the most powerful explanation of our experience of the phenomenon under investigation. It is entirely possible that the best possible inferential explanation of any given phenomenon may be closed to direct empirical verification (e.g. the presence of hydrogen and oxygen in water), challenge previously held notions of rational coherence (e.g. Einstein's abandonment of Newton's notion of absolute time and space), and undermine our established intuitive sensibilities and convictions (e.g. that there is no viable alternative to a capitalist market economy). Retroductive argument is cumulative rather than sequential: it takes the form of a rope made up of many individual strands, none of which are likely to be capable of bearing the full weight of an explanation in isolation, rather than a chain whose strength is limited to its weakest link. Since we must adapt and refine our epistemic tools in response to the ontological reality of the object under investigation, disputes been atheists and theists must be resolved by evaluating the relative merits of their respective explanations of the ultimate order-of-things in relation to one another, rather than in relation to any pre-established external criteria. 'By comparatively evaluating the existing arguments, we can arrive at reasoned, though provisional, judgements about what reality is objectively like: about what belongs to that reality and what does not' (ibid.: 2).

Ultimately the choice between theism and atheism is an act of informed faith, whichever side of the argument we come down on. We reason from prior convictions grounded in real-world environments, and hold fast to our received beliefs until such time as we encounter a more powerful and convincing way of being-and-believing in the world. And we are entirely justified in doing so, provided we evaluate our beliefs attentively, intelligently, reasonably and responsibly to the best of our ability in the light of the available expert testimony. The suggestion that only religious belief requires an act of faith is to attribute unwarranted discursive privilege to secular belief: the alternative to theism is not atheism, but some other substantial secular position, such as materialism or naturalism. There is no neutral ground: to reject the explanatory power of theism is necessarily to put faith in the greater explanatory power of one or other alternative account of the ultimate order-of-things.

Revealed theology rehabilitated

Sean Creaven, in his critique of the work of Archer, Collier and Porpora, notes that that 'religious faith inescapably rests on revelation' contained in sacred scripture, and claims that 'every sensible person understands that these holy books are not truly sacred at all' (Creaven 2010: 398f.). There is no need to dwell further on his startling lack of engagement with apparently sensible people (including university professors of theology and Biblical exegesis) who understand scripture to be genuinely sacred (Wright 2011). Nevertheless, his criticisms of the Christian Bible in particular possess a certain heuristic value for us here, insofar as they reflect some common assumptions expressed in some real-world environments beyond the realm of academic scholarship. Five such criticisms are noteworthy: first, the fact that Biblical revelation is mediated by testimonial authority means that 'the faithful receive it second-hand'; second, the Biblical texts are 'the product of pre-scientific cultures, populated by people who were deeply superstitious'; third, historians, archaeologists and Biblical scholars have shown the Biblical text to be 'not only internally discrepant, but also wrong on every historical fact of importance'; fourth, the Biblical writers naively and irrationally employ myth to depict 'divine intervention on the earthly terrain'; fifth, 'the holy texts are bound by the political and ethical horizons of their time and place' and consequently 'they appear morally stunted by modern enlightenment standards (ibid.: 398f.).

It is remarkable just how close Creaven's position is to the positions of Hume and Paine presented in the previous chapter, especially in view of his failure to engage in depth with either author and his espousal of a critically realistic philosophy at odds with their naive empiricism. Since we have already addressed the issues Creaven raises in the context of our discussion of Hume and Paine, I will restrict my comments here to the following brief observations. First, since the vast majority of our knowledge is dependent on testimonial authority, the issue is not whether the Bible is testimonial in nature, but ontologically whether its testimony is true, and epistemically whether we have good reason to judge it to be true. Second, if to be pre-scientific is to be superstitious and unsophisticated, then there can be no value in reading Homer and Sophocles, Plato and Aristotle, Dante and Shakespeare, or Isaiah and Paul, yet the enduring value of these authors, and many others, lies in their perennial ability to illuminate and enrich the human condition in reference to the social, moral, metaphysical and critical spaces we indwell. Third, contra positivism, the writing of history cannot be reduced to a bare chronology of facts, but rather involves the retroductive explanation of events. Fourth, the notion that the Biblical writers lacked sophistication and failed to self-consciously adopt and refine the various literary forms and modes of expression and representation they employed is naive in the extreme, as is the quasi-positivistic implication that it is illegitimate to utilise tropic language to describe unobservable objects and mechanisms. Fifth, it would be truly remarkable if the Biblical authors did *not* write within and out of the context of the moral and political norms of the cultural milieus they inhabited; nevertheless, one of the reasons for the enduring value of their work lies in the ability to transcend such limitations, as evidenced, for example, in Paul's insight, utterly remarkable for its day, of the absolute equality of *all* people before God, regardless of race, gender or social status.

The Christian Bible is a collection of texts generated over an extensive historical period, employing a range of different literary genres, driven by a range of different concerns in different cultural contexts, and produced in symbiotic relationship with parallel cultures, ideas and literary forms. The individual books are intertextual and cumulative in nature, continuously borrowing from and responding to their predecessors, and collectively telling, through a variety of voices, a common story of the developing relationship between God and his creatures. A standard secular history of the religions of ancient Israel and the early Church will seek to account for the historical origins of the various books. A standard theology of Jewish or Christian scripture will seek to unpack the theological vision of the nature, character and actions of God contained in the Biblical texts and seek to assess their veracity. The former will involve a conversation *about* the Biblical authors and their books, considered of interest in their own right; the latter will involve a conversation *with* the Biblical authors and their books about God and their encounters with God.

Critical realism recognises that beliefs are causal mechanisms which shape the nature and quality of the lives of individuals and communities, for better or worse, in social, moral, metaphysical and critical space. A theological reading of scripture is one that takes seriously the possibility that the account of God contained in the Bible might be true; a secular reading of the Bible will either bracket-out or reject this possibility in advance. The theological task cannot be an arbitrary process: the theologian's exposition of the theology contained in scriptural texts must necessarily be bound by the texts themselves, in precisely the same way that an exposition of Plato must necessarily be bound to what the Platonic corpus actually says. The primary task of both the Biblical theologian and Platonic scholar is that of exegesis rather than eisegesis: reading out of the text that which the text contains rather than reading into the text that which it does not contain. Such exegesis opens the door to the possibility of a critical assessment of what the text actually says, and to the affirmation, rejection or revision of its truth claims. Inevitably such a process will raise fundamental hermeneutical challenges: how to relate the whole to the parts and the parts to the whole, how to distinguish between that which is critically significant and that which is peripheral, how to discern that which is ephemeral and that which is of lasting significance, how to evaluate the claims of the text and apply them to in different cultural contexts.

Just as to read Plato, Marx or Bhaskar is to encounter and respond to powerful philosophical ways of understanding the cosmos and our place in it, so to read the Jewish Torah, the Christian Bible or the Islamic Qur'an is to encounter powerful theological ways of understanding creation and our place in it. Whether we read Plato, Marx or Bhaskar, or the Torah, Bible or Qur'an, insofar as they all proffer truth claims that we might not have previously encountered and which we might potentially find compelling, they constitute for us forms of revelation and provide a reference point around which we might organise our thought and action. Scriptural exegesis thus provides the theologian with a theological resource that, depending on the particular tradition within which he is situated, may take on the status of authoritative revelation. A Christian theologian, situated in the Christian tradition that affirms the basic truth of the accounts of God provided by the Biblical authors, will thus embrace the authority of the Biblical text, in much the same way that the natural scientist embraces the authority of scientific text books, and the Shakespearean scholar the authority of the Shakespearean canon. The crucial difference, however, is that whilst both the natural order and Shakespeare claim only limited authority over us, God claims absolute authority over his creatures; consequently, for Christians the Bible possesses absolute authority, by virtue of its ontological status and role as the divinely appointed mediator of God's self-revelation to humankind in the person of Jesus Christ.

To assert the absolute authority of scripture is not to assert a crude fundamentalism. This is because scriptural texts are always interpreted and assimilated by fallible human readers. The ontic fallacy of seeking to bypass the fallible reader in order to access the scriptural text in its unmediated purity both generates and sustains religious fundamentalism. Once the ontic fallacy is recognised and rejected, the ontological horizon of the authoritative text comes face-to-face with the relativistic horizon of the text's fallible human readers. The epistemic fallacy of allowing the fallible reader to impose his prejudices and preferences onto the scriptural text in acts of eisegesis generates reductive forms of theological liberalism that lead ultimately to forms of theological relativism and anti-realism. A critically realistic exegesis of scripture will seek to allow the text to speak for itself, and in doing so challenge and transform the prejudices and preferences of the reader. Insofar as scriptural exegetes employ judgemental rationality in their pursuit of ontological truth from a situation of epistemic relativity, their exegesis should strive to be attentive, intelligent, reasonable and responsible to the claims of the scriptural text. The Anglican principle that the authority of scripture should always be mediated by the received wisdom of the orthodox Christian tradition and the exercise of reason constitutes an attempt to protect scriptural exegesis from both the ontic and epistemic fallacies.

If the task of scriptural exegesis (Biblical theology) is to identify and explicate the alethic truth claims embedded in scripture, then a secondary theological scholarship (systematic, doctrinal or dogmatic theology) is concerned to generate orderly accounts of the God revealed in scripture. Systematic theology seeks to generate and iteratively refine retroductive explanations of the abductive revelations encountered in scripture, and of the ontological realities scripture testifies to. Thomas Torrance's *Theological Science* seeks to unpack the nature of Christian theology insofar as it seeks to generate powerful secondary retroductive explanations of Christian experiences of the God whose nature is revealed in the person of Jesus Christ and mediated by Christian scripture. First delivered as lectures in 1959 and published a decade later, *Theological Science* constitutes the first extended and substantial discussion of critical realism in the twentieth century (Torrance 1969). In drawing the theological and natural sciences into constructive dialogue, Torrance set out to demonstrate the inherent intelligibility and rationality of the doctrines of classical Christianity.

Torrance argues that since all knowledge is culturally situated, Christian theology necessarily operates from within the Christian tradition. Since we can only ever know as human beings there is an unavoidable personal coefficient of all knowledge, so that theological knowledge is constituted by the *relationship* between God and the human knower. Because we participate in knowledge-relations prior to our reflective understanding of them, knowledge always proceeds from tacit-intuitive understanding. Tacit faith in 'a transcendent reality, independent of our knowledge of it and accessible to all men, is the ultimate determinant of the scientific enterprise' (Torrance 1984: 160). The task of theological science is to infer the best possible explicit-reflective explanation of the Christian community's tacit-intuitive experiential knowledge of God. This is a creative process, in which the theologian seeks to identify the ontological relations and mechanisms that generate and make possible Christian experience of God, and describe it in coherent and consistent theoretical models. Though such retroductive modelling is a fallible process it is not entirely arbitrary, since natural scientists and Christian theologians are under an obligation to place the 'concepts that creatively arise in [their] minds' under 'the compulsion of the objective structures' of nature and divine revelation respectively (ibid.: 111). Affirming 'the concept of ontological stratification', Torrance insists that the ultimate meaning of reality as a whole is irreducible to the laws that govern the ultimate physical particulars of reality; on the contrary, 'as we move up the hierarchy of levels of reality, from the most tangible to the most intangible, we penetrate to things that are *increasingly real and full of meaning*' (ibid.: 159). Since theological knowledge is concerned with the highest strata of reality, namely that of the salvific relationship between human beings and their divine creator, theologians deal with ontological states-of-affairs that are simultaneously elusive to human comprehension and laden with ultimate significance.

Affirming the priority of ontology over epistemology, Torrance insists that the actuality of knowledge-relations necessarily precedes questions of the possibility of knowledge-relations. The basic epistemic problematic is not how to establish knowledge of a reality set over-against us, but rather how to deepen our already established relational knowledge of the world we indwell. The basic epistemic task is to 'begin within the knowledge relation where we actually are, and seek to move forward by clarifying and testing what we already know and by seeking to deepen and enlarge its content' (Torrance 1969: 2). Scientific 'questions as to the *possibility* of knowledge cannot be raised *in abstracto* but only *in concreto*, not *a priori* but only *a posteriori*' (ibid.: 1). Christian theology thus proceeds from the Christian community's mediated experience of the *actuality* of 'the God who actively meets us and gives Himself to be known in Jesus Christ' (ibid.: 26). The *possibility* of such experience can only be explained retrospectively: knowledge of the Trinitarian God is an actuality only because God the Father has freely chosen to reveal himself to us through the incarnation of his Son and the ongoing creative work of his Holy Spirit. Such a circular non-foundational argument is not the last resort of a debunked theology, but rather the necessary epistemic basis of all human knowledge. Knowledge of God is objective, rational, and conceptual: objective, because it entails 'a conscious relation to an object which we recognize to be distinct from ourselves' (ibid.: 13); rational, because it requires us to 'relate our thought and our action appropriate to objective intelligible realities' (ibid.: 11); conceptual, because:

> theological thought consists in developing and clarifying the conceptual structure of this knowledge by constant reference to the object and by advancing in the cognitive modes of rationality set up between us and God as He communicates Himself to us.
>
> (ibid.: 13f.)

As a personal being, the Trinitarian God elects, in the person of Jesus Christ, to reveal himself to us objectively in his own subjectivity, so that knowledge of God takes the form of an inter-subjective and interpersonal relationship. Entry into a personal relationship with another person opens up the possibility of our lives being transformed: in Christian theology 'faith' refers ontologically to the risks and challenges of a transformative relationship with God, rather than epistemically to an extra-rational means of accessing knowledge of God.

Torrance offers a nuanced account of the relationship between theological and natural science that eschews the modern 'conflict' model. The Christian doctrine of creation affirms *both* the essential intelligibility of creation, *and* its ontological otherness-from-God and the God-given freedom to function apart from any divinely imposed necessity. This Christian notion of an ordered-yet-contingent cosmos provided modern a posteriori empirical natural science with its two basic presuppositions: 'an ultimate *orderliness* behind the flux of nature', and an 'element of *contingency* in creaturely existence' (ibid.: 61, emphases added). By virtue of its understanding of God's creation as inherently ordered-yet-contingent, Abrahamic theology can legitimately claim 'to have mothered throughout long centuries the basic beliefs and impulses which have given rise especially to modern empirical science' (ibid.: 57; cf. Foster 1973; Hooykaas 1973; Jaki 1980; Hodgson 2005).

Ironically, given the presuppositions of the 'conflict' model of the relationship between science and theology, it was Greek philosophy rather than Christian theology that threatened the emergence of modern natural science: Platonism, with its negative evaluation of the material world, questioned the orderliness of nature; Aristotelianism, with its deterministic causal nexus, questioned the contingency of nature. If Christianity was culpable in impeding the emergence of modern natural science, this was due primarily to the dual impact of Augustine's Platonic and Aquinas' Aristotelian re-readings of the Christian tradition, and only secondarily on the Church's fundamentally misplaced political manoeuvrings in response to Galileo and Darwin. The Protestant Reformation, insofar as it sought to expunge Platonic and Aristotelian influences on Christian theology and retrieve a Biblical understanding of creation as ordered-yet-contingent, played a significant role in preparing the intellectual ground for the emergence of modern natural science. This process required the abandonment of natural philosophy, which endeavoured to make sense of the natural order-of-things by employing a loose conflation of empirical, philosophical and theological tools. In distinguishing between God and creation, and between the divine economy of grace and the order of nature, Christianity established the ground for the differentiation of the respective objects of study of the theological and natural sciences, and for the recognition of their autonomy vis-à-vis one another. Though theological science and natural science have different objects of study, they share the same generic aims and methods: to generate increasingly powerful understandings of their respective objects of investigation by retroductively constructing and iteratively refining explanatory models in the light of a posteriori experience.

Torrance accepts a distinction between *scientia generalis* and *scientia specialis*: the former concerns the generic principles of scientific discovery applicable to all fields of learning; the latter concerns the actual processes of discovery in distinctive fields, as these are driven and constrained by the specific nature of particular objects of investigation (Torrance 1969: 111ff.). *Scientia specialis* takes priority over *scientia generalis*: though it is legitimate to abstract generic scientific principles from actual scientific practices, it is illegitimate to reify them as an autonomous *scientia universalis*. To attempt to do so will only result in the epistemic fallacy of dislocating scientific method from the objects it seeks to investigate and thereby privileging epistemology over ontology. Torrance identifies four broad features of a *scientia generalis*. First, it assumes the basic intelligibility of the object of investigation, regardless of its contingent nature, and despite the fact that we may not yet be able to fully comprehend it. Scepticism, the a priori assumption of the unintelligibility or putative nature of the object of investigation, is a form of the epistemic fallacy which allows the self-certainty of the investigator to preclude the possibility of scientific discovery. Second, it requires openness, sensitivity, reverence and devotion to the actuality of the object under investigation: the scientifically trained mind must be prepared to allow the ontological givenness of objective reality to mould, shape and transform the epistemic contingency of its subjective understanding. Third, it requires an awareness of the extent and limits of the mind, of the nature and structure of thinking, and of the modes of knowing appropriate to human nature. Such critical self-awareness on the part of the scientific investigator makes possible forms 'of questioning in which we allow what we already know or hold to be knowledge to be called in question by the object' (ibid.: 120). Fourth, it requires formal investigative procedures committed to the rigorous, disciplined and methodical organisation of knowledge. This involves seeking to penetrate beneath surface appearances in order to discern the deep ontic structures and elemental forms of the object of investigation, and to describe and explain its reality retroductively through theoretical modelling. Verification of the truthfulness of a theoretical construct is necessarily relative to the nature of the object it seeks to explain, and as such cannot appeal to any pre-established external criteria: a retroductive model is more likely to be true if it accurately reflects the ontological actuality of the object, is internally coherent, and is more powerful and comprehensive than competing models.

With respect to the *scientia specialis* of Christian theology, Torrance draws a distinction between the ontological truth of being and the epistemic truth of knowing. Ontological truth consists in the totality of reality: the Triune Creator, his Creation, and the relationship between them. In the case of humankind, such truth takes the form, not of mere ideas or statements, but of interpersonal relations between God and human subjects. God's truth 'is Truth which we can meet and know in our concrete existence through personal encounter and rational cognition, yet Truth who retains His own Majesty and Authority' (ibid.: 143). Jesus Christ is the way, the truth and the life:

In Him God turns in Grace toward us and makes Himself open to us, summoning us to be open toward Him and to keep faith and truth with Him in Jesus, so that we may be true as God is true, and learn to do the truth as He does the truth.

(ibid.)

Epistemic truth consists of theological statements regarding these relationships. These are possible only by virtue of God's self-revelation, and as human constructs they are necessarily contingent. Theological statements combine propositions and judgements in a circular relationship: theological propositions affirm theological judgements, and theological judgements assess theological propositions. They are the communal products of the Christian community:

Statements made in response to a Word that is heard, a Truth that is communicated, or an Act that is done to us, a propositional question or rational communication that is directed to us from God Himself in His Son, the Word made flesh, requiring recognition, response, decision for their articulation on our part.

(ibid.: 163f.)

Theological propositions make truth claims about the ultimate nature of reality in response to God's self-revelation as received and discerned by the Christian community. There can be no independent criteria for judging their truth outside of the knowledge-relationship that generates them. Nevertheless, they can be evaluated with reference to their convergence with the historical data of revelation and contemporary Christian experience, their internal coherence, their congruence and fertility vis-à-vis emergent knowledge of other strata of reality, and their comprehensiveness and explanatory power vis-à-vis other religious and secular accounts of the ultimate order-of-things (Wright 2007: 219ff., 2013: 229).

Like all scientific propositions, theological propositions possess a particular logic derived from the ontological actuality of the object they seek to account for. Given the nature of God and limitations of human reason, theologians must grapple with the fact that 'being always breaks through the limits of our statements and outruns their logical forms' (Torrance 1969: 204). Here theology faces a particular challenge, since God cannot be conceived of in the same way we conceive of objects in the created order. The logic of God, as revealed in the person of Jesus Christ, has a number of distinctive dimensions: the logic of *grace*, in which God gives himself to us as the object of our knowledge without ceasing to be the divine subject, so that we know God only as God knows us; the logic of *incarnation*, in which the hypostatic union between God and humanity in Christ provides the normative pattern of all theological statements; the logic of *love*, by which the divine and human natures of Christ are united in one person, establishes love as the proper mode of interpersonal relations and the ontological ground of all reality; the logic of *history*, grounded in the fact that, since God engages ontologically with creation in the specific history of Jesus of Nazareth, he is known only in concrete, communal, historical contexts, and not in abstract, individual spiritual experiences that transcend particular spatio-temporal coordinates.

Natural theology transformed

Natural theology seeks to reason from the facts of nature to the reality of God. Though primarily an exercise in metaphysics, it originally drew on understandings of the natural world provided by natural philosophy. Metaphysics was concerned to account for the deep structures of reality underlying the natural world: not the natural structures investigated by natural philosophy (and later natural science), but rather the deep metaphysical structures presupposed by natural philosophy/science, and which are a condition of the possibility of natural philosophy/science. Prior to the emergence of modern a posteriori natural science, natural philosophy sought to make sense of the natural world through a mixture of a priori philosophical speculation and (largely unsystematic) a posteriori empirical observation (Grant 2007). The remarkable success of natural science, predicated in part on its rejection of a priori philosophical reasoning in favour of a posteriori empirical observation, led in some quarters to the elevation of the methods of empirical observation, mathematical measurement and experimental testing as the only legitimate means of making sense of reality. Consequently, the elimination of philosophical reflection from natural science was extended to a rejection of metaphysics as a viable intellectual discipline. Positivist accounts of the natural world did not need to look beyond surface appearances provided by raw empirical data to discern underlying causal mechanisms, nor did they need to look beyond such causal mechanisms to identify the underlying metaphysical structures of reality. Given this positivistic account of natural science, theological attempts to explain natural phenomena by appealing to some Transcendent source appeared doomed to invoke nothing more than a god-of-the-gaps in current scientific knowledge.

Critical realism's rehabilitation of the disciplines of metaphysics and theology is predicated on two core insights.

First, given that the realm of nature forms only part of a greater stratified reality, and that specific levels of stratification demand explanations appropriate to their distinctive natures, qualities and modes of being, natural science, though properly enjoying autonomy in its investigation of natural phenomena, cannot be employed to explain non-natural phenomena without slipping into the reductionist fallacy. Natural science, metaphysics and theology are concerned to investigate distinctive domains of reality: the realm of nature, the basic ontological structures of being, and the reality of God and his relationship with the created order. Just as each discipline has its own distinctive ontological object of study, so it also possesses its own distinctive epistemic tools and methods, which are not established a priori but rather emerge progressively through a posteriori engagement with its particular object of investigation. The failure to properly demarcate disciplinary investigation of different strata of reality reflects an absence of intellectual seriousness that allows post-modern philosophers to reduce natural science to sociology, 'New Atheists' to reduce theology to biology, and religious fundamentalists to reduce natural science to literalistic scriptural exegesis. The presence of intellectual seriousness enables us to recognise that the natural scientist is no more equipped to explain society, morality and aesthetics than the social scientist is equipped to explain physics, the moral philosopher chemistry or the poet biology.

Second, the principle of the hermeneutical circle, in which individual parts explain the whole and the whole individual parts in reciprocal dialogue, when coupled with the principle of sufficient reason, suggests that the totality of being demands a holistic explanation that combines an understanding of individual strata of reality with an understanding of the ways in which they combine together to constitute reality as a whole. Given the autonomy of specific disciplinary investigations of particular strata of reality, the notion that natural science can produce a total explanation of all reality is essentially reductionist: if reality is greater than the natural order-of-things, then any such total or ultimate explanation necessarily requires either a metaphysics and/or (especially if we follow the ancient Greeks in defining 'God' as the ultimate ground of order, meaning and purpose in reality) a theology. If we accept the existence of both God and nature, then it is reasonable to presume that together they constitute part of the same reality by virtue of their status as existing objects, regardless of any fundamental ontological differences that might divide them. This being the case, we should expect to discover extra-systemic correspondence between the explanations of nature offered by natural science and the explanations of God offered by theological science without any undermining of their disciplinary autonomy. Such correspondence will constitute a significant indicator of alethic truth: since our explanations of the world are cumulative, the greater inclusivity and assimilative power of explanations of one stratum vis-à-vis explanations of other strata, the more powerful the former are likely to be. Put crudely, a creationist theology that rejects the insights of contemporary cosmology is less likely to be true than a theology of creation congruent with them.

Alister McGrath advocates a revisionary approach to natural theology, informed by critical realism, which affirms *both* the essential autonomy of natural science as it seeks to explain the natural strata of reality *and* the legitimacy of metaphysics and theology as they seek to explain reality as a whole. He rejects forms of natural theology that seek to argue from nature to God, and propose instead a 'theology of nature' concerned to bring the theological and natural sciences into constructive conversation in a manner that recognises *both* the autonomy of each vis-à-vis their particular objects of investigation *and* the fact that they are investigating different strata of a single interconnected reality. As previously noted, having obtained doctorates in both molecular biophysics and theology McGrath is better equipped than most to explore the interface of the natural and theological sciences. His *magnum opus* to date, *A Scientific Theology* (McGrath 2001, 2002, 2003; cf. McGrath 2006), draws on both philosophical and theological accounts of critical realism to establish the theoretical ground of his project. Its three volumes broadly follow the basic critically realistic triumvirate: the first volume, *Nature*, is concerned with epistemic relativity; the second, *Reality*, with ontological realism; and the third, *Theory*, with judgemental rationality.

Volume One: Nature focuses on epistemic relativity, and argues that the notion of 'nature' is socially constructed and as such necessarily situated within one or other epistemically relative worldview that will inevitably attribute, whether implicitly or explicitly, a distinctive metaphysical status to the natural order-of-things. Thus naturalism views nature as the self-generating, self-rationalising and self-sustaining bedrock of reality, whilst Christianity affirms nature as the contingent product of a creator God who generates, sustains and rationally orders the world *ex nihilo*. Though such metaphysical and theological claims have no right to impact on the practice of natural science per se (so that we should not anticipate any fundamental dispute between naturalists and theists over the procedures and results of natural science), they do have a vital role to play in our understanding of the nature, extent and limits of the natural world and its relationship to reality as a whole. In line with the foregoing argument, McGrath locates his work in the context of the Christian theology of creation, and rejects the possibility of a natural theology that claims to adopt a neutral standpoint when attempting to reason from nature to God. Natural theology must be replaced with a 'theology of nature' that seeks to explore 'from the standpoint of faith ... the consonance between faith and the structures of the world' (McGrath 2001: 266f.).

Volume Two: Reality turns from the epistemic relativity surrounding our understanding of nature to address questions of its ontological reality. Here McGrath draws on Roy Bhaskar's work in developing a critical theological realism that looks beyond modern objectivism and post-modern subjectivism. Rejecting both foundationalism and tradition-independent enquiry on the one hand, and a thoroughgoing relativism on the other, he contends that 'knowledge arises through a sustained and passionate attempt to engage with a reality that is encountered or made known' (McGrath 2002: 3f.). Contra Kant, there is no dualistic distinction between the world-as-experienced and the world-in-itself: because we indwell the reality we seek to understand, we experience it directly and strive to penetrate more deeply into its mysteries. The primary epistemic task is not to make contact with reality but to better understand that which we are already engaged with. We judge the veracity of our understanding of the world in terms of the internal coherence of our truth claims and their external correspondence with reality. Though different disciplines attend to particular strata of reality, the fact that individual strata combine to form a totality opens up the possibility of intra-systematic investigation, and of employing judgemental rationality vis-à-vis conflicting worldviews. Theological science is the discipline concerned with the identification and representation of the Transcendent, divine and spiritual structures of reality. Though natural science seeks to explain the order and structure of nature, it is far from clear that it can explain *why* nature exists, *why* it is ordered and structured, or *why* it is open to rational investigation. Such questions are essentially metaphysical and theological in nature: they address issues, not about natural science per se, but about the conditions that make natural science possible.

Volume Three: Theory explores the challenge of employing judgemental rationality to express and explain reality. Knowledge is grounded in our experiences in real-world environments and tested in academic settings. Just as natural science assumes a prior engagement with nature, so Christian theological science assumes a prior engagement with the Trinitarian God mediated through the life, worship, teachings, traditions and scriptures of Christianity. As such, both the natural and theological sciences take the form of faith – whether in the reality of nature or the reality of God – seeking understanding. We make sense of our abductive experiences of reality through retroductive explanations and the iterative refinement of our explanatory models. Because the object of investigation of theological science transcends the physical realm of nature, it is necessarily metaphysical in nature. Christian theology generates theoretical accounts of the reality of the Triune God that are relative to the cultural context in which they are produced, and as such are no more than provisional anticipations of the future eschatological fulfilment of our knowledge of God.

In the rest of this section we will unpack McGrath's account of a 'theology of nature' through a concrete case study that explores resonances between so-called 'anthropic phenomena' uncovered by natural science and the Christian doctrine of creation (McGrath 2008: 240ff., 2009). McGrath points out that cosmology, the sub-field of physics concerned with the origins of the universe, is faced with distinctive quantitative and qualitative challenges. Quantitatively, it is concerned with phenomena distant in space and time: the fact that the available evidence is restricted by certain 'selection effects' (e.g. some kinds of matter emit very little radiation) means that it is not necessarily typical and almost certainly incomplete. Qualitatively, unlike other sub-fields of natural science, it is concerned, not with a plurality of events within a clearly identifiable causal nexus, but with a singular event without any obvious cause. At the beginning of the previous century Einstein's field equations and Hubble's observation of spectral redshifts in galaxies beyond the Milky Way suggested that the universe 'was expanding, with increasing speed and apparently irreversibly' (McGrath 2009: 113). Both scientists initially resisted this conclusion: Einstein by adding a 'cosmological constant' to his equations, and Hoyle by positing a 'steady-state' universe without a beginning in which matter was continually created to fill the void left by cosmic expansion. In the 1960s the discovery of background cosmic radiation – the 'afterglow' of the 'Big Bang' – confirmed the greater explanatory power of the retroductive model of an expanding universe, and led to the current consensus that the universe originated 14 billion years ago and has been expanding and cooling ever since.

Iterative refinement of the expanding-universe model has led to a consensus amongst cosmologists regarding the existence of so-called 'anthropic' phenomena.

The existence of carbon-based life on Earth depends upon a delicate balance of physical and cosmological forces and parameters, which are such that were any one of these quantities to be slightly altered, the balance would be destroyed and life would not exist. The smallest variation in the constant of universal gravitation, or the mass of the neutron, or the charge of an electron, would have changed everything, making the emergence of human observers impossible. Initially, anthropic phenomena were identified within cosmology, especially the values of the fundamental constants of nature. Yet in recent years, similar phenomena have been identified in chemistry, biochemistry, and evolutionary biology.

(McGrath 2008: 241)

These physical and cosmological forces are not the result of evolutionary selection: the four fundamental forces of the universe – gravity, electromagnetism, and strong and weak nuclear forces – were already present as constants with specific values *at the very beginning* of the cosmos. In 1974 Brendan Carter proposed what became known as the 'weak anthropic principle', according to which 'the fundamental constants of the universe were such that they appeared to have been "designed" to allow life to come into existence', so that 'the universe appeared to possess an innate propensity to encourage the emergence of life' (ibid.: 240f.; cf. Carter 1974). In 1986 John Barrow and Frank Tipler's *The Anthropic Cosmological Principle* added to the debate by positing the 'strong anthropic principle' that the universe *must* possess the properties conducive to the emergence of life, and the 'final anthropic principle' that intelligent life *must* come into existence and *can never* be extinguished (Barrow and Tipler 1986). The notion of 'necessity' with regard to a singular event without any obvious cause draws us into the domains of metaphysics and theology. Indeed, a common criticism of Barrow and Tipler is that they are arguing metaphysically under the guise of physics. To attempt to explain how nature functions is the task of natural science; however, to attempt explain why nature *as a totality* exists, why it is rationally ordered and open to scientific investigation, and why it is apparently so improbably and counter-intuitively conducive to the emergence of life, takes us beyond natural science into the realms of metaphysics and theology. Natural science is made possible by a particular conjunction of constants ingrained in the very fabric of the universe; and, as Jamie Morgan points out, no scientific theory claims to 'understand where/how those constants and their combinations are created' (quoted in Creaven 2010: 282). The discovery by natural science of anthropic phenomena raises metaphysical *aporiai* that appear to be beyond the scope of natural science to answer: how can we make sense of anthropic phenomena? How can we best explain the vast improbability of the primal forces of the universe possessing values conducive to the emergence of sentient life?

Sean Creaven argues that the turn to metaphysics is nothing more than an illegitimate attempt to plug the gaps in current natural scientific knowledge (ibid.: 282f.). In doing so he commits the epistemic fallacy by claiming to know a priori that the epistemic tools employed by natural science will eventually answer questions about the origins of the natural order-of-things, and therefore to know a priori that the natural order is ontologically self-generating and self-sustaining. The *discernment* of anthropic phenomena is, of course, entirely the province of natural science; however, the *explanation* of anthropic phenomena raises metaphysical and theological *aporiai* that extend beyond the domain of natural science by asking transcendental questions about the existence of being-qua-being, as well as questions about the antecedent conditions necessary for the conduct of natural science. This is not to suggest that Creaven's naturalistic/materialistic ontology is necessarily wrong, merely that he is wrong to predicate it on a form of 'scientism' that privileges the methods of natural science over all other epistemic tools, and as a result generates an ontology on the basis of prior epistemic commitments.

The debate has thrown up at least three potential metaphysical/theological retroductive explanations of anthropic phenomena: (1) Barrow and Tipler defend a panentheistic 'final anthropic principle', rooted in theosophy and bearing remarkable similarities to Bhaskar's philosophy of meta-Reality (Barrow and Tipler 1986). They suggest that from the very beginning the universe was hotwired to generate sentient minds, which can never be extinguished and will eventually be united in a final ground state or omega point. The universe is the product of insentient mechanisms containing the innate potential to generate sentient life and, on the assumption of the priority of potentiality over actuality, it is proper to affirm the final omega point, the moment of realisation of absolute mind, as the sentient postcedent cause of reality. (2) Theists posit both the universe and the emergence of life as the intentional product of the creative act of a self-generating, self-sustaining and self-rationalising God. Anthropic phenomena are 'a marker of our almost exorbitant importance' within the cosmos, and a strong indicator of the fact that we were created by God for a purpose (Porpora 2004: 157). (3) Naturalists and materialists view nature as self-generating, self-rationalising and self-sustaining, and dismiss anthropic phenomena as purely coincidental. We can imagine a counterfactual state of affairs in which different conjunctions of constants generate a universe devoid of sentient life. The far greater probability of this counterfactual actually being the case can be mitigated by identifying the inevitable observational bias of sentient beings inhabiting a universe that *has* generated life. Though we cannot yet explain why the natural world is self-generating, self-rationalising and self-sustaining, we can anticipate natural science proffering a viable solution at some point in the future. Until this happens we must remain silent, since any attempt to invoke theological or metaphysical explanations constitutes an illegitimate attempt to plug the gaps in our current scientific knowledge.

Anthropic phenomena raise fundamental ontological questions: why is there something rather than nothing? Why is that 'something' open to rational explanation? Why – apparently against all odds – is the natural world 'hot-wired' to generate sentient life? If we can imagine counterfactually a universe devoid of sentient life, so we can also imagine an utterly chaotic universe closed to rational explanation, as well as a pure nothingness utterly devoid of time, space, matter, causal mechanisms and rational order. Panentheism, theism and naturalism all proffer metaphysical and/or theological answers to these metaphysical *aporia* which, given the absence of any dispute about the actuality of anthropic phenomena as described by natural science, must be judged in terms of their greater explanatory power vis-à-vis one another.

Anxious to preserve lines of demarcation between the natural and theological sciences, McGrath exercises immense caution in addressing these issues. He prefers the language of 'fine-tuning' to that of 'anthropic principle', and counsels against assuming that the metaphor of a 'fine-tuned' universe implies an extra-celestial 'fine-tuner'. Despite the mathematically astonishing nature of their findings, cosmologists have done no more than identify 'the surprisingly restricted range of values that certain fundamental constants must have to bring about our universe' (McGrath 2009: 116). Nevertheless, like all phenomena the 'fine-tuned' nature of the cosmos demands explanation, and the task of generating the best possible retroductive account of why the totality of reality is-as-it-is falls under the remit of theology and metaphysics as much as natural science.

Rather than reasoning metaphysically from the fine-tuned universe to a fine-tuning God in the style of traditional natural theology, McGrath seeks instead to develop a 'theology of nature' designed to bring the disciplines of natural science and Christian theology into constructive dialogue in a manner that both respects their autonomy and recognises that they are both concerned to explain different strata of the same reality. The concern of natural science for cosmology parallels the concern of theological science for the Christian doctrine of creation. Accounts of the history of the religion of ancient Israel and the early Church tell the story of the emergence, in particular cultural contexts and in response to specific historical events, of a Christian worldview that, like all worldviews, embraces a range of practices, symbols and stories that, taken cumulatively, offer answers to 'the basic *questions* that determine human existence: who we are, where we are, what is wrong, and what is the solution?' (Wright 1992: 123; cf. Walsh and Middleton 1984: 35). Christian theology seeks to give systematic retroductive expression to the Christian worldview's answers to these basic questions, and iteratively test their veracity in the light of the realities they seek to explain, their internal coherence and their explanatory power vis-à-vis alternative explanations. The Christian doctrine of creation draws on the experience of ancient Israel, as expressed in both the 'primal history' contained in the opening chapters of the Book of Genesis and the prophetic and wisdom literature, and subjects such expressions to iterative refinement in the light of the Christian experience of the historical Jesus as the embodiment of the creative 'Word of God' through whom God called creation into being.

When read in the light of other ancient Near Eastern creation myths, it quickly becomes apparent that the account of creation contained in the first chapter of Genesis functions, at least in part, to deliberately subvert and replace the Babylonian understanding of the origins and nature of the cosmos: rather than being the accidental result of conflict between an assortment of dysfunctional gods, creation is presented as the intentional product of one supreme God; whereas the Babylonian gods struggle to control a raft of primal forces of nature, in the Genesis myth these primal forces are utterly dependent on the will of God; and rather than being an afterthought created by the gods for their own benefit, humankind stands at the apex of a created order deliberately designed to provide an environment in which it can flourish (Wenman 1987: xlviff., 1ff.). 'The creation story in Genesis may be metaphorical, but it is not merely a metaphor about the contingency of human life; it is a metaphor about the contingency of creation on a God who created it' (Archer *et al.* 2004: 9). The Genesis story asserts truth claims about intransitive reality that are either true or false: not pseudo-scientific claims about the natural world per se, but theological claims about the Transcendent source and ultimate meaning and purpose of reality as a whole; not the product of the metaphysical reflection of philosophers, but the product of the cumulative historical experience of a spiritual community whose emergent retroductive theology appeared to them to possess greater explanatory power than any other explanation of the ultimate order-of-things available to them. Contemporary Jews and Christians, in affirming the truth of the Genesis story, hold fast to the belief that the cosmos was created by one supreme God who, for the sake of humanity, endowed it, not only with the ordered-yet-contingent structure discerned by contemporary natural science, but also with aesthetic beauty, moral purpose and spiritual significance.

For reasons of space, we must restrict ourselves to teasing out four key features of the Christian doctrine of creation, as explicated in a vast range of literature (e.g. Barth 1958–1961; Gunton 1998; Jenson 1999: 3ff.; Pannenberg 1994: 1ff.).

(1) *The freedom and sovereignty of the Creator.* The Nicene Creed affirms the one Triune God as the creator 'of all things visible and invisible' (Kelly 1950: 215). The doctrine of creation *ex nihilo* serves to affirm God's absolute sovereignty and supreme freedom. God brings *all* that exists into being out of nothing, rather than imposing order onto pre-existent primal matter in obedience to some pre-established rational principle; and he does so freely, not out of any internally imposed necessity. Since the Trinity is a perfect communion of persons existing in loving relationship, there can be no lack, need or unfulfilled desire within God. God creates freely, in a sovereign act of gracious love, not for his own sake but for the sake of creation itself.

(2) *The contingency, order and freedom of creation.* The created realm is utterly contingent on God, both for its coming into being and for its continuing existence: generated by God, not self-generating; sustained by God, not self-sustaining. Creation is also ordered and structured: a stable environment, within which human beings can conduct their lives in meaningful ways, organised by causal mechanisms open to rational explanation. Despite its utter dependence on his will for its continuing existence, God allows his creatures the freedom to be themselves apart from their Creator, sustaining them and proactively engaging with them, but not determining their existence. Because love can never be coercive, God creates an ordered cosmos devoid of necessity, so that human beings are free to choose to

reciprocate or not to reciprocate God's offer of unconditional love as they see fit. Though utterly dependent on God, creation is simultaneously ordered-yet-open: neither anarchically chaotic nor fascistly deterministic.

(3) *The reality, goodness, and meaningfulness of creation.* 'God saw everything he had made, and indeed, it was very good' (Genesis 1:31). The affirmation of the reality of creation challenges idealist notions that the immanent material world is at best an ephemeral and deceptive reflection of a greater immaterial Transcendent reality; the affirmation of the goodness of creation challenges empiricist notions that the cosmos is governed by impersonal and teleologically vacuous natural forces; the affirmation of the meaningfulness of creation challenges notions that the ultimate cause of the universe is an impersonal Platonic 'Form', Aristotelian 'Unmoved Mover', or any natural force or mechanism. Because God is a personal being who creates out of love, the created order is ultimately real, good and meaningful.

(4) *The teleological purpose and future perfection of creation.* Though 'very good', creation is not yet perfect, since God's creatures do not yet live in harmonious bonds of reciprocal love, either with one another or with their Creator. Christian theology looks to the teleological perfection and eschatological consummation of creation, in which the bonds of reciprocal love that unite the three persons of the Trinity will extended to embrace the whole of creation. The Christian doctrine of creation cannot be separated from the Christian doctrine of reconciliation. God created the world with the intention, from the very beginning, that all human beings should participate in the same reciprocal loving relationships that unite the persons of the Holy Trinity. The doctrine of reconciliation insists that God loves *all* human beings unconditionally, and rejects equally unconditionally *all* forces, mechanisms, structures and agential action that separate us from authentic relationships with ourselves, other persons, the created order and our Creator. God's 'yes' to our humanity and 'no' to all that undermines, erodes and destroys our humanity is proactive: the same God who called creation into being enters into creation and in an under-labouring act of uncoercive love (rather than raw coercive power) reveals and actualises the divine love that is the source and perfector of all created being. God's desire to enter into a reciprocal loving relationship with humanity is realised, in anticipation of the final eschatological perfection of creation, in the incarnation: the Word of God, the second person of the Trinity, was united with humankind in the person of Jesus of Nazareth – humanity and divinity in perfect hypostatic union.

> In the beginning was the Word, and the Word was with God, and the Word was God. He was in the beginning with God. All things came into being through him, and without him not one thing came into being.... And the Word became flesh and lived among us ... full of grace and truth.
>
> (John 1:1–3, 14)

What light might the Christian doctrine of creation shed on the anthropic phenomena identified by natural science? McGrath shows remarkably little interest in engaging with the intricacies of the arguments offered by panentheists, theists and naturalists directly, and is happy to acknowledge that anthropic phenomena do *not* provide a sufficient basis for a *proof* of the existence of God. In trying to make sense of the world we employ retroductive explanatory modelling rather than deductive or inductive argument. In any retroductive account of the ultimate order-of-things, anthropic phenomena will constitute just one strand of a broader, cumulative and multifaceted explanatory web. By framing explanations of anthropic phenomena within the Enlightenment-generated discipline of modern natural theology we inappropriately privilege modern atheistic scepticism as a default position, and mistakenly demand that one particular strand of argument provides demonstrable proof that this default position is untenable. Christian theology is grounded, not in any deductive argument from the facts of nature to the reality of God, but rather in retroductive responses to God's historically mediated self-revelation. A Christian theology of nature seeks to explore the extra-systemic correspondence between explanations of God's self-revelation proffered by theological science and explanations of the natural order proffered by natural science. McGrath is content to point out that 'the general phenomenon of fine-tuning is consonant with Christian belief in a creator God', and to suggest that 'observation of the natural world furnishes conceptual resonance with, not deductive proof of, the Christian vision of God' (McGrath 2009: 121).

> It is not argued that such phenomena represent a 'proof' of the existence of a creator God, but they are consistent with the view of God encountered and practiced within the Christian faith. On this approach, the observation of anthropic phenomena resonates with the core themes of the Christian vision of reality.
>
> (McGrath 2008: 243)

McGrath's measured position – despite its paucity when read from the perspective of those who might have expected him to seize an opportunity to argue directly from anthropic phenomena to the reality of God – is highly significant on at least two fronts: negatively, it challenges the assumption that theology and science are embroiled in a competition from which theology can only ever emerge as the loser, exposed as an indefensible pseudo-science; positively, in drawing attention to the consonance between the substantial claims of Christian theology and the anthropic phenomena discovered by natural science it adds significantly to the strength of Christian truth claims, and challenges atheists and panentheists alike to provide a more powerful retroductive explanation as to *why* nature exists, *why* it is inherently rational and self-sustaining, and *why* it is capable of generating sentient life forms despite the remarkable improbability of this being the case. The significance of all of this for the present book is that it serves to underscore the claim that theology is a properly warranted rational activity that cannot legitimately be excluded from the public square in general, and from public education in particular.

5   The fragmentation of education

The philosophy of critical realism raises fundamental questions about truth and truthful living, about our knowledge relationships with the ultimate order-of-things and the implications of these for the task of living the good life. In doing so, it questions the empiricist tendency to reduce knowledge of reality to the identification of recurrent patterns of interaction between observable objects, the idealist tendency to reify values to the status of abstract ideas dislocated from real-world environments, and the pragmatic tendency to shrink the good life to that which meets the parochially perceived needs and aspirations of particular individuals and groups. This dislocation of fact from value forces human beings to muddle through by making the best use of the resources available to them, whether these take the form of objective facts, subjective values, a pragmatically driven volition to maximise happiness, or some combination of the three. This fact–value divide recurs in the theological realm. Religious worldviews and their secular counterparts, insofar as they take the hermeneutical circle seriously and seek to relate the parts of reality to the whole, strive to pursue truth and truthful living *sub specie aeternitatis* in relation to the ultimate order-of-things. In affirming the possibility and importance of such striving, critical realism questions the empiricist tendency to bracket-out questions of Transcendence, the idealistic tendency to generate abstract accounts of Transcendence dislocated from everyday life, and the pragmatic tendency to consign the striving for truthful living in harmony with the ultimate order-of-things to the level of an optional extra, open to those whose personal inclinations happen to draw them in that particular direction. This same pattern emerges in the field of education. The present chapter will tell a story of the disintegration and fragmentation of the realistic and holistic assumptions underlying ancient and medieval *paideia* under the auspices of the Enlightenment, and of the resulting tendency to order education on the basis of epistemic assumptions rather than ontological commitments in a manner that effectively undermined the essential unity of the twin tasks of pursuing knowledge and overseeing personal and social enrichment. The following chapter will seek to show how critical realism opens up the possibility of recovering an approach to education in which the pursuit of truth and the cultivation of truthful living *sub specie aeternitatis* are bound together in an indivisible whole.

The historic unity of education

Prior to the Enlightenment, Western education was not generally tainted by the fact–value divide. The pursuit of knowledge was simultaneously a quest to locate both the individual learner and the learning society within the ultimate order-of-things (Wright 2007: 55ff.). Personal formation and social wellbeing were predicated on the cultivation of harmonious relationships with the ultimate order-of-things. Since such relationships were often discordant there was an educational imperative to search for truth and cultivate truthful living. The perception of the essential unity of these twin tasks was grounded on the assumption that reality is intrinsically purposeful and value-laden. The good life was not dependent on the construction of shared human values against the backdrop of a value-free universe, or on the cultivation of skills and dispositions designed to enable individuals to successfully navigate a pragmatic course through life, but rather on establishing knowledge of, and – which was essentially the same thing – harmonious relationships with, the ultimate order-of-things. In the language of critical realism, the experience of discordant knowledge-relationships (epistemic relativity) generated a pedagogic drive to pursue truth and cultivate truthful living (judgemental rationality) with respect to the actuality of the ultimate order-of-things (ontological realism).

(1) *Judaism.* Education in ancient Israel was grounded in the ontologically actuality of God: 'The fear of the LORD is the beginning of wisdom' (Proverbs 1: 7). Awe, wonder and humility in the face of the reality of God constituted 'the necessary premise to the understanding of truth and the acquisition of learning' (Scott 1965: 37). The quest for knowledge and understanding 'comes back to the question about commitment to God.... One becomes competent and expert as far as the orders of life are concerned only if one begins from knowledge about God' (Rad 1972: 67). To understand God was simultaneously to understand oneself in relation to God, the created order, the Jewish community and gentile society: 'Education involves the entire person, the totality of his or her life, and it affects all of that person's relationships – with self, with others, with things and with ideas' (Melchert 1994: 49). In affirming the primacy of the ontological reality of God, Judaism recognised the epistemic relativity of attempts to comprehend God and fallibility of attempts to live life in harmony with his will. In the period leading up to the emergence of Rabbinic Judaism, Jewish scripture was established as the primary source of knowledge of God, so that Jewish education focused on 'the reading, interpretation, and application of biblical history, myth, stories, laws and counsels for ordinary life' (Elias 2002: 6; cf. Drazin 1940: 11ff.).

The tension between the ontological reality of God and inevitable paucity of any attempt to comprehend the divine meant that Biblical interpretation required a critical hermeneutic grounded in judgemental rationality: 'To understand God [was] to have a kind of wisdom or *sapientia*' that encompassed contemplation, reflection, feeling, reason and action (Kelsey 1992: 34). The transmission and recitation of the Torah required a proactive engagement on the part of the learner who must, in the tradition of Hebraic wisdom, 'try to "make sense of" the puzzles and mysteries of human and divine behaviour' (Melchert 1998: ix; cf. Deuteronomy 6:6f, 20f.). This dialectical relationship between ontological realism, epistemic relativity and judgemental rationality was embedded in the canonical structure of Jewish scripture, with its tripartite division between the books of the Law, the Prophets and the (historical and wisdom) Writings (Brueggemann 1982). If the Torah reveals the nature and will of God, then the prophetic, historical and wisdom books tell the story of Israel's ongoing struggle to better comprehend and respond to divine revelation. Jewish scripture thus contains not just God's *core testimony* to Israel, but also Israel's *counter-testimony*, in which she subjects God's claim to sovereignty and call to faithfulness to cross-examination and testing by articulating her experience of divine absence, ambiguity and injustice (Brueggemann 1997). This ongoing pedagogical dialect assumes a normative pattern: God calls Israel to hear, obey, discern and trust him; responding to God's apparent hiddenness, ambiguity and negativity, Israel acts freely and responsibly, through complaint and petition, to demand God's fidelity; as her experience of God's hiddenness and ambiguity gives way to a renewed and deeper understanding of God's sovereignty and fidelity, so Israel turns once again to thanksgiving, praise and self-abandonment. This drama of exile and restoration, which was lived out both individually and communally, was driven by hope for 'full knowledge of Yahweh, full communion with Yahweh, and full enjoyment of an abundant earth' (ibid.: 484).

(2) *Platonism.* Greek education has its roots in the pre-Socratic distinction between the 'One' and the 'many'. As we have already seen, Parmenides championed the One, affirming the ontological priority and 'persuasive truth' of an enduring and unchanging Transcendent reality, and rejecting the ephemeral and shifting epistemic 'beliefs of mortals, in which there is no true trust' (Parmenides 1984: 53). Heraclitus, on the other hand, took the side of the 'many', holding reality to be ephemeral and in constant state of flux, so that it is impossible to step in the same river twice (Heraclitus 2001: 51). The Sophists, itinerant teachers offering instruction in rhetoric with a pragmatic edge designed to enable the student to be successful in public affairs, stood firmly in the tradition of Heraclitus (Kerferd 2003). Thus Protagoras, having asserted the impossibility of penetrating beyond the realm of perception to establish knowledge of the real world, made a virtue out of necessity by proclaiming that 'man is the measure of all things' (Copleston 1985: 87). Taking the side of Parmenides against Heraclitus, and rejecting Protagoras' anthropocentric epistemic scepticism, Plato insisted on the possibility of securing knowledge of reality and living virtuously in harmony with the actual order-of-things.

'Meno's Paradox' raised a fundamental pedagogic problem:

> But how will you look for something when you don't in the least know what it is? How on earth are you going to set up something you don't know as the object of your search? To put it another way, even if you come right up against it, how will you know that what you have found is the thing you didn't know?

> (Plato 1963b: 363)

Socrates' solution holds that knowledge is latent in the mind, so 'that what we call learning is really just recollection': because we know implicitly what we are looking for we *are* able to recognise it when we find it (Plato 1963c: 55). This is the doctrine of *anamnesis*, 'by which all learning and inquiry is interpreted as a kind of remembering' (Kierkegaard 1967: 11). The role of the Socratic teacher is not to transmit positive knowledge, but to act as a 'midwife who brings others' thoughts to birth' or, in the case of reluctant learners, 'a "gadfly", stinging the sophists into an encounter with truth' (Pattison 1999: 68). In the post-Enlightenment era this maieutic pedagogy has been assimilated into various anti-realistic forms of progressive education concerned to free pupils to construct their own realities and identities according to their personal desires and preferences, which can occlude the fundamentally realistic thrust of Socrates' argument. Prior to their physical embodiment, our immortal souls participated in the Platonic Forms, and consequently retain possession of a latent spark of the Transcendent reality from which they emanated: 'every human soul has, by reason of her nature, had contemplation of true being' (Plato 1963d: 496). As a result, recollection cannot be reduced to a process of self-expression and self-assertion, whose effectiveness is judged against the criterion of the self as the measure of all things. On the contrary, the knowledge latent in the mind is knowledge of the enduring and unchanging ontological reality of the Platonic Forms, which constitute the only proper measure of truth.

This epistemology had profound educational implications. The 'true lover of knowledge must, from childhood up, be most of all a striver after truth in every form' (Plato 1963a: 722). The maieutic task is 'to prove by every test whether the offspring of a young man's thought is a false phantom or instinct with life and truth' (Plato 1963e: 855). Personal flourishing is thus dependent on the pursuit of knowledge of the ultimate truth of the Forms. This personal quest for a knowledgeable and harmonious relationship with the ultimate order-of-things possesses a social dimension. Plato's *Republic* provides a blueprint for the reformation of Athenian schooling, in which education is designed to empower citizens to live virtuous lives within a just and harmonious city-state (Nettleship 1935; Wright 2007: 69ff.). The essence of virtue (ἀρετή, *arête*) is goodness, and to be shaped by virtue is to achieve a deep knowledge of the Form of the Good, and of one's own humanity in relation to that Form (Kelsey, 1992: 66f). The philosopher-rulers of Plato's ideal republic were to undergo an education designed to establish a shared understanding of the good life rooted in the ontological reality of the Platonic Forms. This would enable them to understand the first principles of all that is virtuous and true, and utilise that understanding in their political decision-making. Personal and social wellbeing is thus predicated on the pedagogic occlusion of ignorance (epistemic relativity) via the pursuit of truth and truthful living (judgemental rationality) in harmony with the ultimate reality of the Platonic Forms (ontological realism).

(3) *Christianity.* The early-Christian era saw an increasing convergence between Abrahamic theology and Greek philosophy, as Christian theologians followed the lead of the Jewish philosopher Philo in seeking a rapprochement

with Hellenistic philosophy (Philo 1993; cf. Grant 1988). At the same time, Platonic education underwent a 'scholastic turn' in which, under the influence of the practices of other Graeco-Roman philosophical schools, direct instruction in the Socratic maieutic method gave way to the study of Platonic texts. Plato himself was revered in some circles as a semi-divine figure, and his writings approached as an authoritative scriptural source of ancient perennial wisdom.

> In the Graeco-Roman world, especially during the Hellenistic and Roman periods, what gives philosophical movements their cohesion and identity is less a disinterested common quest for the truth than a virtually religious commitment to the authority of a founder figure.
>
> (Kooten 2010: 7; quoting Sedley 1989)

Thus both the Platonic, Jewish and emergent Christian traditions appealed to authoritative texts as the primary source of knowledge of the ultimate order-of-things. This convergence of the philosophical and theological traditions around scriptural exegesis was reinforced by the tendency of the first Christians to identify Christianity as a philosophy rather than a religion. 'Religion' in the Roman world referred primarily to cultic practices and rituals that 'bind fast' (*religare*) the pious worshipper and God (the modern notion of religion as discrete faith system only emerged in the thirteenth century). Philosophy, on the other hand, was primarily concerned with the pursuit of knowledge of the ultimate order-of-things:

> To the casual pagan observer the activities of the average synagogue or church would look more like the activities of a [philosophical] school than anything else. Teaching or preaching, moral exhortation, and the exegesis of canonical texts are activities associated in the ancient world with philosophy, not religion.
>
> (Kooten 2010: 7; quoting Alexander 1994)

The ancient concept of '*paideia*', from which the modern term 'pedagogy' derives, referred to 'the formative task of transmitting a cultural heritage in order to school virtue and cultivate character', rather than to technical issues surrounding 'the principles and practices of teaching' (Walker and Wright 2004: 58; cf. Jaeger 1986). The primary aim of *paideia* was 'to shape persons in such a way that they are literally "in-formed" by virtue' (Kelsey 1992: 68). Such information had both a social and a personal dimension: *paideia* was 'to form in the souls of the young the virtue or arête they needed to function as responsible citizens' (ibid.: 65). Since the virtues were deemed to have a Transcendent source in God or the Platonic Forms, students must be given access to them, either through a Socratic pedagogy of *anamnesis*, or more commonly through a process of cultural transmission grounded in the study of authoritative texts. 'One essential feature of Greek *paideia* ... is that it not only contemplated the process of development in the human subject but also took into account the influence of the object of learning' (Jaeger 1961: 91). Contra Plato's denial of a place for Homer and the poets in his ideal republic, Hellenistic *paideia* tended to place them alongside the works of Plato at the centre of the curriculum, thereby establishing a humanistic education grounded in the arts and humanities. This classical notion of liberal education was predicated on the pursuit of truth and cultivation of truthful living *sub specie aeternitatis* via the transmission, reception and assimilation of authoritative scriptural knowledge pertaining to the place of humankind in the ultimate order-of-things.

The first Christians seized on classical *paideia's* notion of the essential unity of the pursuit of knowledge of the ultimate order-of-things and personal and collective spiritual formation. In 'calling Christianity the *paideia* of Christ' they sought 'to make Christianity appear to be a continuation of the classical Greek *Paideia*', whilst at the same time implying 'that the classical *paideia* is being superseded by making Christ the centre of a new culture' (ibid.: 12). The aim of classical *paideia*, to bring self and society into a harmonious and knowledgeable relationship with the ultimate order-of-things, remained firmly in place. However, there were fundamental changes in the curriculum and in pedagogy: the new curriculum replaced the Platonic Forms with the Trinitarian God as the primary object of knowledge, and substituted the works of the ancient philosophers and poets with Christian scripture; the new pedagogy replaced maieutic learning grounded in the recollection of a spark of divinity latent in the soul with a form of learning committed to the transmission and assimilation of the Christian Gospel.

Despite their considerable differences, there was a basic commonality between Jewish, Platonic and Christian approaches to education. All three affirmed that knowledge of the reality of the ultimate order-of-things constitutes the necessary basis for the educational task of personal and social formation, and recognised that knowledge of ultimate reality (ontological realism) was not a given, but rather something that must be struggled for through the pursuit of wisdom (judgemental rationality) in the face of human ignorance and sin (epistemic relativity). Despite the presence of a range of incommensurable worldviews, each with their own distinctive ontological commitments and epistemic procedures, pre-modern Western education historically tended to embrace a set of common presuppositions: namely – in the terminology of contemporary critical realism – ontological realism, epistemic relativity and judgemental rationality. The twin tasks of promoting personal flourishing and social wellbeing were indistinguishable from the task of establishing harmonious knowledge-relationships with the ultimate, and intrinsically value-laden, order-of-things. Since the values on which the good life depends were assumed to enjoy realistic ontological status independent of human cognition, an education that left pupils to construct their own value systems or 'muddle through' pragmatically inevitably fell short of what is actually required, namely an education grounded in, and driven by, the realistic pursuit of truth and truthful living.

The challenge of the Enlightenment

How did the Enlightenment-generated dislocation of fact from value impact on education? It is important to understand the nature of this dislocation and avoid reading it over-simplistically as merely a denial of the ontological status of values. To speak of the 'dislocation of fact from value' is to recognise a state of affairs in which the moral, aesthetic and spiritual values on which the good life depends are not ontologically grounded in, or generated by, either the realm of nature or in some greater Transcendent reality, but are rather personal or social constructs. This does not deny such values an ontological status: on the contrary, since they function as causal mechanisms that impact directly and unavoidably, for good or for ill, on the quality of our lives, they are nothing less than 'real'. However, it does mean that, given the absence of any Transcendent reality and the reduction of the natural world to a value-free causal network, there can be no legitimate appeal to any source of value beyond that provided by personal experience and social convention, consensus or covenant. We have already noted Doug Porpora's concerns regarding the negative impact of the failure to locate ourselves meaningfully in the cosmos on our sense of self. Though the occlusion of God and devalualisation of nature has certainly functioned to undermine our sense of possessing a meaningful place in reality as a whole, this need not be the case: even if we are the products of a godless and purposeless evolutionary process, we are still, presumably, capable of locating ourselves critically in the metaphysical space of a teleologically vacuous universe, and of seeking to live the good life whilst fully aware of the constraints and possibilities afforded to us by a Transcendence-devoid and value-free cosmos.

The occlusion of any divine or natural teleology and subsequent affirmation of values as human constructs has profound educational implications. In particular, it immediately rules out any notion of an education grounded in the pursuit of a higher Transcendent or naturalistic truth capable of providing an ontological basis for the good life. This leaves education with the options of either inducting pupils into a particular social construction, consensus or contract with regard to values, or empowering pupils to pursue their own subjective visions of the good life. Of the two educational philosophers who dominated the initial stages of Enlightenment, John Locke took the former route of seeking to induct pupils into an established set of social norms, whilst Jean-Jacques Rousseau followed the latter path of seeking to empower individual pupils to follow their own personal visions of the good life. The danger of overstating the case here must be acknowledged: both philosophers recognised that moral and aesthetic values possess a divine source and are visibly present in the natural order. Nevertheless, their tendency to focus attention on personal experience and social convention, and in doing so pay mere lip-service to the realms of Transcendence and nature, is a clear indication of the emergent intrusion of the fact–value divide into educational thought.

(1) *John Locke.* The rejection of Christian *paideia* evident in John Locke's philosophy of education is grounded in the Enlightenment's epistemic turn, in

which the authority of scripture and ecclesiastical tradition gave way to the authority of autonomous reason. Knowledge for Locke is the product, not of the reception and assimilation of the received wisdom of tradition, but of the rational mind's close observation, systematic description and critical analysis of raw empirical sense data. What his colleague Isaac Newton was achieving in relation to the natural world, Locke sought to achieve in relation to the mind. Sense experience impacts on our minds and forms simple ideas, from which the mind is able, through a process of generalisation and abstraction, to generate complex ideas and thereby establish universally valid knowledge.

Locke's account of human flourishing focuses on human fears and aspirations rather than obedience to God's will. The good life consists of seeking happiness and striving to avoid suffering: 'Things then are Good or Evil, only in reference to Pleasure or Pain' (Locke 1975: 229). However, attempts to pursue happiness can result in an increase in suffering. This is generally the result *either* of poor judgement *or* of an inability to control the passions. Consequently, the moral person requires *both* a rational understanding of the nature of moral obligation *and* the possession of a virtuous disposition. With regard to the former, Locke sought to look beyond both the simple ideas of pleasure and pain, and the complex ideas of good and evil, and identify the universal principles, or natural laws, on which human conduct should be based. With regard to the latter, he developed an educational philosophy predicated on the cultivation of moral character.

Though Locke claims that natural law is open in principle to rational demonstration, and offers a brief sketch of how this might be achieved, he does not develop any detailed account of the source of our moral obligations. His brief sketch begins by positing knowledge of the existence of God derived from rational argument: since God is the creator on whom we depend for our existence, he possesses rightful authority over us; since God is benevolent and desires our happiness, we are under an obligation to do his will; since obedience to God's benevolent will is the ultimate ground of our happiness, it is irrational not to seek to obey his commands (ibid.: 351ff.). However, this skeletal chain of argument does not offer any additional substance to Locke's somewhat underdetermined understanding of the nature of happiness, nor does it identify any specific moral obligations that human beings might be duty bound to follow. His reference to divine commands implies an appeal to divine revelation and Christian scripture; however, though he views Jesus as a great moral teacher, he also subscribes to the deistic view that the nature of goodness can be discerned independently through rational reflection. At best his attempt to provide natural law with a theological grounding did little more than offer a pre-established set of moral ideals the veneer of religious legitimation. Ultimately, Locke takes the established norms of bourgeois society as given, and offers a somewhat halfhearted attempt to relate them to the order of nature and will of God. Not surprisingly, given the paucity of Locke's argument, it was Bentham's secularised account of natural law, grounded in the notion of humanity as the creator of its own values, which came to dominate the modern natural law tradition.

Locke recognised that moral obligations involve civic responsibilities. In their natural state individuals live self-sufficient lives; however, in the social realm individual rights and duties need to be pooled and transferred to communal agencies responsible for overseeing social justice for the benefit of all. The need for a higher authority to oversee social order cannot be based on the historical claims of hereditary monarchs to possess a divine right to rule. Rather governments must operate with the consent of their citizens, and are mandated to do so via civil contracts. Governments have a responsibility to oversee the flourishing of their citizens, and as such are accountable to them. In plural societies, in which there is no common understanding of human flourishing, governments have an obligation to maximise the freedom of individuals to pursue their own distinctive visions of the good life. The right of individuals to hold diverse beliefs and pursue dissimilar visions of the good life carries with it a duty of toleration. Such toleration has its limits, since governments must not tolerate individuals whose understanding of the good life constitutes a direct threat to the security and well-being of the commonwealth. Regardless of which particular account of the good life individuals might choose to pursue, the realisation of their ambitions requires the prudent application of the liberal principles of reason, freedom and tolerance. This in turn requires an education designed to cultivate character and engender virtue.

Locke's belief in the power of enlightened reason generated a positive understanding of the effectiveness of education: 'of all the Men we meet with, Nine Parts of Ten are what they are, Good or Evil, useful or not, by their Education' (Locke 2000: 83). He had no time for the medieval doctrine of original sin, or the Christian belief that humankind is incapable of engineering its own salvation apart from divine grace, and subscribed instead to the Enlightenment's 'doctrine of man's original innocence', which 'pervasively testified to the efficacy of education in man's renewal' (Gay 1973b: 511). His *Thoughts Concerning Education*, first published in 1693, consists of a series of occasional pieces offering advice to his friend Edward Clarke on the upbringing of his son (Locke 2000). Practical in nature, they present 'not so much a generalized pedagogical credo as a custom built body of theory designed to suit the particular educational requirements of the gentleman's son' (Meyer 1975: 127). Geoffrey Bantock detects a 'tension between his humanistic views of conduct and manners and his new "scientific" conception of understanding and utility' (Bantock 1980: 245f.). Locke drew the substance of his vision of an educated citizen schooled in virtue mainly from the tradition of Renaissance humanism; however, once filtered through his empiricist philosophy, it generally took on a practical and pragmatic hue alien to Renaissance pedagogy. Renaissance educators followed the tradition of *paideia* in seeking to cultivate virtue by inducting students into the classical literary canon and thereby providing them with an understanding of their place within the ultimate order-of-things. Locke sidestepped the task of imparting such knowledge and attended instead to the task of cultivating virtuous character *in abstracto*. In effect he dislocated pursuit of knowledge of the 'facts' of the ultimate order-of-things from the cultivation of the values of a virtuous disposition.

Locke's vision of education was grounded in a distinctive, if somewhat limited and parochial, vision of the good life: 'A Sound Mind in a Sound Body, is a short, but full Description of a Happy State in this World' (Locke 2000: 83). The educated gentleman must be taught 'to have the Knowledge of a Man of Business, a Carriage suitable to his Rank, and to be Eminent and Useful in his Country according to his Station' (ibid.: 156). He will display a mixture of reason and self-discipline in exercising the virtues of modesty, politeness, prudence, civility and generosity: 'the Principle of all Vertue and Excellency lies in a power of denying ourselves the satisfaction of our own Desires, where Reason does not authorize them' (ibid.: 107). Locke viewed the mind as a *tabula rasa* devoid of innate knowledge, waiting to be filled by empirical experiences and trained to act on them in useful ways. It is the tutor's responsibility to ensure that good habits are instilled before bad habits become ingrained. Virtue 'is to be got and improved by Custom, made easy and familiar by an *early* Practice' (ibid.: 107). The child's mind is best 'made obedient to Discipline, and pliant to Reason' when it is 'most tender, most easy to be bowed'; though the paternalistic influence of the tutor is be progressively relaxed as self-mastery is gradually achieved (ibid.: 103).

Locke pays relatively little attention to the content of the curriculum. Teaching must focus on the cultivation of virtuous character capable of reasoned and disciplined self-improvement rather than the acquisition of knowledge: 'I do not propose it as a variety and stock of knowledge, but a variety and freedom of thinking; as an increase in the powers and activity of the mind, not as an enlargement of its possessions' (Locke 1922: 216). In contemporary parlance, he replaced a subject-centred curriculum with a skills-based pedagogy. Specific subjects – geography, history, law, religion, philosophy, etc. – are subservient to the acquisition of the basic skills of reading, writing and grammar, and the advanced skills necessary for the mastery of a profession and enrichment of recreational activities (dancing, fencing, travel, etc.). Locke thus championed a shift from a scholastic-humanistic to a pragmatic-utilitarian education: it is better to teach a pupil

> to judge right of Men, and manage his Affairs wisely with them, than to speak Greek and Latin, or argue in Mood and Figure; or have his Head fill'd with the abstruse Speculations of Natural Philosophy, and Metaphysicks.
>
> (Locke 2000: 155)

Throughout the *Thoughts* Locke's given understanding of our place in the ultimate order-of-things functions normatively: the educational task is not to better understand Locke's worldview, nor to question its veracity and consider viable alternatives, but rather to equip pupils to function efficiently within it.

(2) *Jean-Jacques Rousseau.* Locke's tendency to equate morality with social convention, and somewhat indifferent attempt to provide it with any naturalistic or theological warrant, raises the question of its ontological status. This was to become increasingly problematic in a society not yet willing to identify values as

human creations, yet increasingly hesitant about appealing to traditional theological accounts of their origins. Bantock places Rousseau at the forefront of reactive romantic attempts to recover a moral ontology by attempting to ground value in the realm of human nature, and suggests that in doing so he faced a fundamental dilemma:

> Neutralize the universe, demythologize nature's laws so that they function purposelessly (in human terms) driven by their own morally neutral internal momentum, and it is only possible for him to reintroduce the inescapable moral dimension in the education of human beings by literally making a virtue of necessity.
>
> (Bantock 1980: 274)

Rousseau discovered this necessity in the givenness of our natural state, the determinate structures of our developing physical and mental constitution, over which we have little control.

Despite the emerging tendency of natural science to devalue nature, deists continued to insist that the cosmos was designed and created by a higher power who imbibed the natural world with value. Whilst Hume's sceptical empiricism sought to undermine rational attempts to demonstrate the divine origins and intrinsic value of the universe, Rousseau spearheaded the romantic attempt to uphold this claim by appealing not to reason but to intuitive sensibility. He viewed the divinely ordained natural realm as self-evidently ordered, harmonious and value-laden: 'God makes all things good' (Rousseau 1986: 5). His deistic God was the supreme creator and preserver of nature, and the universal principle underlying the physical, moral and aesthetic order inherent in the cosmos. He had little time for the self-revealing personal God of the Judaeo-Christian tradition, and subscribed instead to a natural theology that inferred the existence of a deity from the observation of nature. Such inference departed from traditional rationalist demonstrations of the existence of God by virtue of its appeal to romantic intuition. Though spiritual sensibility generated in Rousseau a 'feeling of gratitude and thankfulness to the author of my species', he tended toward theological agnosticism and retained a deep suspicion of the doctrinal claims of institutional religion: 'In a word: the more I strive to envisage his infinite essence the less so I comprehend it; but it is, and that is enough for me; the less I understand, the more I adore' (ibid.: 240, 249).

Ultimately Rousseau's God played only a functional role in his ontology: though it was important that the cosmos had a higher source and purpose, knowledge of human nature provided a sufficient foundation for the good life. Human beings existing in the state of nature are essentially good: 'the first impulses of nature are always right; there is no original sin in the human heart' (ibid.: 56). Since spiritual sensibility has priority over rational reflection, good acts undertaken in our natural state are driven by a pre-linguistic and pre-rational *pitié* or sentiment through which we distinguish pleasure from pain and happiness from suffering. Human beings are by nature free and self-sufficient; however, as communal creatures they find themselves embroiled in unnatural power-structures generated by society, which make them dependent, competitive and susceptible to manipulation. Society curtails freedom and pollutes natural goodness. Though it is true that 'God makes all things good', it is equally true that 'man meddles with them and they become evil' (ibid.: 5). Once corrupted by this social 'fall', we cannot simply exempt ourselves from society and return to our original state of primal innocence; rather, we must learn to exercise natural reason in our moral judgements, and thereby transform ourselves and the social structures that surround us. If 'all of Rousseau's works concentrate upon a single theme, the utopian desire to reconstruct society by means of a new theory of natural order', then his educational writings are concerned to oversee the preservation and enhancement of natural goodness (Bowen 1981: 186).

For Rousseau education is primarily *moral* education: 'that is, education of a person's active psychology: his fundamental needs, the habitual direction of his imagination and sentiments, his ability to reason and to act from reason' (Rorty 1998: 238). This was not to be achieved by the pursuit of knowledge predicated on the transmission of a received intellectual heritage. Here Rousseau follows Locke in accepting Descartes' vision of the isolated and dislocated self employing a hermeneutic of suspicion to challenge any intellectual authority other than that of the self's own cognitive faculties. However, in rejecting Locke's pragmatic appeal to social convention he produces a more radical account of the Cartesian legacy. If education cannot appeal to the authority of the intellectual heritage of the past, neither can it appeal to the authority of present social norms; instead, the self must learn to rely on his own resources. Though Rousseau follows through the logic of the Cartesian *cogito* with greater consistence than Locke, he does so by recasting it within a romantic framework: *cogito ergo sum* becomes *sentio ergo sum* – sentiment replaces reason as the cardinal epistemic and pedagogic principle. Rather than engage with unresolved philosophical debates we should learn to trust our own intuitive 'inner light'.

Bantock suggests that Rousseau's appeal to the natural state of humanity is largely devoid of any substantial content:

> In effect, 'natural goodness' constitutes simply a rallying point for disengagement from the traditional culture thought necessary by the Enlightenment ... a reason for abstraction from current social pressures.
>
> (Bantock 1980: 282)

Whatever might be usefully learned need not come from outside, since it is already latent within the natural grasp of the learner; hence Rousseau's startling confession 'I hate books', which he justifies on the ground that they 'only teach one to talk about things we know nothing about' (Rousseau 1986: 147). Education consists 'not in teaching virtue or truth, but in preserving the heart from vice and the spirit of error' (ibid.: 57). Rousseau espouses a negative education in which the freedom of pupils is preserved by protecting them from all external forces, and avoiding all forms of instruction and direct teaching. John Darling identifies three fundamental principles in Rousseau's account of pedagogy: the tutor must provide the pupil with unlimited scope for play; stimuli appropriate to their natural being; and encouragement to think things through for themselves and draw conclusions according to their natural reason (Darling 1985). Such pedagogy will equip pupils to fulfil their innate potential, act as autonomous agents, find their proper place in the natural order, and face the challenge of living in a social world urgently in need of reconstruction. In the early years of childhood the natural order, operating under the law of natural necessity, will teach the child to distinguish between pleasure and pain, differentiate between appropriate and inappropriate desires, and discriminate between self-love and selfishness. The cultivation of natural habits, operating in harmony with nature, will provide the foundation for the moral responsibilities of adult life; a life guided, not by the pre-reflective intuition of the child, but by the adult exercise of autonomous reason operating not rationalistically but in harmony with nature. The true freedom of the educated adult lies in their ability to live a life grounded in the autonomous exercise of natural reason rather than the hegemony of social convention.

Rousseau's educational philosophy paved the way for forms of progressive child-centred education that seek to maximise personal autonomy and view the power structures endemic in society in general, and educational institutions in particular, with deep suspicion. However, insofar as progressive education embraces a set of implicit ontological and epistemological assumptions that are rarely made explicit, it is particularly vulnerable to ideological reification. On this reading, progressive education consists of little more than a paternalistic and uncritical transmission of the romantic worldview of the counter-Enlightenment, in which the Cartesian self in its natural state constitutes the highest ontological object in the universe and hence the ultimate measure of all things. Despite his insistence on the freedom and autonomy of the child, Rousseau is at times remarkably candid about the authoritarian role of the tutor, and his task of inducting pupils into a specific, pre-established worldview:

> It is true I allow him a show of freedom, but he was never more completely under control, because he obeys of his own free will. So long as I could not get the mastery over his will, I retain control of his person; I never left him for a moment. Now I sometimes leave him to himself because I control him continually.
>
> (Rousseau 1986: 298)

Ultimately Rousseau's educational philosophy sets out to enable pupils to think and act as he does: 'what is fostered is an alternative culture stimulated by the indirect intervention of the tutor' (Bantock 1980: 274).

(3) *The pragmatic turn in education.* What light can the under-labouring tools of critical realism shed on the educational philosophies of Locke and Rousseau? Both affirm specific, though closely related, ontologies that identify the existence of a deistic God who creates an ordered cosmos and is the ultimate source

of all value. Though Locke pays lip-service to the possibility of divine revelation and appeals to the moral teachings of Jesus (albeit only after stripping them of any theological content), Rousseau is highly suspicious of all forms of institutional religion and theological dogma, and claims to find 'in natural religion the elements of all religion' (Rousseau 1986: 260). Ultimately both infer the divinely ordained values that ground their accounts of education from their observation of human nature and avoid substantial appeals to either natural theology or divine revelation. Locke and Rousseau both recognise that our observation of nature provides us with knowledge of pleasure and pain, from which more elaborate accounts of personal integrity and duplicity, social propriety and impropriety, and good and evil flow. For Locke appeal to the theological and natural ground of value tends to be purely functional: the urgent need to transform society obscures the need to demonstrate the validity of the values he advocates. Rousseau, on the other hand, retains a deep suspicion of social convention, which he views as unnatural and corrosive, and consequently stresses nature as the source of value. Negatively, both reject the medieval doctrine of original sin, together with the traditional Christian belief that humankind cannot engineer its own salvation apart from the grace of God. Positively, both insist that the flourishing of humanity is dependent on human effort, and affirm the potential efficacy of education in achieving this goal. The material content of their moral vision is remarkably similar, despite the fact that they approach the issue from radically different vantage points. Locke's starting point is society: whilst affirming human autonomy and linking it to the duty to act rationally, he stresses the urgent need to do so in a manner that is tolerant of a range of different opinions and belief systems. His liberal values of freedom, reason and tolerance provide a blueprint for the establishment of a network of harmonious relations reflective of the harmony intrinsic to the natural order. Rousseau's starting point is the individual: only by learning to act autonomously and responsibly in harmony with the natural order can individuals hope to contribute to the common good and oversee the restoration of a fragmented society.

Neither Locke nor Rousseau expresses any fundamental doubts regarding their ontological commitments. As children of the Enlightenment they embraced the Cartesian notion of the dislocated self, affirmed personal autonomy, insisted on the centrality of natural reason, and rejected all appeals to external authority. Having displaced God from the centre of reality, they view the good life in terms of harmonious living in the here-and-now, driven by pragmatic utility and devoid of any eschatological end or teleological goal. The only viable alternatives accessible to them were those provided by the theological heritage of the Abrahamic religions and the philosophical heritage of classical Greco-Roman culture. With regard to the former, their adoption of the Cartesian hermeneutic of suspicion ruled out any possibility of encountering revealed theological truth in sacred scripture or ecclesial authority. Institutional religion and religious dogma were treated as superstitious products of the Dark Ages preceding the dawning Enlightenment. With regard to the latter, they regarded the classical heritage as, up to a point, both 'useful' and 'beloved': not because classical antiquity had anything substantial to teach them, but because its 'spirit of criticism' – most visible in Lucretius' and Cicero's insistence of the triumph of reason over myth – mirrored the critical modes of thinking embraced by the Enlightenment (Gay 1973a: 31ff.). Consequently, epistemic relativity was confined to the internal structures of their ontological worldviews. Insofar as individuals failed to act rationally in accordance with nature (Rousseau), or failed to contribute to the stability and wellbeing of liberal society (Locke), they were deemed to fall short of, and function as discordant elements within, the idealised vision of a harmonious natural (Rousseau) or social (Locke) order.

As we have seen, neither Locke nor Rousseau had any interest in exposing pupils to the ontological presuppositions underlying their educational philosophies, or opening them up to the alternative ontologies provided by the Jewish, Christian and Islamic traditions. Consequently judgemental rationality could only be exercised within the constraints of their specific ontologies. This meant that there was little utility in exploring the non-negotiable givenness of the ontological norms within which their education systems operated. In Christian *paideia*, knowledge of the ultimate structures of reality, as revealed in the divine economy of salvation, was a necessary prerequisite for living a good life oriented towards a harmonious relationship with the Triune God. In the educational philosophies of Locke and Rousseau such knowledge was deemed unnecessary: one did not need explicit knowledge of either God or nature in order to live a good life in harmony with either individual moral dispositions or established cultural norms. For Rousseau 'the philosophical aspects of the physical universe as the ordered system of a divine Creator are far less important than the spontaneous response of human sensibility to its spiritual essence' (Grimsley 1973: 74). For both Locke and Rousseau the primary task of education was to form pupils' virtuous moral dispositions: they must learn to be effective participants within an established-yet-implicit moral order. For Locke this meant actively training pupils to replicate a set of social conventions, whilst for Rousseau this meant passively allowing pupils to be taught by nature to replicate the moral values inherent within the natural order-of-things. Both anticipated that eventually their pupils would come to accept, on rational grounds, their personal responsibility to internalise the moral norms into which they had been, either actively or passively, inducted.

The modern dislocation of fact from value has its roots in the Enlightenment, specifically in the emergence of foundational epistemologies that claimed access to objective knowledge of scientific 'facts' in the natural world, and consigned moral, aesthetic and spiritual 'values' to the status of subjective beliefs and opinions. Romanticism contributed to this divide by questioning the moral, aesthetic and spiritual utility of scientific fact, and giving priority to the expression of subjective values. Contrary to received opinion, this did not generate a non-realistic value system; rather, it constituted the transposition of values-realism from the realms of God and nature to the realms of personal intuition and cultural construction. The philosophies of Locke and Rousseau reflect the beginning of this process: both reduce God to the functional role of providing warrant for human values, and though Rousseau insists on grounding values in the natural order Locke is content to appeal to social convention. The educational implications of this shift also begin to emerge: if values are ultimately human constructs, and if as a consequence the ultimate meaning of human life is found only in the here-and-now and does not extend into eternity or have any Transcendent ground, then an education concerned with the pursuit of knowledge of our place in the ultimate order-of-things and/or with the structures and workings of nature, has little relevance to the task of moral education, since the good life is now predicated exclusively on human constructions, dispositions and actions. In such a situation, the pursuit of knowledge of our place within the ultimate order-of-things appears increasingly irrelevant to the pursuit of the good life, and as a result education comes to focus on the formation of moral character apart from the pursuit of truth and cultivation of truthful living *sub specie aeternitatis*. The educational philosophies of Locke and Rousseau reflect in embryonic form the modern pragmatic and utilitarian turn in education, in which the pursuit of truth is effectively dislocated from, and made subordinate to, the pursuit of truthful living predicated on humankind's self-constructed values.

Kant and modernity

Classical and Christian *paideia* assumed that the good life consisted in living in harmony with the ultimate order-of-things, and that consequently education must strive to enable the learner to locate themselves, not just in personal and social space, but also *sub specie aeternitatis* in metaphysical and/or Transcendent space. The demise of Christianity and devaluation of nature opened the door to a world from which God was excluded and in which nature was deemed morally neutral. This threw human beings back on their own personal and social resources: if moral, aesthetic and spiritual values are human constructs, then the good life must consist in living in harmony with oneself and with others-in-community. In such a situation neither theology nor natural science could offer guidance for moral education. The pursuit of truth was reduced to the attainment of the knowledge provided by the natural and social sciences, whilst the pursuit of truthful living was reduced to the pragmatic task of living well in harmony with oneself and with others-in-community. Thus the fact–value divide came to constitute the fundamental framework for post-Enlightenment education. The pursuit of knowledge for its own sake, achieved through the induction of pupils into a cultural and intellectual heritage, became an increasingly tenuous exercise. Increasingly those committed to the transmission of knowledge were called to justify their position at the bar of pragmatic utility.

The relevance and value of education was judged according to its personal and social utility. Progressive child-centred educators in the tradition of Rousseau appealed to the importance of maximising autonomy and producing self-aware and self-confident entrepreneurial citizens at ease with themselves and others. Traditionalist subject-centred educators tended to look to the good of society as a whole, and sought to transmit only that knowledge conducive to the cultivation of citizens capable of contributing to the common good. At its most ideal this meant producing tolerant and autonomous citizens through programmes of personal and social education; at its most pragmatic this meant providing forms of vocational and professional training, viewed either in terms of preparation for specific social and domestic roles (formerly Woodwork, Metalwork and Home Economics, latterly Information Technology), or the attainment of a set of generic transferable intellectual, social and personal skills.

Consequently, subject disciplines were increasingly called to account for the utility of their subjects: physics, chemistry and biology, for example, were able to represent themselves as offering the necessary groundwork for scientific careers, and had no need to argue that knowledge of the natural order was of intrinsic interest and value. Religious education, on the other hand, recognising that there was little value in claiming to be laying the groundwork for the careers of religious ministers, was forced to reinvent itself as a form of moral education. Increasingly the subject was justified through appeals to its ability to enhance moral understanding (by exploring generic moral issues addressed by different religious traditions), social cohesion (by increasing understanding across religious divides), and the core virtues of freedom and tolerance (by cultivating spiritual and moral sensibility). The perceived failure of traditional subject disciplines to adequately justify themselves against pragmatic and utilitarian criteria led, in places, to their replacement by new subject disciplines deemed to be more immediately relevant to the needs of pupils: media studies, information technology, etc. Thus the fact–value divide generated a split between the traditional academic pursuit of truth for its own sake, and emergent forms of education oriented towards personal development and the preparation of future citizens. If this division is implicit in the educational philosophies of Locke and Rousseau, it becomes explicit in the educational philosophy of Immanuel Kant and its impact on the educational aims and curricular design of the new modern University of Berlin.

(1) *The Conflict of the Faculties.* First published in 1789, Kant's *Conflict of the Faculties* was occasioned by the replacement of the liberal regime of Friedrich the Great by the reactionary policies of his successor Friedrich Wilhelm II (Kant 1992). As a theological conservative Wilhelm II took exception to Kant's reductive account of Christianity as an ethical system stripped of theological dogma, and sought to censor his views by restricting lecturing on his philosophy of religion in the universities. Kant, as a child of the Enlightenment, was committed to the exercise of a universal reason grounded in the exercise of autonomous rational judgement and capable of transcending all cultural contexts and eclipsing all external authorities. The politically driven attempt to subject Kant's religious philosophy to the authority of Christian scripture and dogma was a direct affront to his understanding of universal reason. Kant's response was to develop an educational philosophy grounded in the twin canons of universal reason and academic freedom (Howard 2006: 125). This led him to remove the task of pursuing truth and knowledge from the faculties of theology, medicine and law, and place it wholly in the hands of the faculty of philosophy. *The Conflict of the Faculties* offered

an unabashed defence of the philosophical faculty as the bearer of Enlightenment rationality and a vindication of its right to freedom of expression, the right to have its members' rational arguments answered by rational arguments rather than by coercion or appeals to religious authority.

(ibid.: 125)

Having identified the 'lower' faculty of philosophy 'as an autonomous, self-confident dispenser of liberal, rational enquiry within the university', he conceded to the state political control over the 'higher' faculties of theology, medicine and law (ibid.: 125). In doing so he reasoned that the state had a legitimate pragmatic and utilitarian interest in the wellbeing of society, and recognised that the primary interest of the three higher faculties lay in the professional training of priests, doctors and lawyers. If graduates of the philosophy faculty were defenders of reason, then graduates of the higher faculties were legitimate 'tools of the government' whose primary task was to maintain social order: 'the lawyer and judge established security for persons and property, the doctor attended to the health of the body, and the clergy provided spiritual comfort in this world and guidance towards the world to come' (ibid.: 126). The faculty of philosophy had no utilitarian or pragmatic role, but rather was to operate as 'a free spirit whose only task was to tend the flame of rationality by looking after "the interests of science"' (ibid.: 126). Because philosophy was grounded in autonomous reason it could attend to and critique all knowledge claims, including those embraced by the three higher faculties. Rather than enjoying an ivory tower existence, 'the philosophy faculty should perform a watchdog function over the other faculties, criticizing and thus improving them when they failed to comply with the universal canons of rationality' (ibid.: 126). Thus the state, provided it learnt to look beyond its immediate short-term interests, could find in the philosophy faculty a blueprint for a progressive society grounded in science, reason and freedom (ibid.: 127). Kant thus 'dangled before the government a powerful new carrot of legitimation', rooted in autonomous reason rather than authoritarian force (ibid.: 128).

The carrot was simply that science itself offered a promising new 'epic', not the old 'biblical narrative' or 'story of salvation' (*historia sacra* or *Heilsgeschichte*), but a new Enlightenment story of overcoming the obscurantist past through rationale critique and the expansion of knowledge.

(ibid.: 128)

Unlike the old Christian epic, which had provided an ontological account of the ultimate order-of-things, the new Enlightenment epic offered an epistemic account of the criteria through which an alternative ontology might be constructed. In the interim, the urgent task of organising and safeguarding society could not be avoided. Thus the conflict between the lower and higher faculties reflected a tension between fact and value, pure and practical reason, the disinterested pursuit of knowledge and the political interests of the state.

(2) *The University of Berlin.* Founded in 1810 by the academic and statesman Wilhelm von Humboldt, the University of Berlin quickly assumed the status of *the* archetypal modern university, despite having important precursors such as Halle, Gottingen and Erlangen. Humboldt's original vision was rooted in Kant's educational philosophy, and influenced both by the reformist philosopher Johann Gottlieb Fichte, who went on to become the first Vice Chancellor of the University, and by the theologian Friedrich Schleiermacher, who was responsible for drawing up the foundation documents. Berlin was to be a modern progressive research university, holding as its defining goal 'rigorous "scientific" research or *Wissenschaft*' (Kelsey 1992: 78). It was to be driven by the intellectual values of ordered and disciplined study, with reason as the final arbiter. This required the critical testing of all alleged sources of truth for their coherence, clarity and logical validity, as well as their empirical fit to reality in accordance with the model provided by Newtonian physics. Such inquiry must be free from all external authority, and only its established results could legitimately claim the status of knowledge.

Despite the insistence on academic freedom, there was an inevitable political compromise with the state, which retained responsibility for both university funding and academic appointments. The idealistic expectation was for a positive reciprocal relationship between the pure reason driving disinterested academic research and the practical reason driving the pragmatic and political interest of the state: 'if the state provided the university with space for independent inquiry, the students educated that way would provide the state with enlightened servants through whom the state itself would become progressively enlightened' (ibid.: 82). Humboldt insisted on the essential unity of research and teaching, and had little time for the notion of a non-teaching research institution. If the task of the secondary school Gymnasium was to transmit established knowledge and the principles on which it was grounded to the next generation, then the research university was to operate at the epistemic cutting edge: committed both to research programmes designed to discover new knowledge and its underlying principles, and to teaching programmes designed to transmit such knowledge and principles to the intellectual elite of the next generation. The activities of research and teaching were closely related, with teachers and students working together as co-partners in the ongoing pursuit of truth. This marked a further departure from classical *paideia*. In the new master–apprentice relationship in which teachers and students 'cooperate in the promotion of knowledge', the 'teacher does not exist *for* the student, as was the case in *paideia*'; instead, 'the teacher needs the student to achieve the goal of research' (ibid.: 80).

Wissenschaft was not limited to the natural sciences, but rather included all spheres of knowledge opened to ordered and disciplined research, including both the arts and the social, psychological, and life sciences. Consequently, the University of Berlin sought to offer a generic all-round humanistic education prior to more specific professional training. In effect the arts and sciences functioned as a version of Kant's 'lower' faculty of philosophy, preparing the way for later professionally oriented vocational study in the faculties of law, medicine and theology. Study in the lower faculties of arts and sciences eschewed a narrow professionally oriented curriculum in favour of a broad humanistic education oriented toward the transformation of character. However, the formation of character was no longer *ontologically* grounded in a Christian or classical account of the good life predicated on a clear understanding of humankind's place in the ultimate order-of-things. Instead, it was *epistemically* grounded in the Enlightenment's ideal of rational autonomy: 'To have one's character "transformed" is to have one's rational capacities brought out and honed through learning how to be an expert researcher', a process that required recognition of 'reason's independence from all authority and its innate responsibility critically to scrutinize any claim to authority' (ibid.: 81). What ultimately mattered was not the *ontological substance* of the knowledge discovered and transmitted, but rather the *epistemic process* through which knowledge was sought and pursued. Where classical *paideia* understood personal formation ontologically, in terms of a developing harmony between the self and the ultimate order-of-things, the new education understood personal formation epistemically, in terms of the progressive realisation of rational autonomy and self-determination. True, the humanistic education espoused by the University of Berlin opened up the possibility of making the wisdom of the past available to students through the study of ancient texts such as the Christian Bible and the works of Plato. However, where classical *paideia* recognised the possibility of encountering transformative truth, knowledge and moral insight in such texts, in the new educational order they were subject to historical-critical methods of investigation, designed to answer questions about their historical origins, cultural location and literary form, that effectively forced any meaning inherent in such texts into the procrustean straitjacket of the researchers' and students' prior rationalistic expectations.

(3) *Theology in the University of Berlin.* Schleiermacher's proposal that the University of Berlin include a Protestant Faculty of Theology faced a fundamental problem: Christian theology was dependent on the twin authority of the Bible and Christian dogma, but in a modern research university such authority must be subject to critical testing according to the canons of universal reason. It was by no means clear that theological study could remain a viable academic option once the Bible and dogma lost the status as normative sources of truth and became instead objects of critical scrutiny. Schleiermacher inherited a fourfold theological curriculum: *biblical exegesis* identified the core truths of Christianity, *dogmatic theology* organised these truths into a coherent system, *historical theology* investigated the historical development of biblical exegesis and dogmatic theology, and *practical theology* sought to apply the propositional truths of Christian dogma to Christian life and practice. Once the Bible was subject to critical historical scrutiny and read not as a source of divine revelation but as an all-too-human cultural product, then the entire theological edifice threatened to collapse in on itself. Schleiermacher sought to resolve this dilemma by removing theology from the 'lower' faculties of the arts and sciences committed to the unrestricted and dispassionate pursuit of truth, and relocating it, alongside law and medicine, in the higher faculties concerned with the professional training of the future

leaders of society (Schleiermacher 1966, 1991; cf. Howard 2006: 197ff.; Kelsey 1992: 86ff.). Just as the university exists for the good of the state, so theology enjoys a place in the university insofar as it contributes to the wellbeing of society. The needs of the state could be served either indirectly through the autonomous pursuit of truth, or directly through professional training and vocational formation.

According to Schleiermacher theology is not a pure science engaged in the pursuit of universal truth, but rather a positive science grounded in the local cultural practices of the Church. Consequently, the theological curriculum is not grounded in universal truths drawn from the Bible, but is instead 'unified by virtue of its goal to train professional church leadership for their indispensable social roles' (Kelsey 1992: 88). As such, its object of investigation is not the ontological reality of God, but the empirically observable realities of the historical church and the spiritual experiences of Christians. This led Schleiermacher to posit a new threefold structure for the theological curriculum. *Historical theology* was to generate a rational and ordered account of the historical phenomenon of the Christian faith, including its scriptures and creeds, in accordance with the methods of rational historical criticism. *Philosophical theology* was to address the question of the value of Christianity, not by assessing the truth of theological propositions regarding the ontological reality of God, but by addressing the correlation between Christian spiritual experience and 'the structure and dynamics of human consciousness' (ibid.: 89). *Practical theology* was to be concerned directly with the professional training of Christian ministers, grounded in a normative body of theological knowledge derived from an understanding of the historical development of Christianity and of the distinctive nature of Christian spiritual consciousness. This curricular shift, which effectively replaced the authority of the Bible with the authority of rational accounts of the historical, cultural and psychological phenomena of Christianity, enabled Schleiermacher to establish 'the hegemony of critical, orderly, disciplined historical research in theological schools as the model of rationality and excellence in schooling' (ibid.).

Knowledge, identity and utility

(1) *Pedagogic fragmentation.* The curriculum of the University of Berlin came to embody a pedagogic division between pure and practical knowledge: between the transmission of universally valid objective knowledge, and the transmission of knowledge relative to particular cultural contexts and thereby tainted, whether to a greater or lesser extent, by human subjectivity. The long-term task of the lower faculties was to find ways of recasting the practical-relative knowledge purveyed by the higher faculties into a pure universal form. In the interim, the immediate pragmatic needs and utilitarian concerns of society dictated that the higher faculties should continue to work as best they could with the practical knowledge available to them. This strategy, predicated on an epistemic division between the realms of fact and value, generated a further pedagogic division

between the transmission of (universal and/or pragmatic) knowledge and the formation of character. If the natural sciences could account for the ultimate order-of-things in value-neutral terms, from which the realms of moral, aesthetic and spiritual value were necessarily disassociated, then education could no longer be concerned to bring students into a harmonious moral, aesthetic and spiritual relationship with ultimate reality. In the light of this twofold division, the unity of the pursuit of truth and cultivation of truthful living, so central to classical *paideia*, effectively disintegrated. Consequently, in the lower faculties education for personal formation took on the lesser task of equipping students for the pursuit of knowledge by providing them with the cognitive skills required of rationally autonomous agents. In the higher faculties education for the formation of lawyers, doctors and religious ministers was faced with the need to balance the specific transmission of professional knowledge and skills with the general cultivation of virtuous character. As the role of the higher faculties became ever more pragmatic and utilitarian in outlook, so the increasingly explicit requirements of professional training began to take precedence over the increasingly implicit concern to cultivate character. This resulted in a further narrowing of classical *paideia*'s holistic understanding of personal formation: the dislocation of personal formation from the pursuit of truth gave way to a further dislocation between professional training and personal formation.

This emergent educational perspective was grounded in a shift from ontology to epistemology: the task was not to transmit knowledge of reality but to equip students with the intellectual, vocational and personal skills necessary to live the good life effectively. However, this epistemic turn carried with it a set of implicit ontological assumptions. The belief that society was moving progressively from the dark ages of religious superstition and metaphysical speculation into a golden age of enlightened reason was predicated on the ontological assumption that humankind constitutes the highest ontological reality in the cosmos. This in turn generated the belief that education is able to produce rationally autonomous citizens capable of engineering their own salvation. 'To believe in the importance of education was to believe, at least implicitly, in its power' (Gay 1973b: 511). There was no room for the Christian understanding of the ontological fallenness of human nature: 'The myth of original sin, which the philosophes thought they had exploded, made much of man's incapacity to change fundamentally through his own efforts: education could not do the work of grace' (ibid.: 511).

> Even the most optimistic Christian was not free to assert that education, no matter how thoroughgoing, could ever erase the effects of Adam's fall ... the philosophes' doctrine of man's original innocence, though it did not necessarily imply, persuasively testified to the efficacy of education in man's renewal.
>
> (ibid.: 511)

Ultimately the fundamental problem facing the educational vision emerging from the University of Berlin was the poverty of the project of rational autonomy itself.

The objective knowledge generated by disinterested reason proved unable to provide an adequate account of the moral, aesthetic and spiritual values on which personal and social flourishing depends. Increasingly romanticism, with its commitment to self-authenticating moral, aesthetic and spiritual experience, plugged the gap left by rationalist accounts of the human condition. The romantic tradition of *Bildungsroman*, which narrated stories of the moral and spiritual development of the romantic hero through the medium of poetry and fiction, provided more powerful models of personal formation, more akin to the ideals of *paideia*, than accounts provided by rationalistic philosophy. This, however, only served to exacerbate the divide between fact and value, sense and sensibility, reason and faith.

> By limiting scientific knowledge to what is observable and phenomenally determinate, Kant severed the connection between science and faith, depriving faith of any objective or ontological reference and emptying it of any real cognitive content.
>
> (Torrance 1980: 27)

The affirmation of personal autonomy and the subjectivity of values opened the door to a potential clash of individual interests that threatened to undermine the stability of the state. Peter Gay suggests that this presented educationalists seeking to fuse personal autonomy and social reform with a 'dilemma of heroic proportions' (Gay 1973b: 497). 'The realities tore this alliance apart: with the overpowering presence of the illiterate masses and the absence of the habit of autonomy, freedom and reform were often incompatible' (ibid.: 497). The dilemma was increasingly resolved by giving social reform precedence over personal freedom.

> The road to the realisation of the philosophes' political programme thus led through the devious and embarrassing detours of repression and manipulation that were a denial and mockery of the world they hoped to bring into being: the very methods used to distribute the fruits of enlightenment seemed to be calculated to frustrate the Enlightenment itself.
>
> (ibid.: 497)

In effect, political control over the higher faculties was extended to embrace the lower faculties as well. Given the burden of practical demands placed on the state, and in the absence of a genuinely rational bureaucratic and political apparatus, the aspiration for a creative synergy between disinterested reason and political interest proved little more than a form of misplaced 'romantic heroism' (Kelsey 1992: 82; quoting Fallon 1980: 36). As government progressively asserted 'politically inspired direct state influence, especially in regard to opinion and policy' on the university, so it became an increasingly conservative and reactionary institution (Kelsey 1992: 82). According to Karl Barth, the widespread support amongst German intellectuals for Kaiser Wilhelm's war policy in

1914, including many eminent liberal theologians such as Adolf von Harnack, revealed a political subservience and academic sterility that underlined both the failure of the Enlightenment's project of universal reason, and the sterility of theological attempts to forge an alliance between Christianity and the culture of modernity (Busch 1976: 81). His critique was to prove prophetic as, two decades later, more than 20,000 books written by so-called 'degenerates' were removed from the University of Berlin's library by the Nazi regime.

The realm of value, once made dependent on romantic sensibility and stripped of any reflective sense, lost any objective ontological anchor and became a free-floating subjective domain prey to manipulation by totalitarian forces and ideologies. Once emancipated from any external constraint, the subjective self's pursuit of epistemic certainty and personal security 'turned brutish and competitive, and a false individualism soon began to inhabit the descendants of the monadic Cartesian ego' (Levin 1988: 3f.). Not surprisingly, the isolated individual in search of security tended to seek refuge in the collective. At the same time reason, once dislocated from any viable value system, 'turned totally instrumental, a function solely of power (ibid.: 4). This heady mixture of subjective values, a shared desire for security, and instrumental reason proved fertile ground for totalitarianism: in the attempt to recover an idealised past or engineer a utopian future, values were imposed through the manipulation of the masses, aided by the technological products of scientific investigation.

Locke's original liberal vision presented the twin values of freedom and tolerance as the basis of an interim ethic, operating 'independently of any wider comprehensive religious or philosophical doctrine', designed to establish the social conditions necessary for an informed pursuit of truth in a context of ontological ambiguity and epistemic diversity (Rawls 1993: 32; cf. Wright 2007: 29ff.). However, as a result of the urgent need to secure a stable society, Locke's interim values came to be seen as ends in themselves, rather than as the means to a greater end. Consequently freedom ceased to function as a pragmatically useful basis for the pursuit of truth and became instead the core ontological marker of the modern and post-modern self. Whereas Locke's political liberalism approached freedom as an epistemic tool, comprehensive liberalism identified freedom as the ontological essence of humanity: human beings are essentially self-determining creatures.

The post-modern response to the totalitarian dilemma was to abandon the pursuit of truth and any concern for epistemic certainty. Once emancipated from the fear of descending into the chaotic dream world imagined by Descartes, individuals were free to construct their own imaginary identities and utopias at will, unconstrained by any external factor other than the pragmatic need to tolerate the freedom of others to do likewise. This post-modern turn legitimated the abandonment of the pursuit of truth and cultivation of a rationally ordered society as educational ideals (Wright 2004: 141ff.). Education was no longer seen 'as the vehicle by which modernity's "grand narratives", the Enlightenment ideals of critical reason, individual freedom, progress and benevolent change, are substantiated and realised' (Usher and Edwards 1994: 2). If there is no truth to pursue, and if attempts to pursue that which is unobtainable inevitably descend into economies of power, then the notion of educational textbooks as receptacles of 'authoritative knowledge claims' could be discarded (Cherrryholmes 1988: 51). In the post-modern economy the task of education was reduced to the purely instrumental, pragmatic and utilitarian. As a result, universities were free to seek 'to transform themselves, or allow themselves to be transformed, into either instrumental agencies for training potential employees in transferable skills or environments for the exploration of alternative lifestyles for virtual sociocultural realities' (Filmer 1997: 57). Given this truncated agenda of striving to meet the economic needs of society and feeding the personal desires of students, the post-modern university faces the prospect of becoming 'so diverse, so fractured and differentiated that it may have become absurd to seek to express any grand organ-isational principle' (Smith and Webster 1997: 3). The post-modern university is the apotheosis of the deconstruction of *paideia*: the unity of the pursuit of truth and cultivation of truthful living *sub specie aeternitatis* gives way, via a journey from Enlightenment rationalism through its romantic mirror-image to its post-modern finale, to a knowledge-free economy of personal and social stultification, driven by the twin values of economic need and personal desire, and policed by the forces of consumer capitalism. The emergence of the post-modern university is a story of education's abandonment of its transformative responsibilities and potential, and acceptance of the task of maintaining and buttressing an arbitrary status quo. It is a story that takes us on a tortuous and convoluted path from Abra-hamic theology ('God relates to me and I relate to God, therefore I am'), via Car-tesian anxiety and scepticism ('I doubt, therefore I am'), to the affirmation of the cognitive Cartesian self ('I think, therefore I am'); and from there, via the roman-tic Cartesian self ('I feel, therefore I am'), to the post-modern Cartesian self ('I desire, therefore I am') and triumph of an atomistic, competitive and fractious capitalism ('I consume – considerably more than you, and in more tasteful ways – therefore I am.') And during that journey education progressively forgets its responsibility to be a force for truth, truthfulness and transformation, and allows itself to be reduced to the status of a tool for reinforcing and sustaining whatever account of the human condition happens to be currently fashionable.

(2) *The 1988 Education Reform Act.* 'Curriculum theory is intrinsically involved with the debate over what counts as valuable knowledge, how know-ledge should be conceived, and how it should be certified' (Shipway 2011: 129). The process of constructing, delivering and assessing the curriculum, requires teachers and policymakers to make decisions regarding curricular aims, the rel-ative merits of particular subject-disciplines and knowledge-domains, the selec-tion of curriculum content from within chosen disciplines and domains, the pedagogical means by which the curriculum is enacted in the classrooms, and the subsequent evaluation of pupil learning, teacher performance and curricular construction. Such decisions are inevitably wrapped up with the interests of poli-ticians, academics, teachers, pupils, parents and society at large. 'Curriculum theory can therefore be seen as involving the wider issue of what types of know-ledge are deemed important by particular groups in society' (ibid.: 129).

The fact–value divide is clearly visible in the 1988 Education Reform Act, which restructured schooling in England and Wales. It identifies a clear set of educational aims: schools must promote 'the spiritual, moral, cultural, mental and physical development of pupils' and prepare 'such pupils for the opportunities, responsibilities and experiences of adult life' (HMSO 1988: Section 1.2). These twin aims of personal development and social enhancement were to be achieved through the transmission of the knowledge set out in the National Curriculum. This inevitably raised the question of the relationship between the values embedded in the general statement of educational aims, the knowledge embedded within the curriculum, and the social and political structures of educational enterprises (Young 1971a). Progressive educators, predominantly on the political Left, had long argued that socially constructed academic curricula tend to favour 'high-status' middle-class ways of knowing that are predominantly individualistic, literate, abstract and dislocated from ordinary life, and consequently discriminate against 'low-status' working-class ways of knowing that are predominantly collective, oral, concrete and grounded in everyday life. Traditionalist educators, predominately on the political Right, argued in turn that knowledge is objective and as such does not favour any particular social class or group.

Educational traditionalists laboured under the positivistic delusion that knowledge is value free, and that to allow 'received facts' to be tainted by so-called 'progressive values' was to open the door to the political manipulation of knowledge. When Prime Minister Margaret Thatcher intervened in the debate surrounding the content of the National Curriculum's history syllabus, she sought to challenge what she saw as a residual left-wing ideological bias in the proposed curriculum by claiming that history can be reduced to 'factual information ... in a clear chronological framework': a position that was roundly condemned as positivistic by her critics (Thatcher 1993: 595; Ross 2000: 71ff.). Little has changed: the revision of the National Curriculum for history in 2013 to ensure a central place for historical chronology led to accusations of a descent into the rote learning of facts, and generated the counter-accusation, from Michael Grove, the Secretary of State for Education, that such criticisms were informed by Marxism (Marsden 2013). At the same time, educational progressives labour under the delusion that knowledge is a human construct grounded in the exercise of power, and that it is the responsibility of education to oversee the redistribution of knowledge in favour of the dispossessed. If educational traditionalists commit the ontic fallacy of reducing curricular knowledge to objective fact, then educational progressives commit the epistemic fallacy of reducing curricular knowledge to constructed values.

Herein lies the dilemma: if the knowledge embedded in the National Curriculum can be reduced to value-free objective facts then the transmission of such knowledge cannot be expected to contribute in any substantial way to the overarching educational aims of personal development and social enhancement. If education is grounded in the transmission of objective factual knowledge, how does such knowledge relate to the broader aspirations of personal development and social enhancement? And if education is grounded in personal development and social enhancement, how do such values relate to the material content of the National Curriculum? The introduction of a range of cross-curricular themes and skills-based approaches to teaching and learning betrays unease about the lack of any clear answer to these questions, and can be read as a retrospective attempt to bridge the gap between a set of value-driven educational aims and a knowledge-driven curriculum.

In 1999 the *National Curriculum Handbook* sought to clarify the relationship between value-driven aims and a knowledge-driven curriculum by locating the pupil at the intersection between the two (DfEE/QCA 1999). Schools would promote personal and social development by delivering the National Curriculum in a manner that provided opportunities for all pupils to learn and achieve. The *Handbook* presents 'a picture of the kind of pupil that the school curriculum can ideally help to foster' by identifying the personal qualities, and intellectual skills, knowledge and understanding necessary for them to be identified as successful learners (White 2004: 4). This, however, simply begs the question of the relationship between personal qualities on the one hand, and intellectual skills, knowledge and understanding on the other. John White suggests that the dominance of the former over the latter reflects an approach to education primarily concerned with 'promoting a certain kind of society' and 'cultivating citizens of an appropriate sort' (ibid.: 5).

> Broadly speaking, the ideal pupil is an informed, caring citizen of a liberal democratic society. He or she is an enterprising, independent-minded, contributor to the well-being of the national community and all its members, respectful of differences in culture and belief, aware of transnational and global concerns and with an understanding of major human achievements in different fields.
>
> (ibid.: 4)

However, this still does not resolve the issue of the relationship between educational aims and curriculum content. White's closer analysis of the relationship reveals patchy results. He finds a best fit in emergent curriculum subjects such as design and technology, information and communication technology, citizenship education, and personal, health and social education. The stated aims of the more traditional subject disciplines, such as geography, history, mathematics, music and science, are far more difficult to relate to the general educational aims of personal development and social enhancement. The music curriculum, for example, focuses on the acquisition of skills of performance, composition, listening and appreciation, 'yet the overall point of this for those children who will not become specialist musicians is not clear' (ibid.: 13). Similarly, though the science curriculum acknowledges the importance of understanding the impact of science on society, its primary focus is on the mastery of 'specific areas of knowledge and techniques of enquiry within science' (ibid.: 14). White concludes that curriculum subjects have an intra-subject orientation: 'their main preoccupation is with helping pupils to acquire knowledge, understanding and skills in their specialised area' rather than helping them develop as well-rounded persons capable of contributing to the wellbeing of liberal society (ibid.: 14).

Faced with this fact–value divide, White takes the general personal and social aims of education as his benchmark, at the expense of the knowledge possessed by specific subject disciplines: 'Schools' first duty is not the preparation of specialists, but with providing a sound general education in line with subject-transcending aims' (ibid.: 14). On this reading, the promotion of liberal values takes precedence over the transmission of knowledge; so long as the fact–value divide remains securely in place, the only viable alternative would appear to be the pursuit of value-free knowledge at the expense of liberal values. The current status quo allows both paths to co-exist in an uneasy alliance: on the one hand the transmission of 'objective' (predominantly empirical) knowledge, on the other the cultivation of 'subjective' (predominantly idealistic) values, with the latter predicated on the pragmatic option of allowing pupils to determine their own values provided they do so within the normative ontological framework of a comprehensive liberalism committed to a vision of reason, freedom and tolerance as the highest human goods.

Attempts to resolve the tensions between facts and values, objectivity and subjectivity, pure and practical knowledge, and curricular transmission and personal formation either advocate one side of the equation at the expense of the other, or else seek to establish a precarious balance between the two. Such responses are moribund, trapped within the epistemic dualism and ontological reductionism generated by the rationalistic, romantic and post-modern fallout from the Enlightenment. The potential of critical realism to provide a viable alternative to this fragmented vision is the topic of the next chapter.

6   Educational realism

The epistemic fallacy of forcing reality to conform to our ways of knowing results in an ontological divide between fact and value that in turn generates a fragmented pedagogy in which education for the transmission of knowledge is disassociated from both education for social flourishing and education for personal development. This chapter draws on the under-labouring resources of critical realism to recover a realistic framework for education grounded in the essential unity of the pursuit of truth and cultivation of truthful living.

Paul Hirst: forms of knowledge

In a speech delivered in 1976 at Ruskin College, Oxford the British Prime Minister James Callaghan raised a basic question: 'What do we want from the education of our children and young people?' (Callaghan 2011). He suggested that the informal methods of progressive child-centred education lack 'sufficient thoroughness and depth' to adequately prepare pupils for the challenges and opportunities of adult life. Callaghan's intervention instigated a debate that was to lead to the 1988 Education Reform Act and the establishment of a National Curriculum for state schools in England and Wales. The 1977 Green Paper *Education in Our Schools* advocated a core curriculum grounded in a basic set of educational aims (DES 1977). Developing this theme *Curriculum 11–16*, issued by Her Majesty's Inspectors of Schools later that year, proposed that education should be concerned with introducing pupils to certain essential areas of knowledge and experience: aesthetic and creative, ethical, linguistic, mathematical, physical, scientific, social and political, and spiritual (DES/HMI 1977).

The proposal reflected the work of Paul Hirst, a leading representative of the analytical school of educational philosophy operating within the broad tradition of linguistic philosophy associated with Russell, Wittgenstein, Moore and Broad. The conceptual analysis of language in the field of education sought 'a clarification of the meanings of educational beliefs and principles by means of a mapping of the concepts they employed' (Hirst 1982: 7). Whilst it was not the philosopher's task to prescribe educational roles and responsibilities, linguistic analysis could provide practitioners with conceptual clarity, and thereby guide their judgements regarding the nature and justification of key educational principles and practice. Eschewing both reductive positivism and speculative idealism, Hirst analysed the educational language employed by practitioners in an attempt to identify both its relation to reality and its underlying logical structure. In doing so he embraced a thoroughgoing realism that viewed knowledge as the point of contact between the mind and reality: 'Knowledge is achieved when the mind attains its own satisfaction or good by corresponding to objective reality' (Hirst 1973a: 90).

Hirst set out to rehabilitate a classical Greek notion of liberal education 'based fairly and squarely on the nature of knowledge itself' (ibid.: 87). The ancient Greeks, he argued, upheld 'the doctrine that it is the peculiar and distinctive activity of the mind, because of its very nature, to pursue knowledge' (ibid.). Since success in the pursuit of knowledge satisfies and fulfils the mind, it is an essential element of the good life: 'the achievement of knowledge is not only the attainment of the good of the mind itself, but also the chief means whereby the good life as a whole is to be found' (ibid.: 88). Because knowledge is a distinctive virtue and an intrinsic good 'liberal education is essential to man's understanding of how he ought to live, both individually and socially' (ibid.: 89). 'A liberal education in the pursuit of knowledge is, therefore, seeking the development of the mind according to what is quite external to it, the structure and pattern of reality' (ibid.: 90). The attainment of knowledge, achieved through the right use of reason, enables the learner to 'know the essential nature of things' and 'apprehend what is ultimately real and immutable' (ibid.: 88). A knowledge-based education avoids deceptive appearances, doubtful opinions and fleeting values by 'freeing the mind to function according to its true nature, freeing reason from error and illusion and freeing man's conduct from wrong' (ibid.: 89).

(1) *Beyond traditionalism and progressivism.* Hirst suggests that 'the debates between progressives and traditionalists in education are largely anachronistic' (Hirst and Peters 1970: 131). Both pay 'too little attention to *public forms of experience* which ... are absolutely central to the development of knowledge and understanding' (ibid.: 32).

Traditionalism, as exemplified by the conventional grammar school education traceable back to Locke, is beset with a number of persistent and insurmountable problems. In seeking to induct pupils uncritically into the beliefs and cultural norms of a particular epistemically relative tradition, it functions paternalistically to breed ignorance and foster narrow-mindedness. In attempting to make pupils passive receptors of knowledge and social norms, traditionalism operates with a concept of mind 'bedeviled by myths largely of an empiricist nature' (Hirst 1969a: 147). The empiricist belief that knowledge is acquired through the passive reception of packets of sense data fails to recognise that to acquire knowledge is simultaneously to develop the mind. Emphasis on the knowledge to be transmitted at the expense of methods of transmission effectively dislocates questions of curricular content from questions of pedagogy. With regard to the curriculum, the lack of any objective criteria for curricular selection means that traditionalism tends to fall back on a variety of subjective criteria: cultural fashion, political expediency, religious authority, personal preference, etc. The absence of any synthetic map of knowledge capable of doing justice to the diversity and depth of our engagement with reality typically results in a fragmented and narrowly specialised curriculum. With regard to pedagogy, the understanding of the mind as an empty receptacle passively receiving empirical sense data means that the mastery of knowledge, acquisition of beliefs, development of skills and nurturing of mental qualities proceeds in a haphazard and disjointed manner. As a result, education is reduced to a process of enculturalisation through the arbitrary and authoritarian transmission of a dominant tradition, in a manner that undercuts the integrity of both knowledge and learners.

> An authoritarian method of teaching is suggested to which the most desirable form of response on the part of the learner is the unquestioning acceptance of doctrines.... Scientific laws and facts were taught rather than the critical attitudes and ways of thinking of a scientist; moral conformity was insisted on, but not moral awareness.... [Traditionalists] valued obedience more than they valued independence of mind.
>
> (Hirst and Peters 1970: 29, 32)

Progressivism, exemplified by the child-centred education that flourished in many British schools in the 1960s and which can be traced back to Rousseau, is similarly beset with problems. Though Hirst recognised the value of the progressive critique of traditionalism's relegation of the learner to the status of passive receptor of knowledge, he had little time for its positive alternative. The uncritical acceptance of the Socratic notion of learning as the recollection of innate knowledge, together with the Aristotelian notion that 'organic change comes through the actualization of innate potentialities', led to an emphasis on the formation of the mind at the expense of any concern for curriculum content (ibid.: 31). The idealist principle that education be adapted to the children's needs and interests was applied not only to the learning process but also to curricular content. As a result, criteria for the selection of curriculum knowledge focused on the perceived needs, interests and mental capacities of pupils rather than external reality. Advocates of progressive child-centred education were fundamentally concerned with the formation of character and development of virtues such as critical thinking, creativity and autonomy. However,

> they did not sufficiently appreciate that these virtues are vacuous unless people are provided with the forms of knowledge and experience to be critical, creative and autonomous *with*. People have to be trained to think critically; it is not some dormant seed that flowers naturally.... Being critical must be distinguished from being merely contra-suggestible, just as being 'creative' must be distinguished from mere self-expression.
>
> (ibid.: 31f.)

The divisions between fact and value, subjectivity and objectivity, sense and sensibility, and internal mind and external world generated a pedagogic suspicion of intellectualism that 'argued that linguistic and abstract forms of thought are only for some pupils', 'assumed that learning took place naturally in unstructured problem-solving situations', and ignored 'the centrality of conceptual development and language in the process' (Hirst 1969b: 44f.). As a result, progressivism reduced knowledge to a form of self-understanding untouched by 'matters of sheer fact' (ibid.: 35). Just as traditionalist education valorised the acquisition of knowledge at the expense of the development of mind, so progressive education valorised the development of mind at the expense of the acquisition of knowledge.

(2) *Forms of knowledge.* Traditionalism and progressivism must be discarded because they both proceed from subjective opinion and lack any substantial grounding in objective truth. In their place Hirst advocates an education grounded in a set of objective 'forms of knowledge' that bridge the gap between mind and reality. In doing so he embraces the classical notion of truth as *adequatio intellectus et rei*, the convergence of the intellect with reality, and confirms 'the doctrines of metaphysical and epistemological realism' (Hirst 1973a: 90). Realistic knowledge of this kind cannot legitimately be reduced to empirical sense data or subsumed within an idealistic metaphysical system. Hirst finds in the work of Gilbert Ryle, Ludwig Wittgenstein and Michael Oakeshott the seeds of an epistemology capable of penetrating beyond the impasse of concrete empirical facts and abstract idealistic concepts.

Hirst argues that knowledge is grounded in our shared experience of ourselves and the world we indwell (ibid.: 95ff.). Private states of mind and forms of awareness are unintelligible apart from the symbolic and linguistic apparatus by which they are articulated in the public sphere. Authentic knowledge is determined by reality, and achieved by ordering and articulating our experience of reality through a range of conceptual schemes. To acquire knowledge is to learn, under the guidance of these emergent conceptual schemes, to experience the world in previously unknown and otherwise inaccessible ways. By using these schemes to examine subsequent experience it is possible to test our assertions and distinguish between more truthful and less truthful accounts of reality. The ongoing formulating and testing of symbolic expressions enables us to probe our experience to identify increasingly complex knowledge relations and draw increasingly fine epistemic distinctions. Knowledge is grounded in the progressive development of conceptual frameworks tested against experience on the basis of publically available criteria. It is the public nature of these criteria that enable us to lay claim to objective knowledge. The nature of such criteria varies across different forms of knowledge: the natural sciences depend on empirical experimentation and observational testing; mathematics depends on deductive demonstrations of certain sets of axioms; moral knowledge and the arts involve distinct forms of critical tests that require levels of intuition and creativity that cannot easily be articulated or formalised, and which are best learnt through immersion in a tradition of discursive scholarship.

Our experience of the world cannot simply be taken at face value: it requires the proactive engagement of the mind in acts of creative imagination, critical thinking, informed judgement and effective communication. Because of this the achievement of knowledge cannot be separated from the development of mind. Hirst justifies his notion of the essential harmony of knowledge and mind not on metaphysical grounds, but in terms of the logical relationship between the concept of mind and the concept of knowledge. The achievement of knowledge is coterminous with the development of mind, so that to acquire knowledge is to become cognitively aware of how our experience is structured, organised and made meaningful on the basis of a reciprocal dialectical relationship between mind and reality. Consequently Hirst has relatively little time for neo-Kantian notions of the natural development of the mind, innate cognitive structures, or pre-determined patterns of thinking.

Hirst's account of the 'forms of knowledge' has passed through progressive stages of development. Early formulations appealed to formal logic and mathematics, the insights of the physical sciences, awareness and understanding of our own and other people's minds, moral judgements, objective aesthetic experience, religious claims, and philosophical understanding (Hirst 1972). By 1973 the list had been revised and the forms identified as mathematics, physical sciences, human sciences, history, religion, literature and the fine arts, and philosophy (ibid.: 105). However, Hirst's identification of four distinguishing features common to all forms remained relatively stable: each form possesses a set of distinctive central concepts that are peculiar in character; the central concepts peculiar to a particular form denote a network of possible relationships through which a particular aspect of experience can be understood; each form, by virtue of its particular terms and logic, contains expressions or statements that are directly or indirectly testable against experience; individual forms have developed particular techniques and skills for exploring their formative experiences and testing their distinctive expressions (ibid.: 102f.).

The nature of the forms and their place in Hirst's philosophy of education becomes more transparent when we consider his account of religious education. Despite identifying religious claims as a form of knowledge, he holds that there can be no justification for faith-based schooling because confessional approaches to religious education necessarily transmit mere belief or opinion. This is because religious doctrines are not open to public verification and testing: 'I do not consider that we do at present have objective tests for such propositions' (Hirst 1973b: 10). It is 'our uncertainties about such claims that necessarily determine our approach to all aspects of religion within education' (ibid.). Despite the absence of criteria for testing Transcendent truth claims, there are publically available criteria for testing our knowledge and understanding of religious phenomena:

> We do know what it is for people to hold Christian or other beliefs, even if we do not know whether these beliefs are true, and our knowledge here is part of a thoroughly objective form of knowledge and understanding.
>
> (ibid.)

(3) *Critiques of Hirst.* Objections to Hirst's position circle around the claim that he fails to provide an adequate account of the objective status of the forms of knowledge.

Daniel O'Connor argues that 'reason (that is, tested methods of assessing and evaluation evidence) is our only guide to problem solving', and appraises Hirst's account of the forms against the criteria of its explanatory power and openness to empirical verification (O'Connor 1972: 109). Hirst sought to sidestep positivism by invoking a form of empirical testing rooted in a holistic assessment of lived human experience rather than the verification of atomistic sense data. Thus moral knowledge is assessed in the light of our experience of interpersonal relationships and the logical coherence of our moral discourse regarding such relationships, in a manner that bypasses the positivist objection that we cannot see, hear, touch, taste or smell 'goodness'. Hirst's apparent unease about such a holistic notion of empirical testing is reflected in his appeal to intuition in relation to artistic knowledge, and suggestion that there are no objective tests for theological truth claims.

Colin Evers, expanding on O'Connor's critique, argues that Hirst's account of empirical testing is inherently subjective and devoid of the objectivity achieved by the scientific verification of truth claims against empirical sense data. He dismisses the forms of knowledge as vague, pragmatic and unscientific, and suggests that 'the desired unity of educational theory' to which Hirst aspires can only be achieved 'by jettisoning all but one kind of knowledge claim from its legitimate corpus', namely the knowledge claim of natural science (Evers 1987: 11). Despite the naiveté of the positivistic assumptions underlying such critiques, the claim that the forms of knowledge lack the epistemic *certitude* apparently required by Hirst's educational philosophy appears valid.

Elizabeth Hindess distinguishes between contingent states of affairs and necessary truths, and suggests that the attempt to identify the forms as both dynamic cultural products and established objective realities constitutes a 'major confusion in Hirst's theory' (Hindess 1972: 172). Hirst holds that knowledge claims are both contingent, insofar as they are generated by a posteriori experiences of reality that require empirical testing, and necessary, insofar as they possess an a priori logical coherence. In Kantian terms they take the form of synthetic a priori statements; however, 'whether there can be synthetic a priori knowledge or synthetic necessary statements is still a controversy in philosophy' (ibid.: 173).

> The statements which Hirst makes about the nature of mind, the structure of experience and the forms of knowledge are both synthetic and necessary; that is, they are contingent because they give information about the world and because they can be denied without self-contradiction but they are also known to be true with as much certainty as tautologies.
>
> (ibid.: 172f.)

Given his insistence that knowledge is a product of our experience of the world, 'presumably Hirst would have to include under the stricture the possibility that what are now thought of *bona fide* knowledge claims may in some future date be dubbed superstition'; however, this does not square with his insistence on the objectivity of knowledge (ibid.: 158).

Brian Scarlett, arguing along similar lines, draws a distinction between formalism and teleology in Hirst's work. His formalism seeks to ground education in the logical properties of knowledge, which take the form of autonomous and irreducible propositions whose rational justification transcends the contingencies of cultural fashion, public utility, vocational intention, personal preference and ideological commitment. His teleology, on the other hand, grounds education in developing social structures and ethical relationships in pursuit of human well-being and the good life. This begs the question: 'How can one be purely formalist in ethics?' (Scarlett 1984: 158). Scarlett argues that Hirst's programme requires the unification of formalism and teleology: 'Hirst accepts the charge of formalism but also asserts (surely correctly) that educational justification essentially involves reference to human welfare' (ibid.: 159). Education must be concerned with the good life whilst remaining securely grounded in objective knowledge. However, since our understanding of the nature of the good life is clearly contingent and its pursuit necessarily teleologically oriented, it makes little sense to insist that an education committed to the cultivation of human flourishing must be grounded in 'purely formal considerations' (ibid.: 159).

O'Connor, Evers, Hindess and Scarlett arrive at similar conclusions from their respective starting points: since Hirst has not sufficiently demonstrated that the forms of knowledge enjoy the objective status required of a knowledge-based liberal education, they must be contingent on the social, geographic, historical and cultural context in which they are generated. Despite Hirst's influence on the establishment of the National Curriculum in England and Wales, his work was subject to trenchant criticisms that drew John White's cursory evaluation:

> Seductive though the argument may be at first sight, it is pretty clearly inadequate on closer inspection ... few, if any, of its original proponents would wish to adhere to it ... there is no need to rake over these dead leaves again.
> (White 1982: 10f.)

Responding to his critics, Hirst accepted in retrospect that his work contained an unjustifiable objectivism, a misplaced prioritising of reason over action, and a lack of sensitivity to changing socio-political contexts. His defence of the forms of knowledge 'mistakenly saw itself as producing objective universal truths' (Hirst 1982: 8). He followed Michael Young and others in accepting that the philosophy of education is 'a necessarily value-laden activity, reflecting implicitly the contingent values of the individual philosopher, his socially relative political values, or even the inevitably conservative values of all philosophical analyses' (ibid.: 8). Nevertheless, he insisted that such criticisms 'do not seem to me to constitute a fundamental challenge to the enterprise that is sometimes claimed' (ibid.). Taking a lead from Jürgen Habermas, he postulated a path beyond the objective–subjective divide towards an understanding of knowledge as contingently rational and warranted. The need for 'greater sensitivity to the social contexts of conceptual use' does not preclude the task of 'developing more sophisticated arguments in claims about universal categories' (ibid.).

Michael Young: bringing knowledge back in

The educational philosophy of Michael Young is a mirror-image of Hirst's: whereas Hirst began with a commitment to ontological objectivity and came to acknowledge epistemic subjectivity, so Young began with a commitment to epistemic subjectivity and came to acknowledge ontological objectivity. The convergence of these originally diametrically opposed voices in the recent history of the philosophy of education is of great significance for the present task of identifying the contours of a critically realistic educational philosophy committed simultaneously to both ontological realism and epistemic relativity.

(1) *Knowledge and Control.* Michael Young's edited collection *Knowledge and Control*, first published in 1971, was in many ways the antithesis of all that Hirst sought to defend (Young 1971a). In dismissing Hirst's position as a priori and absolutist, Young and his fellow authors sought to develop a sociology of education grounded in social constructivism. Though Hirst was appealed to by politicians anxious to challenge educational progressivism and reaffirm traditionalism through the creation of a National Curriculum, it was social constructivism that came to dominate the academy during much of the remainder of the century. The tension between the two was clearly visible in ongoing attempts by traditionalist politicians to shift initial teacher education from the academy to the school, and to emphasise teachers' practical classroom skills at the expense of educational theory. Ironically, their desire to protect classrooms from the insidious influence of predominantly Left-wing intellectuals operating within the constructivist tradition merely reinforced the constructivist claim that, in the absence of secure objective knowledge, education must necessarily be driven by pragmatic considerations devoid of any substantive and secure knowledge-base. Despite being a multi-authored collection of essays, *Knowledge and Control* possessed a relatively coherent agenda. Denis Lawton identifies five recurrent themes: traditional education preserves an unjust status quo; the selection of knowledge for transmission in schools constitutes a problem requiring examination; traditional subject disciplines are arbitrary and artificial assemblages; knowledge is socially constructed; and rationality merely conventional (Lawton 1975: 58ff.).

Young argues that sociology tends to take educational practitioners' definitions of educational problems for granted. Thus the educational failure of many working-class pupils is treated as a form of deviancy traceable back to aspects of the British class system, rather than as a consequence of dominant assumptions about knowledge and its transmission embraced by teachers and policymakers (Young 1971b: 25). The sociology of education should 'make' rather than 'take' problems. Alfred Schutz's reading of 'institutional definitions or typifications ... as the intersubjective reality which men have constructed to give meaning to their world' opens up the possibility of problematising practitioners' accounts of educational problems (ibid.: 27). Once such inter-subjective meanings are recognised as social constructs, there is an imperative to treat them as objects of enquiry rather than as the presuppositions of enquiry. Thus the sociology of education must take into account the 'historical and situationally specific character of both its phenomena and its explanations' (ibid.: 5). This opens up the possibility of explaining the failure of many working class pupils in terms of the dominance of an academic curriculum that favours the intellectual elite, rather than in terms of intellectual incapacity or socio-cultural deprivation. Enquiries into the social organisation of knowledge in educational institutions suggests that knowledge is neither absolute nor arbitrary, but rather the product of constructed meanings. The construction and distribution of such meanings is best traced back to 'the traditions of a centralized intellectual elite with close links to those holding economic and social power' (Young 1971c: 6). This opens up the possibility of the development of alternative constructs, emancipated from elitist power structures and capable of generating educational practices designed to redistribute knowledge and power. Most schools seek to transmit 'high-status' knowledge grounded in the organisational principles underlying academic curricula. Such knowledge is highly literate, individualistic, abstract and dislocated from daily life and common experience, and as such stands exposed as a contingent human construct established by a small, though immensely powerful, subsection of society (Young 1971b: 38). Once the contingent nature of high-status knowledge is recognised, it is not difficult to imagine an alternative construct in which non-academic curricula are organised in terms of oral communication, collaborative group activities, and concrete problem-solving rooted in everyday life; nor, by implication, is it difficult to envisage working-class pupils engaging more successfully with such a construct than their middle-class peers.

Geoffrey Esland's contribution to *Knowledge and Control*, 'Teaching and Learning as the Organization of Knowledge', offers a detailed account of the epistemic assumptions underlying social constructivism. He dismisses as 'anti-humanistic scientism' the view that knowledge is constituted by a set of abstract propositions and structures, grounded in particular classifications of problems, data and verification procedures, that successfully represent ontological realities (Esland 1971: 70). The idea that the 'individual consciousness recognizes objects as being "out there", as coercive, external realities', is artificially detached from the mind of the human subject in which knowledge is 'constituted, maintained and transformed' (ibid.: 75). The 'notion that man's consciousness arises out of his social being is the central proposition of the sociology of knowledge' (ibid.: 79). Knowledge comes to us in the form of an 'agglomeration of phenomena external to the body' that 'has to be subjectively *realized* before it has any meaning' (ibid.: 74). Human beings are thus active constructors of their worlds rather than passive receptors of knowledge. 'Teachers have certain core assumptions about their 'subjects', about pedagogy, the intellectual status of their pupils, and some idea of what constitutes thinking, including its presence and supposed absence in particular learning situations' (ibid.: 78). This stock of knowledge functions as 'the relevance system and interpretative grid' that informs their interior dialogue, engagement with pupils, and attempts at public accountability (ibid.). However, in the real-world environment of the classroom, subject teachers operate not with objective knowledge but with socially realised and constructed knowledge. This means that the 'relationship between teachers and pupils is essentially a reality-sharing, world-building exercise', in which the participants 'inter-subjectively typify and interpret the actions of one another through vocabularies which they take for granted as plausible' (ibid.: 72). This requires an understanding of teaching and learning as the communal construction of meaning, rather than the authoritarian transmission of established and reified forms of information.

Basil Bernstein's contribution to *Knowledge and Control*, 'On the Classification and Framing of Knowledge', sets out to demonstrate the relationship between the ways in which society selects, classifies, transmits and evaluates educational knowledge, and the distribution of power and social control (Bernstein 1971). By identifying and explaining the power structures through which the formal construction, organisation and transmission of curricular knowledge impacts on the creation and maintenance of pupils' identities, it is possible to revise the former for the benefit of the latter. Bernstein uses the concepts of 'framing' and 'classification' to help reveal these power structures in operation. Where framing determines the generic structure of curricular knowledge, classification determines the relationship between different curricular domains. The interplay between framing and classification influences the levels of control teachers and pupils possess over the selection, organisation and transmission of knowledge. Strong framing tends to objectify educational knowledge, whilst strong classification tends to insulate subject disciplines within clear boundaries. The stronger the classification and framing, the more the educational relationship tends to be hierarchical and ritualised, with the teacher acting as master of a body of objective knowledge and pupils viewed as ignorant and of little status. Typically, secondary schools employ strong framing and classification, producing a hierarchical relationship in which the teacher has maximal control and surveillance over both the transmission of domain-specific knowledge and the formation of pupils' identities. But this need not be the case, since we can envisage a secondary school employing both weak framing and classification, for example in programmes of integrated studies in which pupils are free to negotiate knowledge and take control of their own personal formation and educational development. This points to a resolution of the problematic relationship between reified academic knowledge and practical everyday knowledge, and addresses the reality that the former tends to act as an agent of social control that favours educators in positions of power and disempowers working-class pupils. Thus the problem of the relative failure of working-class pupils to succeed educationally can be seen to lie not in any form of intellectual incapacity or social impoverishment, but in the way in which curricular knowledge is classified, framed and distributed. The transmission of educational knowledge inevitably impacts on pupils' identities: at the most basic level educational success or failure impacts positively or negatively on their sense of self-worth. A sense of the sacred, of the 'otherness' of educational knowledge, is best seen as a function of socialisation into subject-discipline loyalty rather than the product of any deep engagement with ontological realities. For educationally 'successful' (predominantly middle-class) pupils, any attempt to weaken the classification strength of their preferred subject disciplines will tend to be experienced as a threat to their emergent identities; conversely, for educationally 'failing' (predominantly working-class) students, such weakening may help affirm their identities and promote their self-esteem. Viewed in this way, the sociology of knowledge pioneered by advocates of the 'new sociology of education' promised to provide a powerful tool for social transformation.

(2) *Bringing Knowledge Back In.* Young's 2008 publication *Bringing Knowledge Back In* offered a fundamental critique of the agenda of *Knowledge and Control*, one that, as the book's subtitle made plain, sought a path 'from social constructivism to social realism in the sociology of education' (Young 2008). Just as Hirst had qualified his commitment to the objectivity of knowledge by acknowledging the contingencies of the social contexts in which knowledge is generated so, in a reverse move, Young now questioned the exclusion of realistic knowledge from his earlier reductive account of knowledge as a social construct. Without abandoning his belief that knowledge is culturally situated, he now insisted that realistic knowledge claims could potentially possess an epistemic warrant transcendent of social interests and economies of power. In doing so he affirmed the importance of realistic knowledge in the cycle of teaching, learning, and assessment, expressed scepticism about the social utility of an education devoid of a sound realistic knowledge-base, and pointed sociologists of education away from 'position-taking and policy advocacy' towards 'scholarship and rigorous analysis' (ibid.: xv). If the sociology of education is to avoid the 'intellectual cul-de-sac of relativism', there can be no avoiding 'the centrality of epistemological constraints and the inescapable reality that acquiring and producing new knowledge is never easy' (ibid.: xvif.).

Young's emergent critique of social constructivism is informed by Bernard Williams' distinction between 'truth' and 'truthfulness' (ibid. 197ff.; cf. Williams 2002). Williams identifies a deep-rooted commitment to truthfulness in contemporary culture, in the form of 'a pervasive suspiciousness, a readiness against being fooled, an eagerness to see through appearances to the real structures and motives that lie behind them'; however this operates alongside an 'equally pervasive scepticism about truth itself', which manifests itself in forms of relativism and subjectivism (Williams 2002: 1).

> These two things, the devotion to truthfulness and the suspicion directed to the idea of truth, are connected to one another. The desire for truthfulness drives a process of criticism which weakens the assurance that there is any secure or unqualified stateable truth.

> (ibid.)

The expectation that others should act honestly towards us ('truthfulness') is juxtaposed with the assumption that secure knowledge is unobtainable ('truth'). In such a culture, critical and transformative social commentary can easily be replaced by debunking and 'muck-raking journalism' that seeks to expose the dishonesty of the powerful with a self-righteous certainty that is itself groundless (Young 2008: 198). The 'tendency to moral self-righteousness and absolute certainty that we find in some campaigning journalists' is replicated amongst some sociologists of education, who assume, in a move apparently devoid of academic seriousness and intellectual warrant, that 'their identification with the powerless or with a particular disadvantaged group brings them automatically closer to the truth' (ibid.).

If the problem is that scepticism about truth inevitably undermines the pursuit of truthfulness, then the solution is to embrace the pursuit of truth as a necessary condition for any serious commitment to truthful living. Young suggests that 'the "new" sociology of education that began, in Williams's terms, with a radical commitment to truthfulness, undermined its own project by its rejection of any idea of truth itself' (ibid.: 199). Though the 'new' sociologists of education were quick to identify the corrosive influence of educational power structures, they were unable to offer any viable option other than their own alternative partisan economies of power. Young recognises and affirms the genuine advances made by sociologists of education: their resistance to totalising and totalitarian accounts of knowledge; their recognition of social power structures and control mechanisms operating within the educational establishment; and their commitment to social justice. Nevertheless, these achievements require the introduction of a substantial theory of knowledge alongside a theory of society if they are not to prove ephemeral. Without a robust theory of knowledge there can be no adequate basis for an alternative, less authoritarian and more equitable curriculum. The failure of social constructivism lay in its inability to differentiate between epistemology and ontology, between 'how we think about the world ... and any notion of "how the world is"' (ibid.: 201). Young holds that 'social constructivism provided teachers and students of education with a superficially attractive but ultimately contradictory set of intellectual tools' (ibid.: 203). The superficial attraction lay in the hope that education could provide intellectual and social emancipation from authoritarian forms of knowledge and mechanisms of social control. The ultimate contradiction lay in the reality that, 'by undermining any claims to objective knowledge or truth about anything, social constructivism ... denies the possibility of any better understanding, let alone of any better world' (ibid.: 204).

Young's begins his move toward a realistic epistemology by acknowledging that the 'social character of knowledge is not a reason for doubting its truth and objectivity' (ibid.: 205). Though it is undoubtedly true that human interests impact on knowledge claims, it is entirely arbitrary to adopt a reductionist position that affirms the desire for power and prestige whilst simultaneously excluding the desire to understand the world in better and more truthful ways (ibid.: 30). The notion that conceptual knowledge is capable of expressing and corresponding to realities and states of affairs in the external world, albeit to greater and lesser degrees, possesses 'a compelling power and a basic common-sense appeal' (ibid.: 6; cf. Moore and Muller 1999). 'Try designing a domestic lighting system without relying at least implicitly on Ohm's law, or designing an aeroplane without knowing the laws of fluid dynamics' (Young 2008: 6). Young follows Émile Durkheim in recognising *both* the social nature of knowledge, *and* the ability of conceptual and symbolic knowledge to transcend ordinary experience and locate it in wider contexts: 'All societies distinguish between the sacred and the profane and between common sense (our everyday response to events) and *theory* (our systems of unobservable concepts)' (ibid.: 43). It is the social reality of theoretical knowledge of unobserved concepts, whether religious or scientific, that enables us 'to transcend the specific instances and circumstances of everyday life' and thereby understand the world better and act within it in better ways (ibid.). However, Young challenges Durkheim's concern to view such knowledge reductively by limiting it to expressions and reflections of social realities. Ernst Cassirer's account of the epistemic function of symbols provides Young with a path beyond Durkheim's identification of the objectivity of 'social facts' to an understanding of the objectivity of 'natural facts' (ibid.: 213ff.). In particular, his classification of symbol in terms of the ways in which different strata of knowledge demand different systematic symbolic representation provides a path beyond attempts to reduce knowledge to the models provided by the natural and social sciences. The tension between the desire to understand external reality and the fact that knowledge is socially constructed is resolved through informed judgements, which take different forms according to the nature of the object of investigation: 'Regardless of the relativist arguments, people in all societies make judgements about good and bad literature as well as about different explanations of natural phenomena, and debate the criteria for making such judgements' (ibid.: 6). The fact that knowledge is rarely certain does not undermine its status as knowledge. Young defends a 'multi-dimensional' epistemology that assesses the warrant of truth claims against three criteria: their external validity and ability to explain something in a convincing way; their internal coherence and consistency; and 'their ability to invoke support from a particular community of experts' (ibid.: 9).

Young goes on to explore the educational implications of his attempt to develop a realist theory of knowledge and provide it with an epistemic warrant. To bring knowledge back into the classroom is not to impose conservative, authoritarian and idealised accounts of reality and human flourishing dislocated from the social and historical contexts in which they are generated. On the contrary, a realistic account of knowledge, precisely because it *is* realistic, requires educators to recognise the provisional and contingent nature of human understanding. However, this does not imply a thoroughgoing relativism: even though knowledge is generated in contexts of 'competing interests and power struggles', the fact that it possesses 'emergent properties that take it beyond the preservation of the interests of particular groups' empowers educators to 'speak about and argue for cognitive or intellectual interests' (ibid.: 88). If knowledge is more than '*just another set of social practices*', then a knowledge-based education must do more than merely induct of pupils into established social norms (ibid.: 89). Instead, the process of differentiating between theoretical and everyday knowledge, and between different stratified fields of knowledge, becomes fundamental to the educational enterprise, despite the inevitable contingency and fluidity of such differentiation.

The school curriculum cannot legitimately be based on everyday knowledge and practical experience, since this would merely recycle the existing knowledge and experience of pupils rather than extend it. If it is to be genuinely transformative, then it needs to be grounded in theoretical knowledge differentiated between discrete disciplinary fields (ibid.). Once again, this is not a recipe for traditionalist or conservative education: since the pursuit of knowledge is necessarily progressive, dynamic, open and contested, so the curriculum should reflect this state of affairs. Hence there is a warrant for a curriculum organised around subject disciplines that reflect the stratified nature of reality itself, provided it also reflects the progressive, dynamic, open and contested nature of the pursuit of truth and truthful living. Such a critically realistic curriculum based on 'specialist research and pedagogic communities' should take precedence over a pragmatic and utilitarian curriculum 'based on the immediate practical concerns of employers or general criteria for employability such as key skills' (ibid.). The task of education is to offer pupils access to transformative knowledge, in the form of conceptual schemes possessing explanatory power 'shared by specialist teachers, university researchers and professional associations' (ibid.: 89f.). 'A "curriculum of the future" needs to treat knowledge as a distinct and non-reducible element in the changing resources that people need access to in order to make sense of the world' (ibid.: 90).

Though Young does not explicitly acknowledge the fact, it is difficult to avoid observing just how close he has moved towards Hirst's account of liberal education, though not, of course, to his specific account of the epistemic grounds and objective status of the forms of knowledge.

Toward a critically realistic education

Both Hirst and Young accept the impossibility of producing a viable universal account of the timeless essence of education, above and beyond the contingencies of particular historic-cultural contexts. Young has held that position consistently, whereas Hirst has come to accept it in the light of criticism of the objective status of his forms of knowledge. The Enlightenment dream of universal reason, of establishing an objective God's-eye view of reality, has turned out to be no more than a figment of the imagination. The legacy of the Enlightenment is not that of the attainment of universal knowledge. Rather, it is a legacy of flawed attempts, within a particular culturally bound intellectual epoch, to achieve that goal; attempts that have been subject to sustained criticism by post-modernists and critical realists alike. It is certainly worthwhile striving for better, more truthful and more powerful accounts of education, and to that end the goal of obtaining *the* perfect account may potentially function as a useful heuristic device; however, given the actuality of epistemic relativity, such a goal can never be more than an idealised teleological hope. The theory and practice of education is unavoidably contingent: bound to specific cultural contexts, though not necessarily limited by them.

At the same time, however, both Hirst and Young reject any thoroughgoing relativism that would reduce education to the status of a nominal product of relativistic, culturally bound and socially dependent constructs and practices. Hirst has held that position consistently, while Young has come to accept it in the light of criticism of his previous understanding of the inherently subjective status of knowledge. The notion that there is no alternative to an education that simply replicates established cultural norms is false. The principle of judge-mental rationality opens up the possibility of an education capable of striving to both transcend relativism and transform culture. By drawing critically on the heritage of educational theory and practice available within a particular cultural context, it is potentially possible to identify and generate more powerful accounts of education. This, indeed, is the strategy adopted in the current chapter: having explored and contextualised one particular strand of educational theory and practice in the previous chapter, the task before us now is to attempt to transcend it by opening up the possibility of generating a powerful critically realistic account.

Because critical realism does not offer a comprehensive worldview, one does not need to 'convert' to it or 'buy into' it wholesale in order to reap the benefits of its philosophical insights. It does not function as a foundational philosophy, into which the worldviews of, say, Christianity, Islam, naturalism and secular humanism must be integrated and assimilated, since it does not prescribe either a particular ontology or a specific set of epistemic practices. Rather, it seeks to under-labour for society, and for the plurality of ontologically incommensurable worldviews present within society, by enabling greater precision and clarity in our intellectual and practical affairs. It does so by identifying a range of critical questions that, it suggests, society and the worldviews hosted by society would benefit from asking of reality. It does not proceed by saying 'This is how reality is', but rather by asking 'What must reality be like for us to experience it in the various ways we do?' Critical realists argue that the most powerful answer to this basic question is threefold: reality exists, for the most part, independently of our knowing (ontological realism); our knowledge of reality, though in places substantial, is nevertheless limited (epistemic relativity); we can distinguish between more and less truthful explanatory accounts of reality and subject them to ongoing iterative refinement (judgemental rationality). These three principles can be restated as a set of questions designed to interrogate, and thereby enrich and enhance, educational theory and practice: what normative understanding of reality, and of our means of knowing reality, is present, whether explicitly or implicitly, in any given educational endeavour (ontological realism)? What alternative accounts of reality are occluded by this norm (epistemic relativity)? How might a particular educational theory and praxis be enhanced and brought into greater harmony with reality (judgemental rationality)?

Alternatives to this triumvirate tend to collapse in on themselves: either into the ontic fallacy of reducing knowledge of reality to reality, or into the epistemic fallacy of reducing reality to knowledge of reality. Both options impose a premature epistemic closure: either we know reality absolutely objectively, as-it-is-in-itself; or we only know reality absolutely subjectively, as-it-appears-to-us. By distinguishing ontology from epistemology, and drawing on judgemental rationality to undermine all forms of premature epistemic closure, including the closures overseen by positivistic empiricism, idealistic essentialism and relativistic nominalism, the pursuit of knowledge can be reoriented towards an open future. Consequently, the idealist and empiricist (naive realist), susceptible to the ontic fallacy, will be empowered to question whether their suspicion of relativity is intellectually serious: am I *really* claiming access to complete and final knowledge of reality? Similarly, the relativist, susceptible to the epistemic fallacy, will be empowered to question whether their suspicion of realism is intellectually serious: am I *really* claiming that I have no access to knowledge of reality? And both parties will be empowered to consider whether the possibility of making informed judgements between conflicting truth claims is not, at the end of the day, a more powerful option than the premature epistemic closure that flows from both naive realism (the ontic fallacy) and thoroughgoing relativism (the epistemic fallacy).

These considerations have fundamental implications for education: both an education that sets out to transmit a closed, pre-packaged understanding of reality to students (an education in objective facts, akin to Hirst's 'educational traditionalism'), and an education that seeks to empower students to construct their own preferred realities (an education in subjective fictions, akin to Hirst's 'educational progressivism'), will inevitably distort their understandings of, and engagements with, the way things actually are in the world. A genuinely critically realistic education will place ontology centre stage, whilst simultaneously recognising both the epistemically relative nature of our knowledge of reality, and the possibility of a judgemental rationality capable of discriminating, however contingently and provisionally, between conflicting, epistemically relative, accounts of ontological realities.

Education, at its broadest, is concerned with the transmission of knowledge, with the formation of persons, and with the flourishing of society. The fragmentation of education in the post-Enlightenment era led to the compartmentalisation of these three tasks: Rousseau's progressive child-centred education bracketed-out the transmission of knowledge and flourishing of society and viewed it as detrimental to personal formation; Locke's traditionalist society-centred education bracketed-out the transmission of knowledge and the formation of the person as secondary to the flourishing of society; Kant proposed a division between the pursuit and transmission of knowledge on the one hand, and the education of professionals for the good of society on the other, and in doing so effectively bracketed-out questions of the educational task of intentional personal formation. Critical realism affirms, on the basis of a retroductive explanation of human experience which it deems to be more powerful than any other available explanation, that the wellbeing of individuals, the flourishing of society, and knowledge of reality and of our place in the ultimate order-of-things are necessarily interconnected: all three exist and have their being as part of a greater connected-yet-differentiated ontological whole. This being the case, powerful accounts of education must take account of the relationship between persons, society and knowledge within this greater whole. Educational theory and practice, that is to say, needs to be ontologically grounded, epistemically humble and rationally astute.

(1) *Education and ontological realism.* A genuinely critically realistic education will place ontology centre stage. Serious learning cannot be artificially cut off from the greater reality that learners and learning communities indwell and participate in. This larger reality both constrains and enables the lives of learners: there are things we cannot possibly achieve, and things that we can potentially achieve; aspects of reality that are closed to change, and aspects of reality that are open to transformation. When the potential for transformation is actually present, learners are further constrained and enabled by virtue of the fact that not all change is necessarily for the good, and some positive changes are better than others. The way things-actually-are, in the singular reality all learners indwell, cannot be reduced to subjective fictions or reified as objective facts. Because reality consists of a multifaceted web of transitive and intransitive objects, forces and events that exist and occur largely independently of learners, it cannot be reduced to subjective fictions. At the same time, the fact that reality includes human beings who enjoy, albeit to different degrees and extents, knowledge-relations with reality, and hence constitute part of the greater whole they seek to understand, means that it cannot be reified as objective fact. The artificial dislocation of learners from the world on epistemic grounds generates forms of dualism – whether between mind and matter, value and fact, opinion and knowledge, subjectivity and objectivity, or reality-as-it-appears-to-us and reality-in-itself – which force the ontological givenness of reality into the procrustean bed of our own preferred ways of knowing. Whether this leads to a phenomenalism that reduces reality to its surface appearances as apprehended by the mind, or a constructivism that recasts reality within the mind's conceptual apparatus, the artificial dislocation of the learner from the world generates epistemic closures that can only serve to distort our understanding of reality. For this reason a realistic education that places ontology centre stage must seek to cultivate an epistemic humility that, by virtue of its recognition of *both* the ontological givenness of reality and its deep structures, *and* the provisional and fallible nature of human knowing, is constantly open to greater discernment, richer explanation and deeper understanding.

We have already had cause to note Karl Popper's distinction between the ontological strata of the natural, mental and cultural domains, and to supplement these with the stratum of the Transcendent. The distinction need not be read dualistically or reductionistically: they do not identify four ontological disconnected realms of being, and no single stratum can be subsumed within any of the others. The critically realistic notion of emergence offers a more powerful alternative to both dualistic and reductionist readings. The domain of the mental, for example, cannot be either separated from or reduced to the domain of the natural. The feelings, thoughts and ideas possessed by self-conscious human minds are dependent on the biological processes within the brain: as such, they cannot exist as disembodied souls dualistically separated from the body; such dependence does not, however, justify the reduction of the mental to the physical (biology can explain how the mind functions at the biological level, but cannot explain the mind's thoughts and feelings without slipping into the reductionist fallacy). The notion of emergence allows us to see that nature, minds and culture are distinctive-yet-interconnected dimensions of reality. This means that any holistic account of reality must necessarily be stratified and polyphonic, capable of providing retroductive explanations of *both* individual strata *and* the complex and dynamic interrelations between them. This has significant educational implications, since any account of education that focuses on a single stratum at the expense of others will necessarily be dualistic and/or reductive: thus Rousseau's progressive child-centred education isolates the natural mind of the learner from culture, whilst Locke's traditionalist society-centred education occludes the individuality of particular minds.

The dimension of Transcendence raises a particular problem for educators. The fact that the Transcendent domain is contested is not in itself problematic, since all strata of reality are contested and without such contestation it would be impossible to exercise judgemental rationality. What is problematic is that such contestation operates at a deep level, raising not merely quantitative questions regarding the nature and scope of Transcendence, but more fundamental qualitative questions regarding the ontological status of the Transcendent realm and the very possibility of obtaining epistemic access to it. Educators can take for granted both the ontological status of nature, minds and culture, and its openness to epistemic scrutiny; the same cannot be said for the realm of Transcendence. This cannot, however, justify the exclusion of Transcendence from the field of education, for at least two reasons.

First, regardless of the ontological status of Transcendence per se, beliefs *about* Transcendence constitute potent causal mechanisms that impact, whether for good or ill, on individuals and society. Human beings, both individually and collectively, subscribe to beliefs about Transcendence and act upon them: some by affirming particular accounts of Transcendence, others by denying its ontological actuality and reducing it to the status of a mental projection. Because such beliefs are potent causal mechanisms, we have a moral, intellectual and spiritual obligation to ask both ontological questions about the truth of such beliefs, and epistemic questions about how we might adjudicate between conflicting truth claims. Since, as Bhaskar's dialectical philosophy points out, both absence and presence are equally powerful causal mechanisms, it follows that the ontological and epistemic negation of Transcendence is as significant for human flourishing as its ontological and epistemic affirmation.

Second, accounts of nature, mind and culture throw up a set of *aporiai* that extend beyond the boundaries of the arts, sciences and humanities to ask ontological questions of the totality of reality, and epistemic questions of our knowledge of the totality of reality. Such *aporiai* take us into the realms of metaphysics and theology. Thus, for example, natural science is concerned with the natural stratum of reality, and employs the epistemic tools of empirical observation, mathematical measuring, experimental testing, and retroductive modelling that emerged from, and are progressively refined through, ongoing a posteriori scientific engagements with the natural order-of-things. In seeking to explain nature, natural scientists work with a number of metaphysical assumptions about the *nature* of nature: assumptions that are forced on them by their abductive encounters with nature, but which are not, apparently, open to explanation *by* nature. It would not be possible to conduct natural science without making certain assumptions regarding the ontological realities of space, time, objects and causal mechanisms, and of the open-yet-ordered manner in which these objects and mechanisms interact together within relative spatio-temporal coordinates. This raises at least two metaphysical *aporiai*: why is there something rather than nothing? And why is that 'something' simultaneously indeterminate-yet-explicable?

Questions about the totality of reality also involve questions about the relationship between different strata of reality. The natural realm has generated sentient beings who are dependent-on yet irreducible-to nature; these sentient beings are capable of explaining (or, at least, partially explaining) the natural order-of-things, and in doing so frequently employ aesthetic intuitions generated by the intrinsic beauty and majesty of nature; these same beings are also capable of asking moral, aesthetic, spiritual, metaphysical and theological questions about the meaning and purpose of their lives, and of the meaning and purpose of the natural environment within which they conduct their lives. Answers to such questions vary. Some naturalists insist that natural science possesses the potential to explain the totality of reality as ultimately emergent from and reducible to nature; some philosophers and theologians insist that a comprehensive explanation of reality must appeal to some greater Transcendent reality. There is a danger here of the naturalist overstepping the proper boundaries of natural science and presenting it as a universal science whose methods are applicable to the investigation of all strata of reality as well as to the explanation of the totality of reality. Just as natural scientists are fully justified in rejecting theological appeals to a 'god-of-the-gaps' in scientific knowledge, so metaphysicians and theologians are equally justified in rejecting scientific appeals to a 'naturalistic-explanation-of-the-gaps' in metaphysical and theological knowledge; just as metaphysicians and theologians cannot legitimately pontificate on natural science, so natural scientists cannot legitimately pontificate on theology and metaphysics.

Unless we are willing to arbitrarily attribute discursive privilege to one or other of the currently available retroductive explanatory models of the totality of reality, we must concede that the question of the ultimate order-of-things stands open, contested and unresolved. This being the case, there can be little warrant for excluding any potentially viable explanatory model from the curriculum, and no warrant whatsoever for excluding metaphysical and theological *aporiai*. Given the dialectical principle that absence and presence are similarly potent causal mechanisms, any such exclusion would function to significantly reshape our understanding of the totality of reality and the ultimate meaning and purpose of life. Until such time as humanity recognises the alethic truth of the ultimate nature of the totality of reality and the ultimate meaning and purpose of life, neither metaphysical nor theological explorations of Transcendence can legitimately be excluded from humankind's intellectual endeavours – other than through acts of intellectual violence and repression.

This has profound implications for education: an education that excludes Transcendence and the twin disciplines of metaphysics and theology from the curriculum will necessarily commit a version of either the ontic or the epistemic fallacy, and in doing so impose a particular, ontologically and epistemically specific, worldview onto the curriculum and treat it as true, despite the fact that it is fundamentally contested by intelligent individuals and groups. Such a move would require the abandonment of at least one of the core principles of critical realism: ontological realism, epistemic relativity or judgemental relativity. We cannot make sense of nature without also seeking to make sense of minds and culture, and we cannot make sense of nature, minds and culture without also seeking to make sense of them *sub specie aeternitatis*, under the aspect of Transcendence. And this is the case whether or not Transcendence is ontologically putative or real, since both the rejection and affirmation of Transcendence has fundamental implications for the pursuit of truth and truthful living in relation to the ultimate order-of-things.

Contra Rousseau, we cannot make sense of our lives by focusing exclusively on our personal and mental space: we must also attend to our relational identities in cultural space (interpersonal, moral, aesthetic, political, economic, technological, historical, etc.), natural space (physical, chemical, biological), and Transcendent space (whether theistic, pantheistic, panentheistic, meta-Realistic or naturalistic). Contra Locke, we cannot make sense of our lives by focusing exclusively on cultural space: we must also attend to our relational identities in personal space, natural space and Transcendent space. Education, most broadly conceived, is the process of understanding who we are and what we might become as individual and communal members of the human race, in relation to our situated existence within the totality of the interlinked natural, personal, cultural and Transcendent orders-of-things, viewed holistically *sub specie aeternitatis*. We indwell a rich and multifaceted universe that cannot be reduced to either brute facts or imaginary fictions. We are the people we are by virtue of our emergent relationships with ourselves, with nature, with other persons-in-community, with the moral, aesthetic, technological, political and economic fruits of human culture, and with the realm of Transcendence (present or absent, putative or real). We relate to the reality we indwell on the basis of a rich intellectual, emotional, moral, aesthetic and spiritual stratification. Because of this, the pursuit of truth is simultaneously the pursuit of truthful living in pursuit of intellectual, moral, aesthetic and spiritual harmony with the ultimate order-of-things, in a manner in which we recognise that which is and is not, that which can be changed and that which cannot be changed, that which ought to be changed and that which ought not to be changed. The critical realist principle of ontological realism demands an education committed to the pursuit of truth and truthful living *sub specie aeternitatis*.

(2) *Education and epistemic relativity*. If an educational commitment to ontology need not result in the ontic fallacy of reifying the curriculum as a set of absolute facts, then a commitment to epistemic relativity need not result in the epistemic fallacy of reducing the curriculum to a set of absolute fictions. Critical realism's appeal to epistemic relativity is not an appeal to a thoroughgoing epistemic relativism: epistemic relativity, as conceived by critical realists, does not affirm the total absence of knowledge of reality celebrated by some postmodernists, merely the absence of the kind of indubitably secure foundational knowledge dreamt of by the modern philosophers of the Enlightenment. To invoke a dualistic Kantian distinction between noumena and phenomena, between the world-in-itself and the world-as-it-appears-to-us, is to tread an artificially sceptical path that ignores our embeddedness within reality. We are, from the start, intimately engaged with a reality we already know a great deal about: enough to perform open-heart surgery, appreciate the sublimity of Mozart's music, and identify the Holocaust as a great evil. Nevertheless, our knowledge is always partial and incomplete. One of the paradoxes of the epistemic quest appears to be that the greater the depth and breadth of our knowledge of any given object, the greater our awareness that its richness and complexity transcends our understanding. This is clearly evident in the progress of natural science: Newton understood the natural world better than Aristotle, and Einstein understood the natural world better that Newton; yet we are more aware today than we have ever been of the partial and incomplete nature of our knowledge of nature.

Learning is dependent on our embeddedness in established knowledge-relationships. To learn more about reality is not normally to come to know that which was previously completely unknown, but rather to come to know that which is already known in new ways previously unavailable to us. We learn by attaining deeper and richer insight into realities we already partially know. Meno's paradox, which asserts 'the impossibility of learning something because the learner either must already know the stuff or is otherwise unable to recognise it when encountered', assumes a dualistic separation between the knower and the object of knowledge (Marton and Booth 1997: 178). In the general course of things we learn by encountering better ways of understanding things we already know; and if we do happen to stumble across things we did not previously know and were not necessarily looking for, we do not generally have a problem recognising it as something new. The encounter with things we did not previously know takes the form of an abductive revelation: we may not have known what we were looking for but we can recognise it as something new, both because its ontological reality reveals itself to us and because we recognise it as some other than that which we already know. If we can only see red and green and then stumble across blue, we do not need to have been looking for blue in order to recognise that we have encountered blue, and we learn to know blue both because it reveals itself to us and because we recognise it as different to red and green (Marton and Tsui 2004: 14f.; cf. Hella 2007: 50ff.).

The quest for knowledge involves 'taking the experiences of people seriously and exploring the physical, the social, the cultural world they experience' (Marton and Booth 1997: 13). The expansion of knowledge involves the expansion of awareness of the richness and depth of that which we already partially know.

> There is 'not a real world "out there" and a subjective world "in here". The world [as experienced] is not constructed by the learner, nor is it imposed upon her; it is *constituted* as an internal relation between them.'
>
> (Hella 2007: 42; quoting Marton and Booth 1997: 13)

Knowledge expands and deepens as we experience *variation* in our relationships with different objects of knowledge (Hella 2007: 50ff.). Learning takes place when we come to experience the world in different ways: the experience of variation in ways of seeing the object of knowledge allows understanding to expand the lifeworld of the learner. Learning is not a process of identifying basic facts and constructing more complex meanings out of them, but of moving 'from an undifferentiated and poorly integrated understanding of the whole to an increased differentiation and integration of the whole and its parts' (Marton and Booth 1997: viii). Constructivist models of learning invite learners to construct subjective meanings from objective facts; realistic models of learning invite learners to attend to different ways of experiencing and explaining the same object, and begin to differentiate more and less powerful ways of understanding, insofar as these are demanded and warranted by the object of knowledge itself. This will involve working out from their own limited horizons of understanding toward richer horizons of understanding gifted to them by their teachers. Since 'one way of experiencing the world can be judged to be better than another way', it follows that 'some people must have become better at experiencing the world – or have experienced the world in a better way, or have gained better knowledge – than others' (Marton and Booth 1997: 13).

The problem with comprehensive liberal education is not the absence of ontology, but rather the imposition of a singular subterranean ontology. Contrary to its own self-understanding, and despite its attempted exclusion of both metaphysics and theology, comprehensive liberal education is far from being ontologically neutral. It harbours two clear, if generally unstated and implicit, ontological commitments: first, to the ontological givenness of a value-free natural order-of-things; second, to the ontological primacy of individual persons as unique moral, aesthetic and spiritual beings.

With regard to the former, the affirmation of the ontological givenness of a value-free natural order-of-things leads to the assumption that secure knowledge of the world is largely restricted to the fruits of the natural and, albeit to a lesser extent, social sciences. Such knowledge is deemed to be objectively grounded in a posteriori empirical observation of natural and social 'facts' in a manner that tends to lack ontological depth, so that patterns of meaning identified in the interactions between objects tend to be viewed as human constructs only nominally related to the objects themselves, rather than as the product of underlying causal mechanisms. This applies especially to the discernment of moral, aesthetic and spiritual meaning in nature and society, which is frequently assumed to reside, not in the natural and social facts themselves, but rather in the values attributed to them by constructive human agents. Despite the human tendency to construct subjective meaning out of objects' facts, the facts themselves constitute ontological constants that cannot be avoided and which place certain unavoidable constraints on human being and action. In so far as natural and social facts are deemed to be self-evident givens, grounded in the secure epistemic foundation of the empirical experience of the Cartesian ego, their identification tends to constitute a form of the ontic fallacy that rejects epistemic relativity and minimises judgemental rationality.

With regard to the latter, the attribution of ontological primacy to individual persons, by virtue of their status as the highest entities known to have emerged from the impersonal natural order, goes hand-in-hand with their identification as the ultimate source and final arbiters of all moral, aesthetic and spiritual meaning. Moral, aesthetic and spiritual values are deemed not to be intrinsic to reality as a whole, since the natural order-of-things is value-neutral, but rather to possess the status of subjective human constructs, albeit constructs that can take on the authority of non-negotiable moral norms (e.g. in declarations of universal human rights). Two key consequences flow from the assumption of the ontological primacy of the individual Cartesian self. First, the central importance of personal flourishing, understood in terms of personal freedom *from* all external constraint (apart, that is, from the unavoidable brute facts of nature) and freedom *for* self-realisation, self-determination and self-construction. Second, the need to reconcile the freedom of each individual with the freedom of all others, which takes the form of a duty of tolerance designed to ameliorate the threat posed by the inevitable clash of human interests that flows from an individual's exercise of their rights to freedom of thought, expression and action.

These twin features of the liberal self, the right to autonomy and the duty of tolerance, tend to generate various forms of pragmatism. If right action equates with that which 'works' or is deemed 'effective', then some or other criteria for judging what 'works' or what is 'effective' needs to be put in place, since what works for one person may be detrimental to another and what is effective for one community may be counterproductive to another. However, since we construct our own values (whether individually or collectively), and since by-and-large such values are deemed to be essentially subjective, what 'works' or counts as 'effective' will vary according to the perceived needs, desires and aspirations of particular individuals and groups. On this reading, any notion that individual and collective choices *could* be or *ought* to be established on the basis of ontological considerations regarding our individual and collective relationship to the ultimate order-of-things appears to be ruled out a priori. However, this is not the case, since it is precisely the twin ontological assumptions that the natural world is value-neutral and that human beings are therefore free to construct their own values that provide the liberal polity of freedom and tolerance with its (albeit frequently implicit) ontological underpinning. In so far as the Cartesian self is deemed to be free to construct his own moral, aesthetic and spiritual values without recourse to any external influences or constraints, this polity tends to constitute a form of the epistemic fallacy that rejects ontological realism and minimises judgemental rationality.

Educationally, this liberal polity pans out in a range of educational imperatives: first, to transmit those natural and social 'facts' deemed necessary for a competent understanding of and engagement with the world; second, to maximise the freedom of individuals to fulfil their own innate potentials, follow their personal desires, and construct their preferred realities; third, to cultivate the kind of politically stable, socially cohesive, culturally tolerant, aesthetically vibrant and economically wealthy society deemed necessary for the successful practice of personal autonomy; fourth, to generate the skills (personal, social, cognitive, practical, moral, aesthetic, spiritual, etc.) each individual requires in order to pursue their own goals effectively and avoid inhibiting the freedom of others to do the same.

Philosophically this comprehensive liberal polity is empiricist with regard to natural and social 'facts' and idealist (in predominately romantic and postmodern guises) with regard to moral, aesthetic and spiritual 'values'. It espouses a naturalistic account of the natural world and a secular humanistic account of human beings as autonomous arbiters of their own values and destinies. Since comprehensive liberalism's ontological commitments tend to be subterranean, functioning as unacknowledged norms within an intellectual economy inherently suspicious of ontological claims, they tend to be closed to alternative ontologies. This ontological monophony runs against the grain of the polyphonic reality of the actual make-up of liberal societies, which tend to host a plurality of religious and secular traditions that subscribe to a range of ontologically incommensurable worldviews. As a consequence such alternative ontologies tend to be colonised and subsumed within comprehensive liberal praxis, so that comprehensive liberalism is happy to host alternative cultural traditions provided they conform to the core non-negotiable values of freedom and tolerance and restrict their nonliberal ontological commitments to the private sphere.

The net effect is the ideological imposition of an implicit ontology by default, and colonisation of other ontologies within that implicit ontology. Despite the liberal rhetoric of freedom and tolerance, genuine voices of alterity and otherness tend to be comprehensively and systematically excluded. There is no room here for epistemic relativity, which is excluded in favour of an amalgam of the ontic and epistemic fallacies: the ontic fallacy of assuming epistemically secure knowledge of both nature and self in a manner that bypasses epistemic relativity and minimises judgemental rationality; and the epistemic fallacy of assuming that moral, aesthetic and spiritual values can be constructed by the Cartesian self on the basis of personal preference in a manner that bypasses ontological realism and occludes judgemental rationality. If we learn by encountering variation in ways of experiencing the object of knowledge, then with regard to questions of ultimate meaning and truth a comprehensive liberal educational polity is systemically opposed to learning *sub specie aeternitatis*, by virtue of the fact that it systematically excludes all ontological accounts of the ultimate order-of-things other than its own.

A critically realistic education, operating within the politically liberal context of modern democratic societies, must necessarily eschew the educational programme of comprehensive liberalism. This need not, however, result in the eclipse of liberalism per se, since the rejection of comprehensive liberalism as an ideological construct (in so far as it embraces its ontological commitments uncritically and even unconsciously) opens the door to a recovery of John Locke's original vision of a non-comprehensive political liberalism designed to enable plural societies, hosting representatives of a diverse range of ontologically incommensurable worldviews, to pursue truth and truthful living in an open and tolerant environment without any need to impose a comprehensive liberal ontology. On this reading, a critically realistic education will, so to speak, out-liberal liberalism by informing a *genuinely open* liberal education system committed to the cultivation of freedom and tolerance, not as ends in themselves, but rather as a means to the greater liberal end of the pursuit of truth and truthful living. Just as to affirm ontological realism is not necessarily to reduce education to the task of transmitting epistemically secure objective facts (the ontic fallacy), so to affirm epistemic relativity is not necessarily to reduce education to the task of enabling learners to construct their own subjective values (the epistemic fallacy). Rather, the simultaneous affirmation of ontological realism, epistemic relativity and judgemental rationality makes possible a critically realistic education driven by the pursuit of truth and truthful living informed by both an epistemic humility open to ontological actualities and a judgemental rationality responsive to such actualities.

Though the focus here is on educational realism in liberal societies, we may note at this point – though, for lack of space, only in passing – that there is no obvious reason why a critically realistic education might not also flourish in non-liberal and non-plural societies: for example, Islamic education might be grounded in the intransitive ontological constant of the Qur'an as divinely revealed (ontological realism), whilst also acknowledging that the Qur'an is subject to epistemically diverse transitive interpretations within the Muslim community (epistemic relativity) that are open to rational debate (judgemental rationality) (Wilkinson 2015; Demirel 2015).

(3) *Education and judgemental rationality.* 'Critical', when used in the context of a critical education guided by the under-labouring tools provided by critical realism, refers to the importance of identifying a set of critical (crucial, vital, decisive) aspects or dimensions of education, namely ontological realism, epistemic relativity and judgemental rationality, rather than to any neo-Kantian concern to cultivate students' cognitive faculties and critical thinking skills. The latter option, of an education primarily oriented towards generic epistemic processes abstract from ontological realities, is one product of the fragmentation of post-Enlightenment occidental education described in the previous chapter. There we observed how classical Jewish, Christian and Platonic approaches to education were in the main holistic and ontologically grounded, so that the

pursuit of knowledge was *simultaneously* the pursuit of personal wellbeing and social flourishing. The fragmented education of modernity and post-modernity viewed the traditionalist induction of learners into socio-cultural norms and the progressive nurturing of the innate potential of individual persons as binary opposites, and placed the pursuit of knowledge on one side in favour of the cultivation of the social and personal skills deemed necessary for individual and communal flourishing.

Neo-Kantianism invites an understanding of judgemental rationality as a process of critical thinking oriented around the mind's capacity to construct meaning out of a set of given (empirical or idealist) 'facts'. The primary task of education is to generate generic and subject-specific thinking skills. If the 'facts' are value-neutral, then educational value lies in the ability of the learners to draw such objective facts into their subjective inner space and construct meanings out of them in ways appropriate to their own dispositions and aspirations, and the pragmatic needs of society. An education limited to brute 'facts' will necessarily be cold, objective and existentially irrelevant to the learner: a mere assimilation of useless information. An education that requires learners to draw the brute 'facts' into their subjective lifeworlds and construct patterns of meaning out of them will become immediately and existentially relevant to their lives. Such neo-Kantian constructivism constitutes a combination of the ontic and epistemic fallacies: it commits the ontic fallacy by supposing that the brute 'facts' of reality, the primary foundations of knowledge, are immediately accessible to the knower; and it commits the epistemic fallacy by requiring learners to utilise their own cognitive faculties in imposing subjective meaning onto the brute 'facts' of empirical data, idealistic concepts and romantic experiences. On this reading, knowledge is achieved by forcing the brute 'facts' of reality (the ontic fallacy) into the procrustean straitjacket of the mind's cognitive faculties (the epistemic fallacy).

Critical realism, in resisting both the ontic and epistemic fallacies, advocates a progressive deepening of knowledge, capable of passing beyond descriptive knowledge of the surface appearance of states of affairs towards explanatory knowledge of the underlying causal mechanisms that constitute and generate them. Contra constructivism, knowledge is not properly generated by a neo-Kantian process of employing the mind's cognitive apparatus to configure empirical data, linguistic concepts and pre-linguistic sensibilities into satisfying patterns. Rather, it involves relating to reality and allowing reality itself to shape understanding in deeper, more comprehensive, inclusive and powerful ways. Though it is certainly true that we construct accounts of reality, such constructs have validity only to the extent that they identify, discern and explain reality itself. It follows that a stratified curriculum, shaped by a stratified reality, should seek to provide learners with increasingly rich knowledge-relationships that will enable them to not only to *experience* and *describe*, but also – and more fundamentally – to *explain* reality.

Under normative circumstances we learn such explanations by being inducted into intellectual traditions rather than creating such traditions from scratch: we learn natural science not by replicating for ourselves centuries of scientific exploration, but by immersing ourselves in the textbooks that present to us the fruits of such exploration; similarly, we learn theology not by speculating about God *in abstracto*, but by engaging *in concreto* with the cumulative heritage of the religious and spiritual wisdom of the past, and placing ourselves at the feet of theological, philosophical and spiritual experts. Learners in the main are not giants, but rather those who stand on the shoulders of giants. Of course, there are always learners who are themselves giants, operating at the cutting edge of our expanding knowledge of reality and generating original insights and understanding. However, such people are few and far between, and normally work in research institutes and institutes of higher education at doctoral and post-doctoral level. The fact that most learners do not reach such heady heights is reflected in the fact that 'originality', however welcome, is not normally a criterion for assessing students' work prior to doctoral level research.

For the vast majority of learners, education is a process of induction into traditions of knowledge, and learning a process of responding to testimonial authority. This is not to suggest that such learning involves merely the passive induction of students into such traditions; on the contrary, it requires their active engagement with the traditions into which they are being inducted, so that they assimilate for themselves the various ways of experiencing and understanding the world embodied within them. Nor does it imply the authoritarian imposition of one particular way, to the exclusion of other available ways, of experiencing and understanding reality: since knowledge is contested, effective learning requires students to learn to navigate around contested ways of experiencing and understanding objects of knowledge. Neither does it imply that learners have no need to construct accounts of their developing knowledge: however, such constructs need to be driven, not by the exercise of generic cognitive skills in abstract isolation, but rather by the subservience of the cognitive faculties to the ontological primacy of objects of knowledge. Judgemental rationality, when applied in the sphere of education, is the process of inducting students into contested traditions of knowledge in a manner that enables their experience and understanding of the world to be progressively deepened and expanded in conformity with the actual nature of reality. This means that the formation of mind and understanding of the world constitute part of a single, ontologically grounded, epistemic process.

7 Liberal religious education

Given the impossibility of inhabiting a genuinely neutral space, the religious educator is 'under an obligation to expose for examination the fundamental axioms, the prior decisions about what is allowed to count as evidence, which underlie his way of understanding' (Newbigin 1982: 99). This opens up the possibility of 'a *critique of ideology* that aims at freeing the subject from his dependence on "hypostasized powers" concealed in the structures of speech and action' (McCarthy 1984: 94). Bernard Lonergan argues that 'the basic form of alienation is man's disregard of the transcendental precepts, Be attentive, Be intelligent, Be reasonable, Be responsible', and that 'the basic form of ideology is a doctrine that justifies such alienation' (Lonergan 1973: 55). We have also seen how post-Enlightenment versions of the epistemic fallacy generated a closed liberal worldview that seeks to colonise theological and educational discourse, and religious and pedagogic practices, within its own normative frame of reference. This has resulted in the disintegration of classical *paideia* and the privatisation of the public truth claims of the Abrahamic faiths. The situation presents a profound challenge to the religious educator operating within a liberal environment: how to do justice to the non-liberal self-understanding of the vast majority of the world's religious traditions within a cultural and pedagogic space dominated by liberal norms and assumptions. The present chapter explores the thesis that liberal religious education, which has dominated the subject in state-funded schools in England and Wales since the early 1970s, is culpable for a widespread ideological misrepresentation of religion. The following chapter will propose that critical realism offers a heuristic framework capable of meeting the challenge of doing pedagogic justice to non-liberal worldviews and belief systems.

Confessional religious education

The provision of mass education in England and Wales has its roots in the Christian churches (Worsley 2013). The National Society of the Church of England was founded in 1811 to provide education for the children of working-class families employed in the factories, mills and mines of the newly industrialised nation, and within 40 years there were over 12,000 church schools operating across England and Wales. The Elementary Education Act of 1870 (the 'Foster Act'), which made primary education compulsory for all, marked the state's first major intervention in mass education. Whereas the Christian nature of Anglican church schools had been taken for granted, the new state-sponsored board schools were obliged to follow the Cowper-Temple clause, the so-called 'conscience amendment', which forbade the use of any religious catechism distinctive of a particular religious denomination. In effect, this meant that the religious education provided in board schools generally took the form of a common-denominator Protestantism acceptable to both the Anglican establishment and non-conformist churches.

The 1944 Education Act (the 'Butler Act'), which consolidated the dual system of state support for both 'non-religious' county schools and 'religious' voluntary aided/controlled schools, was a watershed in the provision of mass schooling in England and Wales. Broadly speaking (and placing on one side the differences between voluntary aided and controlled schools for reasons of space), 'religious' voluntary aided and controlled schools retained control over religious instruction and school worship, while 'non-religious' county schools were required to provide both regular religious instruction and a daily act of collective worship in a manner not distinctive of any particular religious denomination. Opt-out clauses enabled parents to withdraw their children, and teachers to exempt themselves from, both activities in county schools on grounds of conscience. Whilst religious instruction in aided and controlled schools remained the responsibility of the sponsoring religious foundation, religious instruction in county schools was to be delivered in accordance with a locally agreed syllabus, drawn up by a local Agreed Syllabus Conference consisting of four panels representing the Church of England, other religious denominations, the local authority and teachers' organisations. Though the 1944 settlement is sometimes represented as the result of horse-trading between church and state, with both parties requiring the support of the other in order to achieve their respective educational goals, a more generous estimate views it as a reflection of a widespread concern, amongst politicians, church leaders and society at large, to address the moral and spiritual vacuum at the heart of European civilisation exposed by the Second World War.

From a political perspective, the 1938 Spens Report, which prepared the ground for the 1944 legislation, can be read in part as a response to the rise of National Socialism in Germany (Loukes 1965: 22f.). The Report's fundamental concern was to establish a moral and spiritual basis for the life of the nation. In arguing for the place of Christian education in all state-sponsored schools it recognised the contested nature of Christianity, acknowledged the dangers of proselytisation, and accepted the need to respect pupil autonomy. An entire chapter was devoted to defending the teaching of Christian scripture in secondary schools in a manner that raises 'issues relating to the meaning of life and to human destiny which in the world outside the school are the subject of profound disagreement' (Spens Report 1938: 206). No pupil 'can be counted as properly educated unless he or she has been made aware of the fact of the existence of a religious interpretation of life' (ibid.: 208). Study of the Bible must attend to its primary theological meaning and avoid reductive interpretations that would limit it to 'mere' moral, historical or literary levels of meaning: 'the Biblical literature contains a body of perfectly intelligible [theological] ideas, which can be systematically presented and studied' (ibid.). Such a theological reading of scripture should be objective, that is to say, grounded in academic scholarship, and make the same intellectual demands on pupils as any other subject in the curriculum. The religious interpretation of life is controversial, and there is no significantly 'large body of opinion definitely favourable to an entirely secular secondary education' (ibid.). The focus on Christian scripture is justified because of the central place of Christianity in the life of the nation, and because 'the Bible is the classic book of Christianity and forms the basis of the structure of Christian faith and worship' (ibid.). Though there is no suggestion that scripture lessons should seek to convert pupils, 'it is reasonable for those who teach the Bible to make it clear that the religion contained in the New Testament challenges us to faith and worship' (ibid.: 216).

From a religious perspective, Archbishop William Temple, speaking in 1941 on behalf of the Anglican establishment, expressed 'an ever-deepening conviction that in this present struggle we are fighting to preserve those elements of human civilisation and in our own national tradition which owe their origin to Christian faith' (Loukes 1965: 23). In the light of the struggle against Nazism, it was necessary for the nation to take stock and recognise that 'the standards of our social, commercial, and political life are not even professedly the standards of Christ' (Baker 1946: 159). Rather than 'fighting a rearguard action in perpetual retreat', the established church should seek to be a positive influence on the State for the good of society (Iremonger 1948: 571). To that end, there was 'evidently an urgent need to strengthen our foundations by securing that effective Christian education should be given in all schools to the children, the future citizens, of our country' (Loukes 1965: 23). 'We are not training children according to their own true nature or in relation to their true environment unless we are training them to trust in God' (Temple 1942: 69). Since there is no possibility of neutrality, 'education should throughout be inspired by faith in God and find its focus in worship' (ibid.: 73). 'Education is only adequate and worthy when it is itself religious ... therefore our ideal for the children of our country is the ideal for truly religious education' (Iremonger 1948: 571).

The theory and practice of religious instruction and collective worship in schools in the 1940s and 1950s paid little attention to secularism, and tended to address issues of religious pluralism only in relation to internal differences within the broad Protestant tradition. The underlying assumption was 'that every child is a Christian and comes from a Christian home' (Cox 1966: 16). As Harold Loukes points out, 'the church's theory of education was a theory not of instruction or enlightenment but of community' (Loukes 1965: 27). The ultimate aim of religious instruction and collective worship was 'not to get over to the child a body of facts – or "inert ideas" ... but to inculcate and foster a comprehensible Way of Life' (London County Council 1947: 29). Christianity was to be assimilated by pupils through a hermeneutic of cultural immersion: Christian belief and practice should so permeate the ethos of a school that it 'provides an environment in which the child may acquire the elementary virtues unconsciously' (ibid.: 21). Collective worship 'can quicken the spirits of the children who take part in it, fixing their roots in the Christian faith, and giving them direction and inspiration for life' (ibid.: 26). Religious instruction was dominated by the study of Christian scripture, supplemented with introductory primers in Christian doctrine, church history and ethics. Classroom pedagogy, in line with other subject areas, adopted 'classic authoritarian practices ... chalk-and-talk, the dictating of notes, the working of mechanical exercises, learning for tests, rote-learning' (Loukes 1965: 166).

If such a conservative, traditionalist and apparently paternalistic pedagogy cut across the grain on the Enlightenment's commitment to the critical assimilation of information and autonomous construction of meaning, it had the partial virtue of retaining the vestiges of a rich vision of Christian *paideia* deeply rooted in the ancient past (Brueggemann 1982; Melchert 1994, 1998; Wright 2007: 55ff.). The early church learnt from its Jewish roots a set of fundamental educational principles: that theological knowledge is constituted by the relationship between the subjectivity of the learner and the objective reality of God; that such a relationship requires the commitment of the whole person, in thought, word and deed; that the human side of this knowledge equation is vulnerable to intellectual error, moral failure and spiritual ignorance; and that under the guidance of God's Holy Spirit, as mediated by scripture and tradition and driven by worship and study, human beings could engage in the pursuit of ultimate truth and truthful living *sub specie aeternitatis*. At the same time, the early church learnt from the educational practices of Hellenistic culture the central importance of cultural induction (Farley 2001; Jaeger 1961; Kelsey 1992; Wood 1985). Only by immersing pupils in the wisdom of the past and empowering them to assimilate it for themselves was it possible to follow the examples of Jacob and Job – and, indeed, the collective experience of Israel as a whole, via a historical dialectic of rebellion and trust, exile and restoration – and wrestle with God in a pedagogic process of trial, testing and transformation.

Implicit religious education

Though groundbreaking, and despite inadvertently preparing the ground for the emergence of liberal religious education in the 1970s, the 'implicit' approach to religious education that emerged in the 1960s did not challenge the confessional status quo, but rather sought to make it more effective. The 'implicit' label derives from the assumption that the starting point for religious education should be the (often unrealised) potential for religious experience and spiritual insight latent in pupils' minds. John Hull describes implicit religious education as a 'Christian nurture model along liberal and progressive lines', and Dennis Bates observes that 'however liberal in intention, Loukes' suggestions clearly constitute a programme of Christian nurture' (Hull 1984: 29; Bates 1984: 80). The model of implicit religious education was dominated by two figures: Harold Loukes and Ronald Goldman.

(1) *Harold Loukes.* In *New Ground in Christian Education* Loukes identified a crisis of relevance facing religious education and highlighted its failure to relate Christian faith to pupils' lifeworlds (Loukes 1965). However, he put this down primarily to inadequate teaching methods, rather than to the ambiguous and contested status of Christianity in an increasingly secular and plural environment. Loukes found support for this judgement in his earlier study *Teenage Religion*, which had presented empirical evidence of students' experiences of religious education (Loukes 1961).

> I reported the confusion and ambivalence of mind and heart created among fourteen-year-olds by their religious education. They were confused, it will be remembered, rather than hostile, ambivalent rather than rejecting. The subject matter, they agreed, was interesting: the manner and method were 'totally boring'.
>
> (Loukes 1965: 11f.)

Loukes recognised that the pupils he interviewed were beginning, albeit hesitantly, to interpret their Christian education in the light of their own experiences, and to construct their own understandings of ultimate reality and the mystery of life. He thought it reasonable to 'expect [teenage] children – even less able children – to be capable of ... "autonomy" in religious ideas' (Loukes 1961: 100). However the empirical evidence revealed widespread religious illiteracy, and consequently Loukes invited his readers to 'view with ... alarm a religious education that results in a total inability to think about religion' (Loukes 1965: 12). Dismissing Ronald Goldman's suggestion that young pupils lack the cognitive apparatus necessary for an adult understanding of religion, and ignoring secular claims that religious insight is an unobtainable goal because religious beliefs are cognitively bankrupt, Loukes laid the blame for high levels of religious illiteracy on inadequate teaching. If 'when children hear their elders talk about God, they not only fail to understand, but so radically misunderstand that their whole view of reality may be distorted for life', then the problem lies not with them but with the failure of their teachers to communicate effectively (Loukes 1963: 4).

Loukes insisted that 'religious education should be conducted in an atmosphere of realism and relevance', in which the question of the meaning of Christianity is intimately connected with the question of its truth (Loukes 1961: 11). He identified as a 'cardinal principle, that pupils should be personally and actively concerned with reality' (Loukes 1965: 98). Consequently, he resisted any reduction of religious education to moral education: 'religious belief is concerned first with truth and only later with moral consequences' (ibid.: 76). Loukes recognised the tensions between theological and secular accounts of reality generated by the Enlightenment, and accepted that these impact on pupils. Under the influence of empiricism and positivism, 'we have, in the last thirty years, become frightened of using words that do not refer to some kind of sense experience, or to public, openly demonstrable techniques of thought that relate, in their beginning or end, to "things" ' (Loukes 1963: 5). However, if theological language is approached metaphorically rather than literally, and understood as the expression of personal experience of the being and presence of God, then it can lay claim to an intellectual warrant immune to empiricist and positivist critiques. In effect, Loukes appealed to a romantic liberal Protestant apologetic that employed an experiential-expressive model of religious language in preference to a cognitive-propositional one: if religious language is the secondary expression of the primary self-authenticating spiritual experience of the Cartesian ego, then it is misunderstood if it is taken to be making objective truth claims that are open to empirical verification. If we teach Christianity in a literalistic manner, then 'we are failing to convey through the study of the Bible what we ourselves believe the Bible to say' (ibid.). Hence the challenge for religious educators is 'to convey to the young that our "pictures" of God are all analogical', and to enable them to see that Christianity makes 'statements that intelligent men will, whether they agree or not, take seriously' (ibid.).

This anti-empiricist hermeneutic requires the gulf between ordinary language and theological language to be overcome, and this is to be achieved by showing pupils the connection between their own personal experiences and religious experience. Hence the central task of religious education is to demonstrate to pupils the relevance of Christianity by drawing attention to the convergence between their immanent existential lifeworld experiences and Transcendent religious experience, and between ordinary language and religious language.

> We must be ready to describe *his* [God's] *impact upon us* in language so human, so full of experiential meaning, so personal that they recognise in our talk something that they have known but not understood in their encounter with life.
>
> (Bates 1984: 76)

(2) *Ronald Goldman.* Like Loukes, Goldman was concerned with the failure of confessional religious instruction to engage and convince pupils: 'far from promoting the religious sensibilities of children, the diet of Bible study and church history required by the syllabuses was resulting in boredom, confusion, and even rejection of religion by the majority of pupils' (Slee 1992: 133). The problem, according to Goldman, lay not in the nature of religion itself, but the way in which it is presented in the classroom without reference to the child's cognitive and linguistic development. Adopting an experiential-expressive model of religious language, Goldman identified religious thinking as 'the process of generalizing from various experiences, previous perceptions and already held concepts to an interpretative concept of the activity and nature of the divine' (Goldman 1964: 14). Religious 'language is almost entirely based upon analogy and metaphor, inferring from other non-religious experience the nature of the divine' (ibid.). This has significant pedagogic and hermeneutical implications, since if

religious language is essentially an expression for human experience, then it follows that religious thinking is 'dependent upon understanding the original experience upon which the analogy or metaphor is based' (ibid.: 15). Goldman offers a Piagetian account of cognitive development in which undifferentiated sensory experience of the material world leads to the emergence of thought and language, which then passes through distinct developmental stages. Initially children employ concrete-operational thinking to use language to name and label particular empirical objects; and later, normally at the stage of early adolescence, they begin to employ formal-operational thinking to use abstract conceptual language.

Goldman's empirical research suggested that when presented with the biblical story of Moses and the Burning Bush, pupils wedded to concrete-operational thinking seek quasi-scientific or magical explanations as to why 'the bush was blazing, yet it was not consumed', whereas pupils capable of formal-operational thinking recognise the blazing-yet-unconsumed bush as symbolic of the numinous presence of God and focus on Moses' spiritual experience rather than its linguistic expression. Unlike the literal-minded concrete thinkers, the abstract thinkers have begun to grasp a crucial theological truth:

> In the last resort, religion is a mystery and speaks of matters and experiences which are not easily communicable. Some religious experiences are so profound and personal and mysterious that it is doubtful if they are communicable at all, except through the emotional language of the arts.
>
> (Goldman 1964: 2f.)

Goldman insists that, provided we recognise that religious language is properly analogical and expressive, religion cannot properly be dismissed as pseudo-science; rather, it is grounded in a profound, intuitive and pre-linguistic experience *sub specie aeternitatis* of our place in the universe as a whole. He quotes, with approval, William James' understanding of religion as 'the feelings, the acts and experiences of individual men ... so far as they apprehend themselves to stand in relation to whatever they may consider the divine' (ibid.: 4).

This experiential-expressive understanding of religion has important hermeneutical and pedagogic implications: since any interpretation of religious expression dislocated from religious experience will inevitably lead to literalistic misunderstandings, religious understanding requires both a spiritual sensitivity towards religious experience and an ability to interpret religious expression abstractly and metaphorically. Goldman held that the widespread teaching of the Bible to young children at the concrete-operational stage encourages naive literalistic readings of the Bible that they are unable to shake off when they progress to formal-operational thinking. As a result they learn to dismiss the Bible as a quasi-scientific or magical document, and attribute an identical ontological status to Santa Claus and Jesus Christ. If confessional religious education is to achieve its intended objectives, then it must restrict the teaching of the Bible to pupils capable of formal-operational thought, whilst religious education of concrete thinkers should be directed to the stimulation of their pre-linguistic spiritual sensibilities. To bring pupils to an appreciation of religious thinking requires a form of religious education sensitive to the nature of religious experience and its linguistic expression, and to the stages of pupils' cognitive development (Goldman 1965).

The implicit religious education championed by Loukes and Goldman remained within the framework of Christian confessionalism. As such, it assumed a Christian ontology and paid little attention to epistemic relativity, both internally within the broad Protestant Christian tradition, and externally in relation to alternative religious and secular worldviews. Its primary focus was on epistemology, specifically on the suggestion that the inability of pupils to perceive the truth and relevance of Christianity was a direct result of inappropriate teaching that failed to identify the analogical and expressive nature of religious language, relate it appropriately to pupils' lifeworlds, and/or take account of their cognitive and linguistic development. The underlying assumption was that Christian teaching could not be reduced to a set of propositional statements, since to do so was to invite literalistic readings vulnerable to empiricist critiques and represent Christianity as an abstract and reified doctrinal system devoid of any existential relevance to pupils' lives. The proposed solution to this problem was to recognise that Christian teaching takes the form of expressions of religious experiences rather than propositional descriptions of Transcendent realities. It followed that to understand Christianity it was necessary to understand the spiritual experiences that generate religious expressions, and this required the adoption of an approach to teaching and learning sensitive to the experiences of pupils within their given lifeworlds and capable of demonstrating lines of convergence between these experiences and the experiences of religious adherents. If Christianity is grounded in spiritual sensibility, then the sensibility of pupils carries with it the implicit potential to converge both with Christian experience and its expression.

Loukes' curriculum proceeded from pupils' existential experiences, questions and concerns, and sought to demonstrate the ways in which Christian teaching reflected, answered and responded to them. This effectively replicated Paul Tillich's method of theological correlation, which sought to demonstrate the correspondence between the ultimate concerns of humankind and the ultimate reality of God, between human existential questions and divine answers visible in God's self-revelation, between secular language and theological language, between the realms of the finite and infinite, between immanence and Transcendence (Tillich 1978: 59ff.). This entire strategy reflects the romantic approach of liberal Protestant apologetics, which, in the light of the perceived failure of empirically and rationally grounded natural and revealed theology, followed the romantic tradition in affirming the epistemic priority of self-authenticating pre-linguistic aesthetic, moral and spiritual experience. The implicit turn in religious education shifted attention from the ontological object of Christian faith to the epistemic subject, and made the question of the epistemic means through which ontology might be appropriated, comprehended and made relevant central.

Moreover, in doing so it effectively imported into religious education the subjective turn in theology, with its ongoing struggle to demonstrate the relationship between subjective conviction and objective reality.

Counterfactually, we might imagine a scenario in which Loukes and Goldman, without letting go of their commitment to ontological realism and the pursuit of truth and truthful living *sub specie aeternitatis*, acknowledge the reality of epistemic relativity vis-à-vis Protestant Christianity, both internally within the Christian tradition and externally in relation to alternative religious and secular traditions, rather than take a generic Protestant ontology as given. This would have the virtue of opening up the question of the truth and relevance of all religious and secular worldviews, thereby freeing religious educators from the task of seeking to persuade pupils of the relevance of Protestant Christianity in its liberal guise and enabling them to address the actuality of disputed religious and secular accounts of the ultimate nature of reality and ultimate meaning and purpose of life. It would also open up questions of judgemental rationality no longer restricted by the constraints of the liberal Protestant experiential-expressive religious apologetic.

Phenomenological religious education

Though the secular study of religion first emerged in the nineteenth century, it was not until the 1960s in Britain that university departments of Religious Studies were established in parallel to more traditional departments of Theology. Though these new departments celebrated their freedom from the hegemony of any controlling theological meta-narrative, in retrospect it is clear that claims to have established a neutral perspective from which to scrutinise religious phenomena failed to recognise the normative status attributed to the epistemic and ontological assumptions of modernity (Fitzgerald 2000; Cady and Brown 2002). The use of disciplines such as history, sociology, psychology and phenomenology to investigate religious culture tended to reduce theological exploration of Transcendence per se to the investigation of *human beliefs about* Transcendence, and generate reductive immanent explanations of religious belief and practice. However, this was not necessarily the case. Ninian Smart, who established the first British Department of Religious Studies in the new University of Lancaster in 1967, whilst recognising that 'religious studies should emphasise the descriptive, historical side of religion', insisted that it had an intellectual responsibility to 'enter into dialogue with the parahistorical claims of religions and anti-religious outlooks' (Smart 1968: 106). In *Secular Education and the Logic of Religion* he argued the case for an interdisciplinary critically realistic approach to religious education.

> Thus if one starts with the sociology of religion, one is soon confronted with questions in the sociology of knowledge and about the 'rationality' of religious behaviour. But one cannot estimate this realistically without adopting some kind of philosophical position. This in turn implies a realistic appraisal

of the meaning of religious institutions, practices and claims. In regard to the latter, one needs to take seriously what religion seriously says: and this in part is discoverable in theology, including, for example, contemporary kerygmatic [revealed] theology (far removed, at first sight and yet illusorily, from the concerns of the philosopher). In brief, there is a chain of logic from the empirical study of religion to the parahistorical.

(ibid.)

In seeking to *explain* religious phenomena, the various disciplines operating under the umbrella of Religious Studies have an intellectual responsibility to avoid reductionism by addressing questions of ultimate meaning and truth.

Smart played a major role in developing the liberal 'phenomenological' approach to religious education that emerged in the 1970s in response to explicit and implicit forms of confessionalism. As the key contributor to the Schools Council's working paper *Religious Education in Secondary Schools*, he advocated a phenomenological approach to religious education that rejected the extremes of confessionalism and reductionism (Schools Council 1971). Though religious education must avoid promoting any particular religious viewpoint, it should nevertheless seek to 'transcend the informative ... in the direction of initiation into understanding the meaning of, and into questions about the truth and worth of, religion' (Smart 1968: 105). Since 'every form of religion involves passionate commitment', it is intimately and unavoidably related to that which 'a person, or a community, regards as supremely valuable' (Schools Council 1971: 22). Such passionate commitment to ultimate truth claims demands critical evaluation. If the 'special function of academic communities is to create schemes for the critical evaluation of interpretations originating in non-academic communities', then a central task of religious education is to disseminate the methods and fruits of such labours in the fields of religion, spirituality and theology (ibid.: 26). Given epistemic relativity, religious education cannot legitimately present a single explanation, whether religious or secular, 'as though it were absolute and unquestioned fact'; instead, it must 'admit the possibility of alternative patterns of interpretation', and present evidence for beliefs 'so that they may be accepted or rejected freely and intelligently' (ibid.: 24). 'It is not sufficient to parade alternatives before the eyes of the imagination and to leave it at that, as if there were no objective ways of judging their relative truth or adequacy' (ibid.: 26). Further, since the search for objective truth cannot be separated from the subjectivity of the searcher, religious education should enable students to participate in the search for 'true knowledge and understanding' in a way that becomes 'part of [their] interior mental life', so that their 'convictions are arrived at by personal discovery' (ibid.: 28).

Smart's vision departs from both the ontological and epistemic assumption of implicit religious education: rather than assuming a Christian ontology as given, it employs epistemic relativity to problematise the relationship between ultimate reality and a range of ontologically incommensurate religious and secular accounts of the ultimate order-of-things; rather than reduce judgemental rationality to the level of romantic feeling and sensibility, it assumes a cognitive engagement with the pros and cons of different truth claims; and rather than attempting to demonstrate the relevance of Christianity, it leaves the question of the relevance, meaning and truth of different religious and secular worldviews open to informed scrutiny, and thereby encourages pupils to pursue truth and truthful living *sub specie aeternitatis* by cultivating appropriate levels of religious, spiritual and theological literacy.

Remarkably, given his apparent unawareness of critical realism, Smart employs the triumvirate of ontological realism, epistemic relativity and judgemental rationality to set out the contours of an approach to religious education clearly commensurate with the model of critical religious education defended in the following chapter. Regrettably, the history of the various forms of liberal religious education that have dominated the curriculum since the mid-1970s can be read as the history of the failure to realise Smart's embryonic vision of a genuinely critically realistic religious education. The phenomenological approach to religious education, captivated by implicit religious education's pedagogic concern to demonstrate a correlation between pupils' lifeworlds and the beliefs and practices of religious adherents, developed along a significantly different trajectory to that originally envisaged by Smart. The enduring legacy of implicit religious education as it impacted on liberal religious education was twofold: first, it generated a shift in focus from the ontology of the ultimate order-of-things to an epistemic and hermeneutic concern to demonstrate the *relevance* of religion; second its recognition of a gulf between Christian ontology and pupils' lifeworlds sowed the seed for the future rejection of the primacy of Christian ontology and the introduction of a plurality of religious and secular ontologies into the religious education curriculum. If the latter is demanded by epistemic relativity, the former is not: epistemic relativity opens up the possibility of recognising that if there is no Transcendent realm then religion *is* fundamentally irrelevant. However, the political pressure for liberal religious education to demonstrate its enduring relevance to the curricula of plural and increasingly secular education systems, when coupled with the liberal assumption that Transcendent truth claims are not open to critical scrutiny, resulted in a new search for relevance predicated not on the potential truth of conflicting religious and secular worldviews, but on the liberal norms of freedom and tolerance.

J. W. D. Smith's *Religious Education in a Secular Setting* marked a significant point of transition from confessional to liberal religious education (Smith 1969). He was breaking new ground, both in seeking to replace Christian theology with secular philosophy as the controlling discourse of religious education, and in advocating a plural multi-faith curriculum (Schools Council 1971: 39). Smith's primary concern, inherited from implicit religious education, was with questions of epistemic and hermeneutical relevance: How might religious education contribute to the flourishing of pupils in their real-world environments in a context of religious diversity? Influenced by existential philosophers and theologians such as Martin Heidegger and Rudolph Bultmann, Smith argued that the existential dilemmas encountered by pupils in their real-world environments draw them to 'the threshold of profound questions about the nature of man and the conditions of human existence' (Smith 1969: 41). These questions raise issues of ultimate meaning which give life depth and poignancy, and reflect 'the dimension of mystery ... in human experience' (ibid.: 53). However, despite having affirmed the importance of ontology and identified the actuality of epistemic relativity, Smith failed to identify judgemental rationality as a pedagogic means of responding to the tensions inherent between the two. Instead, he sought a pragmatic response to such tensions. Despite the divisive nature of contested religious beliefs, recognition of our common humanity offers the basis for a common cooperative policy for religious education in state schools: 'Christian and non-Christian alike confront the ultimate mystery of human existence' (ibid.: 100).

This proposed cooperation did not take the open form of an interim ethic designed to support the pursuit of truth across incommensurable ontological worldviews, but rather the closed form of pre-established agreement amongst religious educators regarding the nature and value of religion. Smith argued that all religions, despite their apparently incommensurable truth claims, are united in a common commitment to the universal experience of the mystery of self-forgetful love, of which 'the life and death of Jesus have been the supreme example and inspiration ... in our western tradition' (ibid.: 54). 'Christian and non-Christian', he contended, 'could surely agree on a common intention to recognize this dimension of mystery in educational planning' (ibid.). In effect, the practice of judgemental rationality was foreclosed: rather than seeking to empower pupils to explore contested religious and secular interpretations of the ultimate order-of-things, it was deemed necessary for religious educators to provide *pre-packaged solutions* to disputed religious questions at the stage of syllabus construction prior to classroom teaching and learning. Rather than grapple with contested truth claims, pupils were to be introduced to a diversity of religious traditions, taught that despite their apparent differences they are united in subscribing to the ethical primacy of disinterested love, and encouraged to recognise that their own personal existential quest could find resolution in the same ethical framework.

Once again, this replicates classical liberal Protestantism: replace a cognitive-propositional model of religious language with an experiential-expressive one, utilise it to demythologise and neutralise the contested truth claims of the various world religions, and one is left with monolithic and reductionist understanding of religion as a universal capacity for spiritual intuition. It also reflects the moral economy of secular liberalism: if recognition of the common moral vision of diverse religious traditions serves to foster interpersonal tolerance, so recognition that the personal existential quests of individual students can legitimately find resolution in *any* religious or secular tradition (provided it subscribes to the ethical primacy of disinterested love) serves to foster personal autonomy.

The 1975 *City of Birmingham Agreed Syllabus* was the first 'to abandon the aim of Christian nurture and to embrace a multi-faith, phenomenological model of religious education' (Barnes 2008: 75; cf. City of Birmingham Education Committee 1975). It was also the first 'to require a *systematic* study of non-religious "stances for living", such as Humanism' (ibid.). The notion of 'life-stance' employed in the Syllabus drew on the work of the secular humanist Harry Stopes-Roe, who used the term to refer to the 'style and content of an individual's or a community's relationship with that which is of ultimate import-ance; the presuppositions and commitments of this, and the consequences for living which flow from it' (Stopes-Roe 1988: 21). This begs the question of the relationship between ontology and epistemology: between the epistemic discern-ment of that which is *deemed* ultimately important, and the ontological reality of that which is *actually* ultimately important. Counterfactual reflection suggests that, had the authors of the *Birmingham Syllabus* recognised the value of judge-mental rationality and deployed it to explore the tensions between ontological realism and epistemic relativity, they might have worked their way towards a genuinely Critical religious education. However, this opportunity was not grasped; instead, the tensions between ontology and epistemic relativity were seen as problems that required resolution at the stage of syllabus construction *prior* to classroom teaching and learning, in a manner designed to reinforce the twin liberal values of freedom and tolerance. In effect, students were introduced to a range of different religious and secular life-stances, encouraged to identify or choose their own, and taught to tolerate the choices of others.

The *Birmingham Syllabus* launched a phenomenological approach to religious education that was content to familiarise pupils with a range of equally valid religious and secular life-stances, which they were free to choose between according to personal preference and inclination, provided they respected the choices and life-stances of others. If the presentation of different religious and secular traditions as equally valid stances for living promised to help cement social cohesion, then the freedom of pupils to choose between them in construct-ing their own preferred stances for living served to reinforce their spiritual auto-nomy. If the problem, first highlighted by implicit religious educators, of the *relevance* of the study of religion for pupils remained centre stage, its resolution was now radically reconfigured. The perceived value of the subject no longer lay in its ability to demonstrate lines of convergence between pupils' existential questions and the answers proffered by Christianity; instead, it was grounded in the subject's ability to underpin the key principles of secular liberalism. The emergent programme of liberal religious education, committed as it was to the twin values of tolerance and freedom, identified the relevance of the subject with its ability to promote personal autonomy and maintain social cohesion. If a central concern of pre-liberal religious traditions was to pursue truth and culti-vate truthful living *sub specie aeternitatis*, then this concern was increasingly marginalised by a liberal tradition whose agenda was driven by the maintenance of its own socio-political economy through effective policing of non-liberal tra-ditions that might, potentially, threaten the liberal status quo. In effect, pheno-menological religious education oversaw an ideologically driven colonisation of religious traditions within a secular liberal polity: the ontological question, 'Is this true?' was replaced with the pragmatic question, 'How can this be made useful?'

Phenomenological religious education, in appropriating aspects of the philosophical tradition of phenomenology, identified two hermeneutical 'moments' in the process of religious understanding (Sharpe 1975; Marvell 1976). First, a moment of *epoché*, in which the process of bracketing-out of prior presuppositions enabled phenomena to be observed objectively in their 'pure' form; second, a moment of *eidetic vision*, in which understanding penetrated beneath the surface appearance of phenomena to discern their *sui generis* universal essence. The intention of this dual hermeneutic within the philosophical tradition of phenomenology was to avoid reductionism:

> It is only by bracketing the uncritically accepted 'natural world', by suspending our beliefs and judgements based on our unexamined 'natural standpoint', that the phenomenologist can become aware of the phenomena of immediate experience and can gain insight into their essential structures.
>
> (Allen 1987: 275)

In the phenomenology of religion, the essence of religious phenomena, that which made it distinctively 'religious', was discerned as its intentionality towards, or experience of, the realm of the Transcendent or sacred (Eliade 1987). Paul Ricoeur argues that this reading was wedded to an experiential-expressive model of religion: religious phenomena are essentially culturally bound expressions of a universal Transcendent experience (Ricoeur 1995: 48ff.). This effectively ruled out in advance the self-understanding of all three Abrahamic faiths, whose understanding of revelation appeals not to generic universal experience but to unique revelatory acts of God within history. According some critics,

> not only is the phenomenology of religion not historical, it is even antihistorical, both in terms of a phenomenological method that neglects the specific historical and cultural context and with regard to the primacy – methodologically and even ontologically – it grants to non-historical and non-temporal universal structures.
>
> (Allen 1987: 280)

Daniel Hardy argues that the particularity of the experiences of adherents of discrete religious traditions is effectively undermined by the claim that such experiences are variants of a common generic phenomenon: the process of reifying the concept 'religion', and explaining it in the categorical framework provided by neo-Kantian idealism, effectively dissolves the particularity of particular religions and occludes their ontologically incommensurable truth claims (Hardy 1975, 1976, 1979).

Phenomenological religious education's appropriation of philosophical and religious phenomenology was somewhat idiosyncratic. The moment of *epoché*, rather than revealing religious phenomena in their 'pure' form, tended to generate typological descriptions of the surface appearances of religious culture, frequently ordered around Smart's own sixfold categorisation of the ritualistic, mythical, doctrinal, ethical, social and experiential dimensions of the phenomenon of religion (Smart 1969: 15ff.). The moment of *eidetic vision*, rather than acting as a tool for revealing the intentionality or essence of religious phenomena vis-à-vis Transcendence, tended to take the form of attempts to encourage pupils to empathise with the experiences and lifeworlds of religious adherents by walking for a time imaginatively, as it were, 'in their shoes'. This reduction of *eidetic vision* to psychological empathy reflected the assumption that the primary task of the pupil was to learn to be sensitive towards, and thereby respect and tolerate, the religious 'Other', rather than understand, explain and evaluate Transcendent accounts of the ultimate order-of-things.

Thus empathy had a dual function: to encourage tolerance of religious adherents and communities, and help stimulate a greater openness to spiritual experience. Of the two, the former came to dominate popular conceptions of the place of post-confessional religious education in public education. Liberalism recognises both the problems and possibilities religion affords to the wellbeing of liberal society: 'the history of religion is a story of conflict and dissent, often bloody, as well as of striving for peace and reconciliation' (Yates 1988: 143). Against this background, *Education for All*, the Swann Report on the education of children from ethnic minority groups, expressed the opinion that:

> Religious education can play a central role in preparing pupils for today's multi-racial Britain ... challenging and countering the influence of racism in our society ... the phenomenological approach to religious education reflects most closely the aims underlying 'Education for All', in laying the foundation for the kind of genuinely pluralist society which is envisaged at the opening of this report.
>
> (Swann Report 1985: 496)

In effect, phenomenological religious education was appropriated as a tool for buttressing a liberal society committed to the twin values of tolerance and freedom. The tasks of providing objective descriptions of religious phenomena and encouraging empathetic engagement with religious adherents promised to both help maintain social cohesion and secure individual spiritual autonomy.

Spiritual religious education

Though advocates of the phenomenological approach to religious education were concerned both with the external phenomena of religion and with its impact on the moral and spiritual lives of pupils, there was a constant danger of reducing the subject to the transmission of objective phenomenological 'facts'. The concern that pupils should not merely learn 'about' religion, but also learn 'from' religion led to an increasing interest in the spiritual dimension of the subject in the 1980s. As we shall see, this spiritual turn in religious education embraced an understanding of spirituality implicitly couched in a broad neo-Kantian constructivist framework. The spiritual development of pupils was understood in terms of an increasing self-awareness of their internal spiritual space, in a manner that frequently lacked any overt reference to, or concern for, the external objects of spiritual experience.

The place of religious education in the curriculum was bolstered by the stipulation of the 1988 Education Reform Act that schools have a responsibility to promote the spiritual development of pupils (HMSO 1988: 1). Her Majesty's Inspectors of Schools (HMI) contributed to the debate leading up to the 1988 legislation by proposing, in line with Paul Hirst's notion of 'forms of knowledge', that education should be grounded in a set of core domains of knowledge and experience: aesthetic and creative, ethical, linguistic, mathematical, physical, scientific, social and political, and spiritual. A supplement to HMI's discussion paper *Curriculum 11–16* offered an epistemically oriented account of spirituality that focused on subjective awareness and sensibility:

> The spiritual area is concerned with the awareness a person has of those elements in existence and experience which may be defined in terms of inner feelings and beliefs; they affect the way people see themselves and throw light for them on the purpose and meaning of life itself.
>
> (DES/HMI 1977; cf. Wright 1998: 14f.)

It went on to offer a second ontologically oriented account that identified God as the primary object of spiritual awareness: 'The spiritual area is concerned with everything in human knowledge or experience that is connected with or derives from a sense of God or of gods' (Wright 1998: 14). According to this latter definition spirituality 'is a meaningless adjective for the atheist and of dubious use to the agnostic' (ibid.). HMI's preference was for the former definition: spirituality is fundamentally about inner feeling and sentiment, regardless of the external objects that might generate them.

> Often these feelings and beliefs lead people to claim to know God and glimpse the transcendent; sometimes they represent that striving and longing for perfection which characterises human beings, but always they are concerned with matters at the heart and root of existence.
>
> (ibid.)

The primacy of epistemology over ontology is transparent. In the first account the objects of spiritual awareness are identified as 'elements of existence' that are immediately qualified as 'inner feelings and beliefs', thereby marginalising the significance of any external objects that might evoke such feelings or generate such beliefs. In the second definition God is identified as one possible object of spiritual awareness. However, this is immediately qualified as an epistemic 'claim' generated, not ontologically by divine revelation, but epistemically by the experience of human 'striving and longing'.

Elsewhere I have argued for a critically realistic definition of spirituality that assumes a relational understanding of knowledge which takes ontological intransitivity and epistemic transitivity seriously:

> Spirituality is the developing relationship of the individual within community and tradition, to that which is – or is perceived to be – of ultimate concern, ultimate value and ultimate truth.

(ibid.: 88)

A generous reading of the HMI's second account might find a reflection of such a relational account of Transcendent spirituality ('to know God and glimpse the transcendent'), albeit one grounded in a liberal Protestant epistemology of universal spiritual experience ('these feelings and beliefs lead people to claim to know God') rather than a pre-liberal Abrahamic epistemology of divine revelation grounded in particular historical events and mediated through received tradition. However, the same cannot be said of HMI's first account, which presents a non-relational spirituality in which the *object* of spiritual awareness is *identified*, in a circular manner, with the inner feelings of the spiritual *subject*. On this reading spirituality is nothing more than the spiritual subject's self-awareness: any external object of spiritual experience, if it exists at all, is only of marginal significance. Spirituality is thus understood primarily in epistemic rather than ontological terms: the primary focus falls on the categories of human 'awareness', 'experience', 'feelings', 'beliefs', 'strivings', and 'longings', rather than on God, Transcendence or the natural order-of-things. This choice of focus would be inconceivable without the anthropological and epistemic turns instigated by Descartes and the philosophers of the Enlightenment.

HMI posited a reductive spirituality, concerned primarily with a person's inner feelings abstracted from any deep concern for the external world and the ultimate order-of-things. Whether or not spiritual sensibility is interpreted in terms of the ultimate (Transcendent or immanent) order-of-things is largely immaterial. What *really* matters here is the subjective epistemic capacity for spiritual awareness and experience, rather than its objective ontological source, cause or referent. So long as pupils feel deeply, it does not matter too much what it is that they feel deeply about, or whether such feelings are in harmony with the way things actually are in the world. A comprehensive liberal ontology of the Cartesian self as the highest entity known to exist, and consequently the autonomous arbiter of its own reality, is implicit throughout the document. This reading is reinforced by the inspection regime introduced following the implementation of the 1988 legislation, which required school inspectors to report only on the *provision* schools make for the spiritual development of pupils and not on their *actual* spiritual development. It was enough to take steps to cultivate students' openness to and capacity for spiritual experience and feeling: by implication, any examination of the actual substance of their spiritual understanding of their place in the ultimate order-of-things would constitute a direct attack on their autonomy, since it would open up the possibility of suggesting that their spiritual feelings are inappropriate to the way things actually are in reality. This effectively denies both ontological realism and judgemental rationality a place in spiritual education, leaving only a thoroughgoing epistemic relativism in which pupils are free to adopt whatever spiritual stance they like, regardless of its potential truthfulness and inner coherence, provided they do so sensitively and autonomously.

David Hay, a zoologist and educator concerned with the relationship between biological science and spiritual experience, has been an influential figure in the field of religious education since the mid-1980s. In *Exploring Inner Space* he presented empirical evidence suggesting that a significant majority of the adult population of Britain report spiritual experiences and are aware of a spiritual dimension to their lives (Hay 1982a). Building on this evidence, Hay claims that the capacity for spiritual experience is 'a built-in, biologically structured dimension of the lives of all members of the human species' (Hay 2006: 49). Spirituality 'is rooted in universal human awareness' and as such 'is "really there" and not just a culturally constructed illusion' (Hay and Nye 2006: 18). Because spiritual awareness is universal, it cannot be restricted to religious adherents and need not be expressed in religious language. Despite his initial reliance on the metaphor of 'inner space' to designate the location of spiritual sensibility, in his later work with Rebecca Nye he identified spiritual experience as the 'relational consciousness' of the self in relation to nature, cultural objects, other people and God (ibid.: 131ff.). Hay's determination to affirm *both* the ontological reality of the Transcendent object of spiritual experience *and* the universality of the human capacity for spiritual experience, leads him in the direction of a universal natural theology that runs counter to the self-understanding of the revealed Abrahamic faiths: the Transcendent is known not because God chooses to reveal himself in particular historical contexts and circumstances, but because the human mind is biologically hot-wired to sense the presence of the Transcendent in any given context and circumstance.

Hay recognises a widespread suspicion of spiritual experience in post-Enlightenment culture, and attributes this to rationalistic and empiricist modes of engaging with reality spawned by the Enlightenment: 'we have difficulty hanging onto the spiritual, because "really" the fundamentals of the world are particles and space' (Hay 1985: 140). This ignores the empirical evidence of the widespread prevalence of spiritual experience, and generates a hermeneutic of suspicion that imposes reductive explanations on such experience and refuses to accept it at face value. Hay offers an embryonic natural theology in which the empirical evidence of the human capacity for Transcendent experience demands the conclusion that the Transcendent must therefore exist.

Turning to religious education, Hay works from the premise that pupils have an innate capacity for spiritual experience. In an argument that echoes that of Rousseau, he contends that human beings in their natural biological state enjoy a capacity for spiritual experience that modern culture has progressively eroded under the influence of a hermeneutic of suspicion. Hay follows implicit religious educators in recognising that 'religion, as it has been presented to [pupils], bears little or no relation to their personal experience of reality' (Hay 1985: 140). Pupils retain a capacity for spiritual experience that is under threat to such an extent that they already struggle to recognise the spiritual dimension of religious traditions. This leads Hay to his central pedagogic claim, that religious education has a primary responsibility to challenge the 'suppression or repression of the religious aspect of children's experience' (ibid.: 144). Utilising the experiential-expressive model, Hay understands religious language as a means of expressing spiritual experience rather than offering cognitive-propositional accounts of divine revelation and Transcendent reality. This leads him to suggest that the phenomenon of religion should be presented in the classroom at face-value 'for what it claims to be – the response of human beings to what they experience as sacred' (ibid.: 142).

Hay is clear that his insistence on the objective ontological reality of the Transcendent, albeit one filtered through subjective epistemic feeling, neither implies nor requires a return to confessional religious education. On the contrary, his advocacy of a universal natural theology allows him to argue that religious education should embrace a multi-faith agenda and recognise the 'relativity of all belief systems' (Hay 1982b: 47). Religious education must approach 'the historical faiths as the cultural expression of personal religious experience' (ibid.: 48). The importance of religious traditions does not reside in their *particular* understandings of the ultimate order-of-things, but in their shared possession of a universal spiritual experience that generates a range of culturally relative and non-cognitive expressions of belief. Whilst religious beliefs and doctrines are culturally relative and as such cannot be transmitted as normative, universal spiritual experience is an empirically verifiable fact that, despite the opposition of secular materialists, should be treated as normative in the classroom.

Since religious beliefs are secondary to spiritual experience, it is necessary 'to refer back constantly to our direct experience of the world, as the criterion by which to judge the validity of our beliefs' (ibid.: 47). The task of religious education is to enable pupils to look beyond the culturally relative expressions of religious culture and discern behind them a universal experiential core. In order to achieve this, pupils must be taught to 'enter empathetically the experiential world of the religious believer' (Hay 1985: 145). This process will 'help pupils to open their personal awareness to those aspects of their experience which are recognised by religious people as the root of religion' (ibid.: 142). However, such empathy is only possible if pupils already possess a sufficient depth of spiritual sensibility. Consequently, Hay's practical advice to religious education teachers, presented in *New Methods in RE Teaching*, focuses on ways of stimulating and enriching their pupils' spiritual sensibilities as a prolegomenon to an empathetic engagement with the spiritual experiences of religious adherents (Hammond *et al.* 1990). The classroom exercises suggested in the book seek to stimulate pupils' imaginative capacities and affective sensibilities in a manner designed to 'to loosen the grip of the "fact stratum" [and] demonstrate that there are many possible ways of interpreting reality in which we find ourselves, including the religious way' (Hammond and Hay 1992: 146). This is in essence a replication of the pedagogy advocated by the implicit approach to religious education, albeit one now re-contextualised within a universal natural theology rather than a liberal Protestant interpretation of revealed Christian theology.

Adrian Thatcher views Hay's position as essentially dualistic: the claim that 'experience necessarily requires an inner world where some series of internal events parallels some series of external events … is clearly based on a philosophical dualism which lacks credibility' (Thatcher 1991: 23; cf. Hammond and Hay 1992). He suggests that Hay is unaware of his dependence on the Enlightenment tradition that seeks to establish an inner private realm in parallel to the external public realm, a tradition that Richard Rorty, Michel Foucault, Jacques Derrida and other post-modern philosophers set out to deconstruct. Regardless of whether one accepts the thoroughgoing relativism embedded within much post-modern philosophy, it is increasingly clear that

> expressing my own mental states or feeling states is impossible without a shared publically-owned language and considerable induction into its use, with the result that descriptions of sensations and feelings rely on prior social realities, provided by a linguistic community.
>
> (Thatcher 1991: 23)

Though Thatcher's critique predates Hay's later advocacy of a relational spiritual consciousness, it still retains its power, insofar as the relational consciousness remains grounded in the subjective self-awareness of the knower rather than the *relationship* between the subjective knower and the objective reality of external objects of knowledge. Ultimately the claim that spiritual experience is experience of a Transcendent ontological reality is not intrinsic to the experience itself since, as Hay himself recognises, there are many who understand their spiritual experiences in immanent non-Transcendent terms. Hay's defence of the ontological reality of the Transcendent is clearly dependent on a secondary culturally bound linguistic *explanation* of primary pre-linguistic experience, rather than on the intrinsic nature of the experience itself. Hay is implicitly dependent on the heritage of the Enlightenment: philosophically, on the romantic turn that affirmed the epistemic priority of the aesthetic, moral and spiritual experience of the sovereign consciousness; theologically, on the romantic rejection of cognitive-propositional theology and its replacement with an experiential-expressive understanding of religious language and experience. We have already had occasion to note that, given the human capacity for self-deception and misplaced projection, the romantic reliance on subjective sensibility leads inexorably into forms of relativism and anti-realism. Neither a person's inner conviction that their deepest subjective spiritual experiences converge with an objective Transcendent reality, nor empirical evidence of the widespread prevalence of spiritual experience, constitute sufficient criteria to justify Hay's universal natural theology claiming normative status in religious education programmes in religiously plural and increasingly secular classrooms.

Given the problems inherent in relating subjective feeling to external objects, it was probably inevitable that Hay's account of spiritual education would be recast within a post-modern relativistic framework. The key figures here are Clive and Jane Erricker, whose early work advocated a non-realistic spiritual pedagogy that, in the name of personal autonomy, sought to free pupils to create their own virtual spiritual realities (Erricker and Erricker 2000). This was seen as a necessary antidote to the dangerously intolerant attitudes implicit in the exclusive truth claims of many religious traditions. Hay's desire to cultivate and stimulate pupils' openness to spiritual sensibility remained firmly in place; what changed was the explicit rejection of any external ontological source of referent for such experience. Clive Erricker did not temper his assertion that knowledge is necessarily situated in socio-political power structures with an appeal to judgemental rationality as a means of challenging ingrained hegemonic forces and progressing towards more truthful ways of understanding and engaging with the world (Erricker 2001; cf. Wright 2001). Rather, he followed the mainstream post-modern tradition in assuming that the prevalence of such power structures necessarily precludes any possibility of the pursuit of truth. Given that all knowledge is saturated by economies of power, the only viable means of resisting them is to empower the recently deconstructed Cartesian self to avoid the futile and restrictive pursuit of truth, whether in the external world or in the internal realm of the mind. This exclusion of judgemental rationality led directly to the appropriation of a thoroughgoing anti-realistic and relativistic meta-narrative as the basis for Erricker's post-modern account of spiritual education. By encouraging pupils to deepen their spiritual sensibilities, Erricker sought to free them to construct their own spiritual identities apart from any external constraints: 'Learning starts by avoiding the objectification of children and the mythologies that we introduce them to … what we are concerned with here is … helping children to construct their own enabling metaphors' (Erricker 1993: 146).

Ultimately, the work of Robert Jackson, though he rejects anti-realism and accepts the virtue of pursuing truth, is best located within this emergent tradition. Jackson is relatively disinterested in the 'inner space' of spiritual experience, and focuses instead on the socio-cultural dimensions of religious expression. Ethnographic evidence of the internal diversity and fluid boundaries of religious traditions rules out any essentialist account of religion. Operating implicitly within a broadly nominalist neo-Kantian tradition, in which the noumenal object-in-itself is always obscured by the phenomenal object-as-it-appears-to-us, he argues that the concepts 'religion' and 'religions' are Western and Christian constructs that have generated the reified notions of religions as self-contained 'belief systems' and religion as 'a generic category with an essence' (Jackson 1997: 60). Jackson points out 'the dangers of representing religious worldviews as bounded systems of belief' and proposes 'a more personal and flexible model allowing for the uniqueness of each person, while giving due attention to the various influences which help shape any individual's sense of personal and social identity' (Jackson 2004: 88; cf. Jackson 2008, Wright 2008).

This, perhaps inadvertently on Jackson's part, opens the door to a constructivist reading of religion, according to which any attempt to view religious traditions as anything more substantial than the contingent convergence of a diverse range of cultural objects and forces will necessarily constitute an illegitimate will to power. If religious traditions are not primarily belief systems and if religion is not an essential entity enjoying a secure ontological status, then religious truth claims become marginalised to the extent that they cannot be saved by appeals to a source in either the particularities of divine revelation or the generality of universal spiritual experience. The phenomenological reality of those aspects of culture we label 'religious' cannot be ignored, since they are potentially sources of both great good and great evil. Hence the pragmatic task is to put the phenomena to good use within a broad liberal socio-political economy. Religious phenomena can be saved, not by seeking to discover any substantial truth beneath their surface appearances, but by constructing, attributing and applying pragmatically useful meaning to them. Ultimately, meaning, truth and value do not reside deep *within* the phenomena, but rather in the space *between* the phenomena and the constructive human observer.

For Jackson, the aim of religious education is 'to help children and young people to find their own positions within the key debates about religious plurality' (2004: 87). Though acknowledging affinities with the critically realistic approach advocated in this book, Jackson seeks to distance himself from it by claiming that his 'interpretive' approach, unlike a critically realistic one, 'recognizes the inner diversity, fuzzy edgedness and contested nature of religious traditions as well as the complexity of cultural expression and change from social and individual perspectives' (ibid.). However, this does not square with critical realism's commitment to epistemic relativity, which acknowledges and seeks to do justice to the rich diversity of religious phenomena and ways of making sense of religion. The more fundamental difference appears to be that whilst critical realism seeks to penetrate *beneath* the surface appearance of phenomena in order to expose and engage with their deep ontological structures, Jackson appears content to negotiate constructed meanings in the space between the phenomena and the interpreter.

Where the constructivist finds only disguised, and ultimately power-driven, attempts to reify and essentialise in the interpretative endeavours of critical realism, the critical realist finds in constructivism yet another version of the epistemic fallacy of forcing reality to conform to the constructs of the interpreter. If it is impossible to penetrate beneath the surface appearance of phenomena and expose underlying ontic structures and forces, then reality is effectively reduced to an amalgam of brute phenomenological facts onto which interpreters overlay fluid sets of value-laden constructs. Since such constructs are necessarily relative to their constructors, there is a constant danger of their becoming reified, essentialised, and hegemonised. Consequently, the potential clash of interests generated by conflicting hegemonic constructions must be mitigated through the liberal economy of freedom and tolerance. On this constructivist reading, the danger inherent in the project of Critical religious education lies in its failure to recognise that its pursuit of truth *beneath* the surface of phenomena is actually nothing more than the construction of meaning in the space *between* the critical realist and the phenomena under scrutiny, accompanied with the false claim to be exposing deep ontic truths. The failure to recognise that truth itself is nothing more than a human construct leads directly to the reification, essentialisation and hegemonisation of truth claims. And this constitutes a direct threat to the established liberal order-of-things.

What are the implications of Jackson's position for the spiritual dimension of religious education? As we have seen, unlike Hay and Erricker, Jackson is relatively disinterested in spiritual experience and focuses instead on the socio-cultural aspects of 'religious' traditions. He identifies two basic aims for religious education: first, 'to develop an understanding of the religious world-views of others, their religious language and symbols, and their feelings and attitudes'; second, 'helping pupils to reflect on their studies of ways of life that are different in some respects from their own' (Jackson 1997: 112). Jackson expresses the hope that the latter aim might prompt 'some form of re-assessment of their understanding of their *own* ways of life, or some insight into the human condition in general' (ibid.). Jackson unpacks such reflection and re-assessment in terms of Richard Rorty's notion of 'edification' (Jackson 1997: 112, 130f., 2004: 11; cf. Rorty 1980). Drawing an analogy between edification and spiritual development, he presents edification as a potentially transformative process: 'To be edified, in this sense, is to be taken out of one's own self'; by accepting 'the challenge of "unpacking" another worldview one can, in a sense, become a new person' (Jackson 1997: 130f.).

It is notable that Jackson gives no further guidance to teachers here: he apparently deems it sufficient to enable students to engage with religious worldviews in the *hope* that edification may take place. 'Of course, whether a person feels edified through reflecting on issues and questions raised through interpreting another's way of life is a personal matter, and it is impossible to guarantee it through activities provided in curriculum materials' (ibid.: 116). His insistence on the spontaneity of students' responses and refusal to provide pedagogic guidance and support falls significantly short of the sustained pursuit of truth and truthfulness, utilising the disciplines of philosophy and theology, advocated by Critical religious education. The reasons for this become clear when we look more closely at Rorty's understanding of edification: as a pragmatist he holds that true beliefs are 'those beliefs which are successful in helping us to do what we want to do'; as a post-modernist he holds that there 'can be no absolute truth beyond each way of life'; and as a constructivist he holds that personal identities 'are socially constructed in relation to others' (Jackson 2004: 11; cf. Rorty 1980: 10, 175). Ultimately for Jackson the edificatory spiritual dimension of religious education is not concerned to empower students to locate themselves intelligently in Transcendent space (putative or real) through the pursuit of ultimate truth and truthful living *sub specie aeternitatis*; rather he is concerned to create space within which students can, if they so desire, construct their own preferred identities and worldviews in response to the identities and worldviews of others.

The distinction drawn by implicit religious education between religious experience and religious expression, coupled with its desire to correlate pupils' experiences with religious experiences and expressions in order to show the relevance of religion in their lives, was taken up by phenomenological religious education and generated a dualism that came to dominate liberal religious education. The distinction between two complementary attainment targets, 'learning about religion' and 'learning from religion', is now embedded in the vast majority of locally agreed syllabuses (Hella and Wright 2008). In 1971 the Schools Council distinguished between explicit and implicit religious education: the former was concerned with the cultural phenomenon of religion, the latter with pupils' experiential and existential self-understanding, which may or may not be expressed in an explicitly religious manner (Schools Council 1971). Edwin Cox distinguished between 'understanding religion' and 'religious understanding': the former required 'a relatively detached knowledge of the externals of faith … accessible to any rational being … [that] will probably not significantly alter the student's lifestyle'; the latter was altogether 'more penetrating, requiring experience of the quality of a faith's beliefs and practices, an emotional response to its cult objects, and an ability to perceive and respond approvingly to its ultimate function' (Cox 1983: 5). Michael Grimmitt distinguished between 'dimensional' and 'experiential' approaches to the subject: the former involved the exploration of explicitly religious phenomenon, the latter was concerned with existential themes and experiences directly related to the lives of pupils (Grimmitt 1973).

In this situation appeals to the contribution of the subject to the spiritual flourishing of pupils regardless of their religious convictions (whether positive or negative) carried more weight than appeals to its contribution to the understanding of Transcendence and pursuit of truth. According to John Wilson the 'metaphysical or doctrinal superstructure [of religion] is, in one very real sense, unimportant in itself: it is the kind of emotions to which it has been witness that we have to detect and educate' (Wilson 1971: 171). Similarly, according to Raymond Holley, religious education is not 'simply concerned with imparting information about the religions of the world', rather 'religiously educational activities [should] provoke intellectual understanding of the spirituality of personality in all its extensiveness and dynamism' (Holley 1978: 65f). Such dualism plunged religious education into a 'permanent identity crisis' in which the future survival of the subject appears to be at stake in an increasingly secular society: 'What appears to be a discussion about the nature of religious education is really about curriculum politics … in this search for survival and status, the method of legitimation becomes all important' (Day 1985: 59). Edwin Cox relates the emergence of liberal religious education directly to its need to adapt and change in order to survive:

> In the past two decades religious education and theories of religious education have been greatly modified because it has had to operate in a greatly modified culture. It has been trying to adapt itself, so that it makes

sense in the new, harsher, diverse, humanistic and acquisitive society that has emerged.

(Cox 1983: 7)

My contention is that the subject's search for legitimacy took the form of an accommodation to comprehensive liberalism and its core values of personal autonomy and tolerance, and that this entailed an acceptance of its privatisation of religious truth claims and assertion of an implicit liberal ontology. The strategy is fundamentally flawed for at least two reasons. First, considered on its own terms, liberal religious education's search for legitimacy is likely to prove futile: since the promotion of liberal values can be conducted effectively within secular programmes of moral, social and personal education, it is far from clear that religious education warrants a place in the curriculum as a discrete subject. Second, considered in terms of the self-understandings of religious adherents, it entails a significant and ideologically grounded occlusion of all accounts of the ultimate ontological order-of-things other than that proffered by comprehensive liberalism.

The ideology of liberal religious education

What ontological assumptions, whether explicitly acknowledged or implicitly present, underlie liberal approaches to religious education? Given that the object of study is religion, and that most religious adherents subscribe to beliefs regarding Transcendent reality, the issue of Transcendence is the obvious and most appropriate starting point. It is possible to trace a relatively clear line of development in the ontological assumptions regarding the ultimate order-of-things presented to pupils in liberal religious education classrooms.

In the heyday of Christian confessionalism reality was ultimately understood in Trinitarian terms: confessional teachers recounted an orthodox narrative of the economy of creation and reconciliation that culminated in the incarnation of God the Son in and through the power of the Holy Spirit. This narrative tended to be shorn of any denominational emphases and presented in the form of a generic common denominator Protestant orthodoxy rooted in notions of revelation and scripture. Implicit Christian confessional religious education's replacement of a cognitive-propositional understanding of theological language with an experiential-expressive model led to the increasing marginalisation of this narrative. Though the new approach continued to reference scripture and received Christian doctrine, these were no longer seen as bearers of cognitive-propositional accounts of the ultimate order-of-things generated by God's revelatory acts in history, but rather as mythical expressions of Christian spiritual experience. As a result the nature and role of Christian doctrine was effectively reconfigured: the orthodox task of providing true accounts of Transcendent reality that demanded truthful responses from Christian congregations gave way to the liberal Protestant task of providing a vehicle for the stimulation of a pre-linguistic spiritual sensibility attuned to Transcendent reality. Christianity provided a means of enabling believers to sense the reality of God, but not a means of describing and explaining the nature of God. Instead of ontological explanations of the ultimate order-of-things grounded in the core Christian doctrines of Trinity and incarnation, pupils were offered access to a romantically inspired emotive sense of the presence of God in which core Christian doctrines were treated as largely superfluous mythical expressions devoid of cognitive content.

Liberal religious education, committed to the belief that theological accounts of Transcendent reality could no longer legitimately claim scientific status, focused instead on religion as a cultural phenomenon. If Transcendent truth claims were closed to scientific investigation, the religious traditions that proffered such claims were not: there may be no access to knowledge of God, but there is access to knowledge of those religious individuals, communities and institutions who *claim* knowledge of God. This entailed a significant ontological shift from Transcendence to immanence: if religious education possessed a body of knowledge worthy of transmission to pupils, then it consisted of knowledge of immanent religious phenomena rather than knowledge of Transcendent noumenal realities. This shift in focus, which directly paralleled the emergence of departments of Religious Studies in the universities, was not, however, the full story. If liberal religious education was committed to the intellectual rejection of the scientific status of theology, it was equally committed to a moral concern to maintain equity by avoiding privileging Christianity over other religious traditions.

Despite its suspicion of theological science, liberal religious education's advocacy of the study of world religions allowed for a partial retrieval of Transcendence. We have already seen how liberal Protestantism identified pre-linguistic spiritual experience, rather than divine revelation, as the source of Christian faith; noted how this paved the way for forms of universal theology that affirmed a common *sui generis* spiritual experience as the ground of *all* religious traditions; and observed how this theology claimed to dissipate the cognitive dissonance between conflicting truth claims by reducing them to the status of culturally bound expressions of religious experience rather than cognitively rich descriptors of Transcendent reality. This opened the door to the presentation of all religious traditions as equally valid vehicles for the stimulation of spiritual experience of Transcendence, regardless of the apparent incommensurability of their different truth claims. This universal theology was imported into liberal religious education, albeit with varying degrees of explicitness. By affirming the theological equality of all religions in this way, liberal religious educators sought to counter the twin charges of reductionism and indoctrination: they claimed to be open to the possibility of Transcendence, albeit on an intuitive rather than cognitive basis, yet not guilty of indoctrinating children into any given religious belief system. This, of course, served to buttress the liberal principles of reason, autonomy and tolerance: reason, because the non-scientific basis of theology was acknowledged; autonomy, because pupils were free to subscribe to whichever religious tradition they chose without fear of coercion; tolerance, because of their insistence on the equality of all religious traditions.

However, this partial retrieval of Transcendence was relatively short-lived. The notion that religious education should support some form of Transcendence, however universal, gradually imploded under the pressures of secularism. As naturalistic, materialistic and secular humanist worldviews were increasingly accommodated within the economy of liberal religious education, so Hay's commitment to a universal natural theology gave way to Erricker's post-modern rejection of Transcendence. The anti-realistic turn in liberal religious education marked the death knell of any sustained and substantial concern for Transcendence.

A clear, if implicit, *comprehensive liberal ontology* is at work here: the realms of nature, sentient minds and human culture are affirmed, the former two as sacrosanct ontological givens, the latter as the site of contested meanings; the domain of Transcendence remains a private option, albeit one devoid of any viable cognitive support. The realm of nature provides the fundamental basis of human life, to be controlled whenever technology allows, and accommodated whenever technological control proves impossible. In the mental realm individuals, as the highest entities known to inhabit the cosmos, are free to determine their own lives, construct whatever identities they prefer, and believe whatever they want, regardless of the presence or absence of any intellectual warrant, provided they do so in a tolerant manner that avoids cruelty and harm to others. In the cultural realm the twin principles of freedom and tolerance are sacrosanct: not merely the basic means through which human beings pursue the good life, but also, and more fundamentally, its substantial content. This ontology is supported by a specific *liberal epistemology* grounded in the dualistic distinction between fact and value: cognitive knowledge of the world is limited to the fruits of the natural and social sciences; whilst the value-laden realms of aesthetics, morality and spirituality are closed to scientific investigation. Devoid of a scientific basis, the latter are governed by the twin principles of freedom and tolerance: we are free to adopt whatever aesthetic, moral and spiritual stances and beliefs we prefer, provided that in doing so we avoid doing harm to others.

The task of liberal religious education is to police and reinforce this comprehensive liberal ontology and specific liberal epistemology. The subject's claim to a place in the curriculum of liberal schools is dependent on its ability to uphold the liberal principles of reason, autonomy and tolerance: the principle of reason limits the study of religion to the study of religious phenomena through the secular disciplines of history, sociology, psychology, phenomenology and analytical philosophy, and disqualifies theology and the philosophical disciplines of ontology and metaphysics; the principle of autonomy allows for the adoption of any belief system and construction of any preferred spiritual identity; the principle of tolerance dissipates conflict generated by the clash of autonomous interests by foregrounding the central importance of social cohesion. Read in the light of the preceding chapters, my contention is that liberal religious education is insufficiently attentive, intelligent, reasonable, and responsible, and as such inadvertently falls into the trap of reifying its commitments so that they obtain an ideological status.

8   Critical religious education

The theory and practice of religious education is broad-ranging: it entails issues of curriculum construction and development, of classroom teaching and learning, of pupil assessment and teacher development, of politics and economics, etc. The present chapter does not aim to present a comprehensive account of critical religious education. Rather, it is concerned to establish a basic philosophical framework for the subject, informed by the under-labouring support of critical realism. The triumvirate of ontological realism, epistemic relativity and judgemental rationality identify three critical questions that inform the basic philosophy of critical religious education: what is reality ultimately like? What is the extent and scope of our knowledge of ultimate reality? How might our knowledge of ultimate reality be enhanced and expanded? Realistic answers to these questions enable the emergence of a philosophy of the subject that stands in continuity with the historical focus of traditional religious education, takes religious and secular worldview pluralism seriously, and strives to generate religiously literate pupils and a religiously literate society.

Ontological realism

(1) *Ultimate reality.* Our best (currently) available retroductive account suggests that we participate in a single reality that is constituted by the totality of all that exists, once existed and potentially might exist. We experience and explain this reality as stratified, emergent, transfactual and causally efficacious. Though everything is interconnected in a thick web of causality, the fact that higher strata are irreducible to the lower strata from which they emerge requires us to recognise the existence of distinct-yet-related domains of being. There is near unanimity that the three basic domains of reality are nature (organic and inorganic matter), sentient minds (possessing conscious mental states) and culture (the product of the interplay of sentient minds and nature) (Popper 1972; Niiniluoto 1999: 23ff.). Different academic disciplines seek to interrogate different strata of reality: broadly speaking, natural science interrogates nature, psychology interrogates sentient minds, and social science, the arts and the humanities interrogate culture. The basic principle of the hermeneutical circle requires parts to be understood in relation to wholes and wholes to be understood

in relation to their constituent parts, in an ongoing dialectical process. Thus interpretation of Shakespeare's *Othello* must seek to discern the meaning of individual verses *in relation* to the play as a whole, and the meaning of the play as a whole *in relation* to individual verses. Because different strata are causally connected, a holistic explanation must seek to understand the relationship between different strata. Thus a total explanation of Othello's suffocation of Desdemona would need to refer to, amongst other things, its location in the plot of the play as a whole, the psychology of human jealousy and the biology of the human respiratory system. The principle runs deep: to explain the *totality* of reality is to explain being itself in relation to its constituents parts (nature, sentient minds and culture), and to the constituent parts of each constituent part and so forth. In a world of increasing academic specialisation, questions of the totality of reality tend to be occluded by questions about its constituent parts. In the history of Western thought, accounts of the totality of reality have traditionally been provided by the disciplines of metaphysics and theology. The positivist insistence that neither discipline provides meaningful knowledge by virtue of the unverifiable nature of their truth claims served to further occlude questions of the whole. The critically realistic assertion of the potential truth-bearing nature of both metaphysics and theology opens the door to a recovery of retroductive explanations that take the hermeneutical circle seriously.

To ask the question of the totality of reality is to ask the question of our place in the ultimate order-of-things, and hence of the ultimate meaning and purpose of our lives. Wittgenstein's observations towards the end of the *Tractatus-Logico-Philosophicus* are apposite here, though not his conclusion that the questions raised by them must be passed over in silence:

> It is not how things are in the world that is mystical, but that it exists. To view the world sub specie aeterni is to view it as a whole – a limited whole. Feeling the world as a limited whole – it is this that is mystical.
>
> (Wittgenstein 1974: 73)

The principle of the hermeneutical circle requires us to ask questions about ultimate truth and truthfulness: about the ultimate nature of reality and the ultimate meaning and purpose of life lived *sub specie aeternitatis*. To ask such questions does not necessarily require a religious response: Nietzsche's entire philosophy was predicated on addressing questions of ultimate meaning in a world devoid of God, and it is now generally recognised that to live spiritually *sub specie aeternitatis* does not require us to posit any greater reality than the domains of nature, sentient minds and culture. Thus Bhaskar's philosophy of meta-Reality sought ultimate meaning in the realisation of a ground state ingrained within these three domains. In traditional theological language, Bhaskar defended a form of panentheism (not to be mistaken for pantheism), in which 'God' (a heuristically useful yet equally dispensable term) is simultaneously ingrained within and emergent from the matrix of nature, sentient minds and culture. There is, however, no avoiding the fact that many religious traditions insist on an expanded account of reality in which the matrix of nature, minds and culture are dependent on a greater Transcendent reality. Thus, for example, the Christian doctrine of creation holds that the Trinitarian God created the domains of nature and sentient minds *ex nihilo* (out of nothing), and gives them the freedom to be themselves and generate culture apart from God, whilst simultaneously holding them in being and engaging with them immanently through the person of the incarnate Christ and omnipresent Holy Spirit.

Morgan suggests that to retroductively posit a fourth primal domain in addition to the triumvirate of nature, minds and culture leaves realists divided by realism (Morgan 2015). Precisely so, but this does not warrant any pedagogic occlusion of the fact that the ontological nature of the ultimate order-of-things, and hence also the question of the ultimate meaning and purpose of life, is both epistemically contested and open to rational scrutiny. It is certainly undeniable that the question of the ultimate nature of reality and ultimate meaning of life are occluded from the lifeworlds of many. Porpora offers compelling evidence that many contemporary American citizens struggle to locate themselves in what he terms 'metaphysical space', and that this leads to a void in their sense of self: 'we cannot lose our place in the cosmos without losing ourselves as well' (Porpora 2001: 152). However, the problem may not reside in the absence of a worldview, but rather in the possession of an implicit, and hence poorly articulated, worldview. If we retroductively infer naturalism (the natural world as the self-generating and self-sustaining bedrock of reality), secular humanism (human beings as the greatest entities to have emerged from the bedrock of nature), and secular liberalism (human beings as free to determine their own values and destinies – within the constraints imposed by nature, provided they avoid doing harm to others – by virtue of their status as the greatest existing entities), then the values and life choices espoused by many of Porpora's interviewees make perfect sense: 'I don't need to look beyond myself or my immediate network of friends to live an authentic life, other than for the purposes of generating the capital necessary for my chosen way of life.' Some understanding of the ultimate order-of-things and our place in it, however implicit, would appear to be difficult to avoid.

Our ways of being in the world necessarily assume basic beliefs, whether implicit or explicit, about our place in the ultimate order-of-things. Actions guided by such beliefs are causally efficacious: they necessarily impact, for better or worse, on ourselves, other people, human culture and the natural world. The complex morphogenetic interplay of causal mechanisms across different domains of reality activated by such efficacious beliefs need not detain us here. It is sufficient simply to note that, for good or ill, beliefs generate change. This being the case, there would appear to be a moral, intellectual and spiritual imperative to strive to bring our beliefs about the ultimate nature of reality and the meaning of life, and the actions that follow from them, into conformity with the way things actually are via an ongoing pursuit of truth and truthful living. Or, should we prefer existential rebellion against the ultimate order-of-things – as in Ivan Karamazov's infamous decision to rebel against a God whose existence he does not question – to do so reasonably, responsibly and attentively (Dostoevsky 1997: 236ff.). Moral decisions and actions are the result of a complex interplay of natural, personal and cultural mechanisms, including the beliefs of agents and the values embedded in social structures. Whether such beliefs reflect commitment to (religious or secular) deontological values, or to instrumental (pragmatic, utilitarian) reasoning, some form of moral ontology will inevitably be present. Broadly speaking, a deontological ethic will tend to assume some normative moral order, whether grounded in God, nature or universally valid human constructs, whereas an instrumental ethic will tend to assume a fluid moral order in which moral choices are relative to the needs, desires and aspirations of specific individuals of groups. The notion that instrumental or pragmatic decision-making is a consequence of epistemic uncertainty about moral ontology begs the question, 'Why then privilege an ontology in which individuals are sovereign over their moral values?' and invites the answer, 'Because in such instances epistemic relativism gives way, by default, to a specific moral ontology.' Since we cannot avoid acting on some form of basic belief about the ultimate order of things, and since our actions will inevitably impact on ourselves and on the world we indwell, there is a direct link between our beliefs about the ultimate nature of reality and the problems and possibilities of human flourishing.

Applying the hermeneutical circle to primal ontology suggests that reality has an ultimate nature: different strata and domains of being interlink to form a greater whole. This is the case even if the ultimate order-of-things is essentially chaotic, so that the order we currently discern in reality is nothing but an accidental, arbitrary and ephemeral configuration destined to collapse back into disorder and meaninglessness. This is also the case if reality is in the process of becoming, so that the phenomenon of emergence will eventually generate hitherto unimagined orders-of-being. And this is also the case whether or not the domains of nature, minds and culture are underpinned by a fourth Transcendent domain of being. Such ontological realism about the ultimate order-of-things goes hand-in-hand with epistemic relativity: different religious and secular worldviews offer ontologically incommensurable accounts of the ultimate order-of-things and hence of the ultimate meaning and purpose of life. Such ontological incommensurability runs parallel to epistemic commensurability: that is to say, we can understand conflicting accounts of our place in the ultimate order-of-things whether or not we agree with them. Contra romanticised forms of neo-Kantianism, we can as 'outsiders' understand worldviews other than our own despite lacking the experiential privileges of 'insiders'. To argue otherwise, by suggesting that only Muslims can truly understand Islam and only secular humanists can truly understand secular humanism, is to fall foul of the epistemic fallacy of reducing reality to our given experiences of reality. Given that we can understand conflicting accounts of ultimate reality, it is but a short step to affirming that we can make rational judgements between them. This is a self-evident state of affairs: adherents of conflicting religious and secular worldviews cannot avoid affirming the greater truth of their accounts of the ultimate order-of-things over available alternatives, and if this were not the case the phenomenon of conversion from one worldview to another would be incomprehensible. Read in the light of critical realism, the positivist claim that religious and metaphysical truth claims are meaningless because unverifiable takes the form, not of the closure of judgemental rationality vis-à-vis ultimate reality, but of an act of judgemental rationality marked by intellectual poverty.

To sum up this sub-section, it is reasonable to suppose: that there is an ultimate order-of-things; that we cannot avoid either implicitly or explicitly living life *sub specie aeternitatis* in relation to it; that because our ultimate beliefs are efficacious we have a moral, intellectual and spiritual responsibility to pursue truth and truthful living; and that we are capable of both understanding and adjudicating between conflicting accounts of the ultimate order-of-things.

(2) *Accessing ultimate reality: cultural mediation.* The Cartesian cogito, in identifying immediate consciousness as epistemically foundational, suggested two basic ways of accessing ultimate reality. The first way was by generating rational proofs of the existence/non-existence of God. Here reason was sovereign: its autonomous exercise promised a secure path to truth. Scholastic attempts to better understand God ('demonstrations') gave way to modern attempts to prove or disprove the existence of God ('proofs'). The artificial dislocation of the Cartesian ego from its cultural roots and relocation in a neutral space of pure reason meant that the scholastic task of faith-seeking-understanding was transformed into the modern task of understanding-seeking-faith. The second way was shaped by the Romantic reaction to an arid rationalism that sought to relegate aesthetic, moral and spiritual experience to the epistemically dubious status of arbitrary convention or personal taste. Emotive experience was sovereign: immediate unmediated experience of beauty, goodness and divinity was deemed epistemically self-authenticating. The noumenal realm of ultimate reality-in-itself must be experienced before it can be expressed and, given the nature of such experience, poetry, art and music provided mediums of expression far superior to rational argument. Of the two, noumenal experience proved more durable than rational argument. Given the positivist occlusion of unverifiable-hence-meaningless metaphysics, and the deep gulf between the God of Abraham and the God of the philosophers, rational proof failed to provide secure epistemic foundations for knowledge of ultimate reality. Noumenal experience, immune to rational and empirical critique, yet consistent with the Cartesian epistemic privileging of the immediate awareness of the autonomous self, dominated modern accounts of religious experience and post-modern accounts of spirituality as the expression of primal desire. On the surface level, neither provides a secure epistemic foundation for knowledge of the ultimate order-of-things: rational proofs are fundamentally contested and noumenal experience appears inherently subjective. On a deeper level, the entire strategy of seeking a neutral space in which human reason and/or feeling can reign supreme is fundamentally misplaced, as is the notion that epistemic certainty can provide secure foundations for the conduct of everyday life. Cartesian ways of understanding fail in their attempts to bypass epistemic relativity: sentient minds cannot ignore their embodiment in the vagaries and complexities of culture.

Because sentient minds are embodied in the natural and cultural domains, knowledge of the ultimate order-of-things is necessarily mediated through them. Even if we accept the possibility of direct unmediated mystical experience of ultimate reality, both the presuppositions the apprehender brings to such experience and the ways in which such apprehension are expressed will necessarily be culturally located. And because the ontological question, 'What must reality be like for us to experience it in the ways we do?' necessarily precedes the epistemic question, 'How can we be certain our knowledge is true?' the possession of epistemically relative knowledge is necessarily antecedent to the exercise of judgemental rationality. This being the case, the pursuit of ultimate truth and truthful living *sub specie aeternitatis* necessarily proceeds from established understandings of our place in the ultimate order-of-things. Judgemental rationality under-labours for the iterative refinement of knowledge we already possess; it does not over-labour for the construction of secure epistemic foundations on which to build knowledge we do not yet possess. The expansion of knowledge proceeds from that which we already (fallibly) hold to be true: faith seeks understanding. This being the case, the pursuit of ultimate truth takes the form of the interrogation of the beliefs we already subscribe to and the beliefs of others that we do not subscribe to. These beliefs emerge from the collective practice of ordinary life and form part of the habitus of our lifeworlds. Pedagogic engagement with them in schools, colleges and universities is secondary to our primary engagement with them in the ebb and flow of culture.

Knowledge of the ultimate order-of-things is always mediated by cultural beliefs and practices. Attempts to represent beliefs and practices oriented towards ultimate reality in terms of discrete institutionalised traditions seriously misrepresent a far more complex cultural reality. To identify such beliefs and practices under the headings 'world religions' (Christianity, Buddhism, Hinduism, Islam, Judaism, Sikhism, etc.) and their 'secular alternatives' (Humanism, Marxism, etc.), and attribute to each common typological dimensions (say, doctrinal, mythical, ethical, experiential, institutional and material) is to impose an artificial construct derived from one dominant post-Enlightenment understanding of Christianity. There may be some vague affinity between being a Marxist, a Christian or a Hindu, but to push the comparison further is to risk reification. Certainly the matrix of naturalism, humanism and liberalism that prevails in much contemporary global culture cannot properly be described as a secular version of Christianity. Attempts to overcome the dangers of reification by generating thick descriptions of culture that seek to avoid both over-simplification and the imposition of pre-ordained interpretative frameworks, such as that advocated by Geertz, tend to privilege description over explanation: description gives way to further description in an infinite regress that ultimately excludes questions of truth. This opens the door to forms of nominalism in which culture is reduced to a web of symbolic expressions and exchanges whose significance does not transcend the recognition of regular occurrences of similar symbols and exchanges. If to represent beliefs and practices in essentialist terms is to ignore epistemic relativity, then to represent them in nominalist terms is to bypass judgemental rationality. Emergent configurations of beliefs and practices cannot be reduced to the sum total of their constituent parts, but at the same time such emergence takes many different forms irreducible to a single interpretative framework.

The notion of 'worldview' provides a powerful interpretative tool for the exploration of beliefs and actions oriented towards the ultimate order-of-things. Smith's critically realist account of 'personhood' identifies a person as a 'conscious, self-transcending center of subjective experience, durable identity, moral commitment and social communication', the 'efficient cause of his or her own responsible actions and interactions' (Smith 2011: 61). We are separated from animals by virtue of our possession of an inescapable moral and spiritual dimension. As moral beings we inevitably interact with others within some form of moral order (sociopaths being the rare exceptions that prove the rule), and do so regardless of its merits (perpetrators of gangland revenge killings inhabit a moral order informed by notions of honour, self-respect and vindication) (Smith 2009: 13f.). As spiritual beings we are 'centres of purpose' in our engagement with self, other persons, culture, nature and the ultimate order-of-things. As persons, we are capable of addressing basic questions that underlie any given world view: who am I – what is the ultimate nature of humankind and ultimate meaning of life? Where am I – what is the ultimate nature of the reality we indwell? What ultimately is wrong – what gets in the way of the good (however conceived)? What ultimately is the remedy – how can the good (however conceived) be increased? (Walsh and Middleton 1984: 35). Collectively, human beings generate worldviews, defined by Hiebert as the 'foundational cognitive, affective, and evaluative assumptions and frameworks a group of people makes about the nature of reality which they use to order their lives' (Hiebert 2008: 25f.). Hiebert's analysis of worldviews identifies synchronic structures and diachronic characteristics. Viewed synchronically, worldviews possess depth: visible cultural products and patterns of behaviour are dependent on underlying belief systems that presume particular assumptions regarding category sets, logic, signs, causality and epistemology. 'Because worldviews are deep, they are generally unexamined and largely implicit. Like glasses, they shape how we see the world, but we are rarely aware of their presence' (ibid.: 46). As human constructs, worldviews are sites of internal and external contestation, form more or less integrated systems, have generative powers, and possess cognitive, affective and evaluative dimensions. Viewed diachronically, worldviews are dynamic and emergent entities that change over time, and most possess narratives, myths and stories that help explain the process of change to their adherents. Crucially for present purposes, the expansive notion of 'worldview' limits the dangers of misrepresenting religious traditions within pre-conceived typological frameworks and restricting accounts of them to thick cultural descriptions devoid of explanatory power. Critical realism sees reality as emergent, stratified, transfactual and value-laden. Representing religious traditions and secular alternatives through the interpretative frame of worldview studies promises to open up core questions of ontological realism, epistemic relativity and judgemental rationality.

(3) *Accessing ultimate reality: academic mediation.* Access to ultimate reality is culturally mediated. The heuristic notion of 'worldview' provides a means of identifying and explaining culturally grounded accounts of the ultimate order-of-things. Hence the ontology of the ultimate order-of-things, mediated by culturally relative accounts of that reality, is open to judgemental scrutiny. We can, and often do, apply wisdom and discernment regarding our place in the ultimate order-of-things in the course of everyday life within our given lifeworlds. Education provides a powerful means of refining and enhancing our capacity for wisdom and discernment. The academic fruits of research and scholarship mediated through education serve to enhance our understanding of our place in the ultimate order-of-things, illuminate the contextually relative nature of that understanding and open up the possibility of pursuing truth and truthful living in more powerful ways. Universities, by etymological definition, are concerned with generating and transmitting knowledge of reality as a whole (*universitas*) in order to enable individuals and society to flourish *sub specie aeternitatis*. The academic pursuit of truth and truthful living takes reality and our place in reality as its object, recognises that knowledge of both is partial and contested and seeks through programmes of research to generate more truthful knowledge (including practical knowledge), and through programmes of teaching to mediate the fruits of research to individuals and to society at large. With regard to knowledge of the totality of reality, contemporary universities frequently fail to relate increasingly specialised research into individual strata of reality to the totality of reality as a whole. The problem is exacerbated by the fact that investigation of particular strata frequently requires interdisciplinary methods, so that, for example, many social scientists seek to master not just the discipline of sociology, but other disciplines such as anthropology, ethnography, social psychology and philosophy. The challenge of interdisciplinary investigation of particular strata militates against cross-stratum investigation (though there are, of course, many notable exceptions to this tendency), which in turn militates against investigation of the relationship between interconnected strata and reality as a whole. Three curriculum areas buck this trend: theoretical physics, metaphysics and theology. For present purposes (and without denying that there is a debate to be had here) we can discount theoretical physics: attempts to find a master 'theory of everything' in the strata of reality investigated by physicists appears, from a critical realist perspective, inherently reductive, closed to the phenomenon of irreducible emergence and to metaphysical questions concerning the primal conditions that make the natural order-of-things and knowledge of nature possible. To claim that physics will one day provide a 'total theory of everything' is to commit oneself in advance to the naturalist belief that the natural order-of-things constitutes the fundamental bedrock of reality. This leaves the two disciplines of theology and metaphysics as the primary means through which academics seek to understand the totality of reality.

From its outset the tradition of Western metaphysics sought to address questions about the ultimate order-of-things. Heraclitus understood the reason (*logos*) underlying all things to be in a state of perpetual flux, whereas Parmenides contrasted epistemic experience of flux ('the way of opinion'), with an ultimate, timeless, uniform and unchanging ontological order ('the way of truth'). Plato viewed the material world as the work of the Demiurge, who shaped primal pre-existent matter using the eternal Forms as blueprint. Aristotle saw metaphysics as the investigation of being-qua-being, and traced causation, matter and form back to a Prime Mover. The Platonic Forms and Aristotelian Prime Mover permeated Jewish, Christian and Islamic theological scholarship in the medieval period. Early Enlightenment rationalist philosophers expanded the purview of metaphysics beyond the question of God (the Form of the Good or Unmoved Mover) to embrace issues raised by Abrahamic theologies (the relationship between mind and body, the immortality of the soul, the freedom of the will, theodicy, etc.), and in so doing set the agenda for the distinctly modern discipline of the 'philosophy of religion'. Leibniz and Kant shifted metaphysical attention from the noumenal realm of 'things-in-themselves' to the phenomenal realm of 'things-as-they-appear-to-us', thereby foregrounding the metaphysics of the mind and the presuppositions of conceptual thought. Thus the ontological question, 'What must the world be like for us to experience it in the ways we do?' gave way to the epistemic question, 'What must the mind be like for us to think, reason, reflect, desire, etc. in the ways we do?' Scepticism about our ability to ask questions about the ultimate order-of-things came to a head in logical positivism, which dismissed theological and metaphysical truth claims as nonsense by virtue of their unverifiability. This scepticism was carried over into various post-modern philosophies. Critical realism oversaw the rehabilitation of metaphysics: the ontological question 'What must reality ultimately be like for us to experience it in the ways we do' was seen to be an entirely valid question open to retroductive explanations and their ongoing iterative refinement. Metaphysics asks the question of the ultimate nature of the world presupposed by natural and social science and other human activities, and 'seeks to show the way the world must be for scientific and other practices as conceptualized in experience to be possible', by elaborating 'the philosophical ontology or categorical structure of the world that they logically presuppose' (Hartwig 2007: 353).

Theology stands alongside metaphysics as the second major academic mediator of knowledge of ultimate reality. We must proceed with caution here. Theology, understood as the self-consciously intellectual exploration of the reality of God or Transcendence whose natural home is the religious academy, is largely a product of the Abrahamic traditions. Though non-Abrahamic religious traditions certainly engage in conversations about ultimate reality, such discourse tends to take the form of primary religious discourse rather than secondary discourse about primary religious discourse. Theology as an intellectual enterprise emerged in early Christianity and Rabbinic Judaism in the context of attempts to articulate the meaning of received authoritative scriptures (Neusner and Chilton 1997). The core Christian doctrines of incarnation and Trinity take the form of iteratively refined retroductive interpretations of Christian scripture interpreted in the light of the ongoing spiritual life and worship of the Christian Churches. Theology thus functioned to explicitly articulate the implicit worldview assumptions of the early Church: the

New Testament's monotheistic insistence on the unity of God, when read along-side its insistence on describing the *relationship* between God the Father, God present in Jesus Christ and the Spirit of God guiding the lives of Jesus and the first Christians, demanded a Trinitarian formula. The distinction between primary worldview and secondary theology should not be reified as a set of binary opposites. Wright argues that Paul was forced to radically revise his received Jewish worldview in the light of his encounter with the life, death and resurrection of Jesus Christ. After rereading Jewish scripture in the light of this encounter, he 'effectively invented "Christian theology" to meet a previously unknown need' (Wright 2003; Paul 1:26). That our knowledge of Paul's theologising is derived from pastoral letters designed to encourage and guide Christian communities, and that those extant letters now form part of Christian scripture, should warn against the dangers of simplistically equating 'theology' with scholarly activities conducted in modern, largely secular, universities. Theology, understood as the intentional articulation and refinement of core beliefs concerning the ultimate order-of-things, in the form of faith-seeking-understanding, constitutes a vital mediator of human understanding of our place in the ultimate order-of-things.

Both metaphysics and theology are necessarily emergent from more basic religious and secular traditions and worldviews. Study of these traditions and worldviews, including the study of 'religions' as distinct cultural objects, emerged during the Enlightenment. The study of religion, for long under the tutelage of the disciplines of theology and metaphysics, only gradually emerged as a field of investigation in its own right. Departments of Religious Studies, as opposed to Departments of Theology, were only established in British universities in the 1960s. Such departments sought to interpret and explain religion as a cultural phenomenon through a multidisciplinary approach that utilised the tools of, amongst others, historical, sociological, psychological, anthropological, ethnographical and phenomenological research and scholarship. A key driver was the desire to understand religion apart from the hegemonic assumptions of theology. Frequently this led to reductive accounts of religion that artificially bracketed-out questions of ultimate truth and failed to countenance any suggestion that religions might possibly engage in truthful ways with the ultimate structures of reality. This, however, was certainly not universal: as noted earlier, Smart amongst others envisaged the interpretation of 'religion' in terms of a continuum from historical to para-historical explanation. Unsurprisingly, Religious Studies remains a contested field of study. In particular, the use of the term 'religion' to identify relatively discrete and comparatively institutionalised social entities is generally recognised to be a product of European colonialism and Christian missionary activities in the nineteenth century. Fitzgerald suggests that, despite its attempt at emancipation from theology, the comparative study of religions functions as a neo-colonial ideology and post-Protestant ecumenical theology complicit in the generation and reproduction of occidental, and hence hegemonic, representations of reality (Fitzgerald 2000). Flood suggests that the study of religion has been dominated by a phenomenology of consciousness and religious experience, and advocates a hermeneutical turn more sensitive to language and culture and more open to interdisciplinary research at the interface of religious studies, theology and the social sciences (Flood 1999). Regardless of the future direction of these and other debates, any understanding of culture as the primary mediator of know-ledge of the ultimate order-of-things must of necessity draw on the conflicting insights of academic research and study conducted under the umbrella of 'Reli-gious Studies', alongside those of theology and metaphysics.

(4) *Critical religious education and ontological realism.* Critical religious education, drawing on the under-labouring services of critical realism, advocates an approach to religious education grounded in the pursuit of truth and truthful living. The two are envisaged as an essential unity: to pursue knowledge of the ultimate order-of-things (truth) is simultaneously to seek to live *sub specie aeter-nitatis* in relation to that order (truthfulness). The classical notion of *paideia* assumed a fundamental pedagogic unity between the pursuit of truth and truthful living: to understand the world truly was simultaneously to flourish truthfully both as individuals and as a society. Thus a holistic classical curriculum consist-ing of science, ethics and logic sought to *generate knowledge* of the world and human persons (science), enable *social flourishing* (ethics), and oversee the *per-sonal formation* of individuals capable of wise discernment (logic). As we have seen, one legacy of the Enlightenment was the fragmentation of this holistic vision of the pedagogic integration of knowledge generation, social flourishing and personal formation. This fragmentation continues to permeate contemporary schools and universities, which struggle to identify organic connections between education for knowledge transmission (teaching) and expansion (research), per-sonal formation and social flourishing; and it is reflected in established forms of liberal religious education. Given that few pupils aspire to religious vocations, the notion of religious education for professional training is excluded from the agenda. However, the cultivation of personal autonomy and social cohesion (learning 'from' religion) *is* firmly embedded in curricula. At the same time, pupils are expected to assimilate information about the beliefs and practices of religious traditions (learning 'about' religion) via a hermeneutic that emphasises the importance of empathetic engagement. Education for knowledge of the ulti-mate nature of reality is conspicuous only in its absence. The dominant values of liberal religious education are the secular liberal values of freedom and toler-ance, and the implicit worldview that frames the subject is that of the post-Enlightenment matrix of naturalism, secular humanism and secular liberalism. Departures from this matrix are tolerated (since we are free to believe whatever we like provided we avoid doing harm to others), but frequently in a patronising manner that rarely treats their truth claims as serious options. Ironically, a liberal religious education predicated on resistance to religious confessionalism finds itself embroiled in a secular confessionalism that effectively inducts pupils into the norms of the post-Enlightenment matrix.

Critical religious education, supported by the under-labouring services of crit-ical realism, is committed to the pursuit of ultimate truth and cultivation of per-sonal and social flourishing *sub specie aeternitatis*. As a disciplinary subject, it takes as its primary object of knowledge the ultimate ontological order-of-things.

This marks a significant step beyond confessional Christian Religious Education's identification of the Triune God as the primary object of knowledge, and liberal religious education's identification of religious phenomena (frequently presented within in the implicit framework of a naturalistic ontology) as the primary object of knowledge. Critical religious education, whilst accepting the inappropriateness of public education in a plural society subscribing exclusively to Christian ontology, rejects liberal religious education's response to Christian confessionalism. Identifying religious phenomena as the primary object of knowledge tends either to occlude questions of the ultimate nature of reality, assume a naturalistic ontology by default, or implicitly embrace a universal theology in which all religious traditions are equally valid expressions of a common experience of the 'Ultimate'. All three outcomes lack pedagogic integrity: to exclude questions of the ultimate nature of reality is to occlude the hermeneutical circle of the relationship between parts and wholes and thereby give discursive privilege to post-positivist and post-modern assumptions that the circle is closed to rational investigation; to implicitly affirm either naturalism or universal theology is to revert to a form of confessional religious education in which the 'truth' of naturalism or theological universalism replaces the truth of Christianity as the subject's implicit non-negotiable 'given'. Identifying the ultimate ontological order-of-things as the primary object of knowledge affirms the traditional disciplinary orientation of religious education towards Transcendence (ontological realism), recognises that the object of knowledge is fundamentally contested (epistemic relativity), and opens the door to the cultivation of religious (metaphysical, spiritual, theological) literacy (judgemental rationality).

Knowledge is constituted by the *relationship* between knowing subjects and objects of knowledge. To progressively understand the ultimate order-of-things is to progressively understand one's place and the place of society within that order. Confessional Christian education sought to cultivate the spiritual formation of pupils and the spiritual wellbeing of society within a Christian framework. Liberal religious education distinguished 'learning about religion' and 'learning from religion': between the generation of knowledge of religious phenomena, and the cultivation of personal formation and social flourishing. The intentionality underlying the distinction was certainly praiseworthy; it sought to overcome the Enlightenment divide between knowledge acquisition, personal formation and social flourishing. However, the outcome was problematic: given the reduction of the primary object of knowledge from the ultimate order-of-things to immanent religious culture, personal formation and social flourishing were addressed in terms of pupils' relationships to religious culture rather than their relationships with the ultimate order-of-things. In the absence of a cultivation of judgemental rationality vis-à-vis ultimate reality, personal formation tended to be construed in terms of secular liberal notions of personal autonomy and freedom of expression, and social flourishing in terms of secular liberal notions of tolerance and social cohesion. Thus 'learning from religion' tended to take the form of expressions of personal opinion coupled with expressions of tolerant attitudes towards religious adherents (or, more accurately, expressions of tolerance towards religious adherents who had not undergone radicalisation). Critical religious education's recognition of the indivisibility of the relationship between knowing subjects and objects of knowledge disallowed any divide between learning 'about' and 'from': to understand ultimate reality was simultaneously, and unavoidably, to understand oneself and one's society in relation to ultimate reality. Identifying the necessary relationship between knowledge of the ultimate ontological order-of-things and individual and collective self-knowledge affirms the traditional disciplinary orientation of religious education as the pursuit of ultimate truth and cultivation of truthful living *sub specie aeternitatis*, but in a manner that recognises the contested nature of ultimate reality and hence the contested nature of personal formation and social flourishing.

To the best of our knowledge, everything in reality is ontologically related. If alternative realities other than our own exist then they must be ontologically related to our reality, even if that relationship is a negative relationship of absolute disconnectedness. That being the case, we necessarily enjoy an ontological relationship to the ultimate order-of-things, whether we are aware of that fact or not. Critical religious education is maximally committed to ontological realism, and maximally resistant to reductive accounts of the ultimate nature of reality. At the same time it seeks to be maximally committed to epistemic relativity, and maximally resistant to all forms of premature epistemic closure. This is in sharp contrast to both confessional and liberal approaches to the subject. Confessional religious education is maximally committed to ontological realism, but only minimally committed to epistemic relativity: the Transcendent reality confessed is treated as a given norm, and questions about its veracity are downplayed. Liberal religious education, on the other hand, is maximally committed to epistemic relativity, and only minimally committed to ontological realism: scepticism about Transcendent reality effectively excludes the pursuit of ultimate truth. Critical religious education's commitment to ontological realism frequently brings the charge of neo-confessionalism. However, this charge makes little sense when read in the light of critical religious education's equally trenchant commitment to epistemic relativity: particular theologies, universal theologies, the secular matrix of naturalism, humanism and liberalism, and indeed any other account of the ultimate order-of-things – including forms of ontological anti-realism – are all firmly on the agenda for debate. Thus the first 'critical' feature of critical religious education is its commitment to ontological realism about the ultimate order-of-things and our relation to it.

Epistemic relativity

(1) *Relativity 'all the way down'*. The labels 'judgemental rationality' and 'epistemic relativity' are open to misunderstanding by the casual observer not conversant with the broad vision of critical realism. 'Judgemental rationality' resonates with the modern notion of the Cartesian ego making rational choices in the expectation of overcoming epistemic relativity and achieving epistemic

certainty. 'Epistemic relativity' resonates with the post-modern notion of the ephemeral self playfully negotiating the ebb and flow of life without any expectation of exercising judgemental rationality or desire to achieve epistemic certainty. Both options impose premature epistemic closure: the former by claiming epistemic certainty, the latter by claiming, somewhat paradoxically, epistemic certainty that epistemic certainty is unobtainable. The critical realist response is to insist that judgemental rationality and epistemic relativity do not exist in isolation, but rather in dialectical tension, both with one another and with ontological realism. Thus for the critical realist 'epistemic relativity' asserts that knowledge is always relative to the perspective of the knower or community of knowers and marked by their specific spatio-temporal locations. This means that there can be no neutral 'view from nowhere' from which to generate pure perspective-free knowledge. At the same time 'judgemental rationality' asserts the possibility of identifying some perspective-limited ways of understanding the world, and our place in the world, as more truthful than others. Crucially both epistemic relativity and judgemental rationality are answerable to ontological realism: the way things actually are in reality constitutes the benchmark against which the dialect of relativity and reason must be played out.

When measured against ontological reality, conflicting knowledge claims cannot all be equally true. On the contrary, some *are* more truthful than others, and some *may be known* to be more truthful than others. Geertz argues that 'thick' descriptions of human culture are constantly open to still-thicker descriptions, and that, since there can be no final description, the generation of progressively thicker descriptions is a never-ending process: description is operative 'all the way down'. For the critical realist, thick description must give way to rich causal explanation: it is not sufficient merely to *describe* the world, rather the more basic task is to *explain* why the world is-what-it-is and behaves-as-it-does. Though one explanation may be more truthful than another explanation, the fact that all explanations are necessarily relative to the perspective of the knower means that even the most truthful explanation currently available to us must remain open to the possibility of a yet-more-truthful explanation. If some explanations are more truthful than other explanations, and if all explanations are open to better explanations, then explanation is operative 'all the way down'. Thus there is no contradiction between the impossibility of epistemic closure on the one hand, and the actuality that some explanations *are*, and under certain circumstances may be shown beyond reasonable doubt *to be*, more truthful to the realities they seek to explain than others.

Any object or event, however mundane or bathed in significance, is open to multiple explanations. Critical realism distinguishes between the domains of the empirical, actual and real. That is to say, between: that which may be *empirically* observed and reported by the persons present at any given event (say, the birth of a child); all *actual* human births that have previously taken place, are currently taking place and may potentially take place; and the *real* causal mechanisms involved in the process of childbirth. Neither of these three domains is open to comprehensive, total or definitive description and/or explanation. The persons present will experience the same event from different perspectives, report their experiences in different ways, and highlight different critical aspects of it. Knowledge of the totality of all actual births, past, present and future, whether experienced directly or through various forms of mediation, is simply impossible. Causal explanations will have recourse to different strata of the same event: physical, chemical, biological, psychological, social, cultural, moral, aesthetic, spiritual, etc. Each individual stratum is dependent on lower strata but irreducible to them. Causal mechanisms operate together, both within particular strata and across different strata, in complex morphogenetic ways. Since any event will be situated at a particular spatio-temporal location, it will form part of a causal web linked to all other spatio-temporal events. Because all things are related, a truly comprehensive account of any particular object or event will require a truly comprehensive account of the totality of all objects and events in the whole of reality. Thus explanation is truly operative 'all the way down'. And the unavoidable actuality of epistemic relativity precludes the possibility of human beings generating a total explanation of reality: only an omniscient, omnipotent and omnipresent God could possibly do so. And even if such a God were to make such an explanation available to a particular human being, their account of the totality of everything would be relative to the fact that they are recounting, from a particular spatio-temporal location a total account of everything bequeathed to them by God at a particular spatio-temporal location. There can be no epistemic closure. All our knowing is necessarily and unavoidably related to our perspective as knowers. But this does not rule out the fact that we possess substantial knowledge of ourselves and the world we indwell. Nor does it preclude the possibility of progression from less truthful to more truthful knowledge.

This assertion of the simultaneous actuality and contingency of knowledge diverges from comprehensive liberal attempts to bridge the gulf between epistemic relativity and epistemic certainty. Liberalism recognises a plurality of moral, aesthetic and spiritual beliefs that (unlike, supposedly more secure, objective scientific 'knowledge') it deems inherently subjective and closed to epistemic verification. The liberal commitment to the sovereign autonomy of the individual knower generates a parallel commitment to the authenticity of the sovereign knower's beliefs (the exception being beliefs deemed intrinsically intolerant and hence detrimental to the common good). The fact that incommensurable beliefs cannot all be equally true when measured against ontological realities, coupled with the insistence that nevertheless all beliefs must be *treated* as equally authentic, generates an inconsistency that cuts through the heart of the liberal project. Insofar as a moral commitment to the authenticity of all perspectives undermines an intellectual commitment to the pursuit of truth, liberalism falls foul of the epistemic fallacy of forcing reality into the straightjacket of its preferred (moral) ways of knowing. In effect, the commitment to respect and tolerance serves to occlude the exercise of judgemental rationality concerned to differentiate between more and less truthful beliefs. But this need not be the case:

there is nothing to preclude respect for a particular knower and a particular knower's beliefs running hand-in-hand with the reasoned presentation of an alternative perspective that claims greater truth. Indeed, the absence of the latter opens the door to the possibility of patronising attitudes that fail to respond to the knower's claims with the seriousness they may demand. However the practice of respect-and-criticism can be difficult, particularly in closed liberal societies in which the defence of sovereign autonomy overrides all other concerns. This is perhaps most clearly visible in liberalism's suspicion of enthusiasm: the enthusiast being the person who insists on treating their subjective beliefs as if they enjoyed the status of objective knowledge, and seeks to persuade others of the truth of their commitments. In the religious sphere, this generates a division between acceptable and unacceptable forms of religious belief: acceptable belief being belief that is held without undue enthusiasm and hence largely confined to the private sphere; unacceptable belief being belief that is proclaimed zealously in the public square. Such antipathy towards enthusiasm frequently gives discursive privilege to dominant value systems, so that to be enthusiastic about a dominant set of values is deemed acceptable whilst similar enthusiasm about a minority set of values is deemed less acceptable: contrast, for example an enthusiastic defence of (say) human rights and a similarly enthusiastic defence of (say) evangelical Christianity. The simultaneous affirmation of both epistemic relativity and judgemental rationality demands *both* respect for the authenticity of different perspectives *and* commitment to the ongoing pursuit of truth: one can respect a position even though one has good reason for considering it to be less truthful than an alternative (though this need not rule out justifiably disrespecting a position judged unworthy of respect). The absence or presence of enthusiasm is irrelevant, both to the duty of respect and commitment to the pursuit of truth. Enthusiasm is a significant mechanism of change, both for good and for bad, and as such is itself morally neutral: enthusiasm can be a source of great harm, but equally a source of great good. Without enthusiasm the status quo would simply be accepted as normative, regardless of the presence or absence of good or ill. What matters is not the degree of enthusiasm, but the relative truth of the cause to which the enthusiast subscribes. We cannot avoid fundamental commitments to truths, despite the fact that the truths we are committed to are always contingent and not necessarily the best truths available to us. The way forward is not to preclude enthusiasm (since to do so is to weaken the possibility of transformative change for the better) but to ensure that enthusiastic commitment to epistemically relative beliefs is guided by a concomitant exercise of judgemental rationality. In short: the simultaneity of epistemic relativity and judgemental rationality means that *all* knowing takes the basic form of faith-seeking-understanding.

(2) *Causes of relativity.* If knowledge is constituted by the relationship between knowing subjects and objects of knowledge, then empirical experience of external objects is fundamental to our ways of knowing. Empiricism construes empirical experience as possession of isolated packets of sense data, and empiricist pedagogy suggests that epistemic relativity is partly a consequence of the

learner's limited possession of such data. Hence the key pedagogic task is to provide for the quantitative expansion of experienced data. This generates a 'banking' model in which knowledge is equated with possession of information. Though many constructivists accept this basic empiricist model, they staunchly reject any reduction of knowledge to possession of information. Sense data only becomes meaningful when empirical data is assimilated to learners' frames of meaning via a process of active construction. Though learners require raw data from which to construct meaning, knowledge is generated, not through the passive reception of data, but through the active construction of meaning from data. Hence constructivism's identification of the cultivation of cognitive processing skills as the principal means of overcoming epistemic relativity. The nature and scope of cognitive processing skills is contested: modernists advocate rational thinking skills, romantics favour forms of emotional intelligence, while post-modernists celebrate the creative imagination. Constructivism's central conflation of empirical data and cognitive processing assumes two basic ways of overcoming epistemic relativity: the quantitative expansion of information available to learners and the qualitative enhancement of their cognitive processing skills. Realist pedagogy questions the centrality of both assumptions: *expansion* and *cognitive processing* must give way to *insight* and discernment. First, expansion of information in the domain of the 'actual' (the totality of objects, events and states of affairs in the world) must give way to the deepening of insight in the realm of the 'real' (the underlying causal mechanisms that constitute objects, events and states of affairs). Second, knowledge produced by cognitive processing designed to generate meaning from neutral data must give way to the active discernment of meaning inherent in objects of knowledge.

The modernist picture of the isolated Cartesian self dislocated from the world as a consequence of a thoroughgoing hermeneutic of suspicion, assumes an epistemic gulf between the knowing subject and objects of knowledge, and construes the epistemic task as that of finding ways of bridging that gulf. Given the gulf, we have no access to noumenal objects-in-themselves, only to phenomenal objects-as-they-appear-to-us. In sharp contrast, the post-modern picture of the embodied ephemeral self embedded in the ebb and flow of culture (as opposed to the alternative post-modern picture of the disembodied ephemeral self trapped in a web of linguistic signifiers) suggests that we are intimately related to things-in-themselves despite our inability to understand them truthfully. This notion of the embodied self resonates with critical realism's understanding of knowledge as constituted by the *relationship* between knowing subjects and objects of knowledge. If there is no epistemic gulf between ourselves and the world, if we are already intimately related to the reality we seek to understand more truthfully, then the epistemic task is not to *establish* knowledge relationships but to *generate more truthful* relationships with that which we already partially know.

Knowledge is not constituted by the possession of information but by the relationship between knowing subjects and objects of knowledge. Hence epistemic relativity is reduced, not by the quantitative expansion of information about the world, but by the development of deeper insight into the world the learner already relates to. The primary school pupil and post-doctoral researcher trying to make sense of one or other aspect of world are both engaged with and related to the same reality, despite significant differences in their levels of understanding. We are not dealing here with the binary opposites of present and absent knowledge, but in qualitatively different levels of established knowledge. The primary pupil learning to spell simple words and the post-doctoral researcher seeking deeper understanding of Shakespearean metaphor are both related to and engaged with the same reality: language. That the primary pupil may never have heard of Shakespeare, and almost certainly has never read a line of Shakespeare's poetry, does not mean that he is unrelated to Shakespeare. Rather, his knowledge of language in general, and of the language of poetry in particular, is rudimentary, and may not yet be sufficiently informed to allow for explicit knowledge of Shakespeare per se. Both pupil and researcher indwell the same world and engage with the same reality (language), but at different levels of sophistication. It is not so much that the primary pupil is ignorant of Shakespeare (though, of course, he may never have heard of him), but that his understanding of language is insufficiently complex and differentiated to allow (at this stage in his education) for any deep or expansive knowledge of Shakespeare. If epistemic relativity operates 'all the way down', it does so not via leaps from the known to the previously unknown, but through the progressive move from less differentiated and less complex to more differentiated and more complex insight.

The move towards more differentiated and complex insight is simultaneously a move towards discernment of the real causal mechanisms that constitute objects, events and states of affairs in the world. Ontological realism recognises that meaning resides in objects independently of our knowledge of them. Objects do not exist in splendid isolation, but are unavoidably and causally linked to other objects. Hence the intrinsic meaning of objects resides primarily in their status as objects in relation to other objects and as objects located in a matrix of events. The establishment of a knowledge-relationship with independent objects enhances their intrinsic meaning because they become objects of knowledge in relation to other objects that are now known by knowing subjects. When an object is known, so relational identity extends to its relationality with the knower. The meaning of an object does not reside in its surface appearance, nor does it reside in either the space between object and knower or the mind of the knower. Descriptions of surface appearances and expressions of the knower's experience of the object must give way to explanations of the underlying causal mechanisms that constitute the object in reality. Such explanations take the form of retroductive explanations of abductive encounters that are progressively itera- tively refined by learning communities. Learners cannot reasonably be expected to generate retroductive explanations for themselves, but instead must be intro- duced to retroductive explanations that have already been generated. Learning, say, natural science, takes the form of induction into communal tradition: stu- dents left alone in a science laboratory with a Bunsen burner cannot reasonably be expected to replicate the knowledge contained in scientific text books that has been accumulated over centuries of scientific endeavour. If epistemic relativity is reduced by learning to better explain the world we inhabit, then such learning must necessarily take the form of induction into received traditions of explanation. This means that the constructivist prejudice against knowledge-transmission must be stringently resisted. The fear of indoctrination and/or reduction of knowledge to brute objective facts is misplaced, because retroductive explanations are complex entities subject to contestation. Knowledge-transmission cannot be reduced to the transmission of brute facts or meaning-free information, but rather involves the transmission of contested meaning and the transmission of received wisdom regarding the ways in which the process of meaning discernment takes place. Thus cognitive skills such as critical thinking, emotive intelligence and creative imagination are not primary pedagogic tools for meaning construction, but rather secondary pedagogic tools under-labouring in support of the epistemic virtues of attentiveness, reasonableness, intelligence and responsibility vis-à-vis objects of knowledge.

(3) *Spiritual formation.* Since we indwell reality, we necessarily exist in ontological relation to the ultimate order-of-things and cannot avoid living life ontologically *sub specie aeternitatis.* This is the case regardless of whether we are epistemically aware of it or not. Earlier we identified spirituality as the developing relationship of the individual, within community and tradition, to that which is – or is perceived to be – of ultimate concern, ultimate value and ultimate truth. Spirituality is not the unique preserve of religious adherents and religious traditions that subscribe to a Transcendent ontology. Even if the ultimate order-of-things does not contain a Transcendent domain, an ultimate order-of-things still exists and we still unavoidably live life *sub specie aeternitatis.* We are inescapably spiritual beings, though the extent of insight into and discernment of our spiritual relationships varies enormously. That being the case, it is far better to be aware of the contested nature of ultimate reality, recognise our faith commitments vis-à-vis ultimate reality, and seek to exercise judgmental rationality with respect both to our understanding of ultimate reality and our conduct of life *sub specie aeternitatis.* Greater insight and discernment is preferable to lesser insight and discernment: far better be a discontented philosopher than a contented sheep. We are better people for taking responsibility for our spiritual lives, regardless of whether we envisage our lives as a modern or pre-modern spiritual quest for some ultimate goal or as a post-modern nomadic wandering in a world devoid of any ultimate goal. Education for spiritual insight and discernment brings education for knowledge of the world, education for personal formation, and education for social flourishing into a coherent whole. We cannot understand the ultimate order-of-things without beginning to understand ourselves and the communities we belong to in relation to it.

The process of spiritual formation is extraordinarily complex: it is the process of a unique individual making sense of their lives in relation to the ultimate order-of-things, of discerning their relations to self, others, culture and nature in the light of the totality of everything. Given epistemic relativity 'all the way down', this can only ever be a process of faith-seeking-understanding. We are stratified beings inhabiting a stratified world, and the hermeneutical circle requires a dialectical interplay between discernment of individual strata and discernment of the totality of everything. We are emergent beings in an emergent world, and the hermeneutical circle requires a dialectic interplay between discernment of all that has been, all that is and all that might potentially be, and discernment of the individuals we once were, the individuals we are and the individuals we might become. We live in a transfactual and causally efficacious world, in which the morphogenetic interplay of natural, sentient, cultural and (possibly) Transcendent causal mechanisms generates an ordered-yet-dynamic reality in which, despite the fact that secure prediction and effective control are absent, we carry the burden of living good lives *sub specie aeternitatis* and face the constant risk of failure and promise of success. Kierkegaard suggested that 'purity of heart is to will one thing': an allusion to the words of Christ in the Sermon on the Mount: 'Blessed are the pure in heart, for they shall see God.' To make the best of our lives, to live in purity of heart, is to will the very best: that is to say, to will truthful living in relation to the ultimate order-of-things. Education for spiritual formation is education for truthful relationship with the ultimate order-of-things. Ontologically, we are already related to ultimate reality, whether we are aware of that fact or not. Epistemically, we already possess, however embryonically, some level of insight and discernment into our spiritual relationships. In the context of spiritual formation, epistemic relativity does not imply scepticism allied to a pragmatic affirmation of the prevailing status quo, but rather faithful commitment to our received understanding of who we ultimately are and what reality ultimately is like, coupled with a similarly faithful commitment to strive for more complex, more differentiated, more truthful insight and discernment of that which we are already related to and that which we already partially understand.

(4) *Critical religious education and epistemic relativity.* Critical religious education, drawing on the under-labouring services of critical realism, identifies the ultimate order-of-things and our relationship to it as the primary ontological object of study. Its commitment to epistemic relativity rules out any misidentification with neo-confessionalism: the fact that the ontological object of study is epistemically contested rules out any possibility of premature pedagogic closure. We have seen that epistemic relativity runs 'all the way down'. There can be no dualistic distinction between present and absent knowledge, because we already possess knowledge of reality in general and ultimate reality in particular, however embryonically, implicitly and partially. Consequently, the primary pedagogic task is not to establish new knowledge, but to strive for deeper insight and discernment into that which we already know, and to seek to do so in increasingly complex and differentiated ways. To discern the ultimate order-of-things is to discern ourselves in relationship to ultimate reality. Such discernment is essentially spiritual. Because our lives matter, because each individual is irreplaceable and hence infinitely valuable, the spiritual quest is a vital process and the pursuit of ultimate truth and truthful living *sub specie aeternitatis* an intrinsic good.

Prior to formal teaching and learning students already inhabit worldviews bequeathed to them by the cultures they participate in, already possess embryonic understandings of themselves in relation to the ultimate order-of-things, and hence are already nascent philosophers and theologians. Prejudice and presupposition is an essential dimension of learning: insight and discernment emerges when we project potential meaning, derived from our prejudices and presuppositions, onto unfamiliar objects, and allow such objects to resist our projections and suggest alternative meanings. That being the case, critical religious education's commitment to epistemic relativity begins with a commitment to enabling students to recognise and identify their prejudices and presuppositions: in effect, to become self-consciously aware of the implicit worldview spectacles through which they already make sense of the world and of themselves in relation to the world. There is no imperative to bring about qualitative changes in students' worldviews: because ontological realism trumps epistemic relativity, it is entirely possible that a naive and poorly discerned knowledge relationship with the ultimate order-of-things may be more truthful than a more critical and sophisticated knowledge-relationship – everything is dependent on what, ultimately, reality is actually like. There is, however, a pedagogic imperative to bring about deeper insight and discernment of students' worldviews and primary commitments. Because we always understand what something is in relation to what it is not, insight and discernment of a particular worldview requires insight and discernment of alternative worldviews. Thus there is an imperative to enable students to discern their received worldviews in relation to alternative worldviews. This opens up the possibility of qualitative changes in worldviews: of conversion from one particular religious or secular worldview to another. However, this possibility is not a pedagogic imperative: because epistemic relativity identifies the possibility of potential truth in a range of different religious and secular worldviews, critical religious education is not justified in seeking any form of conversion. It is, however, fully justified in striving to ensure that students' understanding of their own worldviews and of the worldviews of others is increasingly complex and differentiated.

Deeper, more complex and more differentiated discernment necessarily transcends both naive description of the surface appearances of the cultures that sustain different worldviews, and naive projection of constructed meaning onto surface appearances. Description must give way to explanation: it is necessary to penetrate beneath the *empirical* and *actual* realms of surface appearances and projected constructs and engage with the *real* causal mechanisms that underlie them. To achieve this the cultural mediators of ultimate reality must be understood in the light of academic mediators. Hence critical religious education is an academically grounded subject: drawing on academic insight and transmitting academic insight. There is, of course, a genuine danger of academic rationalisation and reification here, but this is an issue, not for the fundamental structures of the theory of critical religious education, but for the process of pedagogic delivery: good pedagogic delivery will avoid reification, poor pedagogic delivery may not. In this, critical religious education takes its stand alongside other school disciplines. As curriculum subjects physics, sociology and English literature must be grounded in the best possible academic insight, whilst pedagogic delivery must seek to avoid reification and connect appropriately with students' lifeworlds. If physics, sociology and English literature were to seek to disconnect from their respective academic bases their integrity as disciplinary subjects would be seriously compromised. Precisely the same holds for critical religious education. The notion of education as transmission of academic knowledge does not, contra constructivism, undermine epistemic relativity by reifying knowledge into objective facts. This is because academic knowledge is itself contested and hence epistemically relative.

Epistemic relativity enables the pursuit of deeper insight and discernment into that which is already partially known. Hence the second 'critical' feature of critical religious education is its commitment to epistemic relativity about the ultimate order-of-things and our relation to it.

Judgemental rationality

(1) *Critical thinking and critical religious education.* As noted earlier, when read in isolation from epistemic relativity, judgemental rationality resonates with the modern notion of the Cartesian ego making rational choices in the expectation of achieving epistemic closure. The modern dream of reason has been fundamentally challenged by post-modern philosophers. Critical realism's response is not to abandon reason per se, but to affirm reason as the most effective means of making sense of the world known to us whilst simultaneously insisting on the contingency of our rational endeavours. Angela Goodman's detailed survey of the reception history of critical religious education reveals a tendency to interpret it within a neo-Kantian framework that equates judgemental rationality with modernist accounts of 'critical thinking' in a manner that effectively loosens its relationship to epistemic relativity (Goodman 2014; cf. Goodman 2013). The word 'critical' is taken by many commenters as a reference to 'critical' thinking rather than, as originally intended, an attempt to identify the most crucial ('critical') aspects of realist religious education, namely ontological realism, epistemic relativity and judgemental rationality. Goodman identifies three key critiques of critical religious education generated by scholars operating within a broad liberal framework.

First, criticism of the notion that religious education 'should be fundamentally concerned with opposing truth claims' (ibid.: 3). According to Patricia Hannam, critical religious education only deals with propositional truth claims (Hannam 2013: 433). Geoff Teece proposes that critical religious education align itself with Hick's pluralistic theology of religions, which affirms religious traditions as culturally relativistic expressions of a common universal religious experience (Teece 2005; cf. Barnes and Wright 2006). Jackson notes that '"religion" and "religions" are social and cultural constructs, the meaning of which has changed over time' and suggests that, though this does not preclude the pursuit of ultimate truth, it places a significant question mark over notions of religions as bearers of stable propositional truths (Jackson 2008: 20). Goodman notes that the central thrust of these critiques is to place a question mark over the viability of orienting religious education towards the pursuit of ultimate truth, on the grounds that it is questionable whether religions uniformly proffer stable propositional truth claims.

Second, criticism that critical religious education is 'too academic and rationalistic to be accessible to all students' (Goodman 2014: 3). Jackson notes a 'heavy rationalism' in critical religious education and questions whether it pays due attention to the emotions (Jackson 2004: 84). He suggests that this

> is rather like being told that one must go through the discipline of learning chords in jazz before being allowed to play or sing, or having to do a course in the history of art before one's enjoyment of a picture can be authentic.
>
> (ibid.: 84; cf. Wright 2003)

> It is hard to see his approach working over all the years of schooling. The approach appears to be demandingly academic. His own experience is very much in secondary education, and it is difficult to imagine his project working with younger children or with less able young people. Moreover ... there will be young people who do not feel psychologically ready to face the tensions involved with resolving inconsistent intellectual positions.
>
> (Jackson 2004: 85f.)

Third, 'many commentators have criticised the lack of practical examples of [critical religious education], calling for evidence of how the theory can be translated into practice' (Goodman 2014: 3, referencing Grimmitt 2000, Jackson 2004, Teece 2005, Hannam 2013). Thus, for example, Jackson notes the 'feeling of distance from the classroom (especially in relation to young or less able pupils) that comes across in [Wright's] writing' (Jackson 2004: 86).

The cumulative picture emerging from these critiques is of a pedagogy committed to the critical assessment of conflicting propositional truth claims in a rationalistic manner likely to challenge the competencies of some teachers and many pupils. On this reading, critical religious education promotes critical thinking skills in order to empower students to 'make their own judgements about questions of truth' and 'express and formulate their own positions' (Jackson 2004: 34, 36, 86). This foregrounding of critical thinking is held to spawn a range of unwelcome consequences: the reduction of religious beliefs to propositional statements; the reification of religion in a manner that ignores the messy reality of religious habitus; the introduction of an academic curriculum inaccessible to less-able students; and the prioritising of rational thought over the emotions. This reading of critical religious education emerged in the context of liberal religious education's increasing reliance on relativistic post-modern pedagogies. Thus Erricker argues that students should be free to assimilate information about religion within their own subjective frames of reference without recourse to questions of objective truth (Erricker 2001). Similarly Jackson, despite acknowledging the importance of critical thinking for understanding religious culture and affirming the importance of the pursuit of truth, identifies 'edification' as a key pedagogic goal, and understands it as a subjective process of 'grasping another's way of life ... and pondering on the issues and questions raised by it' in a manner closed to formal teaching and unfettered by rationalistic thought (Jackson 1997: 123, 130f.). Read in this context, critical religious education was understood as a modernist reaction to liberal religious education's postmodern turn, rather than as an attempt to transcend the modern–post-modern divide.

(2) *Critical Thinking and Education.* Discussion about the place of critical thinking in religious education forms part of a wider educational debate. John Dewey's pragmatic pedagogic turn helped generate a shift in emphasis from curriculum content to the critical thinking skills required for the effective assimilation of curriculum content. He argued that the transmission of disciplinary knowledge and vocational skills via rote learning and imitative repetition failed to prepare students for life in an increasingly complex, dynamic and challenging democratic society. If students were to make their way effectively in such a world they must be offered an education capable of generating reflective thinking, considered expression and flexible action in a manner sensitive to their given lifeworlds and experiences. Dewey defined 'reflexive thinking' as 'active, persistent, and careful consideration of a belief or supposed form of knowledge in the light of the grounds which support it and the further conclusions to which it tends' (Dewey 1991: 6). In the wake of Dewey's work, critical thinking became a central plank of mainstream pedagogic theory and practice. It is standard practice for curricular documents at all levels of education to specify the subject specific and generic thinking skills deemed necessary for the effective assimilation of curriculum content. A common truncation of Bloom's taxonomy of educational objectives in the cognitive domain ('knowledge, comprehension, application, analysis, synthesis and evaluation') differentiates between knowledge, understanding and evaluation: raw *knowledge* only becomes meaningful when *understood* within students' own cognitive frames of reference, and only gains validity when subjected to critical *evaluation* (Bloom 1965). Piaget advocated a form of central conflation in which learners both *accommodate* themselves to the objective constraints of the external world and *assimilate* the external world to their own subjective frames of meaning (Piaget 1977; cf. Fosnot and Perry 2005: 16ff.).

Dewey's work gave birth to a rich tradition of thinking about critical thinking in education, pioneered by John Passmore, Israel Scheffler and Robert Ennis, and developed by, amongst others, Harvey Siegel, Richard Paul, Matthew Lipman and John McPeck (Passmore 2010; Scheffler 1973; Ennis 1962, 1996; Siegel 1990; Paul 1990; Lipman 2003; McPeck 1981), The range of issues addressed under the umbrella of 'critical thinking' is vast: the logical structure of critical thought; argumentation and informal logic; inductive and deductive reasoning; sources of knowledge and information; freedom and authority; methods of interpretation and evaluation; criteria for rational evaluation; credibility and warrant; universal versus culturally relative reason; the relation between rational thought, emotive intelligence and practical wisdom; the connection between thought, expression and praxis. Accounts of critical thinking frequently take the form of taxonomies of cognitive objectives, and the assessment of critical thinking frequently employs analytic measures grounded in multiple-choice tests (Ennis 1993). There is widespread recognition that effective critical thinking is dependent on the possession of underlying dispositions, such as open-mindedness, self-awareness, and empathy (Facione *et al.* 1995).

Robert Ennis's *Critical Thinking* is an influential example of the application of critical thinking to educational contexts. It aims to enable learners to make reasonable decisions about belief and action (Ennis 1996). In line with similar textbooks, it combines an account of the nature of critical thinking with practical exercises designed to encourage students to *think critically for themselves* rather than merely learn about critical thinking. Ennis identifies six basic elements of critical thinking gathered under the acronym FRISCO: Focus, Reasons, Inference, Situation, Clarity and Overview (ibid.: 4ff.). Critical thinking begins by identifying the central issue, question or problem underlying a particular argument (Focus). It then identifies the evidence and reasons offered in support of the argument and assesses their validity (Reasons). Since evidence and reasons deemed valid in themselves may not necessarily support an argument's conclusion, the plausibility of the inferences drawn from them must be evaluated (Inference). Critical thinking occurs in concrete situations ('the people involved and their purposes, histories, allegiances, knowledge, emotions, prejudices, group memberships, and interests') that may impose specific situational rules: in a court of law, for example, critical thinking must obey the rule that the burden of proof lies with the prosecution rather than the defence (Situation) (ibid.: 7). Arguments and counter-arguments require precision of thought and simplicity of expression (Clarity). Once these five stages of an argument have been worked through systematically, it is vital to view the sequence as a whole, check the validity of each stage, and monitor the critical thinking process itself, prior to reaching a final judgement (Overview). To follow this process effectively requires possession of certain dispositions: critical thinkers must take care to ensure 'that their beliefs are true', 'that their decisions are justified', that all positions are honestly represented and that the dignity and worth of all parties is respected (ibid.: 9).

Post-Dewey, there is little dispute in educational circles that students must be active assimilators of curriculum content and not merely passive receptors. However, the nature of assimilation remains a contentious issue. Advocates of critical thinking tend to align themselves with modernist pedagogies that understand education as the transmission of objective truths given in the curriculum that must nevertheless be critically assimilated and assessed by students if they are become meaningful and valid *for them*. On this reading, the active assimilation of objective truth via critical thinking employs judgemental rationality to *overcome* epistemic relativism. Constructivists, on the other hand, tend to align themselves with post-modern pedagogies that affirm the subjectivity of all truth claims, identify curricular content with the vested interests of privileged elites, and advocate knowledge construction as 'a reality-sharing, world-building exercise' driven by questions of pragmatic utility rather than objective truth (Esland

1971: 72). This leads them to construe assimilation as an extra-rational process driven by personal preference and desire in a manner that affirms a thorough-going epistemic relativism and rejects both ontological realism and judgemental rationality. This paves the way for the accusation that modernists are guilty of the authoritarian transmission of supposedly objective truth. Modernists respond by claiming that critical thinking disallows any possibility of the authoritarian transmission of truth: the exercise of judgemental rationality serves to help secure objective knowledge of the world in a manner that avoids authoritarian transmission.

To interpret critical religious education's commitment to judgemental ration-ality as advocacy of critical thinking is to locate critical religious education firmly in the modernist camp. This helps explain the recurrent suspicion that crit-ical religious education is a form of neo-confessional religious education, com-mitted to the surreptitious advocacy of religious (specifically Christian) truth claims behind the smokescreen of 'critical thinking'. However, critical religious education insists on the delicate balance of ontological realism, judgemental rationality *and* epistemic relativism as critical features of effective pedagogy. The appeal to epistemic relativity enables critical religious education to retain maximal openness to conflicting religious and secular truth claims, including the truth claims of post-modern anti-realists. If judgemental rationality is equated with critical thinking, and critical thinking seen as a viable means of bypassing epistemic relativism, then the entire critical religious education framework col-lapses in on itself. Maintenance of the balance requires an account of judge-mental rationality that preserves the viability of adjudicating between conflicting truth claims in a manner that respects epistemic relativity and affirms ontological realism. Since a neo-Kantian account of critical thinking that presumes the ability to bypass epistemic relativism is not up to this task, an alternative must be found.

(3) *Critical thinking and rational choice.* Critical thinking claims to possess privileged understanding of the 'nature of knowledge', of 'man-as-knower', of 'mental processes' and of the 'activity of representation' that enables it to suc-cessfully 'underwrite or debunk claims to knowledge made by science, morality, art, or religion' (Rorty 1980: 3f.). Its self-appointed task is to establish increas-ingly accurate representations of reality via 'conceptual analysis' and 'explica-tion of meaning' informed by the 'logic of language' and the 'structure of the constituting activity of consciousness' (ibid.: 12). If 'to know is to represent accurately what is outside the mind', then 'to understand the possibility and nature of knowledge is to understand the way in which the mind is able to con-struct such representations' (ibid.: 3f.). Rorty traces this epistemic model back to the Enlightenment: Descartes' invocation of a mind–matter dualism; Locke's construal of knowing as a mental process of constructing complex ideas from atomistic sense data; Kant's affirmation of critical thinking 'as the tribunal of pure reason, upholding or denying the claims of the rest of culture' (ibid.). Rorty's identification of the metaphorical base of the model (the mind as 'mirror' of reality) exposes a set of primal assumptions that warrant further investigation.

First, *dislocation*. The notion of 'accurate representation' assumes the dislocation of mind from nature. We have already seen how Descartes' hermeneutic of suspicion, designed to strip away all false and unwarranted knowledge, dislocates the mind from received intellectual traditions and sources of empirical sense data and forces it to turn in on itself and identify the immediate self-consciousness of the Cartesian ego as the only secure epistemic foundation of knowledge. The ontological dislocation of the mind from the external world provides epistemology with its two basic tasks: to distinguish between true and false ideas contained in the vestibule of the mind, and to reconnect such ideas with external realities. The modern stand-off between idealist notions of truth as internal coherence and empiricist notions of truth as external convergence reflects this Cartesian dualism. In both cases possession of truth is dependent on our cognitive endeavours: whether in actively assessing the coherence of the ideas in the mind's possession (idealism), or actively assessing the convergence of such ideas with external realities (empiricism). When formulated in this way, the epistemic task becomes vulnerable to the prioritising of epistemic procedures over ontological realities: ontological realities are made to conform to our ways of knowing, rather than our ways of knowing made to conform to the ontological actuality and epistemic demands of the realities we seek to know.

Second, *autonomy*. Such epistemic dislocation places the burden of epistemic responsibility on the mind: truthful knowledge is dependent on the exercise of critical thinking. Because prejudice, presupposition, opinion and authority serve only to cloud rational judgements, the dislocated mind must establish a neutral perspective conducive to the pursuit of objective knowledge where the mind is answerable only to its own autonomous reasons. *Sapere aude*, have the courage to think for yourself, don't let others do your thinking for you. This has significant ontological ramifications: conflation of the epistemic notion of the sovereignty of reason with the need to protect the mind from potentially corrosive forces and power structures generates an ontological *identification* of selfhood *with* rational autonomy: to be truly human is to exercise rational autonomy, to be irrationally dependent on others is to be less than fully human.

Third, *parsimony*. The pursuit of accurate representation suggests the need for clarity and simplicity. Because perception can be deceptive, it is necessary to focus on what is actually there to be seen and avoid either inferring invisible realities beneath surface appearances or projecting imagined realities onto surface appearances. In order to ensure perceptual clarity, observation must proceed from parts to wholes: atomistic sense data generates simple ideas, which the mind then constructs into complex wholes. Because both our initial perceptions and subsequent constructs may be mistaken, it is necessary to verify them: is perception of particular units of sense data in particular conjunctions a regular occurrence, so that we may reasonably infer they are triggered by external objects and not generated by either indolent perception or over-fertile imagination? Parsimony of perception extends to parsimony of language: if accurate perception is dependent on observation of atomistic sense data, then accurate description is dependent on linguistically simple ostensive labelling. Metaphor is the enemy of accurate description, since it obscures the connection between words and objects and invites imaginary constructions disconnected from reality and closed to verification. Effective reasoning requires simple axioms, theories and propositions: the notion that people make self-interested rational choices from stable sets of preferences opens up the possibility of statistically grounded predictive models of economic behaviour that would be impossible given a more complex model of human nature. Once again, epistemic procedures carry onto-logical consequences: reality is reduced to that which can be perceived by the senses and described in a manner open to empirical verification. The principle of parsimony, which limits reasoning to the fewest assumptions, postulates and conceptual entities, overrides the principle of sufficient complexity, which requires models of reality to reflect the intricacy of reality.

Fourth, *disenchantment*. The notion of verifiable perception invites a distinc-tion between external objective 'facts' and internal subjective values. The Abra-hamic traditions nurtured an understanding of the world as God's intrinsically meaningful, purposeful and value-laden – and hence 'enchanted' – creation. Newton's reading of the natural world against the grid of absolute time and space enabled him to 'bring mathematical order into phenomena, and so expound the immutable laws of nature in terms of the causal and mechanical connections' (Koyré 1957: 276). This resulted in 'the discarding by scientific thought of all considerations based upon value concepts, such as perfection, harmony, meaning and aim' (ibid.). However the disenchantment of the world was not due to natural science per se, but rather to the naturalistic reduction of reality to the stratum of reality explained by natural science, and the reduction of that stratum to objects open to empirical observation and measurement. Nature may still be experienced in aesthetic, moral and spiritual terms, but such experience is not objective experience of nature as-it-is-in-itself, merely subjective experience of nature as-it-appears-to-us. The latter were deemed closed to empirical observa-tion and verification, and explained away as culturally relative social conven-tions or subjective mental constructs projected onto the surface appearance of reality. Though they may possess pragmatic or utilitarian value, they remain ephemeral entities that do not form part of the 'real' world. These empirical assumptions generate ontological results: the 'facts' of nature become the natu-ralistic bedrock of a self-generating, self-ordering and self-sustaining reality; the projection of values onto nature is possible because human beings, as the great-est entities known to have emerged from the bedrock of nature, are free to do so; the recognition that values are subjective and culturally relative generates a liberal polity designed to maximise the freedom of individuals and groups to live according to their own preferred value systems. It is not that the post-Enlightenment world is devoid of enchantment, but that the spells of enchant-ment cast by individuals are tragically subjective, and hence destined to be consumed by the hegemony of disenchanted nature: ashes to ashes, dust to dust.

Fifth, *authority*. The epistemic task of making sense of the world is our responsibility and we have the authority to carry it out to the best of our ability by employing critical thinking in an appropriate manner. Kant suggests that we are able to do so effectively by virtue of our innate possession of a priori cognitive categories (quantity, quality, relation, and modality with respect to space and time) that provide the rational tools that enable us to bring order and attribute meaning to our experiences. And our status as autonomous thinkers with possession of innate rational categories *authorises* us to do so.

> Reason only perceives what it produces after its own design.... It must not be content to follow, as it were, in the leading-strings of nature, but must proceed in advance with principles of judgement according to unvarying laws, and compel nature to reply to its questions.... It is only the principle of reason which can give to concordant phenomena the validity of laws, and it is only when experiment is directed by these rational principles that it can have any real utility. Reason must approach nature with a view, indeed, of receiving information from it, not, however, in the character of a pupil who listens to all that his master chooses to tell him, but in that of a judge, who compels the witness to reply to those questions which he himself thinks fit to propose.
>
> (Kant 1934: 10f.)

Critical thinking focuses on key issues, identifies evidence and reasons, checks the plausibility of inferences, takes account of epistemic contexts, strives for clarity, and seeks reflective awareness of the argumentative process. In doing so, it employs twin criteria for identifying a true statement or warranted argument: is its convergence with empirical reality verifiable? And is it coherent, simple and consistent? All this is virtually inconceivable apart from the notion of accurate representation, and concomitant notions of dislocation, autonomy, parsimony, disenchantment and authority. In so far as critical thinking bears the burden of generating objective truths its fundamental flaws are recognised by post-modernists and critical realists alike.

(4) *Beyond rational choice.* To question the viability of making sense of the world and our place in it via autonomous rational choices is not to follow the post-modern route of relinquishing reason per se. Rather it is to seek to open the door to a more powerful account of reason, one attuned both to the complexity of ontological reality and to the epistemic relativism of our knowing. Notions of 'humanity-as-knowers' and 'mental processes' need to be contextualised. We participate in the world we seek to understand, and if we seek reflective distance from the ebb and flow of our lifeworlds we cannot legitimately transform such distance into an epistemic gulf. The complexity of the stratified, emergent, causally efficacious and transfactual ontological reality we indwell mitigates against simplistic representations. And the unavoidability of epistemic relativity means that we need to exercise epistemic humility by recognising the limits and provisionality of all attempts to 'underwrite or debunk claims to knowledge'. Given the priority of ontology over epistemology, we need to see the epistemic task as that of adjusting our minds and their cognitive faculties to accord with the way things actually are, rather than forcing reality to conform to our given ways of

knowing. Such considerations generate an alternative set of primal assumptions: participation replaces dislocation, relationality replaces autonomy, complexity replaces parsimony, enchantment replaces disenchantment and responsibility replaces autonomy.

First, *participation*. The notion of the 'pursuit of truth' and 'truthful living' in the context of our engaged participation in the world undermines ideas of dislocation and accurate representation. The notion of a hermeneutic of suspicion designed to strip away all false knowledge and generate secure epistemic foundations is unobtainable. Because we know the world as we engage with it as embodied participants, knowledge is not located in a mirror situated in the vestibule of the mind, but in our established knowledge-relationships with reality. We cannot escape our given cultural environments and received intellectual traditions, and there is no epistemic virtue in seeking to do so. Because our thoughts, words and deeds change the world, however minimally, the notion of accurate representation must give way to that of truthful participation. Knowledge is not grounded in secure foundations, but emerges from the ebb and flow of our ongoing engagement with reality. The mind does not adjudicate reality indirectly from a distance, but wrestles directly with it in close combat.

Second, *relationality*. As previously noted, the primacy of ontology over epistemology means that the epistemic virtues of attentiveness, reasonableness, intelligence and responsibility take precedence over critical thinking skills. The task is not to force reality to conform to our ways of knowing, but to allow our ways of knowing to be shaped by the epistemic demands reality imposes upon them. The burden of epistemic responsibility may still remain with the mind, but the fact that such responsibility requires subservience to the epistemic demands ontological objects impose on us means that the notion of cognitive autonomy requires radical deconstruction. Thinking is not an autonomous activity: we think in the context of thinking communities, and in doing so learn from one another and where necessary accept the authority of experts. The fruits of our thinking can only claim objective status if we artificially dislocate them from socio-cultural, spatial-temporal, and interpersonal and inter-subjective considerations. It is not the case that prejudice, presupposition, opinion and authority serve only to cloud rational judgements. On the contrary, our retroductive responses to abductive encounters *require* the projection of potential meaning derived from prejudices, presuppositions, opinions and authorities. Crucially, the epistemic demands made by ontological objects require us to progressively refine our pre-understandings so that they are shaped by those objects and brought into line with them. If pre-understanding is unavoidable, it makes more sense to proceed with notions of participation, relationality, enchantment and responsibility that resonate with our actual ways of knowing rather than with the artificial constructs of dislocation, autonomy, parsimony and disenchantment. Iterative refinement of provisional retroductive models is more likely to be effective if it proceeds from our actual ways of knowing rather than from accounts of how we ought to know.

Third, *complexity*. Coherence and convergence are weak criteria for truth: coherence is trumped by the fact that the world is complex, stratified and emergent and consequently closed to coherent comprehensive understanding; convergence is trumped by the fact that causal mechanisms cannot be read directly from surface appearances. Answers to the four basic worldview questions (Where ultimately am I? Who ultimately am I? What ultimately is wrong? What ultimately is the solution?) cannot possibly be reduced to mere 'representations', however coherent and verifiable. To articulate an otherwise implicit worldview is not to provide an accurate representation of reality, but to self-consciously embrace retroductive explanations that are generated by our abductive encounters with reality and which are constantly undergoing iterative refinement. A complex reality demands complex vocabulary and complex grammar. Art, music and poetry provide insights into reality and our place within it that are irreducible to mere ostensive definitions. History, narrative and story cannot be reduced to sequential ostensive facts. 'God', 'goodness' and 'beauty' cannot be reduced to narrow linguistic definitions. Understanding Christian theodicy requires more than accounting for the logical possibility or impossibility of an all-powerful and all-loving deity who allows evil and suffering to exist. Rather it requires close attention to the Biblical narrative, to the discourses of Christian and non-Christian theologians, to Christian art, music and poetry. In short, attention to a complex web of linguistic and artistic expression and meaning whose nuances cannot possibly be encapsulated in overly simplistic linguistic definitions. By the same token a person's spiritual biography cannot be reduced to coherent statements of their primal beliefs coupled with factual descriptions of the sequence of their lives. Spiritual biographies are, unavoidably, provisional attempts to find meaning in complex relational webs of meaning, in which the existential parts unique to the individual are related to a partially known whole. Reading a person's spiritual biography is more akin to reading a *Bildungsroman* than reading a chronology or almanac. It is faith-seeking-understanding 'all the way down'.

Fourth, *enchantment*. Life, as they say, is a mystery. We cannot avoid attributing meaning to our world and to our lives, and cannot avoid the fact that whatever meaning we attribute will always fall short of the way things actually are, and of the people we are actually becoming. If knowledge is constituted by the relationship between knowing subjects and objects of knowledge, and if knowledge relationships are dynamically morphogenetic, then all knowledge is personal knowledge possessing existential significance for the knower. It is not the case that deepening knowledge of ourselves and our world generates increasing epistemic clarity and hence increasing disenchantment. On the contrary, the deeper our knowledge of ourselves and the world, the more mysterious ourselves and our world reveal themselves to be. It is not the case that expanding knowledge of the natural world generates disenchantment; on the contrary, the more we understand the complexities of nature the more mysterious and wondrous it reveals itself to be. By the same token, it is not the case that expanding knowledge of human psychology generates disenchantment; on the contrary, the more we learn about the complexities of the human mind, the more mysterious and wondrous we discover ourselves to be. It is not that either ourselves and our world lack enchantment, but that the poverty of our epistemic tools, especially those tools that promise yet fail to deliver epistemic closure, generates the illusion of disenchantment. Ontologically, both ourselves and the world we indwell are enchanted, and the epistemic task is to allow our minds to be shaped and formed by the wonder of reality. And it is precisely at this point that the arts and humanities come into their own, no longer as purveyors of cultural norms or expressions of sentimental preference, but as revelators of the profound mystery of being. What Shakespeare can tell us about the mystery of life is irreducible to what Einstein can tell us.

Fifth, *responsibility*. The idea of rational autonomy, when coupled with notions of the power of reason to overcome epistemic relativity, provides the knower with unbounded epistemic authority. Hence the Kantian picture of the knower as a judge who compels reality to answer whatever questions she see fits to ask. This is directly linked to the similarly Kantian notion that the basic structures of knowledge are derived from the mind of knowing subjects rather than from ontological objects of knowledge. However, if we take ontological realism seriously by recognising the priority of ontology over epistemology, and if we acknowledge that epistemic relativism precludes certain knowledge and epistemic closure, then the epistemic table is effectively overturned. Critical realism holds that knowledge is constituted by the relationship between knowing subjects and objects of knowledge, and that knowledge is dependent on the mind conforming to the epistemic claims made by such objects. It is not that reality must be accommodated within the cognitive structures of the mind, but that the cognitive structures of the mind must be accommodated to reality. Hence epistemic authority resides not in the mind of the knowing subject but in the reality of the object of knowledge. This requires an epistemic shift from arrogant *authority over* the object of knowledge to humble *responsibility towards* it. Hence the centrality of the epistemic virtues of attentiveness, reasonableness, intelligence and responsibility. Insight and discernment is conditional on our *attending responsibly* to the object of knowledge, and responding *reasonably* and *intelligently* to the demands it makes of us. In pedagogical terms, the primary task is to instil epistemic virtues in learners by making objects of knowledge available to them and showing them how to engage with them appropriately, rather than seeking to cultivate abstract critical thinking skills.

(5) *Critical religious education and judgemental rationality*. If students find themselves cast into a world whose ultimate structure, meaning and purpose they only partially understand, then the primary task of critical religious education is to generate deeper insight into their situation. Ontological realism about ultimate reality, when coupled with epistemic relativity about ultimate reality, generates a spiritual, moral and intellectual imperative to cultivate judgemental rationality. In this context 'religious literacy' refers to the capacity to exercise judgemental rationality vis-à-vis the ultimate order-of-things and our place within it: the capacity to pursue ultimate truth and live increasingly truthful lives *sub specie aeternitatis*. The notion of 'religious literacy' needs qualification in three directions. First, 'religion' is used here, not to refer exclusively to religious culture, but as shorthand for literacy about the ultimate order-of-things and our place within it,

and as such may be qualified as both 'spiritual' and 'worldview' literacy. Such qualification foregrounds both the existential orientation of the individual learner ('spiritual') and the fact that ultimate reality does not necessarily contain a Transcendent element (religious *and* secular 'worldviews'). Second, though 'literacy' carries the narrow connotation of linguistic capacity, it is used here as shorthand for the capacity to think (reasonably, rationally, emotionally, intelligently, wisely) communicate (linguistically, and through other mediums of expression such as the creative arts) and act (towards ourselves, others, society, culture, nature and the presence/absence being/non-being of Transcendence) in increasingly attentive, intelligent, reasonable, and responsible ways. Third, though 'religious literacy' also carries a narrowly academic connotation, it is being used here to identify *both* the academic study (through the disciplines and fields of Theology, Philosophy and Religious Studies) of worldviews (both religious and secular) insofar as they mediate ultimate reality (whether Transcendent or non-Transcendent), *and* the exercise of the fruits of such study in the habitus of our ordinary (and, at times, extraordinary) everyday lifeworlds.

When understood in this expansive manner, a strong case can be made for the claim that we live in a profoundly religiously illiterate society. We have already had occasion to note empirical evidence that many people struggle to locate themselves in 'metaphysical' space and make sense of their lives *sub specie aeternitatis* (Porpora 2001). Secular attacks on religion frequently display an astounding lack of engagement with religious and theological literature, and an equally astounding ignorance of even the most basic beliefs and practices of particular religious worldviews (Wright 2011). This is not the place to attempt to explain in detail the reasons for such widespread religious illiteracy, though the immediate cause would appear to be positive and negative aspects of the legacy of the Enlightenment. Positively, the Enlightenment generated the currently dominant worldview matrix of naturalism, secular humanism and secular liberalism: nature is the bedrock of reality, and by virtue of the fact that human beings are the greatest entities to have emerged from nature they are permitted to establish their own goals and values (freedom) provided they avoid doing harm to others in the process (tolerance). Negatively, the Enlightenment generated a still-dominant account of the intellectual, moral and spiritual poverty of religious belief and practice, predicated on empiricist, positivist, rationalist, idealist and pragmatic assumptions. Critical realism has exposed the fragility of both aspects of this Enlightenment legacy: ontological realism recognises that reality possesses ultimate order, meaning and structure; epistemic relativity recognises that our understanding of ultimate reality (including the understanding generated by the legacy of the Enlightenment) is necessarily provisional and open to contestation; judgemental rationality recognises that (contra much post-Enlightenment thought) it *is* possible to be attentive, responsible, reasonable and intelligent with regard to our primal beliefs and practices. The problems and possibilities occluded by the legacy of the Enlightenment and restored by critical realism matter, because our primal beliefs and practices irrevocably impact on our identities (personhood), on our relationships with others (morality), on society (political, economic, etc.), on culture (both 'high' culture and 'ordinary' culture), on our engagement with the natural order-of-things and on the task of living good lives (whether in harmony with, or responsible rebellion against the ultimate order-of-things). That being the case, the moral, spiritual and intellectual imperative to pursue religious literacy is both urgent and undeniable.

Critical religious education offers a redefined notion of religious literacy that seeks to take up and transcend previous understandings of the aims and purposes of religious education. It has a close affinity with confessional approaches to the subject, insofar as they hold fast to a Transcendent object of learning and seek to cultivate personal and social flourishing in relation to that object. However, it departs from confessionalism, insofar as it recognises the epistemic relativity of all human understanding, and hence seeks to problematise the Transcendent object as an object of fundamental contestation. In plural classrooms operating in open-liberal contexts, this requires an openness to a diversity of religious and secular accounts of the ultimate order-of-things. This does not preclude the application of critical religious education to non-plural and non-liberal faith community schools. Because it is impossible to inhabit a neutral space claiming a 'view from nowhere', religious education cannot avoid operating out of one or other set of religious or secular faith commitments. In faith community schools the open-liberal presuppositions of plural classrooms simply give way to the faith-specific presuppositions of faith schools. Given that epistemic relativity runs 'all the way down', there can be no good reason for precluding religious education operating within some particular faith settings but not others. This does not, however, immunise faith-based classrooms from epistemic relativism: on the one hand, not every student in a faith school will necessarily subscribe to the school's primal commitments and presuppositions, and on the other students who do subscribe to them will necessarily lack total understanding of them. Thus critical religious education operative within faith-based contexts must recognise that the faith commitments undergirding their provision for religious education are always contingent on deeper insight and discernment (though not for that matter necessarily untrue), and take seriously the faith commitments students bring with them to the classroom, regardless of whether these are in harmony with the commitments of the school or not. With the proviso that epistemic relativity runs deep, critical religious education resonates strongly with confessionalism. The proviso is, however, vital: lose it and religious education risks becoming indoctrinatory, and epistemic relativity risks giving way to the ontic fallacy of claiming total knowledge of the ultimate order-of-things. Even the most committed subscriber to a particular religious or secular worldview necessarily sees through a glass darkly and does not yet see face-to-face. It is precisely because of its commitment to epistemic relativity that critical religious education cannot justifiably be branded 'neo-confessional'.

Critical religious education's affinity with forms of liberal religious education is more dubious. The notion that students 'learn about' religion by amassing greater quantitative information about religious culture and 'learn from' religion by projected constructed meanings onto objective facts is anathema to critical religious education. It is not the case that a religiously literate person is one who possesses a large quantity of information about religion, and is capable of articulating and expressing their personal opinions confidently and effectively, and demonstrates empathetic and tolerant attitudes to religious adherents (provided that they are not radicalised). This notion of religious literacy is parochial within the dominant worldview matrix of naturalism, secular humanism and secular liberalism. This precludes taking alternative accounts of the ultimate ontological structure and meaning of reality seriously, affirms a thoroughgoing epistemic relativism (as opposed to epistemic relativity), and occludes the exercise of judgemental rationality. This is not to suggest that critical religious education seeks to exclude the dominant matrix of naturalism, secular humanism and secular liberalism from the curriculum. On the contrary, as the dominant and, in the eyes of many, most persuasive worldview currently available to us, it must be engaged with and explored in the classroom. A religious education that excludes secular alternatives to religion from the curriculum cannot possibly be 'critical'. Problems only arise when the matrix is provided with implicit default privilege: a trap liberal religious education regularly falls into. That is not to say that critical religious education cannot function in liberal contexts. On the contrary, it was initially designed precisely for liberal contexts, and sought to out-liberal liberalism by being *genuinely* liberal about the contested nature of religious and secular worldviews (epistemic relativity) and about the importance of attending to these wisely and intelligently (judgemental rationality). It is, however, to say that if the liberal context is a 'closed' (as opposed to 'open') liberalism that seeks naive induction into liberal norms and values, then the result will be, not religious literacy, but a confessional induction into a non-negotiable worldview conducive to religious illiteracy.

Religious literacy thus eschews any form of naive induction that bypasses the critical issues of ontological realism, epistemic relativism and judgemental rationality. To be religiously literate, in the sense outlined above, is to be critically engaged with question of the ultimate order-of-things and our place within it, critically engaged with the reality of epistemic relativity (as opposed to epistemic relativism) and critically engaged with the practice of judgemental rationality.

Judgemental rationality cannot properly be construed as a process of making rational judgements in a manner designed to secure objective knowledge and occlude epistemic relativity. Such a notion attributes too much authority to human reason and too little authority to the fact that epistemic relativity runs 'all the way down'. This does not, however, denude judgemental rationality of legitimate and appropriate authority and thereby enforce a thoroughgoing relativism. It is not that we cannot make judgements between conflicting truth claims about the ultimate order-of-things, but that such judgements do not normally take the form of definitive rational choices that impose premature closure on the ongoing pursuit of truth.

What then might the exercise of judgemental rationality look like in critical religious education classrooms? First, to employ judgemental rationality is to seek to reduce epistemic relativity by generating more truthful knowledge of the ultimate order-of-things and enabling more truthful living *sub specie aeternitatis*. This requires the pursuit of more explicit, complex and differentiated knowledge-relationships with ultimate reality as mediated through worldview cultures and academic explanations of them. Students will bring their worldviews with them to the classroom. The task of the teacher is to enable students to make their primal worldview beliefs explicit, recognise how these vary from other conflicting worldviews, and understand both their worldviews and the worldviews of others in increasingly complex and differentiated ways.

Second, to employ judgemental rationality is to acknowledge the unavoidability of epistemic relativity and recognise that the achievement of more complex and differentiated knowledge-relationships is necessarily an ongoing process resistant to epistemic closure. The fact that the emergence of deeper understanding immediatly opens up the possibility of still-deeper understanding precludes forms of critical thinking that claim epistemic closure on the basis of singular acts of rational judgement. The achievement of more truthful knowledge-relationships is an ongoing and open-ended process.

Third, to employ judgemental rationality is to recognise that deeper discernment proceeds from faith, through faith, to faith. It is impossible to avoid primal worldview assumptions, or to think, speak or act apart from a set of implicit or explicit primal faith commitments. That being the case, we are entitled to hold fast to our beliefs and act on them, since they are the most truthful beliefs currently available to us. At the same time, we are under an intellectual, moral and spiritual obligation to seek to iteratively refine our primal commitments in the pursuit of greater truth and more truthful living.

Fourth, to employ judgemental rationality is to recognise that understanding of the ultimate order-of-things and our place within it is the product of a complex web of meaning. Because reality is stratified, emergent, transfactual, value-laden, causally efficacious and morphogenetic, the relationship between parts and the whole, and between the existential individual and the ultimate order-of-things, is intrinsically complex and irreducible to simple propositions open to binary yes/no judgements. Increased discernment of a part of reality may demand a revision of our understanding of reality as a whole, but not necessarily a *fundamental* revision necessitating the abandonment of one worldview in favour of another. However, it is entirely possible that the cumulative weight of evidence *may* demand such a fundamental revision, and hence conversion from one worldview to another.

Fifth, to employ judgemental reality is to respond to the epistemic demands reality makes on us. This requires us to be attentive and responsible towards reality, and intelligent and reasonable in our engagements with it. The emergence of deeper discernment will normally be a slow and largely implicit process: deeper discernment of an object of knowledge, and of conflicting ways of explaining its nature, will normally be a cumulative process in which explicit recognition of our developing understanding follows on from the fact that our discernment has actually changed. Rather than make the punctiliar critical judgement that one way of explaining an object is more powerful than another, we will tend to find ourselves *discovering* that our understanding *has* progressively changed over time by virtue of the fact that our knowledge-relationships have become increasingly complex and differentiated.

Sixth, to employ judgemental rationality is to recognise that we have no secure epistemic criteria on which to make rational judgement calls. The priority of ontology over epistemology means that epistemic criteria are necessarily subservient to ontological realities and emerge from our engagement with them. To claim secure epistemic criteria and adjudicate between those aspects of reality that conform to such criteria and those which do not is to commit the epistemic fallacy of forcing reality to conform to our established ways of knowing. This does not preclude the acceptance of generic epistemic indictors such as attentiveness, inclusivity, congruence, coherence, fertility, simplicity (or appropriate complexity) and depth (Wright 2013: 254ff.). Judgements between conflicting worldviews cannot be judgements made against independent epistemic criteria; rather, they involve the comparison of conflicting worldviews in an attempt to discern which of them enjoys greater explanatory power.

In conclusion, critical religious education is critical insofar as it affirms three critical features of the pedagogic process. First, the critical nature of the object of study, namely the ultimate order-of-things and our emergent relationships with ultimate reality. Second, the critical nature of epistemic relativity, which recognises the contested nature of ultimate reality and acknowledges that the pursuit of greater truth and truthfulness is an ongoing process resistant to premature epistemic closure. Third, the critical nature of judgemental rationality, which takes the form, not of punctiliar rational judgements claiming epistemic closure, but cumulative discernment of ultimate reality, as mediated by cultural worldviews and academic traditions, so that ultimate nature of reality progressively reveals itself to us and calls us to more truthful living *sub specie aeternitatis*. To be religiously literate is to be attentive and responsive to reality, and reasonable and intelligent in our dealings with it: it is not to have the courage to think for ourselves and impose ourselves on reality; rather it is to have the courage to humbly open books, both ancient and modern, to humbly attend to founts of wisdom, both religious and secular, and to humbly be prepared to have our understanding of ourselves, of the meaning and purpose of our lives, and of our place in the ultimate order-of-things transformed as a result. Humility in the face of a reality that transcends our ability to fully comprehend it is both a cardinal epistemic virtue and the fundamental basis of judgemental rationality.

Bibliography

Alexander, L. (1994) 'Paul and the Hellenistic Schools: The Evidence of Galen', in T. Engberg-Pedersen (ed.) *Paul in His Hellenistic Context*, Edinburgh: T. and T. Clark, 60–83.

Allen, D. (1987) 'Phenomenology of Religion', in M. Eliade (ed.) *The Encyclopaedia of Religion, Volume Eleven*, London: Collier-Macmillan, 272–285.

Aquinas, T. (1920) *Summa Theologica, Volume One*, London: Burns Oates and Washbourne.

Aquino, F. D. (2004) *Communities of Informed Judgement: Newman's Illative Sense and Accounts of Rationality*, Washington DC: The Catholic University of America Press.

Archer, M. S., Collier, A. and Porpora, D. V. (2004) *Transcendence: Critical Realism and God*, London: Routledge.

Aristotle (1984) 'Metaphysics', in J. Barnes (ed.) *The Complete Works of Aristotle, Volume 2*, Princeton, NJ: Princeton University Press, 1552–1728.

Bacon, F. (1974) *The Advancement of Learning* and *New Atlantis*, Oxford: Clarendon Press.

Bacon, F. (2012) *Novum Organum Scientiarum*, Memphis, TN: Bottom of the Hill Publishing.

Baker, A. E. (1946) *William Temple and His Message*, Harmondsworth, Middlesex: Pelican Books.

Bantock, G. H. (1980) *Studies in the History of Educational Theory, Volume 1: Artifice and Nature*, London: Allen and Unwin.

Barnes, L. P. (2008) 'The 2007 Birmingham Agreed Syllabus for Religious Education: A New Direction for Statutory Religious Education in England and Wales', *Journal of Beliefs and Values*, 29 (1), 75–83.

Barrow, J. D. and Tipler, F. J. (1986) *The Anthropic Cosmological Principle*, Oxford: Oxford University Press.

Bates, D. (1984) 'Harold Loukes: Christian Educationalist 1912–80', *British Journal of Religious Education*, 6 (2), 75–81.

Barth, K. (1958–1961) *Church Dogmatics, Volume Three, Parts One–Four: The Doctrine of Creation*, Edinburgh: T. and T. Clark.

Barth, K. (1975) *Church Dogmatics, Volume One, Part One: The Doctrine of the Word of God*, Edinburgh: T. and T. Clark.

Bedford, R. D. (1979) *The Defence of Truth: Herbert of Cherbury and the Seventeenth Century*, Manchester: Manchester University Press.

Berger, P. L. (1990) *The Sacred Canopy: Elements of a Sociological Theory of Religion*, New York: Anchor Press.

Berlin, I. (1997) *The Proper Study of Mankind*, New York: Farrar, Strauss and Giroux.

Bernstein, B. (1971) 'On the Classification and Framing of Knowledge', in M. F. D. Young (ed.) *Knowledge and Control: New Directions in the Sociology of Education*, London: Collier-MacMillan, 47–69.

Bernstein, R. J. (1983) *Beyond Objectivism and Relativism: Science, Hermeneutics and Praxis*, Oxford: Blackwell.

Berry, P. (1992) 'Introduction', in P. Berry and A. Wernick (eds) *Shadow and Spirit: Postmodernism and Religion*, London: Routledge, 1–8.

Bhaskar, R. (1993) *Dialectic: The Pulse of Freedom*, London: Verso.

Bhaskar, R. (1994) *Plato Etc.: The Problems of Philosophy and their Resolution*, London: Verso.

Bhaskar, R. (2002) *Meta-Reality: Creativity, Love and Freedom (The Philosophy of Meta-Reality, Volume One)*, New Delhi: Sage.

Bhaskar, R. (2008) *A Realist Theory of Science*, London: Verso.

Blond, P. (1999) 'Perception: From Modern Painting to the Vision of Christ', in J. Milbank, C. Pickstock and G. Ward (eds) *Radical Orthodoxy: A New Theology*, London: Routledge, 220–241.

Bloom, B. S. (1965) *Taxonomy of Educational Objectives: The Classification of Educational Goals. Handbook I: Cognitive Domain*, New York: McKay, 1965.

Bowen, J. (1981) *A History of Western Education, Volume 3: The Modern West*, London: Methuen.

Boyne, R. (1990) *Foucault and Derrida: The Other Side of Reason*, London: Unwin Hyman.

Brown, J. (1953) *Subject and Object in Modern Theology*, London: SCM.

Brueggemann, W. (1982) *The Creative Word: Canon as a Model for Biblical Education*, Philadelphia, PA: Fortress Press.

Brueggemann, W. (1997) *Theology of the Old Testament: Testimony, Dispute, Advocacy*, Minneapolis MN: Fortress Press.

Buckley, M. J. (1987) *At the Origins of Modern Atheism*, New Haven, CT: Yale University Press.

Bultmann, R. (1969) *Faith and Understanding*, London: SCM.

Bultmann, R. (1985) *New Testament and Mythology*, London: SCM.

Busch, E. (1976) *Karl Barth: His Life from Letters and Autobiographical Texts*, London: SCM.

Butler, J. (1884) *The Analogy of Religion Natural and Religion Revealed to the Constitution and Course of Nature*, London: George Routledge and Sons.

Byrne, J. (1996) *Glory, Jest and Riddle: Religious Thought in the Enlightenment*, London: SCM.

Byrne, P. (2003) *God and Realism*, Aldershot, Hampshire: Ashgate.

Byrne, P. (2013) *Natural Religion and the Nature of Religion: The Legacy of Deism*, London: Routledge.

Cady, L. E. and Brown, D. (2002) *Religious Studies, Theology, and the University: Conflicting Maps, Changing Terrain*, Albany, NY: State University of New York Press.

Callaghan, J. (2011), 'Towards a National Debate: The Full Text', *The Great Debate: 25 Years On*, http://education.guardian.co.uk/thegreatdebate, accessed 17 October 2011.

Campbell, J. (2011) *The Masks of God*, 4 Volumes, London: Souvenir Press.

Carter, B. (1974) 'Large Number of Coincidences and the Anthropic Principle', in M. S. Longair (ed.) *Confrontation of Cosmological Theories with Observational Data*, Boston: D. Reidel, 291–298.

Cassirer, E. (1951) *The Philosophy of the Enlightenment*, Princeton, NJ: Princeton University Press.

Chambers, F. P. (1932) *A History of Taste*, New York: Columbia University Press.

Cherryholmes, C. H. (1988) *Power and Criticism: Poststructural Investigations in Education*, New York: Teachers College Press.

City of Birmingham Education Committee (1975) *Agreed Syllabus of Religious Instruction*, Birmingham: City of Birmingham Education Committee.

Cobban, A. (1960) *In Search of Humanity: The Role of the Enlightenment in Modern History*, London: Cape.

Coleman, F. X. J. (1971) *The Aesthetic Thought of the French Enlightenment*, Pittsburgh, PA: University of Pittsburgh Press.

Collier, A. (1999) *Being and Worth*, London: Routledge.

Comte, A. (1988) *Introduction to Positivist Philosophy*, Cambridge, MA: Hackett.

Copleston, F. (1985) *A History of Philosophy, Volume One: Greece and Rome*, New York: Doubleday.

Cowdell, S. (1988) *Atheist Priest? Don Cupitt and Christianity*, London: SCM.

Cox, E. (1966) *Changing Aims in Religious Education*, London: Routledge and Kegan Paul.

Cox, E. (1983) 'Understanding Religion and Religious Understanding', *British Journal of Religious Education*, 6 (1), 3–7, 13.

Creaven, S. (2010) *Against the Spiritual Turn: Marxism, Realism and Critical Theory*, London: Routledge.

Cupitt, D. (1980) *Taking Leave of God*, London: SCM.

Cupitt, D. (1985) *Only Human*, London: SCM.

Cupitt, D. (1987) *The Long-Legged Fly: A Theology of Language and Desire*, London: SCM.

Dahlhaus, C. (1993) *Ludwig van Beethoven: Approaches to His Music*, Oxford: Clarendon.

Darling, J. (1985) 'Understanding and Religion in Rousseau's Émile', *British Journal of Educational Studies*, 33(1), 20–34.

Dawkins, R. (2007) *The God Delusion*, London: Black Swan.

Day, D. (1985) 'Religious Education 40 Years On: A Permanent Identity Crisis?', *British Journal of Religious Education*, 7 (2), 55–63.

Demirel, A. (2015) *Improving teaching and learning in Islamic Religious Education based on the framework of Critical Religious Education and Variation Theory: Cases of two secondary girls' schools in London*, unpublished PhD thesis, London: King's College.

Dennett, D. C. (2007) *Breaking the Spell: Religion as a Natural Phenomenon*, London: Penguin.

DES (1977) *Education in Our Schools*, London: HMSO.

DES/HMI (1977) *Curriculum 11–16*, London: HMSO.

Descartes, R. (1967a) *The Philosophical Works, Volume One*, Cambridge: Cambridge University Press.

Descartes, R. (1967b) *The Philosophical Works, Volume Two*, Cambridge: Cambridge University Press.

Descartes, R. (1970) *Philosophical Writings*, London: Nelson.

Dewey, J. (1991) *How We Think*, New York: Prometheus Books.

DfEE/QCA (1999) *The National Curriculum Handbook for Primary/Secondary Teachers in England*, London: HMSO.

Dostoevsky, F. (1997) *The Brothers Karamazov*, London: Alfred A. Knopf.

Drazin, N. (1940) *History of Jewish Education from 515 BCE to 220 CE*, Baltimore, MA: Johns Hopkins Press.

Eliade, M. (1987) *The Sacred and Profane: The Nature of Religion*, San Diego, CA: Harcourt Brace.

Elias, J. L. (2002) *A History of Christian Education: Protestant, Catholic and Orthodox Perspectives*, Malabar, FL: Krieger.

Ennis, R. H. (1962) 'A Concept of Critical Thinking', *Harvard Educational Review* 32, 81–111.

Ennis, R. H. (1993) 'Critical Thinking Assessment', *Theory into Practice*, 32 (3), 179–186.

Ennis, R. H. (1996) *Critical Thinking*, Upper Saddle River, NJ: Prentice-Hall.

Erricker, C. (1993) 'The Iconic Quality of the Mind', in D. Starkings (ed.) *Religion and the Arts in Education: Dimensions of Spirituality*, London: Hodder and Stoughton, 138–147.

Erricker, C. (2001) 'Shall We Dance? Authority, Representation and Voice: The Place of Spirituality in Religious Education', *Religious Education*, 96 (1), 20–35.

Erricker, C. and Erricker, J. (2000) *Reconstructing Religious, Spiritual and Moral Education*, London: Routledge.

Esland, G. M. (1971) 'Teaching and Learning as the Organization of Knowledge', in M. F. D. Young (ed.) *Knowledge and Control: New Directions in the Sociology of Education*, London: Collier-MacMillan, 70–115.

Evers, C. W. (1987) 'Epistemology and the Structure of Educational Theory: Some Reflections on the O'Connor–Hirst Debate', *Journal of Philosophy of Education*, 21 (1), 3–13.

Facione, P. A., Sánchez, G., and Gainen, J. (1995) 'The Disposition Toward Critical Thinking', *The Journal Of General Education*, 44 (1), 1–25.

Fallon, D. (1980) *The German University*, Boulder, CO: Colorado Associated University Press.

Farley, E. (2001) *Theologia: The Fragmentation and Unity of Theological Education*, Eugene, Oregon: Wipf and Stock.

Feuerbach, L. (1957) *The Essence of Christianity*, London: Harper and Row.

Feyerabend, P. (1987) *Farewell to Reason*, London: Verso.

Fichte, J. G. (2010) *Attempt at a Critique of All Revelation*, Cambridge: Cambridge University Press.

Fiddes, P. S. (1992) *The Creative Suffering of God*, Oxford: Clarendon Press.

Filmer, P. (1997) 'Disinterestedness and the Modern University', in A. Smith and F. Webster (eds) *The Postmodern University? Contested Visions of Higher Education in Society*, Buckingham: Open University, 48–58.

Fitzgerald, T. (2000) *The Ideology of Religious Studies*, Oxford: Oxford University Press.

Fosnot, C. T. and Perry, R. S. (2005) 'Constructivism: A Psychological Theory of Learning', in C. T. Fosnot (ed.) *Constructivism: Theory, Perspectives and Practice*, New York: Teachers College, 8–38.

Foster, M. B. (1973) 'The Christian Doctrine of Creation and the Rise of Modern Natural Science', in C. A. Russell (ed.) *Science and Religious Belief: A Selection of Recent Historical Studies*, London: Hodder & Stoughton, 294–315.

Foucault, M. (1971) *Madness and Civilisation: A History of Insanity in the Age of Reason*, London: Tavistock.

Foucault, M. (1972) *The Archaeology of Knowledge*, London: Routledge.

Foucault, M. (1989) *The Order of Things: An Archaeology of the Human Sciences*, London: Tavistock/Routledge.

Freddoso, A. J. (1999) 'Ockham on Faith and Reason', in P. V. Spade (ed.) *The Cambridge Companion to Ockham*, Cambridge: Cambridge University Press, 326–249.

Gadamer, H. G. (1979) *Truth and Method*, London: Sheed and Ward.

Gaukroger, S. (2001) *Francis Bacon and the Transformation of Early-Modern Philosophy*, Cambridge: Cambridge University Press.

Gay, P. (1973a) *The Enlightenment: An Interpretation, Volume One: The Rise of Modern Paganism*, London: Wildwood House.

Gay, P. (1973b) *The Enlightenment: An Interpretation, Volume Two: The Science of Freedom*, London: Wildwood House.

Gerson, L. P. (1994) *God and Greek Philosophy: Studies in the Early History of Natural Theology*, London: Routledge.

Gillespie, M. A. (1996) *Nihilism before Nietzsche*, Chicago, IL: Chicago University Press.

Goldman, R. (1964) *Religious Thinking from Childhood to Adolescence*, London: Routledge and Kegan Paul.

Goldman, R. (1965) *Readiness for Religion: A Basis for Developmental Religious Education*, London: Routledge and Kegan Paul.

Grant, E. (2007) *A History of Natural Philosophy: From the Ancient World to the Nineteenth Century*, Cambridge: Cambridge University Press.

Grant, R. M. (1988) *Greek Apologists of the Second Century*, London: SCM.

Grimmitt, M. (1973) *What Can I Do In RE?*, Essex: Mayhew-McCrimmon.

Grimmitt, M. (1987) *Religious Education and Human Development: The Relationship Between Studying Religions and Personal, Social and Moral Education*, Great Wakering, Essex: McCrimmon.

Grimmitt, M. (2000) 'Constructivist Pedagogies of Religious Education Project: Rethinking Knowledge, Teaching and Learning in Religious Education', in M. Grimmitt (ed.) *Pedagogies of Religious Education: Case Studies in the Research and Development of Good Pedagogic Practice in RE*, Great Wakering, Essex: McCrimmons, 207–227.

Grimsley, R. (1973) *The Philosophy of Rousseau*, Oxford: Oxford University Press.

Groff, R. (2004) *Critical Realism, Post-positivism and the Possibility of Knowledge*, London: Routledge.

Gunton, C. E. (1978) *Becoming and Being: The Doctrine of God in Charles Hartshorne and Karl Barth*, Oxford: Oxford University Press.

Gunton, C. E. (1985) *Enlightenment and Alienation: An Essay Towards a Trinitarian Theology*, Basingstoke: Marshall, Morgan and Scott.

Gunton, C. E. (1991) *The Promise of Trinitarian Theology*, Edinburgh: T. and T. Clark.

Gunton, C. E. (1995) *A Brief Theology of Revelation*, Edinburgh: T. and T. Clark.

Gunton, C. E. (1998) *The Triune Creator: A Historical and Systematic Study*, Edinburgh: Edinburgh University Press.

Gunton, C. E. (2003) *Father, Son and Holy Spirit: Toward a Fully Trinitarian Theology*, Edinburgh: T. and T. Clark.

Hammond, J. and Hay, D. (1992) '"When You Pray, Go To Your Private Room": A Reply to Adrian Thatcher', *British Journal of Religious Education*, 14 (3), 145–150.

Hammond, J., Hay, D., Moxon, J., Netto, B., Raban, K., Straugheir, G. and Williams, C. (1990) *New Methods in RE Teaching*, Harlow: Oliver and Boyd.

Hardy, D. W. (1975) 'Teaching Religion: A Theological Critique', *Learning for Living*, 15 (1), 10–16.

Hardy, D. W. (1976) 'The Implications of Pluralism for Religious Education', *Learning for Living*, 16 (2), 55–62.

Hardy, D. W. (1979) 'Truth in Religious Education: Further Reflections on the Implications of Pluralism', *British Journal of Religious Education*, 1 (3), 102–119.

Harris, S. (2006) *The End of Faith: Religion, Terror, and the Future of Reason*, London: Free Press.

Hay, D. (1982a) *Exploring Inner Space: Scientists and Religious Experience*, London: Penguin Books.

Hay, D. (1982b) 'Teaching the Science of the Spirit', in J. G. Priestley (ed.) *Religion, Spirituality and Schools*, Exeter: School of Education, University of Exeter, 37–53.

Hay, D. (1985) 'Suspicion of the Spiritual: Teaching Religion in a World of Secular Experience', *British Journal of Religious Education*, 7 (3), 140–147.

Hay, D. (2006) *Something There: The Biology of the Human Spirit*, London: Darton, Longman and Todd.

Hay, D. and Nye, R. (2006) *The Spirit of the Child*, London: HarperCollins.

Heelas, P. (1996) *The New Age Movement: The Celebration of the Self and the Sacralization of Modernity*, Oxford: Blackwell.

Hella, E. (2007) *Variation in the Understanding of Lutheranism and its Implications for Religious Education*, Helsinki: University of Helsinki.

Hella, E. and Wright, A. (2008) 'Learning "About" and "From" Religion: Phenomenography, the Variation Theory of Learning and Religious Education in Finland and the UK', *British Journal of Religious Education*, 30 (5), 517–521.

Heraclitus (2001) *Fragments*, London: Penguin Classics.

Hick, J. (1977a) *God and the Universe of Faiths*, London: Collins.

Hick, J. (ed.) (1977b) *The Myth of God Incarnate*, London: SCM.

Hick, J. (1989) *An Interpretation of Religion: Human Responses to the Transcendent*, London: Macmillan.

Hick, J. (1993) *The Metaphor of God Incarnate*, London: SCM.

Hiebert, P. G. (2008) *Transforming Worldviews*, Grand Rapids: Baker Academic.

Hindess, E. (1972) 'Forms of Knowledge', *Proceedings of the Philosophy of Education Society of Great Britain, Supplementary Issue*, 6 (2), 164–175.

Hirst, P. H. (1969a) 'The Logic of the Curriculum', *Journal of Curriculum Studies*, 1 (2), 142–158.

Hirst, P. H. (1969b) 'The Curriculum', *Western European Education*, 1 (1), 31–48.

Hirst, P. H. (1973a) 'Liberal Education and the Nature of Knowledge', in R. S. Peters (ed.) *The Philosophy of Education*, Oxford: Oxford University Press, 87–111.

Hirst, P. H. (1973b) 'Religion: A Form of Knowledge?', *Learning for Living*, 12 (4), 8–10.

Hirst, P. H. (1982) 'Philosophy of Education: The Significance of the Sixties', *Educational Analysis*, 4 (1), 5–10.

Hirst, P. H. and Peters, R. S. (1970) *The Logic of Education*, London: Routledge and Kegan Paul.

Hitchens, C. (2007) *God is Not Great: How Religion Poisons Everything*, London: Atlantic Books.

Hitchens, C. (2010) *Christopher Hitchens v Tony Blair: The Full Transcript*, www.newstatesman.com/blogs/the-staggers/2010/11/christopher-hitchens-tony-blair, accessed 21 March 2011.

HMSO (1988) *Education Reform Act*, London: HMSO.

Hodgson, P. E. (2005) *Theology and Modern Physics*, Aldershot, Hants: Ashgate.

Holley, R. (1978) *Religious Education and Religious Understanding: An Introduction to the Philosophy of Religious Education*, London: Routledge and Kegan Paul.

Hooykaas, R. (1973) *Religion and the Rise of Modern Science*, Edinburgh: Scottish Academic Press.

Howard, T. A. (2006) *Protestant Theology and the Making of the Modern German University*, Oxford: Oxford University Press.

Hull, J. (1984) *Studies in Religion and Education*, London: Falmer Press.

Hume, D. (1902) *Enquiries Concerning the Human Understanding* and *Concerning the Principles of Morals*, Oxford: Clarendon Press.

Hume, D. (1947) *Dialogues Concerning Natural Religion*, Indianapolis, IN: Bobbs-Merrill Educational.

Hume, D. (1963) *Essays Moral, Political and Literary*, Oxford: Oxford University Press.

Iremonger, F. A. (1948) *William Temple, Archbishop of Canterbury: His Life and Letters*, Oxford: Oxford University Press.

Irwin, L. (1997) 'Epistemic and Ontic Fallacies', *The Web Site for Critical Realism: Glossary*, www.raggedclaws.com/criticalrealism/, accessed 31 January 2012.

Jackson, R. (1997) *Religious Education: An Interpretative Approach*, London: Hodder and Stoughton.

Jackson, R. (2004) *Rethinking Religious Education and Plurality: Issues in Diversity and Pedagogy*, London: RoutledgeFalmer.

Jackson, R. (2008) 'Contextual Religious Education and the Interpretative Approach', *British Journal of Religious Education*, 30 (1), 13–24.

Jaeger, W. (1961) *Early Christianity and Greek Paideia*, Cambridge, MA: Harvard University Press.

Jaeger, W. (1986) *Paideia: The Ideals of Greek Culture*, 3 Volumes, New York: Oxford University Press.

Jaki, S. L. (1980) *The Road of Science and the Ways to God*, Edinburgh: Scottish Academic Press.

Jammer, M. (1999) *Einstein and Religion: Physics and Theology*, Princeton, NJ: Princeton University Press.

Janiak, A. (2010) *Newton as Philosopher*, Cambridge: Cambridge University Press.

Jenson, R. W. (1999) *Systematic Theology, Volume Two: The Works of God*, Oxford: Oxford University Press.

Kant, I. (1934) *Critique of Pure Reason*, London: Dent.

Kant, I. (1992) *The Conflict of the Faculties*, Lincoln, NE: University of Nebraska Press.

Kant, I. (1997) 'An Answer to the Question: "What is Enlightenment?"', in H. S. Reiss (ed.) *Kant: Political Writings*, Cambridge: Cambridge University Press, 54–60.

Kant, I. (1998) *Groundwork of the Metaphysics of Morals*, Cambridge: Cambridge University Press.

Kekes, J. (1999) *Against Liberalism*, New York: Cornell University Press.

Kelly, J. N. D. (1950) *Early Christian Creeds*, London: Longmans, Green and Co.

Kelsey, D. H. (1992) *To Understand God Truly: What's Theological about a Theological School?* Louisville, KY: Westminster/John Knox Press.

Kenny, A. (1968) *Descartes: A Study in His Philosophy*, New York: Random House.

Kerferd, G. B. (2003) 'The Sophists', in C. C. W. Taylor (ed.) *Routledge History of Philosophy, Volume One: From the Beginning to Plato*, London, Routledge, 244–270.

Kermode, F. (1971) *The Romantic Image*, London: Fontana.

Kierkegaard, S. (1967) *Philosophical Fragment, or A Fragment of Philosophy, by Johannes Climacus*, Princeton, NJ: Princeton University Press.

Kitto, H. D. F. (1957) *The Greeks*, Harmondsworth, Middlesex: Penguin Books.

Kooten, G. H. van (2010) 'Christianity in the Graeco-Roman World', in D. J. Bingham (ed.) *The Routledge Companion to Early Christian Thought*, London: Routledge, 3–37.

Koyré, A. (1957) *From the Closed World to the Infinite Universe*, Baltimore, MD: Johns Hopkins Press.

Kuhn, T. (1970) *The Structure of Scientific Revolutions*, Chicago, IL: University of Chicago Press.

Küng, H. (1980) *Does God Exist? An Answer for Today*, London: Collins.

Lackey, J. and Sosa, E. (eds) (2006) *The Epistemology of Testimony*, Oxford: Clarendon Press.

La Montagne, D. P. (2012) *Barth and Rationality: Critical Realism in Theology*, Eugene, OR: Cascade Books.

Lawton, D. (1975) *Class, Culture and the Curriculum*, London: Routledge and Kegan Paul.

Leavis, F. R. (1972) *The Great Tradition*, Harmondsworth, Middlesex: Penguin Books.

Leibniz, G. W. (1973) *Philosophical Writings*, London: Dent.

Lessing, G. (1957) *Lessing's Theological Writings*, Stanford, CA: Stanford University Press.

Levin, D. M. (1988) *The Opening of Vision: Nihilism and the Postmodern Situation*, London: Routledge.

Lindbeck, G. A. (1984) *The Nature of Doctrine: Religion and Theology in a Postliberal Age*, Philadelphia, PA: Westminster Press.

Lipman, M. (2003) *Thinking in Education*, Cambridge: Cambridge University Press.

Lipton, P. (2004) *Inference to the Best Possible Explanation*, London: Routledge.

LiverpoolFC.TV (2012) *Bill Shankly in Quotes*, www.liverpoolfc.tv/news/latest-news/bill-shankly-in-quotes, accessed 2 March 2012.

Locke, J. (1922) 'Of The Conduct of the Understanding', in J. W. Adamson (ed.) *The Educational Writings of John Locke*, Cambridge: Cambridge University Press, 181–265.

Locke, J. (1975) *An Essay Concerning Human Understanding*, Oxford: Clarendon Press.

Locke, J. (1993a) 'An Essay Concerning Toleration', in D. Wootton (ed.) *John Locke: Political Writings*, London: Penguin Books, 186–209.

Locke, J. (1993a) 'A Letter Concerning Toleration', in D. Wootton (ed.) *John Locke: Political Writings*, London: Penguin Books, 436–437.

Locke, J. (2000) *Some Thoughts Concerning Education*, Oxford: Clarendon Press.

London County Council (1947) *London Syllabus of Religious Education*, London: London County Council.

Lonergan, B. J. F. (1973) *Method in Theology*, London: Darton, Longman and Todd.

Loukes, H. (1961) *Teenage Religion*, London: SCM.

Loukes, H. (1963) 'Editorial: The Fear of the Blab', *Learning for Living*, 2 (5), 4–5.

Loukes, H. (1965) *New Ground in Christian Education*, London: SCM.

MacIntyre, A. (1988) *Whose Justice? Whose Rationality?* London: Duckworth.

Mackie, J. L. (1982) *The Miracle of Theism: Arguments For and Against the Existence of God*, Oxford: Clarendon Press.

Marsden, S. (2013) 'Michael Gove Attacks His Critics as "Marxist" Opponents of Improvements to Schools', www.telegraph.co.uk/education/educationnews/, accessed 1 April 2013.

Marton, F. and Booth, S. (1997) *Learning and Awareness*, Mahwah, NJ: Lawrence Erlbaum.

Marton, F. and Tsui, A. B. M. (2004) *Classroom Discourse and the Space of Learning*, Mahwah, NJ: Lawrence Erlbaum.

Marvell, J. (1976) 'Phenomenology and the Future of Religious Education', *Learning for Living*, 16 (1), 4–8.

McCarthy, T. (1984) *The Critical Theory of Jürgen Habermas*, Cambridge: Polity Press.

McCormack, B. L. (1997) *Karl Barth's Critically Realistic Dialectical Theology: Its Genesis and Development 1909–1936*, Oxford: Clarendon Press.

McGrath, A. E. (2001) *A Scientific Theology. Volume One: Nature*, Edinburgh: T. and T. Clark.

McGrath, A. E. (2002) *A Scientific Theology. Volume Two: Reality*, Edinburgh: T. and T. Clark.

McGrath, A. E. (2003) *A Scientific Theology, Volume Three: Theory*, Edinburgh: T. and T. Clark.

McGrath, A. E. (2005) *Dawkins' God: Genes, Memes, and the Meaning of Life*, Oxford: Blackwell.

McGrath, A. E. (2006) *The Order of Things: Explorations in Scientific Theology*, Oxford: Blackwell.

McGrath, A. E. (2008) *The Open Secret: A New Vision for Natural Theology*, Oxford: Blackwell.

McGrath, A. E. (2009) *A Fine-Tuned Universe: The Quest for God in Science and Theology*, Louisville, KY: Westminster John Knox.

McGrath, A. E. (2011) *Why God Won't Go Away: Engaging with the New Atheism*, London: SPCK.

McPeck, J. (1981) *Critical Thinking and Education*, New York: St Martin's Press.

Melchert, C. F. (1994) 'What is Religious Education?' in J. Astley, and L. J. Francis (eds) *Critical Perspectives on Christian Education: A Reader on the Aims, Principles and Philosophy of Christian Education*, Leominster: Gracewing, 48–60.

Melchert, C. F. (1998) *Wise Teaching: Biblical Wisdom and Educational Ministry*, Harrisburg, PS: Trinity Press International.

Meyer, A. E. (1975) *Grandmasters of Educational Thought*, New York: McGraw Hill.

Miegge, G. (1960) *Gospel and Myth in the Thought of Rudolf Bultmann*, London: Lutterworth.

Milbank, J. (1990) *Theology and Social Theory: Beyond Secular Reason*, Oxford: Blackwell.

Moltmann, J. (1974) *The Crucified God: The Cross of Christ as the Foundation and Criticism of Christian Theology*, London: SCM.

Moore, A. (2003) *Realism and Christian Faith: God, Grammar, and Meaning*, Cambridge: Cambridge University Press.

Moore, R. and Muller, J. (1999) 'The Discourse of "Voice" and the Problem of Knowledge and Identity in the Sociology of Education', *British Journal of Sociology of Education*, 20 (2), 189–206.

Morgan, J. (2007) 'Emergence', in M. Hartwig (ed.) *Dictionary of Critical Realism*, London: Routledge, 166f.

Nagel, T. (1986) *The View from Nowhere*, Oxford: Oxford University Press.

Nahm, M. C. (1975) *Readings in the Philosophy of Art and Aesthetics*, Englewood Cliffs, NJ: Prentice-Hall.

Nettleship, R. L. (1935) *The Theory of Education in Plato's Republic*, London: Oxford University Press.

Newbigin, L. (1982) 'Teaching Religion in a Secular Plural Society', in J. Hull (ed.) *New Directions in Religious Education*, Basingstoke: Falmer Press, 97–107.

Newman, John H. (1979) *An Essay in Aid of a Grammar of Assent*, Notre Dame, IN: University of Notre Dame Press.

Niiniluoto, I. (1999) *Critical Scientific Realism*, Oxford: Oxford University Press.

Norris, C. (1987) *Derrida*, London: Fontana.

Norris, T. J. (1977) *Newman and His Theological Method*, Leiden: Brill.

Ockham, W. (1983) *Predestination, God's Foreknowledge and Future Contingencies*, Cambridge, MA: Hackett.

Ockham, W. (1990) *Philosophical Writings*, Cambridge, MA: Hackett.

O'Connor, D. J. (1972) 'The Nature of Educational Theory', *Proceedings of the Philosophy of Education Society of Great Britain*, 6 (1), 97–109.

O'Connell, R. J. (1978) *Art and the Christian Intelligence in St Augustine*, Oxford: Basil Blackwell.

Otto, R. (1931) *The Idea of the Holy: An Inquiry into the Non-rational Factor in the Idea of the Divine and its Relation to the Rational*, London: Oxford University Press.

Paine, T. (2004) *The Age of Reason: Being an Investigation of True and Fabulous Theology*, Mineola, NY: Dover.

Pannenberg, W. (1976) *Theology and the Philosophy of Science*, London: Darton, Longman and Todd.

Pannenberg, W. (1994) *Systematic Theology, Volume Two*, Edinburgh: T. and T. Clark.

Parmenides of Elea (1984) *Fragments*, Toronto: University of Toronto Press.

Pascal, B. (1966) *Pensées*, Harmondsworth, Middlesex: Penguin Books.

Passmore, J. (2010) 'On Teaching to Be Critical', in R. S. Peters (ed.) *The Concept of Education*, London and New York: Routledge, 192–211.

Pattison, G. (1999) *Kierkegaard: The Aesthetic and the Religious – From the Magic Theatre to the Crucifixion of the Image*, London: SCM Press.

Paul, R. (1990) *Critical Thinking: What Every Person Needs to Survive in a Rapidly Changing World*, Rohnert Park, CA: Center for Critical Thinking and Moral Critique.

Philo (1993) *The Works of Philo*, Peabody, MA: Hendrickson Publishers.

Piaget, J. (1977) *The Development of Thought: Equilibration of Cognitive Structures*, New York: Viking.

Plato (1963a) 'Republic', in E. Hamilton and H. Cairns (eds) *The Collected Dialogues of Plato*, Princeton, NJ: Princeton University Press, 575–844.

Plato (1963b) 'Meno', in E. Hamilton and H. Cairns (eds) *The Collected Dialogues of Plato*, Princeton, NJ: Princeton University Press, 353–384.

Plato (1963c) 'Phaedo', in E. Hamilton and H. Cairns (eds) *The Collected Dialogues of Plato*, Princeton, NJ: Princeton University Press, 40–98.

Plato (1963d) 'Phaedrus', in E. Hamilton and H. Cairns (eds) *The Collected Dialogues of Plato*, Princeton, NJ: Princeton University Press, 475–525.

Plato (1963e) 'Theaetetus', in E. Hamilton and H. Cairns (eds) *The Collected Dialogues of Plato*, Princeton, NJ: Princeton University Press, 845–919.

Polanyi, M. (1958) *Personal Knowledge: Towards a Post-Critical Philosophy*, London: Routledge and Kegan Paul.

Poole, M. (2009) *The New Atheism: Ten Arguments That Don't Hold Water*, London: Lion Hudson.

Popper, K. T. (1966a) *The Open Society and its Enemies, Volume One: Plato*, London: Routledge and Kegan Paul.

Popper, K. T. (1966b) *The Open Society and its Enemies, Volume Two: Hegel and Marx*, London: Routledge and Kegan Paul.

Popper, K. R. (1972) *Objective Knowledge: An Evolutionary Approach*, Oxford: Oxford University Press.

Porpora, D. V. (2001) *Landscapes of the Soul: The Loss of Moral Meaning in American Life*, New York: Oxford University Press.

Porpora, D. V. (2004) 'The Human Project', in M. S. Archer, A. Collier, and D. V. Porpora *Transcendence: Critical Realism and God*, London: Routledge, 155–167.

Rad, G. von (1972) *Wisdom in Israel*, London: SCM.

Rawls, J. (1993) *Political Liberalism*, New York: Columbia University Press.

Ricoeur, P. (1995) *Figuring the Sacred: Religion, Narrative, and Imagination*, Minneapolis, MN: Fortress Press.

Roberts, R. C. (1976) *Rudolf Bultmann's Theology: A Critical Interpretation*, London: SPCK.

Rorty, A. O. (1998) 'Rousseau's Educational Experiments', in A. O. Rorty (ed.) *Philosophers of Education: New Historical Perspectives*, London: Routledge, 238–254.

Rorty, R. (1980) *Philosophy and the Mirror of Nature*, Oxford: Basil Blackwell.

Rorty, R. (1989) *Contingency, Irony and Solidarity*, Cambridge: Cambridge University Press.

Ross, A. (2000) *Curriculum Construction and Critique*, London: RoutledgeFalmer.

Rousseau, J.-J. (1986) *Émile*, London: Dent.

Russell, B. (1946) *History of Western Philosophy and its Connection with Political and Social Circumstances from the Earliest Times to the Present Day*, London: Allen and Unwin.

Sarup, M. (1988) *An Introductory Guide to Post-structuralism and Postmodernism*, London: Harvester Wheatsheaf.

Sayer, A. (1992) *Method in Social Science: A Realist Approach*, London: Routledge.

Scarlett, B. F. (1984) 'Formalism and Teleological Elements in Hirst's Argument for a Liberal Curriculum', *Journal of Philosophy of Education*, 18 (2), 155–165.

Scheffler, I. (1973) *Reason and Teaching*, London: Routledge & Kegan Paul.

Schleiermacher, F. D. E. (1958) *On Religion: Speeches to its Cultured Despisers*, London: Harper and Row.

Schleiermacher, F. D. E. (1966) *Brief Outline of the Study of Theology*, Richmond, VA: John Knox.

Schleiermacher, F. D. E. (1976) *The Christian Faith*, Edinburgh: T. and T. Clark.

Schleiermacher, F. D. E. (1991) *Occasional Thoughts on Universities in the German Sense*, Lewiston, NY: Edwin Mellen.

Schools Council (1971) *Schools Council Working Paper 36: Religious Education in Secondary Schools*, London: Evans/Methuen Educational.

Schwöbel, C. (1995) 'Imago Libertatis: Human and Divine Freedom', in C. E. Gunton (ed.) *God and Freedom: Essays in Historical and Systematic Theology*, Edinburgh: T. and T. Clark, 57–81.

Schwöbel, C. (2000) 'Theology', in J. Webster (ed.) *The Cambridge Companion to Karl Barth*, Cambridge: Cambridge University Press, 17–36.

Scott, R. B. Y. (1965) *Proverbs and Ecclesiastes*, Garden City, NY: Doubleday.

Sedley, D. (1989) 'Philosophical Allegiances in the Greco Roman World', in M. Griffin and J. Barnes (eds) *Philosophia Togata: Essays on Philosophy and Roman Society*, Oxford: Clarendon Press, 97–119.

Shakespeare, S. (2007) *Radical Orthodoxy: A Critical Introduction*, London: SPCK.

Sharpe, E. J. (1975) 'The Phenomenology of Religion', *Learning for Living*, 15 (1), 4–9.

Shipway, B. (2011) *A Critical Realist Perspective of Education*, London: Routledge.

Siegel, H. (1990) *Educating Reason: Rationality, Critical Thinking and Education*, London: Routledge.

Slee, N. (1992) 'Cognitive Development Studies of Religious Thinking', in J. Fowler, K. E. Nipkow and E. Schweitzer (eds) *Stages of Faith and Religious Development: Implications for Church, Education and Society*, London: SCM, 130–148.

Smart, N. (1968) *Secular Education and the Logic of Religion*, London: Faber and Faber.

Smart, N. (1969) *The Religious Experience of Mankind*, London: Collins.

Smith, A. and Webster F. (1997) 'Changing Ideas of the University', in A. Smith and F. Webster (eds.) *The Postmodern University? Contested Visions of Higher Education in Society*, Buckingham: Open University, 1–14.

Smith, J. W. D. (1969) *Religious Education in a Secular Setting*, London: SCM.

Snow, C. P. (1959) *The Two Cultures and The Scientific Revolution*, Cambridge: Cambridge University Press.

Sonneck, O. G. (ed.) (1954) *Beethoven: Impressions by His Contemporaries*, New York: Dover.

Spade, P. V. (1999) 'Ockham's Nominalist Metaphysics: Some Main Themes', in P. V. Spade (ed.) *The Cambridge Companion to Ockham*, Cambridge: Cambridge University Press, 100–117.

Spens Report (1938) *Board of Education Consultative Committee: Secondary Education, With Special Reference to Grammar Schools and Technical High Schools*, London: HMSO.

Stopes-Roe, H. (1988) 'Humanism as a Life Stance', *New Humanist*, 103 (2), 19–21.

Swann Report (1985) *Education for All: The Report of the Commission of Inquiry into the Education of Children from Ethnic Minority Backgrounds*, London: HMSO.

Swinburne, R. (1971) *The Concept of Miracle*, London: MacMillan.

Swinburne, R. (1993) *The Coherence of Theism*, Oxford: Clarendon Press.

Swinburne, R. (1998) *Providence and The Problem of Evil*, Oxford: Clarendon Press.

Swinburne, R. (2004) *The Existence of God*, Oxford: Clarendon Press.

Swinburne, R. (2005) *Faith and Reason*, Oxford: Clarendon Press.

Swinburne, R. (2010) *Was Jesus God?* Oxford: Oxford University Press.

Taylor, C. (1992) *Sources of the Self: The Making of the Modern Identity*, Cambridge: Cambridge University Press.

Taylor, C. (2007) *A Secular Age*, London: Belknap Press.

Temple, W. (1942) *Christianity and Social Order*, Harmondsworth, Middlesex: Penguin Books.

Thatcher, A. (1991) 'A Critique of Inwardness in Religious Education', *British Journal of Religious Education*, 14 (1), 22–27.

Thatcher, M. (1993) *The Thatcher Years*, London: HarperCollins.

Thiessen, E. (2011) *The Ethics of Evangelism: A Philosophical Defence of Ethical Proselytizing and Persuasion*, Milton Keynes, Bucks: Paternoster.

Tillich, P. (1978) *Systematic Theology, Volume One*, London: SCM.

Torrance, T. F. (1969) *Theological Science*, London: Oxford University Press.

Torrance, T. F. (1980) *The Ground and Grammar of Theology*, Belfast: Christian Journals.

Torrance, T. F. (1984) *Transformation and Convergence in the Frame of Knowledge: Explorations in the Interrelations of Scientific and Theological Enterprise*, Belfast: Christian Journals.

Usher, R. and Edwards, R. (1994) *Postmodernism and Education*, London: Routledge.

Voysey, C. (ed.) (1879) *Fragments from Reimarus, Consisting of Brief Critical Remarks on the Object of Jesus and His Disciples as Seen in the New Testament*, London: Williams and Norgate.

Walker, A. and Wright, A., (2004) 'A Christian University Imagined: Recovering *Paideia in a Broken World*', in J. Astley, L. J. Francis, J. Sullivan and A. Walker (eds) *The Idea of a Christian University: Essays on Theology and Higher Education*, Milton Keynes: Paternoster, 56–74.

Walsh, B. J. and Middleton, J. R. (1984) *The Transforming Vision: Shaping a Christian World View*, Downers Grove, IL: IVP.

Wenman, G. J. (1987) *Genesis 1–15, Word Biblical Commentary Volume One*, Nashville TN: Thomas Nelson.

White, J. (1982) *The Aims of Education Restated*, London: Routledge and Kegan Paul.

White, J. (2004) 'Introduction', in J. White (ed.) *Rethinking the School Curriculum: Values, Aims and Purposes*, London: RoutledgeFalmer, 1–19.

Wilkinson, M. L. N. (2015) *A Fresh Look at Islam in a Multi-Faith World: A Philosophy for Success through Education*, London: Routledge.

Williams, B. (2002) *Truth and Truthfulness: An Essay in Genealogy*, Princeton, NJ: Princeton University Press.

Wilson, J. (1971) *Education in Religion and the Emotions*, London: Heinemann Educational.

Wittgenstein, L. (1968) *Philosophical Investigations*, Oxford: Blackwell.

Wittgenstein, L. (1974) *Tractatus Logico-Philosophicus*, London: Routledge and Kegan Paul.

Wood, C. M. (1985) *Vision and Discernment: An Orientation in Theological Study*, Atlanta, Georgia: Scholars Press.

Worsley, H. J. (ed.) (2013) *Anglican Church School Education: Moving Beyond the First Two Hundred Years*, London: Bloomsbury.

Wright, A. (1998) *Spiritual Pedagogy. A Survey, Critique and Reconstruction of Contemporary Spiritual Education in England and Wales*, Oxford: Culham College Institute.

Wright, A. (1999) *Discerning the Spirit: Teaching Spirituality in the Religious Education Classroom*, Oxford: Culham College Institute.

Wright, A. (2000) *Spirituality and Education*, London: RoutledgeFalmer.

Wright, A. (2001) 'Dancing in the Fire: A Deconstruction of Clive Erricker's Postmodern Spiritual Pedagogy,' *Religious Education*, 96 (1), 120–135.

Wright, A. (2004) *Religion, Education and Post-modernity*, London: Routledge.

Wright, A. (2007) *Critical Religious Education, Multiculturalism and the Pursuit of Truth*, Cardiff: University of Wales Press.

Wright, A. (2008) 'Contextual Religious Education and the Actuality of Religions', *British Journal of Religious Education*, 30 (1), 3–12.

Wright, A. (2011) 'In Praise of the Spiritual Turn: Critical Realism and Trinitarian Christianity', *Journal of Critical Realism*, 10(3), 331–357.

Wright, A. (2013) *Christianity and Critical Realism: Ambiguity, Truth and Theological Literacy*, London: Routledge.

Wright, N. T. (1992) *Christian Origins and the Question of God, Volume One: The New Testament and the People of God*, London: SPCK.

Yates, P. (1988) 'Religious Education: An Anthropological View', *British Journal of Religious Education*, 10 (3), 135–144.

Young, M. F. D. (ed.) (1971a) *Knowledge and Control: New Directions in the Sociology of Education*, London: Collier-MacMillan.

Young, M. F. D. (1971b) 'An Approach to the Study of Curricula as Socially Organised Knowledge', in M. F. D. Young (ed.) *Knowledge and Control: New Directions in the Sociology of Education*, London: Collier-MacMillan, 19–46.

Young, M. F. D. (1971c) 'Introduction', in M. F. D. Young (ed.) *Knowledge and Control: New Directions in the Sociology of Education*, London: Collier-MacMillan, 1–17.

Young, M. F. D. (2008) *Bringing Knowledge Back in: From Social Constructivism to Social Realism in the Sociology of Education*, London: Routledge.

Zizioulas, J. D. (1985) *Being as Communion: Studies in Personhood and the Church*, Crestwood, NY: St Vladimir's Seminary Press.

Index